Language, Thought, and Other Biological Categories

Language, Thought, and Other Biological Categories

New Foundations for Realism

Ruth Garrett Millikan

A Bradford Book
The MIT Press
Cambridge, Massachusetts
London, England

Copyright © 1984 by
The Massachusetts Institute of Technology

This book was set in Palatino
by The MIT Press Computergraphics Department
and printed and bound by The Murray Printing Co.
in the United States of America.

Library of Congress Cataloging in Publication Data

Millikan, Ruth Garrett.
    Language, thought, and other biological categories.

    "A Bradford book."
    Bibliography: p.
    Includes index.
    1. Languages—Philosophy. 2. Semantics (Philosophy)
I. Title.
P106.M52   1984   401   83-22276
ISBN 0-262-13195-1

This book is gratefully dedicated to Charles Morris, the memory of whose warm enthusiasm enabled me to persevere. Dr. Morris did not live to see the rough ideas he so generously encouraged in a young acquaintance grow into a strongly naturalist view and then engender a theory of signs. Those who remember his ground-breaking *Signs, Language and Behavior* will appreciate the irony and my regret at not having finished this project before his death.

Contents

Foreword

In this book, Ruth Millikan presents a remarkably original and ambitious theory concerning the topics that have been at the center of philosophical attention in recent years: language, thought, meaning, reference, intentionality. She achieves this originality, moreover, not by rejecting the spirit and attitude of the mainstream but by adopting it more resolutely than its leading practitioners. One of the happiest trends in philosophy in the last twenty years has been its Naturalization: since we human beings are a part of nature—supremely complicated but unprivileged portions of the biosphere—philosophical accounts of our minds, our knowledge, our language must in the end be continuous with, and harmonious with, the natural sciences. But while striking the Naturalistic Pose is as agreeable and welcome as it is easy, actually *doing* naturalized philosophy has proved difficult—indeed a very unnatural act for a philosopher to perform—and contemporary philosophy of meaning, even where it is most brilliant, has been inconstant in its commitment to naturalism.

Millikan's originality, then, does not consist in launching a scornful attack on the tradition (that's been done before, many times), but in something at once more revolutionary and more constructive: devising in detail an alternative theory of meaning that is more deeply naturalistic, while preserving and amplifying the hard-won gains of the last half century. Thus this book owes profound debts to Frege, Russell, Wittgenstein, Quine, and especially Sellars, while at the same time occupying an arrestingly independent vantage point from which all of them—and Putnam and Fodor and virtually everyone else writing about meaning, reference, and intentionality—can be seen to be failed naturalists, unwitting "Meaning Rationalists" who have never quite managed to wean themselves from their Cartesian heritage.

Contemporary philosophical theory of meaning is something of a black hole. One simply cannot hope to work effectively on the issues without becoming intimately familiar with the technical literature, but that literature is such an intricately interlocked, powerfully argued conglomeration of doctrines that once one has come to terms with it, one is typically caught in its embrace. Millikan has somehow found the centrifugal energy to *leave* the tradition—*after* understanding it. At one point she says, after asking some particularly novel questions about particularly familiar matters, "In order to answer these questions we will have to strike out on our own." And that is just what she does. What she doesn't overturn, she supports with new arguments. Things we had taken for granted as primitives, in effect, are given foundations and explanations. New taxonomies of old friends reveal differences that had been papered over, similarities that had been missed.

Along the way answers are given to just about all the persistent puzzle questions about meaning, intentionality, and representation that currently preoccupy the field. Taken individually, they are often quite compelling, but if they are to escape the gravitational distortions of the standard ways of looking at the issues and establish themselves as part of a genuine alternative, the whole theory must be laid out. That takes a hefty book, but there are ample rewards in every chapter.

Daniel C. Dennett

Acknowledgments

My most immediate debt is to Carol Leary, who typed several drafts of this book with breathtaking speed, accuracy, intelligence, and good will, the last version while on maternity leave from our department.

Hector-Neri Castañeda, Fred Dretske, and Georges Rey (readers for the press) read an earlier draft, each making helpful suggestions in his own style. Richard Lee made good, feisty, page-by-page comments on most of the last half for me. Various of my colleagues at the University of Connecticut, especially Joel Kupperman, Samuel Wheeler III, John Troyer, Jerome Shaffer, Calvin Rollins, and Crawford Elder, have read or heard small bits and snatches of the book over the last few years, offering advice and criticism and, in some cases, taking pen in hand to help make the writing clearer.

I would never have had the courage or stamina to finish without the goodness of Bruce Katz, who sent the first half of the manuscript out to readers before the second half was written, and the encouragement of Daniel Dennett, who with supererogatory kindness independently read unsolicited material sent him by a total stranger. Without Charles Morris (see dedication), another who gave help to a near stranger, I would never have begun at all. Dennett also scribbled invaluable red ink all over the penultimate copy. If he carries his incisive and witty red pen in his breast pocket I will recognize him immediately should we meet.

I am grateful for having studied at Yale at a time when the broad-minded, deeply educated, and historically oriented department that Charles Hendel had built was still intact. I was introduced to most of the problems addressed in this book by a study of their history, not of the current season's solutions.

And, speaking of deep education, thank you Eunice and Wayne Garrett.

Introduction

In the early pages of *Philosophical Investigations*, Wittgenstein compares words to tools. "Think of the tools in a tool box: there is a hammer, pliers, a saw, a screwdriver, a glue-pot, nails and screws.—The functions of words are as diverse as the functions of these objects" (para. 11). Surely he would have said the same about the functions of language devices generally—words, surface syntactic forms, tonal inflections, etc. We might try to carry Wittgenstein's analogy further.

1. Tools "have functions" but do not always serve these functions. Although the function of the screwdriver is driving screws, it sometimes fails in this task. Moreover it is not always used even with the intention of driving a screw but, say, for prying or for poking holes. Language devices "have functions" but do not always serve these functions. Although the function of the imperative mood is to produce action, it sometimes fails in this task. Moreover it is not always used even with the intention of producing action but, say, insincerely, sarcastically, jokingly.

2. It is true that whereas the physical constitution of a tool is usually directly relevant to its function, the physical forms of language devices usually appear to be arbitrary in relation to their functions. There is no sense in which the household screwdriver might have served the pliers function, but "dog" might have served the "and" function and vice versa. But there are exceptions to this observation, most clearly in the case of tools. The key to my front door has a shape that is quite arbitrary within limits in relation to its function of opening my front door. Almost any shape would have done—provided that the lock on my door was adjusted accordingly. And it is in just this sense that almost any sound could have served the "dog" function—provided that the mechanisms within hearers that respond to tokens of this sound were adjusted accordingly.

3. Although the functions of tools are extremely various, there is a uniform manner in which any tool may be described as such: (*a*) describe the purpose of the tool; (*b*) describe how the tool works, hence also

the constitution of the tool, the method of operating or handling the tool, and other conditions normally requisite for the tool to perform its function. Is there a uniform manner in which any language device may be described as such?

The Tarski-Davidson tradition of semantics talks about certain kinds of words, describing these in terms of their effects upon the truth conditions of sentences in which they occur. The Austin-Searle tradition talks about other words and devices, "performatives" and "illocutionary force indicating devices," describing these in terms of conventional rules governing their use. The Grice-Schiffer-Lewis tradition talks about (speaking here very roughly) indicatives and imperatives, describing these in terms of nested speaker intentions. At least it is clear that no accepted manner of description applicable to every language device has *yet* emerged. But why should there be a problem about a uniform manner of description in the case of language devices when there is none in the case of tools? Where does the analogy with tools break down?

When we say that a tool has a certain function, its "own" or "proper" function, which can be distinguished from (1) its actual functions— what in fact it succeeds in doing on various occasions of use—and (2) the functions that various users intend it to perform on various occasions, we are referring to a function, roughly, that the tool type was designed by someone to serve. Natural language devices are not (at least literally) devices once "designed by someone" to serve certain functions. "The function of language device A is to F" does not bear the same analysis as does "the function of tool A is to F."

Consider another analogy. Body organs and instinctive behaviors also "have functions." As is the case with both tools and language devices, not every token of such a device succeeds in serving its "own" or "proper" function. And we can also imagine a person intentionally using such a natural device, say one of his own organs or reflexes, to serve a purpose that does not accord with its proper function. For example, people usually use their hands and arms "as Nature intended" for grasping, manipulating, pushing or pulling, etc. But a person can also use these members as matter upon which to draw, as subjects for physiological experimentation, as objects of aesthetic contemplation, etc. Moreover, some of these natural devices appear, as do all language devices and some tools, to have forms that are relatively arbitrary in relation to their functions. For example, instinctive mating displays, bird songs, and (other) ways of marking out territory are quite specific for the various species yet arbitrary in form within broad limits. And, as is the case with language devices but not with tools, these natural devices have not literally been "designed" by someone to serve their functions. The "functions" of these natural devices are, roughly, the functions upon which their continued reproduction or *survival* has depended.

Do language devices "have functions" that admit of the same kind of analysis? The functions of body organs and instinctive behaviors are radically diversified, yet when known can be described in the same sort of uniform manner in which the functions of tools can be described. Could a similar manner of description be used for language devices?

By "language devices" I mean words, surface syntactic forms, tonal inflections, stress patterns, punctuations, and any other significant surface elements that a natural spoken or written language may contain. We begin with two speculations. First, as is the case with other natural devices that are regularly reproduced by biological systems (e.g., body organs and instinctive behaviors), we suppose that normally a natural-language device has continued to be proliferated only because it has served a describable, stable function or set of functions. Second, as is the case, for example, with mating displays, speaker utterances of a language device presumably are proliferated only insofar as stable overt or covert reactions by cooperating partners (the female, the hearer) are also proliferated. The device type in each normal case, we speculate, should have at least one function—perhaps simple, perhaps complex—that accounts for the continued proliferation *both* of tokens of the device and of corresponding cooperative hearer reactions.

The language device performs this function in cooperation not with a specific hearer's response mechanism but with a random hearer, and the hearer's cooperative response mechanism performs its function in cooperation with a random speaker's utterance. Hence it is necessary that both the language device and its cooperative hearer mechanism be "standardized." Similarly, the mating dance of the male stickleback fish must perform its proper function in cooperation with the response mechanism built into a random female stickleback and vice versa. So the male dance and the female response must be standardized throughout the species if these devices are to perform their proper functions, hence survive. But stabilization of the function of a given language form and standardization within a language community of the form and cooperating response that serve that function must be two sides of a coin. For this reason I will use both "stabilizing (proper) function" and "standardizing (proper) function" for the hypothesized function of a given language device that accounts for the continued proliferation both of speaker utterances and of stable cooperative (overt or covert) hearer responses. (These equivalent terms will be given a more formal introduction in Chapter 1.)

Language devices are often used in secondary or parasitic ways, as in metaphor, sarcasm, or lying. And even when used literally and felicitously, they may still fail to perform standardly. For example, the hearer may not hear, or though having heard may still fail to reply with the proper overt or covert response. Further, speakers sometimes misuse language, as when a speaker says "temerity" but means timidity. The standardizing and stabilizing function of a language device should be thought of not as an invariable function or as an average function but as a function that accords with a critical mass of cases of actual use, forming a center of gravity to which wayward speakers and hearers tend to return after departures. It is because a language device has such a stabilizing and standardizing proper function, which it performs in such a critical mass of actual cases, that it can *survive* incidents in which this stabilizing function fails to be performed, without extinction or change of function.

These speculations are of course extremely vague. Many points will need to be clarified in order to evaluate them. But what they *suggest* is that there is a level upon which the "functions" of language devices can be analyzed that is not found either by averaging over idiolects or by examining speaker intentions. I will argue that public language is to the idiolect rather as the biological species is to the individual. The business of the biological species of staying in business determines standards for individuals of that species, standards which, though they often correspond to averages, are not defined in terms of mere averages over the species. Consider, for example, how few sperm or immature members of most species actually manage to perform all the functions that nonetheless are proper to them—that help account for the survival of the kind. Similarly, the proper functions of natural language devices, considered as elements of public languages such as French or German, are not derived by averaging over the actual functions of these devices within idiolects. The idiolect is not the basic unit of analysis here. The business of the language species of staying in business imposes a standard of correctness upon idiolects that is not a matter of mere averages.

In order to press this analogy, a definition of "function" or "*proper* function" is needed that is broad enough to encompass both the functions of language devices and the functions of biological devices. Producing a definition that will do the work required of it efficiently is a task of medium difficulty, but the rewards are many. One reward will be that human purposes, looked at from a naturalist's viewpoint, turn out to correspond to proper functions of a certain kind, so that a connection between human purposes and the natural purposes of body organs and instinctive behaviors will be established that does not rest on mere metaphor. The purposes or functions of tools and the unconscious purposes or functions of customs will also turn out to correspond to (different kinds of) proper functions. But the main point of developing the theory of proper functions is to use it as a tool for understanding language and other representations, inner and outer.

One result will be an analysis of sentence and word meaning that does not take speaker meaning as base, and an analysis of speaker meaning that does not take sentence or word meaning as base. These two kinds of meaning are entwined to be sure, but neither is *the* root in terms of which the other is to be explicated. Compatibly, I will argue that the meaningfulness of sentences can be described without making reference to the fact that sentences are typically used to express and transmit thoughts, and that what beliefs and desires and intentions are can be explained without making reference to language.

The theory of proper functions is outlined in Chapters 1 and 2. Some easy applications to language of the theory which do *not* bear upon the phenomenon of intentionality are discussed in Chapters 3 and 4. An important result of these chapters will be a new description of how language device tokens are grouped into types.

The key notion that is needed in order to discuss intentionality ("of-ness," "aboutness") will be, in a way, only a by-product of the notion "proper function." This is a quasi-normative (roughly, the biological or medical) notion "Normal." (I will capitalize the technical term "Normal" routinely. Possibly this is unnecessary, but in such contexts as "hence, Normally, such and such happens" it may be too easy to forget that it is not statistics or averages that are referred to but a specific sort of quasi-norm, and often a false reading would prove disastrous.) I will argue that looking for stabilizing proper functions of various language devices—roughly, for functions that explain the survival or proliferation of these devices together with their characteristic cooperative hearer responses—can lend a sharp focus to questions about what language devices *do*. But looking to the conditions under which these devices work when they work in accordance with historically Normal explanations is what reveals the representing or intentional side of language. These conditions are conditions that sentences Normally map. Thus the exact nature of the relation between two traditional kinds of investigations of language forms, the first of which concentrates upon use, performance, speech acts, etc., the second upon semantic value, will also be clarified. Stabilizing proper function, I will argue, is the first aspect of public-language meaning; something more like "semantic value" or "intentional content" or "propositional content," explicated by reference to the notion Normal and by reference to mapping functions, is the second and most important aspect.

I will call this second aspect of meaning "Fregean sense" (to distinguish it from "dictionary sense") or just "sense," various connections with Frege's notion *Sinn* being recognizable. *Fregean sense* is the most basic stuff of "meaning," and in some contexts it will be clarifying just to call it that. Using the notion *Fregean sense*, I will develop a "general theory of signs" roughly in the sense C. S. Peirce envisioned—a theory that covers conventional signs and also *thoughts* (as well as some other things).

This theory of signs and thoughts has an important consequence. Sense, the basic intentional or semantic feature, is neither reference nor intension. Moreover it is not determined by intension. Because it is not determined by intension there is an epistemological problem associated with intentionality. It turns out that we cannot know a priori either *that* we think or what we think *about*, just as we do not know a priori whether what we think is true. But, I will argue, facing up to this disturbing result saves realism.

Just how it saves realism will come out slowly as we proceed to the end of the book. But readers who are philosophers are likely to be impatient here. So let me say some words to these readers, hoping that others will catch the drift if not every detail.

A very striking theme of mid-twentieth century philosophers was that it is possible to reject the notion that our knowledge rests upon a foundation of "givens." It is possible reasonably to deny that incorrigible knowledge of things directly experienced (pains, perceived red patches) is a given; it is possible to deny that there are infallible observations of any sort that come epistemologically first, the rest of our knowledge logically following after. It is also possible to deny that there are any truths of reason or even any analytic truths known infallibly to be true. From this discovery there has emerged a movement that not only rejects the tarnished ideal of Cartesian certainty for knowledge[1] but rejects any attempt to ground our knowledge by stratifying it into layers, some of which serve irreversibly as foundations for others. The movement says of itself that it rejects "foundationalism" in epistemology.

A rejection of foundationalism goes hand in hand with rejection of correspondence as a test of truth for any level of judgment. No longer are there thought to be experiences or sensations or sense data with which one compares protocol sentences to see if these sentences are mapping truly, any more than one compares sentences about genes directly with genes to see if these sentences are mapping truly.

So described, the movement against foundationalism seems to me to be not only challenging but, in essence, right. But certain *conclusions* have been drawn from these new axioms, drawn almost universally, that seem to me to be unhelpful, indeed, dead wrong. The dominant view seems to be that acceptance of these new axioms entails rejection of correspondence (using Brand Blanshard's terms) not only as the "test of truth" but also as the "nature of truth"—that realism, in one rough sense of "realism," must go. It is argued stoutly—indeed, almost all of the most commanding arguments have been on this side—that reference cannot be thought of as a correspondence relation between a word and a thing, and that truth is not the mapping of a sentence onto what the sentence is about. Rather, truth must be understood as a redundant notion (" 'p' is true" just equals "p"), or it must be the same as rational assertability, or semantic assertability, or even just as socially respectable assertability—"what our peers will, *ceteris paribus*, let us get away with saying."[2] The dominant view is also that, once foundationalism has been abandoned, epistemological holism is the only alternative. If our beliefs are not tied and stabilized by a base of incorrigible observation judgments on the bottom and a skyhook of analytic judgments on the top, it must be that they are stabilized only by adhering to one another—by the coherence of the whole.

These popular views are not without paradox. Indeed, there are many problems. One is how to avoid on the one side a wholesale and incomprehensible relativism[3] concerning truth while avoiding on the other the conclusion that we have not yet got any knowledge at all (though we might in some most unlikely but conceivable future time when "our total theory of the world" is complete and consistent and we all agree on it). Another is how to deal with the paradoxes concerning indeterminacy of meaning and translation[4] that grow out of this viewpoint. But the problem to which I wish to draw attention is that of reconciling this view with our view of man as a natural creature and a product of evolution.

If man is a natural creature and a product of evolution, it is reasonable to suppose that man's capacities as a knower are also a product of evolution. If we are capable of believing and knowing things, it must be because these capacities, and the organs in us or organization of us that are responsible for these capacities, *historically* performed a service that helped us to proliferate. Knowing must then be something that man has been doing all along—certainly not something he might get to some day when the Peircean end of inquiry arrives. Knowing must also be something that man has been doing *in the world*, and that has adapted him to that world, by contrast with which not knowing, being ignorant, is something objectively different and less advantageous.

From this standpoint it seems clear that man's knowing must be some kind of natural relation that he often bears to his world. Hence true sentences, being direct vehicles for conveying knowledge, must also bear some kind of natural relation (presumably a relation routed through man) to man's world. If we can understand why singing fancy songs helps song birds, why emitting ultrasonic sounds helps bats, why having a seventeen-year cycle helps seventeen-year locusts, why having ceremonial fights helps mountain sheep, and why dancing figure eights helps bees, surely it is mere cowardice to refuse even to wonder why uttering, in particular, *subject-predicate sentences, subject to negation,* helps man. Surely there is some explanation for this helping that is quite general and not magical. Nodding one's head and saying how it is wonderful that using subject-predicate sentences, subject to negation, helps us creatively-to-develop-evolving-forms-of-social-behavior-and-life while at the same time (mysteriously) adapting us to the environment will not do. Nor will it do to claim that coherence in a set of beliefs is the test of truth without at the same time attempting some explanation of *why* having a coherent set of beliefs rather than an incoherent set has anything to do with adapting to the world—that is, without explaining what coherence is *for*, how it helps. And, if we wanted to remain holists, it would have to be explained how man could have been doing so well for all these eons *without* having an overall coherent set of beliefs—without a consistent, let alone total, "theory of the world."

One more observation.[5] A very tempting theory of man's knowledge is that it consists in part of inner "maps" of sorts or of inner "representations" that model man's outside world inside him. It is hard to see how any a priori or metaphysical argument, such as those of Quine, Putnam, and Rorty, could have established that this is *not* how man does it. So it is hard to see how realism could be so obviously out of the question as is being claimed.[5]

These are not sharply focused difficulties, but I suggest they add to the general feeling that something *has* gone wrong with the newest of the empiricisms.

The main thing that has gone wrong, I will argue, is that the new empiricists have accomplished only half of their own revolution. They have failed to drop the foundationalist theory of *meaning* embedded in the tradition they reject along with the foundationalist theory of truth embedded there.

How simple and watertight the argument against realism can seem:

> To find the meaning of a word or sentence, look to what would justify its application or assertion or, if you prefer the causal to the logical order, look to what would cause it to be uttered. Now consider the meaning of " 'p' is true." Its assertion is justified on the grounds that p, or on grounds that would justify asserting that p; its assertion is caused by prior beliefs and/or stimulations of the afferent nerves. That "p" corresponds to anything obviously plays no role in the justification of " 'p' is true" or in the causal

derivation of its utterance. Hence correspondence has nothing to do with the meaning of "true," and *certainly* it cannot be, as has been claimed by the realists, the very essence or nature of truth.

But suppose we run this argument in reverse, taking the realist claim as premise:

> Correspondence is the very nature of truth and is of course involved in the very meaning of "true." For a sentence to be true is for it to correspond in a certain way to some part of the world. Now consider the sentence " 'p' is true." That "p" should correspond to anything clearly plays no role in the justification of " 'p' is true" or in the causal derivation of its utterance. Hence the meaning of " 'p' is true" has nothing to do with the justification or with the causal derivation of the utterance of " 'p' is true." Generalizing this, there seems to be good reason to think that meaning in other cases may also have nothing to do with justification or causal derivation.

But what could meaning be if it had nothing directly to do with justification or causal derivation? It would be nice, of course, if it were something such that terms and sentences in your idiolect might have the same meanings as same-sounding terms and sentences in my idiolect, despite the fact that our ways of justifying applications and the causal paths that lead to our utterances of these terms and sentences were different. That would help toward soothing our "indeterminacy of meaning and translation" anxieties. And making a *start* in this direction is not too hard.

Assume that what makes a sentence true is that there is something in the world onto which it maps in accordance with certain mapping functions. (The status of these mapping functions would need, of course, to be explained.) Now the *meaning* of a sentence is something which, having itself been made determinate, in turn determines the conditions under which the sentence is true. But, we have said, the sentence will be true under the condition that there *is* something in the world onto which it maps in accordance with certain mapping functions. What determines the meaning of a sentence is then what determines the mapping functions in accordance with which it must map onto something in the world in order to be true. Put roughly, the meaning of a sentence is its own special mapping functions—those in accordance with which it "should" or "is supposed to" map onto the world. (Sentences are supposed to be true, aren't they?) *But* we are rejecting correspondence as the test of truth on any level. So these mapping functions cannot be rules that the *user* of the sentence somehow has in his head and applies. It cannot be the user who "supposes" that his sentences map so. Similarly, the "supposed to" that determines the meaning must be of a different kind from that in which a person is "supposed" in accordance with the expectations of *others* to conform to certain rules when applying a certain sentence or justifying its application.

The *beginning* was not too hard. But now the difficulties are piling up. What kinds of "things" in the world do sentences map onto? What kinds of mapping functions are involved? More crucial, what kind of "supposed to" *is* this? What *does* determine which mapping function goes with a sentence—what the meaning is? Further, if something else than the way I justify my assertions or the way they are causally derived determined my meaning, how on earth could I ever *grasp my own meaning*—know what I or the sentences I used meant? Or teach my children to mean the same as I mean when they used the same English words and sentences?

These questions I will try to answer, step by step and with loving care. At the same time I will place meaning and, in general, intentionality (aboutness, of-ness) in nature alongside sentences and the people who utter sentences. In so doing I will also try to show why sentences that exhibit subject-predicate structure, subject to negation, are of use to man, and how the law of noncontradiction (the essence of coherence) fits into nature. The notion *Fregean sense* is the basic tool that I will use in this construction.

We should not expect the results of dropping a foundationalist theory of meaning to be any less unsettling than those of dropping a foundationalist theory of knowledge have been. True, the results of dropping both together will leave us without the paradoxes that resulted from dropping only one. But ancient dogmas, permeating our philosophical instincts and every traditional and familiar argument, are not easy to rout. In particular, though it will not be comfortable, we must be willing to give up what are perhaps the most cherished of all our dogmas— dogmas that I will lump under the heading Meaning Rationalism. We must be willing to discover that, just as we cannot know a priori or with Cartesian certainty whether any particular thing we think or say is true, so we cannot know a priori or with Cartesian certainty that in seeming to think or talk about something we *are* thinking or talking about—*anything at all*. We cannot know a priori *that we mean*. Nor can we know a priori or with Cartesian certainty *what* it is that we are thinking or talking about. Further, we cannot tell just by armchair reflection whether or not two terms in our idiolect are synonymous, whether a single term is ambiguous, or whether any particular state of affairs is or is not "logically possible" in any interesting or useful sense of that idiom. As man can fail in knowing, so he can fail in meaning; success is not on any level a "given." Putting this another way, our meanings are as much theoretical items as are any other items. Should we have expected to be able to give up all the other givens (including, in accordance with Sellarsian insight, the givenness of knowledge of sensations) while keeping the givenness of meanings?

After this final parting with Descartes we must also be willing to embark on new ventures in epistemology—the adventure of trying to construct a nonfoundational empiricist epistemology of meaning along-side the more traditional sort of empiricist epistemology—epistemology of judgment and truth. I will do this in such a way as to bypass holism. Then we will be able to understand how man, before the dawn of history, (before the dawn of full scale "theories") could still have pro-ceeded in his piece-meal way genuinely to know, in bits and snatches, some things about his world.

The result will be a position that, though the starkest possible an-tithesis of rationalism, will still be close to Aristotelian realism. Properties and kinds will show up only in the actual world. Nominalism will be denied.[6] (If one cannot tell by armchair reflection whether a seeming thought *is* a thought—is of anything at all—then those universals that are *mere* "objects of thought" need not really "be" at all—and certainly need not be somewhere outside of nature.) Also, logic will take an Aristotelian place as, in its way, the first of the *natural* sciences.

Putting ten chapters in a nutshell (though the dangers here may well outweigh the benefits), the sense of an indicative sentence is the mapping functions (informally, the "rules") in accordance with which it would have to map onto the world in order to perform its proper function or functions *in accordance with a Normal explanation.*[7] That is, the "supposed to" to which I made reference earlier will unpack in terms of the notion *Normal* (which, of course, must also be unpacked). *Sense*, in the vo-cabulary I use, is thus to be distinguished sharply from the classical notion "intension," from the (various) Quinean notion(s) of "meaning," and also from Frege's own notion *Sinn* to the degree that the latter tends to merge with the former. Intension, as having to do with a network of inference rules that enmesh a term or sentence, with jus-tifications for or causes of its application, or with its role in a theory, is something quite other than sense. Intension, I will argue, is the third and least important aspect of meaning.

Many though by no means all of the jobs that the notion *intension* has traditionally been thought capable of doing will be taken over by the notion *sense*. But sense will not contrast with reference in at all the same way that intension has traditionally been thought to do. Indeed, *having* a referent, it will turn out, is just one particular way of having a sense. Referents themselves, of course, are another matter; they are things in the world. But the notion *referent* does not serve as the basic partner to the notion *sense* either. The basic partner of sense I will call "real value," and the difference between a real value and a referent will turn out to be at least as great as the difference between sense and intension. Only complete and true sentences, or parts of these, have real values, real value being, roughly, that in the world which makes the sentence true, or that in the world which happens to correspond to a part of a true sentence.

It is in Part II that I will introduce the notions *Fregean sense* and *real value*. I will use these in developing a general theory of signs. Speaking loosely, sense is intentionality. I will argue that thoughts as well as sentences may be interpreted as devices that exhibit intentionality—as inner intentional icons, likely sometimes taking the form of inner sentences. The senses of these inner sentences are not determined by the inference rules or dispositions that connect them to other inner sentences, or by their causes or the stimulations that induce them, but by the "rules" (mapping functions) in accordance with which they map when true. Intentionality is thus divorced from rationality, as sense is divorced from intension.

So I will describe the intentionality of thoughts in naturalist terms. Yet the program is not a physicalist or reductionist program. For, I will argue, the problem of understanding intentionality can and should be divorced from the problem of understanding consciousness. This is done by abandoning the traditional epistemic view of consciousness—by giving up the rationalist view of meaning and intentionality. Intentionality is not harbored within consciousness, nor can consciousness, in the guise of a priori reflection, provide an affidavit for the genuine intentionality of seeming thoughts.

In Part III I will discuss in considerable detail the problem of just *how* language maps onto the world when it does, and cases in which it does *not* map onto the world, applying the theory of proper functions and the theory of sense to devices such as indexicals, definite and indefinite descriptions, sentences asserting identity and asserting existence, negative sentences, and intentional contexts. Here it will come to the fore how very different real value is from reference, and how important having a notion such as that of real value is to an understanding of *indefinite* sense—the sort of sense that indefinite descriptions have and, I will argue, many other devices have as well.

Another important distinction will also figure in Part III—a distinction between intentional devices generally and a special class of these that I will call "representations." Sentences and thoughts are representations; bee dances, though they are intentional devices, are not. Representations are distinguished by the fact that when they perform their proper functions their referents are *identified*. Part IV will begin with a description of the act of identifying the referent of an intentional device element. For the cases of language and thought, this is the same as *knowing what* one is thinking of or *knowing what* a word represents. According to most forms of classical realism, thinking of a thing and knowing what one is thinking of are one and the same act; intentionality is transparent. I will argue that intentionality is not transparent. Many intentional items—items that are "about" other things—do their jobs without their interpreters or the organisms that harbor them having any grasp of what they are about. VonFrisch knew what bee dances are about, but it is unlikely that bees do. Bees just react to bee dances appropriately. Similarly, a thought can be about something without the thinker's knowing what it is about. But for the most part human thought performs its proper functions only insofar as what it is about is *identified* in thought. Inference, I will claim, involves acts of identifying what thoughts are about, and one of the proper functions of beliefs is to participate in inferences. Hence beliefs are *representations*, and the traditional connection between having beliefs and being rational is established.

Certain assumptions about ontology are then sketched, for these are needed in order to understand what general structure the world must have in order that subject-predicate sentences, subject to negation, can map onto it. I will argue that if we as realists understand ontology the right way, we do not have to claim that mapping the world with sentences requires that the world be "cut up" in a way that somehow "gets things right." The realist need only give an account of objective *identity* or selfsameness, which is something quite other than Nature's preferred classification system or Nature's preferred way of carving parts out of wholes or her preferred way of grouping things into unities. The sketch of the ontology of identity that I will give is needed even more urgently in order to understand how epistemology might be reconstructed after this wholesale rejection of foundationalism.

The final chapters introduce a nonfoundationalist and also nonholist epistemology that allows us to understand how we test for validity both our apparent abilities to reidentify things and our seeming meanings. I will argue that we possess a much larger store of observation concepts than is generally supposed and that these concepts have fallible yet effective adequacy tests that are independent of the development even of modest explanatory theories about the world. To test these concepts is the same as to test the most fundamental of our abilities to reidentify things in the world and the same as to test the most fundamental of our seeming meanings for validity. Insofar as these meanings and abilities to identify are real or valid, necessarily a good proportion of our judgments are true. The development of modest and then less modest explanatory theories about the world, the bringing of judgments to interact with one another in groups, gives us additional evidence concerning the truth of individual judgments as well as additional evidence concerning that more basic level of epistemological concern—conceptual adequacy and clarity. And, of course, the development of theories is often associated with the development of new concepts, which may or may not turn out to be testable independently of theory.

Epistemology, ontology, philosophy of mind, and philosophy of language cannot ultimately be separated from one another. There is no way of making significant and convincing moves in one of these areas without adjusting simultaneously in the others. I have promised, rhetorically, to proceed step by step. Yet many of the steps will of necessity rather resemble enthusiastic leaps, the object being to pace off the whole at one stretch so as to take its measure. Like other large-scale theories, *philosophical* theories too do not rest only upon previously secured foundations—upon point-by-point prior arguments. As in the case of other theories, the general coherence of the whole is often the beginning point. Details and also foundations are constructed or perfected later, the value of the theory depending upon whether or not it is in fact possible to accomplish this. My purpose is to argue for a program; the various rough foundations and the details of results that I will sketch, taken distributively though not of course collectively, are tentative.

A good number of new or technical terms are introduced during the course of this book. There is a special index at the back telling where each of these is explained.

PART I

The Theory of Proper Functions with Some
Applications Prior to Introducing Intentionality

Chapter 1

Direct Proper Functions

That a heart is a heart certainly has something to do with pumping blood. But what *kind* of connection with pumping blood must a heart have? Some hearts are diseased and some are malformed in such a way that they are unable to pump blood. Other devices, such as water pumps, are perfectly capable of pumping blood, yet these are not hearts. Devices have now been designed that in fact pump blood in people, but these are only artificial hearts, not members of the biological category "heart." It is not then the actual constitution, powers, or dispositions of a thing that make it a member of a certain biological category.

My claim will be that it is the "proper function" of a thing that puts it in a biological category, and this has to do not with its powers but with its history. Having a proper function is a matter of having been "designed to" or of being "supposed to" (impersonal) perform a certain function. The task of the theory of proper functions is to define this sense of "designed to" or "supposed to" in naturalist, nonnormative, and nonmysterious terms.

If language device tokens and mental intentional states (believing that, intending to, hoping that) are members of proper function or "biological" categories, then they are language devices or intentional states not by virtue of their powers but by virtue of what they are supposed to be able to do yet perhaps cannot do. For example, just as hearts and kidneys are sometimes diseased or malformed, so sentences and beliefs are sometimes false, and words and concepts are sometimes ambiguous and sometimes vacuous. Such sentences, beliefs, words, and concepts are not able to perform their proper functions. Consider, for example, beliefs. The traditional functionalist has assumed that whatever interesting functions make beliefs to be beliefs, these must be found among the actual dispositions or powers of beliefs or of people who have beliefs. True beliefs are beliefs; false beliefs are also beliefs. So false beliefs must have these powers too. But this, I will argue, is like looking for the functions that make kidneys to be kidneys by trying to see what is in common to the powers of *all* kidneys—the normal ones, the diseased ones, and the malformed ones. But, of course, true beliefs, false beliefs, and beliefs containing confused or empty ideas have no powers in common beyond, as it were, their powers to move one another about in the head (inference) or their powers to affect input-output dispositions of the human or his brain. So the traditional functionalist concentrates upon input and output and upon ways the system might work inside, hoping to show what about the insides of this system or about its dispositions constitutes its having beliefs. Intentionality is sought against the background of *possible* worlds or *possible* stimulations and their results. But if, instead, we push the analogy with biological categories, only *true* beliefs are capable of performing the defining functions of beliefs. We will then be free to look for the defining attributes of beliefs among relations between *true* beliefs and the *actual* world outside. False beliefs will then appear merely as things that were "supposed to" have had such and such relations to the actual world.

"Proper function" is intended as a technical term. It is of interest because it can be used to unravel certain problems, not because it does or doesn't accord with common notions such as "purpose" or the ordinary notion "function." My program is far removed from conceptual analysis; I need a term that will do a certain job, and so I must fashion one. However, I have found the growing literature on teleology and teleological explanation, much of which concerns itself with conceptual analysis of terms like "goal," "purpose," and "function," of considerable interest and believe that the notion "proper function" may interest those working in this area reciprocally. For the things that have "proper functions" do seem to coincide with things (omitting God) that have, in ordinary parlance, "purposes."

The first part of the theory of proper functions concerns only the functions of devices that are members of families of devices that are similar to one another—as human hearts are similar to one another, and stickleback mating dances or various tokens of the English word "dog" or various handshakes occurring in greeting are similar to one another. In the second part of the theory I will show how things that are quite new under the sun can also have proper functions—things such as novel behaviors, novel bee dances, and novel beliefs. Devices of the first kind have what I shall call "*direct* proper functions." Devices of the second kind have "*derived* proper functions."

A device that has a *direct* proper function has this function *as* a member of a special kind of family that I will call a "reproductively established family."[1] Things similar to one another form a reproductively established family, in the simplest cases, when these things are similar to one another because something like copying has been going on. I will term the kind of copying I have in mind "reproduction." Hence, I will define first "reproduction," then "reproductively established family," then "direct proper function"—and last, "Normal." In the next chapter I will define "derived proper function."

There is a complication in giving these definitions. I will need to distinguish two kinds of reproductively established families, first-order and higher-order. Only members of first-order reproductively established families are "copies" of one another. Higher-order reproductively established families cannot be defined except by reference both to the proper functions of lower-order families and to the notion "Normal explanation." The definition of "proper function" then applies recursively to higher-order reproductively established families, and the definition of "reproductively established family" likewise applies recursively. What I will do is put the definitions of first-order and higher-order reproductively established families all in one place, even though the definition of higher-order reproductively established families will presuppose understanding of the notions "Normal" and "proper function," defined only later on. I do not believe that this procedure will pose any severe problems for the reader—some rough understanding of what a proper function is and what it is, for example, for a body organ to do its work in accordance with a Normal explanation, rather than by accident or mediated by wonder drugs or artificial devices, can surely be presupposed.

Reproductions

The definition of "reproduction" given below does not correspond exactly to ordinary usage. The ordinary word "copy" probably expresses what I will define somewhat better, but that term has problems of its own; so I have settled on "reproduction." The motivating idea behind the definition of "reproduction" is to capture certain cases in which it can be explained why two things had to be *alike* in a certain respect or respects, say, color, this being quite other than either (1) independently explaining for each why it is, say, *red*, or (2) explaining why, more specifically, given that one is *red*, the other is also *red*. Some explanations explain, rather, why given that one had any certain color, the other had to have *the same* color.

An individual B is a "reproduction" of an individual A iff:

(1) B has some determinate properties p_1, p_2, p_3, etc., in common with A and (2) below is satisfied.

A property is "determinate" relative to some "determinable" property under which both it and a set of properties contrary to it fall. Thus *red* (along with its contraries *green*, *yellow*, etc.) is a determinate property relative to *colored*; *scarlet* is a determinate property relative either to *red* or to *colored*.

(2) That A and B have the properties p_1, p_2, p_3, etc., in common can be explained by a natural law or laws operative in situ, which laws satisfy (3) below.

By a law operative in situ I mean a special law that can be derived from universal natural laws by adding reference to the actual surrounding conditions, in this case the conditions surrounding the production of B. For example, given the presence of a certain kind of properly constructed copying machine, a paper with black marks on it placed in the appropriate spot, presence of paper of the right sort in the machine's paper-supply box, a force of appropriate magnitude and direction applied to the machine's "copy" button, etc. (assuming that all these conditions are described in appropriate physical terms) and given the laws of physics and chemistry, a natural law in situ can be derived that correlates the configuration of black marks on the paper with the configuration of marks that will be produced on the copy that comes out.

(3) For each property p_1, p_2, p_3, etc., the laws in situ that explain why B is like A in respect to p are laws that correlate a specifiable range of determinates under a determinable under which p falls, such that whatever determinate characterizes A must also characterize B, *the direction of causality being straight from A to B*.

Roughly, the law in situ implies that *had A been different* with respect to its determinate character p within a specifiable range of variation, as a result, B *would have differed accordingly*. Everything has *many* causes, of course. For B to be a reproduction of A it is necessary only that there be *some* way of describing B's causal history, holding certain conditions constant (mentioning these as initial conditions or simply as conditions that as a matter of fact entered the scene at this or that point in B's history) such that it is explained why B had to be *like A*, whatever the character of A, within a certain range of character variation.

I will call the properties p_1, p_2, p_3, etc., by reference to which B is a reproduction of A "reproductively established properties" of B. And I will call A "the model" or "a model" for B, sometimes speaking too of B's being "modeled on" A or, informally, "copied from" A.

It is possible for an item to have reproductively established properties derived from several different models. Trivially, if B is a reproduction of A and A is a reproduction of A' with respect to the same properties, then B is a reproduction of A'. More interesting, an item can be a reproduction of numerous unlike things at once, deriving different properties from each. For example, a silver cross, such as many people wear on a chain around their necks, that is made also to resemble a vine of olive leaves has some reproductively established characters derived from earlier examples of Christian crosses and others derived from the olive leaves (or pictures of these) that the artist studied in order to make the cross. The laws operating in situ here are derived in part from the structure and state of the individual nervous system of the artist, just as, in the case of the copying machine, the laws are derived in part from the structure of the insides of the machine.

Sounds produced by recordings and copies of documents, etc., are of course reproductions. Things such as footprints (they are the same shape as the foot) and fossil impressions and mirror images and even shadows are also reproductions, but they are not reproductions that will turn out to be of any interest, for they do not have proper functions. More interesting examples of reproductions are viruses, genes, artifacts that are not of original design, and behaviors that have resulted from imitation. (In the last two cases at least, the relevant laws in situ have different derivations in the case of each new reproduction of a type, for they depend upon the structures of different individual nervous systems through which the type is reproduced.) Sometimes a behavior that occurs because someone has been told to behave so is also re-produced behavior. If a child watches me shake hands with a friend and imitates this behavior with his own friend, his handshaking is a reproduction. And if the child was trained or told by me to shake hands instead of naturally imitating this behavior, his handshaking is still a reproduction—so long, that is, as it is true that if I and others did not shake hands but rather rubbed noses or kissed on both cheeks in greeting, I would have trained or told the child to rub noses or to kiss on both cheeks and he would have done that instead.

Now consider mass-produced products. Items coming off an assembly line are not reproductions of one another. Rather than the character of one item directly producing the character of the next, these items are alike because they have certain causes in common. On the other hand, items produced by mass production are usually reproductions of some prototype not produced on the line—some original experimental model. Biological devices such as dogs, human hearts, and stickleback fishes' mating dances are not reproductions of one another either. (That is one reason why I warned that "reproduction" is not being used here in its ordinary sense.) It is not directly because his father danced so that the stickleback dances so. Had his father been injured and hence danced differently, that would not have caused him to dance differently.

It is not directly because my father and mother had two legs that I have two legs. Mutilated parents can produce normal children; wooden legs are not inherited. Rather, the stickleback's *genes* and my *genes* (tokens) were reproductions of earlier gene tokens harbored by our respective parents, and similar *genes* produced similar *products*. It is this sort of consideration that will later complicate the definition of "reproductively established *family*," causing us to divide these into first-order and higher-order families. Only in the case of first-order families are the members "reproductions" of one another in the sense of "reproduction" we have defined. People and hearts, etc., are members of higher-order reproductively established families.

The respects in which one thing B is a reproduction of another thing A can be relational respects. Coordinately, the production of B that is reproduction need not produce B from scratch. If a child watches me shake hands with a friend and imitates this behavior with his own friend, what is reproduced is not just a bodily movement. What is reproduced is the relational configuration *person shaking the hand of another person*. And, of course, in order to reproduce this configuration, the child does not have to produce his friend (or himself).

Sentences are reproduced items—a fact that will prove to be of considerable importance. Like the silver cross that has more than one model, a sentence token usually has numerous models at once, acquiring different reproductively established properties from each. Each word token in a spoken sentence is a reproduction of some earlier token or tokens of its type that the speaker has heard, stored in his memory, and now reproduces. Had these heard models been different in certain respects, the word token that the speaker produces would have differed accordingly. Moreover, any sentence that is grammatical can, presumably, be described as according with specifiable syntactic rules, according with these rules, whatever they are for a given sentence, being a reproductively established character of the sentence. Just as children copy words from adults, they copy grammar. This is true even if Chomsky is right that there are universals of grammar corresponding to inborn dispositions of children to generalize in quite limited ways from sentences heard. Such universals merely guarantee that there are certain properties of sentences that children will *not* copy. For example, they will not copy from the sentence "John's mother makes quilts" the property "makes" *is placed third* or any other "structure-independent" aspect of the sentence. But all that is necessary for reproduction is that there be *some* variables such that the reproduction has followed its model with respect to the values of these. That speakers copy words and also grammar does not of course imply that speech is mere blind imitation. But for every word token and for every syntactic form token, one among its myriad causal explanations shows how it is a reproduction. And for every sentence token, a collection of such explanations shows how the sentence entire is a reproduction based on a number of models.

First-Order Reproductively Established Families

There are two kinds of reproductively established families, first-order and higher-order. These are reproductively established families for slightly different reasons.

> Any set of entities having the same or similar reproductively established characters derived by repetitive reproductions from the same character of the same model or models form *a first-order reproductively established family.*

Notice that in accordance with this definition the members of a first-order reproductively established family could but need not have been reproduced all in the same way. For example, tokens of the written English word "dog" that have been reproduced by Xerox, by various people's hands (each hooked to a somewhat differently programmed nervous system), and by various kinds of printing presses are all members of a single reproductively established family. Similarly, if a parrot says "hello," granted that he copied from an English speaker's tokens of "hello," his token is a member of the same reproductively established family as are the speaker's tokens of "hello."

Tokens of a specific gene, handshakes occurring in a culture (i.e., not independently derived), household screwdrivers (the same design has been copied over and over), and various tokens of the same word are members of first-order reproductively established families. All sentences in a given language that illustrate the same syntactic form are members of a single reproductively established family. However, sentence tokens are always members of a number of different reproductively established families at once, indeed, one for each significant aspect of the sentence.

In one important sense of "conventional," all conventional devices and behaviors are members of first-order reproductively established families. According to *Webster's Third New International Dictionary,* "conventional" can mean (1) *formed by agreement or compact; stipulated; contractual.* Dub this sense "conventional₁." It can also mean (2) *growing out of, or depending on, custom or general agreement; established or sanctioned by general concurrence or usage.* Dub this sense "conventional₂."[2] Paul Revere's agreement "one if by land and two if by sea" made his signals with lights conventional₁. But these signals were by no means conventional$_2$; indeed, it is of the essence of secret codes that they should not be conventional$_2$. We associate conventions with what is in a certain way *arbitrary*. There is always something arbitrary, specifically, about the connection between a conventional$_2$ device and its function. But the species-typical "chip" of a chipping sparrow is arbitrary in relation to its function, and *it* is not a conventional device. What, besides arbitrariness, is needed to make a device conventional$_2$?

Consider: It is not conventional or customary but "only natural" that we usually write with our hands rather than our feet and that we hold hands rather than holding feet or putting foot in hand. Is it conventional, or customary, or is it "only natural" that we shake hands with the right hand? It is not arbitrary that we do, given the proportion of the population that is right-handed. But in left-handers this behavior is merely reproduced behavior. They do it only because *others* do, rather than naturally. Their behavior is in this respect modeled, either directly or indirectly, upon the behavior of right-handers. Here, I suggest, is where an element of mere custom, or convention$_2$, enters. It enters, of course, *because* of the arbitrariness for left-handers of using the right hand when shaking hands. In general, if a behavior recurs naturally without modeling, it is not conventional$_2$. One thing that is needed, then, to make a behavior conventional$_2$ is that it be a member of a first-order reproductively established family.[2]

Higher-Order Reproductively Established Families

(1)   Any set of similar items produced by members of the same reproductively established family, when it is a direct proper function of the family to produce such items and these are all produced in accordance with Normal explanations, form a *higher-order reproductively established family*.

Also

(2)   Any set of similar items produced by the same device, when it was one of the proper functions of this device to make later items *match* earlier items, and these items are alike in accordance with a Normal explanation for performance of this function, form a *higher-order reproductively established family*.

(*Reminder*: I will define "proper function" and "Normal explanation" using the notion "reproductively established family." We get our first proper functions by reference to first-order reproductively established families. After that the definitions are recursive.)

Hearts and livers are not members of *first*-order reproductively established families because one heart or liver is not a direct reproduction of another. But although my heart is not a copy of my parents' hearts, it was produced under Normal conditions in accordance with the proper functions of certain of my genes which *were* directly copied from my parents' *genes*. Hence my heart and my parents' hearts (and ultimately your heart) are members of the same higher-order reproductively established family in accordance with (1). The various tokens of screech owls' screeches, various tokens of stickleback fishes' mating dances, and various tokens of walking and washing behavior in cats are members of higher-order reproductively established families in accordance with (1). Learned behaviors resulting from training or from a trial-and-error procedure are members of higher-order reproductively established families in accordance with (2), assuming that it is a proper function of the mechanisms that produce such behaviors to turn out again the *same* behavior as was rewarded or found to be successful earlier.

A third condition under which an item may be said to be a member of a higher-order reproductively established family must now be added that will prove of utmost importance. This condition is not an *additional* condition, but a loosening of conditions (1) and (2) above. The point of this new condition is to make room for malformed members of reproductively established families.

> (3)   If anything x (*a*) has been produced by a device a direct proper function of which is to produce a member or members of a higher-order reproductively established family R, and (*b*) is in some respects like Normal members of R because (*c*) it has been produced in accordance with an explanation that approximates in some (undefined) degree to a Normal explanation for production of members of R, then x is a member of R.

The vagueness of the question, in some cases, whether a bit of matter should be called "a malformed eye" or merely "a glob of misplaced organic matter on the forehead" is reflected in the vagueness of "in some respects like" and "approximates in some degree to a Normal explanation."

The properties that are common to all members of a higher-order reproductively established family that have been produced Normally are not, strictly speaking, reproductively established properties. Rather, we can say that they make up the "Normal character" of that family.

Direct Proper Functions

The intuitive idea behind the definition that I will give of a direct proper function is this. A function F is a direct proper function of x if x exists having a character C because by having C it *can* perform F. (Notice how close this is to the idea that x exists in order to perform F.) First interpret "because by having C it *can* perform F" to mean "because there were things that performed F in the past due to having C." But how could it be because F was performed in the past by C as opposed to, merely, because F was performed in the past by something or other, that x was produced? Consider a motor idling. A cyclical process is involved here. Stage A produces stage B which produces stage C which in turn produces stage A again. But it is not because it was A that produced B or because it was A that produced C that A occurs over again. It is merely because B and C were produced at the right time by *something*. How could it ever be because it was A that caused B that A recurred as opposed to being, merely, because B occurred? How can a thing result from a prior *causing* as opposed to resulting from an effect produced via the causing?

My suggestion is that when it is in part because A's have caused B's in the past that a positive *correlation* has existed between A's and B's, and the fact that this *correlation* has existed figures in an explanation of the proliferation of A's, then it does make sense to say that A's exist in part because A's caused B's.

To say that there is a correlation between two things A and B is to say that a higher proportion of A's than of non-A's are B (and—it follows—vice versa). A correlation holds relative to some definite sample of things, and this sample must of course contain things that are not A (as well as things that are not B). In the case of the motor idling it seems clear that no explanation of why any stage A occurs that makes reference to this kind of correlation could be given. Cases in which A stages did not occur or in which B stages did not occur have no bearing upon reasons for recurrence of A stages. (It is true as well, of course, that recurrences of A stages are not in this sort of case reproductions, for there are not ways in which had an A stage differed, other things remaining constant, the next A stage would have differed accordingly.) But in the arena of evolutionary history, there *is* room for such statistical explanations. There are of course many legitimate explanations, some more interesting than others, for every happening in nature. What matters here is only that explanations making reference to correlations of a certain type can be given *at all* for why certain traits of organisms survive.

During the evolutionary process Nature effectively experiments by producing mutations affecting, at one time or another, surely every character of a species. Each trait is thus set in competition not only against the environment but against cases of its absence. (We don't have to think here only of such extremes as things born without hearts. Things born with new variants on hearts is enough. And things having more primitive hearts that were pushed out by things with modern hearts.) Moreover, economy dictates that traits serving no purpose are highly likely to disappear, not necessarily because they get in the way, but because that section of the genetic code *could* serve a useful function if coded otherwise and sooner or later Nature will stumble on this discovery. Historical statistical correlations between organ or behavior structures and the performances or reliability of the performances of certain useful functions thus figure in legitimate explanations of why the modern Normal traits of any species have continued to proliferate, thus culminating in the existence of current exemplars of these traits.

I wish to emphasize this particular aspect of evolutionary theory because it has parallels in other domains of concern to us. Especially important is the fact that many living organisms contain equipments that pick up or react to correlations of various kinds among items in and around them, for example, between their own behaviors and subsequent events. Nearly every macroscopic animal can learn some things by trial and error. Many can learn by observing rather than, as it were, acting out correlations. Some reach the height of simulating use of Mill's method of difference with "one trial" and "one observation" learning.

Putting things intuitively, products of evolution have in common with various other kinds of products the fact that they are reproduced or continue to be proliferated because they, *rather than certain other things*, have been associated with certain functions. If certain other things had correlated better with these functions, the chances are these other things would have been reproduced or would have proliferated instead.

Let me now attempt a definition of "direct proper function" with an eye to exploiting these parallels.

A direct proper function is a function that an item has *as* a member of a reproductively established family. (Of course, not every reproductively established family has proper functions.) First we define the notion "ancestor of a member of a reproductively established family":

(1) Any member of a (first-order) reproductively established family from which a current member *m* was derived by reproduction or by successive reproductions is an ancestor of *m*.

(2) Any temporally earlier member of a (higher-order) reproductively established family which member was produced by an ancestor of the device that produced a present member *m* is an ancestor of *m*.

(3) Any earlier member of a (higher-order) reproductively established family that a present member m is similar to in accordance with a proper function of a producer that produced both is an ancestor of m.

Now we define the notion "proper function."

Where m is a member of a reproductively established family R and R has the reproductively established or Normal character C, m has the function F as a direct proper function iff:

(1) Certain ancestors of m performed F.

(2) In part because there existed a direct causal connection between having the character C and performance of the function F in the case of these ancestors of m, C correlated positively with F over a certain set of items S which included these ancestors and other things not having C.

(3) One among the legitimate explanations that can be given of the fact that m exists makes reference to the fact that C correlated positively with F over S, either directly causing reproduction of m or explaining why R was proliferated and hence why m exists.

It follows that if any member of a reproductively established family has a direct proper function, all members of which this member is an ancestor have this proper function too.

In accordance with this definition, the sorts of purposes that we ordinarily attribute to biological devices such as hearts and inherited behaviors are direct proper functions, granted that our guesses about the evolutionary histories of these devices are correct—our guesses about their "reasons for survival." Artifacts that have been serving certain functions known to those who reproduce them and that are reproduced on this account (e.g., household screwdrivers) have these functions as direct proper functions. Behaviors that result from training or from trial-and-error learning involving correlations of a reward with the behavior have as direct proper functions to produce that reward. Behaviors that result from imitation of behaviors of others because the latter behaviors have correlated, within the observation of the learner, with certain functions have these functions as direct proper functions. (In the latter case, the *intent* of the person who so behaves, it will turn out, affords the behavior *also* a *derived* proper function (Chapter 2) which may or may not accord with its direct proper function. For example, I may shake hands in a skit because shaking hands has often been observed by me to serve a greeting function. I do not in this instance actually purpose that function, for I am not actually greeting anyone. Yet this function is a *direct* proper function of my handshake, and my handshake *is* a member of the social artifact class "handshakes," not a dance gesture or a mere movement.)

Notice that it is not necessary that a device actually serve any direct proper functions of it. For example, very few sperm actually serve their direct proper functions. It is not necessary that a device even be capable of serving any direct proper function of it. Some members of reproductively established families are malformed and unable for this reason to perform properly. Having a proper function depends upon the *history* of the device that has it, not upon its form of dispositions.

The same function may sometimes be proper to quite separate and differently constituted reproductively established families. Consider mating displays or greeting rituals. Also, some members of reproductively established families are malformed. Hence if we classify items simply into proper function categories, these categories will correspond neither to physical structure nor to actual or possible functions of these items. Our ordinary classification of items under headings such as "heart," "kidney," "mating display," or "greeting ritual" tends to correspond to classification in accordance with direct proper functions. For example, it is not difficult to construct examples involving novelties or accidents of nature that might produce (1) heart tokens quite different in form from any existent hearts, (2) heart tokens that do not in fact circulate blood, (3) heart tokens that (because malformed) could not circulate blood (at least not in accordance with a Normal explanation), (4) items that (freakishly) have the exact form of certain existent hearts but that are not hearts (because their history is wrong), (5) items that do (freakishly) circulate blood but that are not hearts, and (6) items that could circulate blood but are not hearts. In the title of this book I used "biological categories" by extension to cover all proper function categories, and I will continue to do so when convenient.

The various aspects of language that we intuitively think of as carrying meaning—words, syntactic forms, inflected word endings, tonal inflections, stress patterns, etc.—all seem to be "reproduced" items in the sense we have defined, for all of these vary among languages. Children do not speak before hearing speech, and when they do speak, how they speak depends upon what they have heard. Tokens of these various significant aspects of language—I am calling these aspects "language devices"—are thus members of first-order reproductively established families. Do these families have proper functions? Can the existence of current tokens of each of these devices be given an explanation by reference to a history during which each has correlated with a certain function or set of functions and for this reason proliferated rather than becoming extinct?

That a device is enabled to perform its proper functions almost invariably depends upon its having a suitable surrounding environment, and often a suitable environment must contain members of other reproductively established families that need it in turn in order to perform properly. Neither your heart nor the rest of your circulatory system can perform properly unless attached to the other; the bee needs to live where there are flowers and vice versa; the male stickleback's dance and the female's response mechanism perform properly only in the presence of one another. If language devices have proper functions, it is clear that the performances of these functions must depend upon there being suitable cooperating response mechanisms or programs in hearers within the surrounding language community. For the moment let us ignore the question of how it happens that any particular hearer responds to a language device in the way or ways he happens to and consider only speakers.

The speaker finds himself surrounded by hearers who are affected in various ways by his speaking. These hearers react differentially to different language sounds. For any given hearer at any given time, granted that he is listening, some differences in what he hears will make differences in how he reacts covertly and even overtly. For example, you may not react overtly sentence by sentence as I tell you a pleasant story. But suppose that in place of one of my sentences the cry "Help!" were substituted, or the sentence "I once committed a murder" or "And then Aristotle, *the* philosopher, asked me for advice on the matter" or any sentence that was nonsensical or out of place in the context or obviously false. Then you probably would react overtly.

Now I think it can be assumed that speakers nearly always speak with purpose—often just for the sake of pleasant times with hearers, but also for the sake of a thousand other ends. Suppose that the overt reactions that hearers in a language community made to language sounds were totally random, varying from hearer to hearer and from time to time for the same hearer. That is, these reactions bore no relation whatever to the sounds speakers uttered, even after taking account of linguistic context, nonlinguistic context, indeed, of the context that is *everything* there is in the world with language. Confronted with such a situation, speakers would, after a time, stop speaking. No child, brought up in such a community, would bother to utter any more than those random sounds that happened to amuse him (babbling), and this only in private, since he would have no way of learning how to make language sounds publicly without producing unpredictable and sometimes very unwanted reactions and results. Speaking is purposeful doing, and one cannot purposefully do things in a completely lawless world. That language devices proliferate must depend upon there being *some* degree of uniformity at *some* level of description at least among *covert* hearer responses that *can* be manifested in overt hearer responses. This is trivial. But this is exactly the same as to say that language devices must have direct proper functions at some level or levels. It must be because they correlate with functions that they proliferate.

Stabilizing and Standardizing Proper Functions

Now let us examine the situation the language hearer is in. We cannot assume that the hearers in a language community will continue to make exactly the same responses under the same conditions to the same language devices regardless of what utterances are typically made by speakers. It is not that hearers have certain inborn responses to language and then speakers learn to use these blind responses in order to manipulate hearers to their own advantage. Hearers who are too often manipulated in ways that go against their own purposes will stop responding to language as they once would have done. Just as speakers will continue to speak only if there is some correlation between what they say and how hearers respond, so hearers will continue to listen and to follow certain patterns of translation into understanding and sometimes into belief or intention and action only if these responses are of some use in relation to the hearer's own projects in the world— of use at least in some critical proportion of cases. And if hearers stop listening or stop responding in ways that show some uniformities, speakers in turn will stop speaking. Hence one of the proper functions of the various language devices must be to do things that keep hearers responding in the old ways with some degree of uniformity. Otherwise the language device would die out.

Now I suppose that it is conceivable that language devices proliferate because of a sort of symbiotic relationship that they establish between speakers and hearers in a critical proportion of cases. As in the case of the bees and the flowers, perhaps what hearers get out of responding standardly to speakers' utterances and what speakers get out of using language in standard ways are quite independent. But it seems much more likely that in the case of standard speaker uses followed by standard hearer responses there is a crossover point or points—certain functions that the various aspects of a sentence perform that contribute both to the speaker's and to the hearer's ends, thus tending to keep speakers speaking and hearers responding in standard ways. I will argue for this point of view by trying to show in the cases of a number of kinds of language devices where this crossover point actually lies.

The stabilizing and standardizing proper function (or functions) of a language device is that hypothesized function (or functions) that tends at the same time to keep speakers using the device in standard ways and to keep hearers responding to it in standard ways, thus stabilizing its function or functions. As I mentioned earlier, such a function should be thought of not as an invariant function or as an average function but as a function performed in a critical mass of cases of actual use, forming a sort of center of gravity to which wayward speakers and hearers tend to return after departures. Without such a center of gravity, uses and responses would diverge in all directions until there would be no motivation for hearers to respond at all or for speakers to use the device at all. A language device that lacked a stabilizing and standardizing proper function or functions would simply die out.

A Note on Changes in Proper Function

Clearly the correlation pattern that is partially responsible for the existence of a device token with a direct proper function may be more or less proximate vs. remote from the time of the production of that token. For example, the historical correlation pattern responsible for the appendix in humans is quite remote from current appendix tokens. Thus a direct proper function of a device may be called "historically proximate" or "historically remote"; the direct proper function of our appendixes is historically remote. If the function accounting for reproduction of its ancestors changed over time, a device may have a stacked series of direct proper functions, each more historically proximate to its current tokens than the last. It is hard to give examples of this from biology, because the structure of an organ usually must change as its function changes, front legs turning into flippers or gills into lungs. But in the case of words, where structure is not directly related to function, the phenomenon is clear. Etymologists study the changes that have taken place over time in the functions of what remain recognizably the same words. Current tokens of these words exist *now* in part because ancestors of these tokens once performed certain functions, but these functions were other than those that currently account for proliferation of the word's tokens. Thus words often have a stacked series of proper functions moving from the most historically remote to the most historically proximate, all of these being, literally, proper functions of current tokens. Our tendency to call also a historically remote function of a word or word root "what it means" or even "what it really means" (e.g., when going back to Latin or Greek), I suggest, reflects this. Thus schoolchildren are told that "transcend" *means* to climb beyond. Our use of the present tense is not anomalous here.

Normal Explanations and Normal Conditions for Direct Proper Functions

A Normal explanation is an explanation of how a particular reproductively established family has historically performed a particular proper function. For each such family and function there are more proximate and less proximate Normal explanations. For example, there are Normal explanations, on various levels of proximity, of how the human heart has managed historically to circulate blood. Begin with the most proximate Normal explanation of how a reproductively established family R performs a proper function F. This explanation is the *least detailed* explanation possible that starts by noting some features of the structure of members of R, adds some conditions in which R has historically been when it actually performed F—these conditions being uniform over as large a number of historical cases as possible—adds natural laws, and deduces, i.e., shows in detail without gaps, how this setup leads to the performance of F. The features of R that must be mentioned in such an explanation are the "Normal functioning properties" of members of R. (Some Normal properties of R may just be along for the ride.) The conditions that must be mentioned are "Normal conditions" for the proper performance of members of R. Less proximate Normal explanations of how R performs F will make reference as well to the historically most usual origins of conditions cited in the most proximate Normal explanation for R's performance of F. For example, the most proximate Normal explanation of how the human heart circulates blood must tell something of how the heart is made (its Normal properties or structure), how it works inside, and note such conditions as the regularity of electrical impulses sent to the heart, the oxygen supply sent to the heart, and the presence of a closed circuit of blood vessels emanating from and returning to the heart which carry the blood to and from the proper places in the heart. A slightly less proximate Normal explanation will tell where the electrical impulses have usually come from, then how they in turn are usually produced. The heart of a person who must wear a pacemaker does not pump blood in accordance with a Normal explanation except on the most proximate level. A less proximate Normal explanation might also tell where the oxygen usually comes from. There is a level upon which the heart of a person swimming underwater with an Aqua-lung does not circulate blood in accordance with a Normal explanation.

Now there may be reproductively established families that have historically performed proper functions in accordance with *alternative* Normal explanations, especially on less proximate levels of explanation. I cannot think of any biological examples where the most proximate

Normal explanation is disjunctive, but possibly the reader can do better. Talk of "uniform conditions," "uniform over as large a number of historical cases as possible" is pretty vague talk. Help formulating better definitions would be gratifying. But the uses to which I will put the notions *Normal explanation* and *Normal conditions* will be clear-cut uses.

A Normal explanation is a preponderant explanation for those historical cases where a proper function was performed. Similarly, Normal conditions to which a Normal explanation makes reference are preponderant explanatory conditions under which that function has historically been performed. In the case of devices that have evolved, these are the conditions to which the device that performs the proper function is biologically adapted. But it is crucial to see that the Normal conditions for the performance of a certain function by a reproductively established family are not at all the same as average conditions under which members of that family have existed. It is for this reason that I capitalize *Normal*—to distinguish it from *normal* in the sense of *average*. Consider again how few sperm have historically managed to realize any but the most immediate functions (say, swimming) proper to them. This is because very few sperm existed under conditions Normal for (*actual*) performance of less immediate proper functions. (Most never find an ovum and have to call it quits.)

Later I will use the notion "Normal explanation" in giving a naturalist description of the intentionality of indicative signs. Such signs have as proper functions to aid "cooperative interpreter devices" or "cooperative interpreter programs" in performing certain further functions. But the "cooperative interpreter devices" can use these signs in performing these functions in accordance with a Normal explanation (rather than performing them by freak accident) only insofar as the signs actually map onto the world in accordance with certain semantic rules. For example, in offering an explanation of how the programs in hearers that use indicative sentences in English have managed to do those things upon which their proliferation, hence also the proliferation of the English indicative mood, has depended, one must say that and how these sentences Normally map. Any explanation that stops short of mentioning this Normal condition must fail to cover any but a minute proportion of historical cases of proper performance for these interpreting programs. (This claim will be explained in detail in later chapters, beginning with Chapter 6.)

Focused Proper Functions

One last notion needs to be on the table before the theory of direct proper functions is applied to language devices. "Focused proper function" is a somewhat vague term that sometimes proves useful in discussion of the various proper functions of a device and is indispensable in examining the functions of language devices. I will not attempt a formal definition of "focused proper function." I will just explain it.

Reproductively established families often have numerous proper functions. Sometimes these functions are quite independent. The feathers of waterfowl, for example, keep them warm, trap air that keeps them afloat and dry, are necessary for flying, and may be shown off during mating displays. Proper functions that are independent of one another in this way might be called "alternative" or "disjunctive." On one occasion the device performs this function, on another occasion it performs that function, all of these alternative functions being useful, hence the device has survived. On the other hand, separate proper functions that a device has may all be performed simultaneously. The blood, for example, carries oxygen and also nutrients and also hormones and also wastes from one place to another in the body. These are not alternative functions, one performed on one occasion, another on another. They are and must be performed all at once. We might call such functions "simultaneous" functions or "conjunctive" functions. Besides disjunctive and conjunctive relations among the proper functions of a device there can also be serial relations. For example, the human heart pumps blood; this causes oxygen to circulate through the blood vessels; this causes oxygen to reach the brain, thus helping brain cells to live, thus helping the brain to think properly, thus causing appropriate human actions and utterances, etc. Call functions that are related to one another in this way "serial functions."

It is very obvious that the more distant or removed of the serial functions of a device are almost invariably performed each with the aid of other, indeed of numerous other, cooperating devices, the contributions of these cooperating devices being Normal conditions for performance of these functions. Thus the human heart performs its proper function of contributing to the production of appropriate utterances Normally only with the aid of the blood vessels, the blood, the brain, the tongue, etc. These in turn do their share only with the aid of still other devices such as the liver, the sense organs, etc. Less obviously, even the most proximate of a device's proper functions are often performed only with the aid of cooperating devices. For example, the heart couldn't pump blood if it were not for the lungs through which its oxygen is supplied or if it were not for the bone marrow that makes the red blood cells that carry this oxygen, etc. Why do we tend to think of *pumping and circulating the blood* rather than *causing appropriate utterances* as *the* function of the heart? And why don't we think of pumping and circulating the blood as *the* function of the lungs or of the bone marrow? Something like "explanatory proximity" seems to be involved here. In the order of explanation, the heart pumps blood first and only therefore can do other things; the lungs do not help pump blood first but first supply the blood with oxygen. But there is another way, too, that a device may be related to one among its various proper functions more intimately than to others.

Sometimes a device has a single set of serial functions (each performed with the aid of cooperating devices) and this series goes on through a number of stages without the device having any additional functions that are simultaneous with or alternative to these. Or if there are simultaneous or alternative functions, these lead right back again to contribute always to this central series of functions and lead nowhere else. The last member of such a series of functions I will call the *focused function* of such a device. This function will be the last function that such a device performs before its serial functions finally diverge for good, being merely disjunctive and/or conjunctive after that point.

I have said that the notion of a focused function is especially helpful when analyzing language function. And it is not easy to think of examples from biology of devices having focused functions except among those devices that strike us intuitively as being akin to language in that they seem to "transmit signals" or "transmit information." Most obvious, the receptors at the ends of our afferent nerves have focused functions. They do just one thing, namely, cause impulses to cause more impulses to cause more impulses all the way up the nerve and finally to cause little inputs to one's brain. Later I will argue that all artifacts have proper functions—usually not direct ones but derived ones. The ignition switch of a car has a focused (derived) proper function. Turning it causes a whole series of things to happen that ultimately result in the car's motor idling, but it has no functions that lie beside this series and only alternative functions beyond. (Is turning the ignition switch how one "tells" the car to start?) The brake pedal has as a focused function to slow or stop the car, further functions that slowing or stopping may have being alternative and diverse. The "add" button on a small hand calculator has as a focused proper function to cause a number to appear on its display that is the sum of the numbers on the buttons depressed just before and just after *it* was depressed. (Does it "tell" the calculator to add?)

Sometimes a device may have several distinct sets of serial functions all of which converge in one focused function. For example, it may be that some special little cells located in the hypothalamus have as a proper function to initiate several series of happenings in the body resulting in (1) more blood flowing through the skin capillaries, (2) the sweat glands secreting sweat, (3) cooling-down behaviors, each of these series ending in the same, namely, in helping to restore the inner body to 98.6 degrees Fahrenheit. After that the functions of these little cells diverge again, a steady inner body temperature of 98.6° being necessary to the proper performance of nearly every other device in the body. Restoring the body to 98.6° is then the focused proper function of these cells.

I do not, however, wish to make it actually *contradictory* that a device *might* have, say, two or even three alternative or simultaneous focused functions or that it might have, besides a central focused function, a number of peripheral functions thrown in for good measure—good survival value. The idea of a focused function, then, is vague. But the general idea is that the device's functions are concentrated in a central series or set of series involving a number of stages and culminating at one point, and that the device doesn't (properly) do much else, except as this else *depends* upon completion of the last of these stages or of the stage where these functions converge. The heart has functions that diverge and diverge again until there is nothing we do or that goes on in the body that our hearts do not properly contribute to. By contrast, where devices have focused functions, any of their functions that may have diverged prior to the performance of these focused functions all converge again, all having had, as it were, a single end in view.

The human eye may be a device with a focused proper function. The various parts of the eye all cooperate with one another and cooperate with the optic nerve, with feedback from the motor system concerning movements of the head and body as well as of the eyes, and with large portions of the brain, etc., to produce, we might speculate, *one* essential product: visual representations. This process, though rapid, is complex and has various stages. Focusing images upon the retina, causing impulse patterns in the optic nerve, causing selective parts of the brain to do various things that help to produce these representations are all more proximate proper functions of the eye than producing visual representations. But all of these more proximate functions contribute at a certain point to one and the same function and to no other unless *beyond* it. The various functions of visual representations themselves are conjunctive and disjunctive. For example, they are used to guide a wide variety of simultaneous or alternative movements, and as a source of many different kinds of theoretical and practical beliefs. They are used, as it were, for anything one happens to need them for. The functions of the eyes thus come to a focus at the point of producing visual representations. At least that *may* be the case, assuming visual representations to exist.

Language devices, I believe, typically have focused proper functions. For example, direct proper functions of uttered sentences cast in imperative mood include producing sound waves, producing vibrating eardrums, producing auditory nerve impulses, producing acts of interpretation on the part of hearers, etc., at least the last of these being also a stabilizing proper function. But I will soon argue that the *focused* stabilizing proper function of imperative-mood sentences qua imperative is the production of acts of compliance on the parts of hearers. Any proper functions that imperatives may have that lie *beyond* this point are disjunctive, imperatives serving one kind of further purpose on some occasions, other kinds of further purposes on other occasions. Sometimes imperatives serve (properly, not accidentally) for giving orders, sometimes they serve for making requests, sometimes they serve for giving cookbook-style directions, sometimes they serve for giving advice, etc., these proper functions coinciding with different kinds of motivations that hearers have historically had for complying with imperatives on alternative occasions. That is what the first part of Chapter 3 will be about.

The Spirit of the "Theory of Proper Functions"

The spirit in which I offer the "theory of proper functions," though I have given it a rather grandiose title, is quite humble. That the definitions I have given are loose in the sense that they don't cut between all *possible* cases does not bother me. For the position that I will take on meaning and on the nature of clarity in thought implies that adequate concepts needs not cut between all possible cases. But I *am* concerned that the definitions may not do the job I need them to do in the clearest and most efficient manner. I need them in order to talk about analogies and disanalogies among things belonging to quite diverse categories— body organs, tools, purposive behaviors, language elements, inner representations, animals' signals, customs, etc. The definitions are, in one way, that upon which the rest of my argument rests. But in another way, it is the rest of my argument upon which these definitions rest. The definitions were conceived in detail *last*, their purpose being to make as explicit as possible analogies among categories of things, which analogies had struck me as useful to reflect upon. Although I will stick to these definitions strictly (as well as is in my power), the spirit in which I offer them to the reader is as a handle by which to grab hold of the analogies rather than as a definitive explication of them. If the analogies are really there, it will undoubtedly take time and an interchange of ideas before they can be explicated entirely adequately. Let us forge ahead then to the theory of derived proper functions.

Chapter 2

Adapted Devices and Adapted and Derived

Proper Functions

Relational Proper Functions

A device has a *relational proper function* if it is its function to do or to produce something that bears a specific relation to something else. Consider a chameleon. The chameleon contains equipment—"a device"—that is supposed to vary its skin color in accordance with the color of what the chameleon sits on. This device arranges pigmented matter in the chameleon so that the chameleon will match its environment. The point, of course, is to make the chameleon invisible to predators. The chameleon's pigment-rearranging device has a relational proper function. It is supposed to produce a color for the chameleon that bears the relation "same color as" to the chameleon's nether environment. Similarly, the amoeba is so constructed that it flows in a direction that is determined by chemical differences in the water on its various sides. Thus it manages to flow toward food and away from certain dangers. The whole amoeba seems to be the relevant "device" in this case. The amoeba has as a relational proper function to flow in a direction determined by a relation or as a function (mathematical sense) of the chemical variations in the water around it. Or consider a bee that has returned home after spotting a particularly succulent supply of nectar. The bee does a bee dance. The device in the bee that is responsible for this dance has as a proper function to produce movements that bear a certain relation to or are a certain function of the direction (relative to the sun), distance, quality, and/or quantity of the nectar spotted. This proper function is a relational proper function. The device that is responsible for producing the bee dance has as a less immediate relational proper function to produce, as a result of the dance, a movement of the bee family in a direction that is so-related to nectar. Also, the mechanisms within interpreter bees that are designed to translate observed bee dances into a direction of flight have as a relational proper function to produce a direction of flight that is so-related to the dance observed and also so-related to nectar.

Adapted Proper Functions

When a device has a relational proper function, *given* some specific thing that the device is now supposed to produce in relation to, the device acquires what I will call an *adapted proper function.*[1] For example, given that the chameleon is sitting on something brown and green blotched, it is an adapted proper function of its pigment-arranging devices to produce a brown and green blotched skin pattern. This is not a *direct* proper function of these devices because these devices have not proliferated as a result of producing, specifically, brown and green skin patterns. It is a proper function only as adapted to a given context. Similarly, once a bee has spotted nectar at a particular place, the dance-choreographing devices in the bee acquire as an adapted proper function the production of a specific dance—the dance that maps the location of this nectar in accordance with the "semantic rules" of B-mese (apologies to Sellars). And they acquire as a further adapted proper function to move the bee family off in a certain direction, say, south-southeast.

Adapted Devices

Now suppose that the chameleon's pigment arrangers and the bee's dance choreographers perform their adapted proper functions correctly. Consider the brown and green skin pattern and the ornamented adagio figure eight and the movement of the bee family south-southeast that result. The configuration "chameleon bearing the relation *same color as* to what it sits on" is a member of a (higher-order) reproductively established family, and so are the configurations "bee dancing a dance that maps thusly onto the location of some nectar" and "bee moving toward nectar." But the brown and green skin pattern and the adagio figure eight and the south-southeast movement are none of them members of reproductively established families. Indeed, any of these might chance to be unique in history (though in these cases it is unlikely). Hence none has a direct proper function. These devices are *adapted devices*. (They are "adapted," of course, in a sense quite different than that in which evolution causes things to be "adapted.")

A properly adapted device bears as such a certain relation to something else. This something else is what the device is *adapted to*. I will call what a device is supposed to be adapted to the *adaptor*[2] for the device. Often an adapted device is adapted both to a prior adapted device and to the adaptor of this prior device. For example, the direction in which the honeybee flies after watching a bee dance is *immediately adapted* to the configuration of the dance, for it is a proper function of the interpreting devices in the watching bee to produce a direction of flight that bears a certain relation to this dance. The dance is an immediate adaptor for the direction of flight. But the line of flight is also adapted to the adaptor of the bee dance—to the place of nectar—for it is a proper function of the dance-choreographing devices to produce a direction of flight in watching bees that bears a certain relation to this place. The furthest removed thing to which a device is adapted is that to which it is *originally adapted*—its *original adaptor*. The site of nectar is the original adaptor for the direction of flight of the gatherer bee after it watches a bee dance. What the chameleon sits on is the original adaptor for the color of the chameleon, and the color has no adaptor that is more immediate.

Many biological devices have proper functions that they perform by varying their performance with conditions so as to produce an invariant end result. That is, they produce first adapted devices or processes, and by so doing achieve always the same ultimate end—e.g., not being eaten or getting in nectar. Of course, the intermediate adapted processes or devices can also be described not as having such and such structure but as bearing such and such relations to the conditions adapted to. Looked at from this point of view, the intermediate stages are invariant too. Activity involving movement through adapted stages seems to be what some have described as "goal-directed activity." But in order to have a proper function a device must be more than merely "goal-directed" as this notion has been (variously) described in the literature. Obviously its "goal-directed" activity must have attainment of its goal as a proper function. (As Bennett remarks, "Every animal is tremendously plastic in respect of becoming dead."[3]) And often a device that has goal-directed behavior as a proper function is in fact considerably *less* than goal-directed. For malfunctioning devices still have proper functions.

Derived Proper Functions

The proper functions of adapted devices are derived from proper functions of the devices that produce them that lie *beyond* the production of these adapted devices themselves. I will call the proper functions of adapted devices *derived proper functions*. These further proper functions of the producer of an adapted device from which the adapted device derives its proper functions may be invariant functions of the producer. Or they may be adapted functions having the same ultimate adaptor as the adapted device itself. In the former case, the derived proper function of the adapted device is not derived from an adaptor. In the latter case, the derived proper function of the adapted device is an adapted derived proper function and is derived, strictly speaking, from the producing device *and* the adaptor. Our chameleon's brown and green pattern has as an invariant derived proper function to make the chameleon invisible to predators, hence to prevent it from being eaten. The adagio figure eight dance has as an adapted derived proper function to get the bee family moving south-southeast, and as invariant derived proper functions to bring them to nectar, hence to get honey into the hive, etc. The south-southeast flight of the bee family has as an invariant derived proper function to bring them to nectar, etc.

The same device that is an adapted device with derived proper functions qua displaying a concrete character may also be a member of a reproductively established family having direct proper functions qua displaying a more abstract character. For example, the specific dance that the bee performs has proper functions that are derived from the choreographing devices that made it plus the adaptor that is nectar sighted in a certain location. But considered merely as a dance that conforms to the syntactic rules of B-mese, this dance also is a member of a (higher-order) reproductively established family having direct proper functions. As such, its most immediate direct proper function is relational. It is supposed to move the bee family off in a direction that bears a certain relation to its own *concrete* form, whatever that may be. Thus it has an adapted proper function that is adapted to its own content. After that, it is supposed to bring the bees to nectar, etc. The fact that the bee dance has two sources of proper function, one derived, the other direct, becomes an important fact only when the dance is incorrectly executed.

Adapted devices, like members of higher-order reproductively established families, are sometimes malformed or abNormal. For we will consider anything to be an adapted device bearing the derived proper functions that its producer plus adaptor have conferred upon it so long as it has been produced in accordance with an explanation that approximates (in some undefined degree) to a Normal explanation of how that producer makes adapted devices.

The characteristic kind of abNormality that adapted devices may display is *maladaptedness*. A device is *maladapted* to a particular adaptor if it does not bear the relation it is supposed to bear to that adaptor. An adapted device is also maladapted if it has no real adaptor. Consider a worker bee that "thinks" it has spotted nectar but has not. It does a bee dance showing the location at which it mistakenly "thinks" nectar to be. Its dance-producing mechanisms do not really have as an adapted proper function to produce this dance, indeed any dance. This dance is *maladapted*, even though there is no adaptor to which it is maladapted. Since there may be several adaptors to which a given device is supposed to be adapted, immediately, less immediately, and originally, a device may be Normal in certain adaptive respects and abNormal in others—adapted properly to some of its adaptors, maladapted to others.

Where adapted devices are maladapted, it can happen that one and the same device acquires *conflicting* proper functions. Suppose that a worker bee spots nectar 2000 feet southeast of the hive but, owing to some abNormality of its dance-choreographing mechanisms or owing to abNormal appearance, say, of the sun, it produces a maladapted dance. The dance it produces displays correct B-mese syntax but, by B-mese rules, is of a kind that should be produced when nectar is north-northwest. This dance has as a derived adapted proper function to move the bee family southeast. But as a member of the reproductively established family of syntactically correct bee dances it has an adapted proper function (adapted to its own concrete form) to move the bee family north-northwest. Also, the interpreter mechanism of any bee that watches the dance acquires the adapted proper function of moving that bee north-northwest, qua being supposed to produce a line of flight that bears such and such a relation to the dance watched. But a further proper function of these devices is to move the bee toward nectar and the nectar is not north-northwest but southeast.

Notice that what we would intuitively take to be what is *represented* in the case of the maladapted bee dance hangs upon the dance's direct proper function, this according with the adapted proper function of the interpreter bee's interpreting mechanisms qua confronted with the dance. It does not hang upon the derived proper function of the dance itself—upon that to which the dance was supposed to be adapted. In Part II I will argue that the most dominant notion of what is signed by signs is derived by reference to *direct* proper functions of these signs themselves, hence to resulting adapted proper functions of interpreting devices qua taking these signs as immediate adaptors. It is not derived by reference to adapted functions of the sign's producing devices. (On the other hand, *sometimes* we do consider a sign to be "about" its original adaptor.)

Normal Explanations for Performance of Adapted and Derived Proper Functions

A Normal explanation is an explanation of how a device has, historically, managed to perform a certain function. But adapted devices and adapted and derived proper functions may be devices and functions quite new under the sun. How can their performances have Normal explanations?

An adapted proper function is a relational proper function adapted to a given context. If the relational proper function is performed Normally, clearly the adapted function is performed Normally too. The

Normal explanation for proper performance of an adapted proper function is thus a *general* explanation that tells how it happens that the device produces or does things that bear certain relations to its adaptors. For example, a Normal explanation of how a chameleon's color arrangers produce brown and green splotches is a general explanation of how these mechanisms produce skin patterns that match what the chameleon sits on, hence derivatively an explanation of the occurrence of these splotches.

A properly adapted device is, as it were, *half* of a member of a reproductively established family. The whole is this-device-plus-its-adaptor-in-a-certain-relation-to-one-another. The Normal explanation of how ths half-device performs its derived adapted functions does not of course make reference to some invariant Normal concrete constitution that the half-device must have. Rather, it explains how the half-device does something that is a function (mathematical sense) of some aspect of its constitution. This explanation is, again, a general explanation. It applies to any adapted half-device produced in the same way by the same producer in response to any adaptor. For example, if we are interested in how a certain bee dance, Opus II no. 4, serves its derived adapted proper function of causing a watching bee to fly off in a certain direction, east-southeast, the Normal explanation is a general explanation that tells how it happens that the direction of flying is determined as a certain function (mathematical sense) of certain variables in the dance pattern. This explanation applies to *any* bee dance, not just Opus II no. 4.

The Normal explanation of how an adapted device serves a derived invariant function sometimes has to tell, first, how the adapted device produces results that are a function (mathematical sense) of aspects of itself. But, second, the Normal explanation must always mention as a *Normal condition* that the adapted device is so-related (i.e., Normally related) to something else—something of the sort it is supposed to be originally adapted to. For example, no Normal explanation of how our chameleon's brown and green splotches prevent its being eaten can be given that does not mention the Normal condition that this color pattern matches what the chameleon sits on. (Suppose that, although the color of the chameleon does not match what it sits on, it does cause the chameleon to look like a snake's head to some predator. So the predator does not eat the chameleon, and a proper function of the color pattern has been performed. The explanation of how this came about, however, is abNormal.)

The most proximate Normal explanation of how the chameleon's color pattern helps prevent its being eaten need not, however, explain how the color pattern *came* to match what the chameleon sits on, any more than the most proximate Normal explanation of how the heart manages to circulate the blood explains where the heart's oxygen supply comes from or where the electrical impulses come from (see Chapter 1, "Normal Explanations and Normal Conditions"). Possibly the color pattern matches not because the chameleon's pigment arrangers operated Normally but because someone has taken pity on the sick chameleon and placed him on something he matches. Still, his color pattern could now prevent his being eaten in accordance with a *proximate* Normal explanation. Similarly, a maladapted bee dance might correctly though accidentally show a place where nectar in fact happens to be. (The dance is, as it were, *true* though it does not express *knowledge*.) If such a dance should then guide fellow bees to nectar, it does so in accordance with a *proximate* Normal explanation. The most proximate Normal explanation of how the line that the bee is flying after watching Opus II no. 4 helps bring nectar to the hive must mention the Normal condition that the bee's line of flight bears a certain relation to a location where honey is. Of course, it bears this relation in accordance with a full Normal explanation only if the flight of the bee bears a certain relation to Opus II no. 4 and Opus II no. 4 bears a certain relation to the location of nectar, etc. But these facts are not mentioned in the most *proximate* Normal explanation of how the line of flight serves its invariant derived proper functions. Later I will argue that the most *proximate* Normal explanation, not for how an indicative sentence produces a belief but for how it produces a *true* belief, must mention that the sentence maps conditions in the world in accordance with certain semantic rules. But it need not mention how this came about. (Hence the sentence can be true without expressing knowledge.)

Some Applications of the Second Part of the Theory of Proper Functions

Plastic behaviors accounted for by closed instincts and also those accounted for by imprinting or open instincts seem to be adapted devices. Behavior patterns can be instinctive adapted patterns with derived proper functions (1) even though when described nonrelationally these patterns may be entirely novel, and (2) even though, due to abNormal conditions under which the devices that produce the behaviors have labored or due to damage to these devices, the behaviors may not bear the relations they are supposed to bear to the environment, hence may not further their own proper functions. Consider the behavior of a duckling that follows after a mechanical toy upon which it has imprinted, moving apparently aimlessly around and around a bare enclosure hour after hour. The duckling's behavior is a maladapted device. Still, the duckling's behavior has all of the same invariant derived proper functions as the behavior of a Normal duckling following its mother.

Just beyond behaviors that result from closed or open instincts, many animals exhibit behaviors that have been learned through trial and error accompanied by reward. These behaviors, I have already pointed out, (Chapter 1, "Direct Proper Functions") have as *direct* proper functions to bring in the rewards that have conditioned them. But, I will now argue, these behaviors have these functions *also* as derived proper functions. (Doubling up of proper functions acquired by different routes, we will find, is very common.)

Skinnerians draw a distinction between behaviors that have been "conditioned to a stimulus" and free or "operant" conditioned behaviors (though the basis of this distinction is considered by some to be questionable). From our point of view, behavior "conditioned to a stimulus" is merely relational behavior. The rat that has learned to push a bar when a light comes on has learned just that—to push-when-light-comes-on. His pushing bears the relation "just after" or perhaps "during the time of" to the light. If there is a mechanism or program in the rat that has as a proper function to produce this relational behavior, it has a relational proper function. I wish to show that all conditioned behavior, whether relational or nonrelational, is behavior that has derived proper functions.

Such behavior will have a derived proper function only if the specific mechanism or program responsible for it has as a proper function to produce it and, by so doing, to perform some function(s) beyond. Whence came the proper function of this *program*? Obviously it has no *direct* proper function. The program is not a reproduction, and it was not hard-wired into the organism at birth. So I must show how such a program is an adapted device, to create it having been an adapted proper function of the mechanisms that made *it*, given some way in which these mechanisms were adapted by a specific context, e.g., a specific kind of environment.

Consider a simple case first. Suppose that the "reward" that conditioned a certain behavior was the "reduction of a need"—roughly, newly full stomach, newly warm body, etc. And suppose further that it was built into the organism to reproduce *any* behavior correlated in the past of the animal with the reduction of a need whenever that behavior is possible and that need is present. The built-in apparatus responsible has a direct invariant proper function—reduction of such needs—that it performs by producing first adapted devices—adapted programs for behavior. These adapted programs are related to the environment in a certain way. (That is, they are related to the environment in this way if the devices that fashioned them were Normally constituted and operating under conditions Normal for them.) If they are fashioned properly, they are programs that produce need reduction under conditions of a sort that the organism is frequently *in*. That is their Normal or properly adapted relation to the environment. These adapted programs and the behaviors they produce have need reduction as a derived invariant proper function.

Suppose, however, that the reward that has conditioned the behavior is not the reduction of a need nor was it built into the animal's system to bring this reward in. Why then is the animal "seeking" this "reward"? Perhaps there *was* built into the animal a controlling device whose job it is to program or instruct the trial-and-error learning mechanisms to treat this rather than that as a "reward" during learning and to trot out the learned behavior under these rather than those conditions. This controlling device must be supposed to have further proper functions that it performs by doing this, and its specific programming operations or instructions must be adapted devices—adapted to something specific in the organism or its environment. In this case the learning mechanisms produce behavior that is adapted twice—once to the instructions of the controller (hence to whatever these instructions are adapted to) and once directly to the world outside. The behavior has as derived proper functions both bringing in the "reward" and whatever further proper functions are conferred upon it by the controlling device that also helped produce it. These further functions will be derived proper functions of the "reward"—ends to which getting the "reward" is a means. If no such controlling device was built into the animal, we can only suppose that the controlling device is itself an adapted device, having been produced by some *higher* controlling device in response to its adaptors, etc., until we *do* reach a system that was built into the animal at birth. Otherwise the animal's learning patterns have no functional explanation at all.

Taking now a great leap, how much of human behavior can be understood as adapted behavior having derived proper functions? The general principles in accordance with which the human nervous system works in adapting behavior to environment are still matters for sheerest speculation. However, plausibly human behaviors *are* adapted to the environment in our defined sense of "adapted." To be sure, humans learn not only behaviors but truths, and they probably learn both of these in accordance with a number of different principles. Humans also explicitly represent to themselves the world in which they live and the goals of their behavior and, sometimes at least, perform inferences during the process of bringing world and goals together. Further, humans not only learn, they also learn how to learn (e.g., develop concepts) and possibly even learn how to learn how to learn (e.g., develop methods of concept formation). But however flexible the human nervous system is, containing systems that are instructed or programmed by other systems that are instructed or programmed by still other systems, still there must come an end to flexibility. Both the outermost systems and principles involved and the kinds of flexibility possible in programming more inner systems must be inherent in the basic brain—the original product of evolutionary design. There must be a way of describing the inherited nervous system and certain very general environmental conditions (e.g., being in the context of a human "society," given an appropriate definition of "society") under which the nervous system has historically operated such that a general explanation can be given of *how* that system has Normally accomplished those ultimate functions that have led to its proliferation.

These ultimate functions, plausibly, are performed by the production first of adapted devices within and out of the brain, adapted to fit the special circumstances of the individual nervous system, including, for example, its special body and social situation. It seems reasonable to speculate that some of these adapted devices are programmings of certain parts of the nervous system, knowings how and knowings that, intentions, and adopted goals that *Normally* (not necessarily on the average) are related to one another and the environment in specifiable ways. It also seems reasonable to speculate that what we identify as various specific purposes in human behavior (proximate and less proximate, conscious and unconscious) correspond to (more and less immediate) derived proper functions of these behaviors. Later I will fill in a good number of details that will clarify and lend more substance to these speculations.

Of course, human purposes are in large part conscious purposes, and this is fundamental to their nature. What consciousness consists in from a naturalist's point of view, if it consists in *anything* from a naturalist's point of view, I have nothing to say about. It is the *intentionality* of human purposes that, I suggest, allows of a naturalist account.

If the specific purposes of human behaviors coincide with derived proper functions of these behaviors, the purpose for which an artifact was designed and made is a derived proper function of that artifact, the artifact being itself an adapted device. So also with language. The purpose or intention with which an individual speaker utters a word or sentence token corresponds to a derived proper function of that token. Thus we have come full circle. The notion "function" as applied to tools, language devices, and body organs has in one sense been given a univocal construction, in another sense not. For some of these proper functions are direct, some are derived, and some are both direct and derived.

Body organs have for the most part only *direct* proper functions. Language-device families, hence tokens of these, have (we speculate) *direct* proper functions too; but tokens of these have also *derived* proper functions—derived from the speaker's intentions. The direct and the derived proper functions of a language token often are not the same, for example, whenever a speaker does not understand how to use a word or uses it sarcastically or metaphorically. Tools that have been reproduced (as have traditional carpenter hand tools) because of their success in serving certain functions have these functions as *direct* proper functions. But all tools have as *derived* proper functions the functions that their designers intended for them. When a tool has both of these sources of proper function, they usually coincide. But the proper function that derives from the intention in design is always there in the case of tools. Tools simply *as such* have only *derived* proper functions. The intent with which a specific user uses a tool on a specific occasion corresponds to still a third proper function, a proper function of the user's behavior, however, rather than of the tool itself.

Appendix: Summary of the Main Terms Introduced in Chapter 2

1. When a reproductively established family has a proper function, this function is always *direct*.
2. Some direct proper functions are *relational*. An item *A* that has a relational proper function is supposed to produce something that bears a certain relation to something else *B*, *B* being "so situated" in relation to *A*.
3. If there is something *B* that is "so situated" in relation to *A*, *A* becomes for the moment *adapted* and acquires an *adapted proper function*. *B* is now the current *adaptor* for *A* and for this adapted function of *A*.
4. Whatever *A* produces qua performing a merely adapted function is an *adapted device*.
5. Functions of *A* that lie beyond the production of any adapted device *D* that *A* produces are *derived proper functions of D*, derived from *A*'s proper function plus, perhaps, *A*'s current adaptor.
6. Some of *D*'s derived functions may be *invariant derived functions* of *D*, so called because they are invariant functions of its producer. Others are merely *adapted derived* functions, adapted first to *D*'s particular constitution but, *originally*, to *A*'s adaptor.

Chapter 3

Indicatives, Imperatives, and Gricean Intentions

"So when it comes dark again, I will steal down into that clachan, and set this that I have been making in the window of a good friend of mine, John Breck Maccoll, a bouman of Appin's."

"With all my heart," says I; "and if he finds it, what is he to think?"

"Well," says Alan, "I wish he was a man of more penetration, for by my troth I am afraid he will make little enough of it! But this is what I have in my mind. This cross is something in the nature of the crosstarrie, or fiery cross, which is the signal of gathering in our clans; yet he will know well enough the clan is not to rise, for there it is standing in his window, and no word with it. So he will say to himsel', the clan is not to rise, but there is something. Then he will see my button, and that was Duncan Stewart's. And then he will say to himsel', The son of Duncan is in the heather, and has need of me."

"Well," said I, "it may be. But even supposing so, there is a good deal of heather between here and the Forth."

"And that is a very true word," says Alan. "But then John Breck will see the sprig of birch and the sprig of pine; and he will say to himsel' (if he is a man of any penetration at all, which I misdoubt), Alan will be lying in a wood which is both of pines and birches. Then he will think to himsel', That is not so very rife hereabout; and then he will come and give us a look up in Corrynakiegh. And if he does not, David, the devil may fly away with him, for what I care; for he will no be worth the salt to his porridge."

"Eh, man," said I, drolling with him a little, "you're very ingenious! But would it not be simpler for you to write him a few words in black and white?"

"And that is an excellent observe, Mr. Balfour of Shaws," says Alan, drolling with me; "and it would certainly be much simpler for me to write to him, but it would be a sore job for John Breck to read it. He would have to go to the school for two-three years; and it's possible we might be wearied waiting on him."

Robert Louis Stevenson, Kidnapped

The moral of this and the next chapter will be that there are more differences between Alan's bouquet of cross, button, and twigs and a spoken or written natural-language message than have been penetrated by some philosophers.

The purpose of this chapter is to show what the relations are among (1) the stabilizing function of a language device, (2) its literal use and, more generally, (3) intentions of speakers that use it. In the next chapter I will argue that one aspect of the *meaning* of a word, syntactic form, or other language device is its focused stabilizing function.

The best way to begin to understand the claim that language devices have standardizing and stabilizing proper functions is to examine some concrete cases. I will begin with those syntactic devices that indicate indicative and imperative moods. From this examination we will learn why "literal use" of a language device does not correspond to stabilizing function and how these two are related. (The category "literal" turns out to be a relatively uninteresting category from the standpoint of the basic theory of language.) Then I will argue that Gricean intentions or, as some have it, "the Gricean mechanism," is not at least the engine that *drives* language use and language understanding.

If our speculations in the Introduction were correct and elementary public language devices such as words and syntactic forms have stabilizing functions, these functions are direct proper functions of first-order reproductively established families of which these devices are members. Words (unless these are just being coined—see Appendix B, Chapter 4) and specific syntactic forms are members of first-order reproductively established families. If these have functions, performance of which functions has historically accounted for their proliferation by accounting for proliferation both of speaker utterances and of cooperative hearer responses, then these functions are direct proper functions. In particular, these functions do not depend upon speaker intentions or purposes. Even when a word is parroted by a parrot, the token produced has a direct proper function. For it is a member of a reproductively established family having a direct proper function. The intention or purpose with which a speaker utters a public language device token does afford that token a *derived* proper function. But this derived proper function is above and beyond its direct or stabilizing function and may or may not be the same as the direct function. Thus it is that a speaker can use a language device, just as he can use a tool or one of his body parts, to perform a function or serve a purpose that is not, however, the language device's *own* function.

But although the stabilizing function of a language device is independent of the purpose of the particular speaker who utters it, it is not independent of speaker purposes in general. The survival of a public language element without change of function must depend upon there being a critical mass of occasions upon which speakers and hearers use the element such that it performs its stabilizing function in accordance with the speaker's and the hearer's purposes. When a language device serves its stabilizing function in accordance with a Normal explanation, the speaker and hearer both purpose this function. But we may not have to think of this "purposing" as corresponding, always, to explicit intentions. It may be enough that the stabilizing function of the language device be the same as a derived proper function of the speaker's utterance and of the hearer's response mechanism or program. This question we will have to examine.

"Imperative mood" and "indicative mood" are not names of reproductively established families. Rather, these labels attach to proper function categories. Similarly, labels such as "noun," "verb," "preposition," "article," and "exclamation" do not attach to reproductively established families but tend to attach to proper function categories. The various grammatical moods take different concrete forms in different languages. Often they take a number of different forms in the same language. To describe the function of a certain grammatical mood is thus the same as to define that mood. It is to tell what proper or stabilizing function any reproductively established family of sentences must have if members of it are to qualify as sentences in that grammatical mood.

A sentence is never a member of just one reproductively established family. Minimally, its syntactic form and each of its content words are members of different reproductively established families. Often its syntax is itself derived from several families, the overall syntax coming from one large family, the syntax of smaller parts (embedded phrases, clauses) coming from other crisscrossing families. For example, we may suppose that "the girl I met," "the boy he saw," "the ball she hit," and "the apple John ate" are all members of a single reproductively established family, members of which sometimes appear in subject place, sometimes in direct object place, sometimes in indirect object place, etc. The full direct proper function of any sentence is derived from the stabilizing functions of its significant elements or aspects, each of which belongs to its own reproductively established family. (How these functions are combined is explained in Chapter IV, Appendix A.) Our job now is to discover for indicative and imperative mood indicators, whatever concrete forms these may take, what contributions these make to the full proper functions of the various sentences in which they appear.

I will conclude that the stabilizing function of the imperative mood is to produce compliance; the stabilizing function of the indicative mood is to convey information, i.e., to produce *true* belief. The specific nature of the information to be conveyed or of the act that constitutes compliance is determined by the stabilizing functions of other aspects of the sentence. The fact that these conclusions are so simple and natural should not occasion scorn. Proving platitudes is not as exciting as posing paradoxes, but these platitudes have often been abandoned in the face of paradox. My purpose is to show how to put foundations under them, at the same time illustrating how the theory of stabilizing functions works.

Discussion of what the indicative and imperative moods do, of their functions, is not at all new. But our approach contrasts with earlier approaches in the way it understands the problem to be solved. We are beginning with a theory that tells us exactly what it is we are looking for in looking for "the function" of a language device. We are looking for a focused function that is of value both to speakers and to hearers that might explain the survival and proliferation both of speaker utterances of and hearer responses to indicative and imperative mood sentences. Contrast this approach with that of looking for something in common that as many as possible literal tokens of a device do. For example, indicatives characteristically produce beliefs—or is it understandings of what speakers mean that they produce? (Or sound waves?) Without an explicit theory of what sort of thing "the function" of a language device type is, as opposed to what its tokens tend on the average to do, no answer can be *supported*. (And unless this explicit theory fits in with a more general theory of functions, *it* cannot be supported.)

Given our speculations about the relation of specific speaker and hearer purposes to the stabilizing functions of language devices, we can easily construct an explicit theory concerning the general kinds of *failure* we should expect to find of language device tokens that do *not* perform their stabilizing functions. We will then be satisfied when these kinds of actual token performances do not fit our descriptions of the stabilizing functions of the indicative and imperative moods rather than casting about trying to fit these kinds in somewhere. Let us begin then by constructing such a theory.

Cases of language device tokens that do *not* perform their stabilizing functions should divide into the following four kinds: (1) cases in which the speaker purposes the stabilizing function but the hearer does not; (2) cases in which the hearer purposes the stabilizing function but the speaker does not; (3) cases in which neither the speaker nor the hearer purposes the stabilizing function; (4) cases in which both the speaker and the hearer purpose the stabilizing function *but this function fails to be performed nonetheless*.

Suppose that we can prove that the stabilizing function of the imperative mood is to produce compliance and that the stabilizing function of the indicative mood is to convey information. Then the following would be examples of these four kinds of nonstabilizing performances for the indicative and imperative moods.

1. The commonest cases in which the speaker purposes the stabilizing function of the indicative or imperative mood but the hearer does not are those in which (*a*) the hearer does not hear or does not understand or (*b*) the hearer is uncooperative, refusing to do or to believe what the speaker says.

2. The commonest cases in which the hearer but not the speaker purposes the stabilizing function are cases of manipulative, lying, or insincere uses that are not detected by the hearer. In these cases, not only does the hearer purpose the stabilizing function, the speaker intends the hearer to purpose it. But the speaker has no intention that the stabilizing function in fact be performed. In the case of the imperative, the speaker may wish the hearer to try to comply but fail. In the case of the indicative, the speaker usually intends the hearer to acquire *mis*information rather than information.

3. Of course, there are insincere uses of language devices where neither the speaker nor the hearer purposes the standardizing function. The hearer may detect the speaker's insincerity, or the speaker may not even intend the hearer to purpose the standardizing function, wanting only that he think that the speaker intends it, etc. But the most common case in which neither the speaker nor the hearer purposes the stabilizing function of a language device is the case of parasitic function. Here the speaker purposes a secondary function that bears a conventional relation to the stabilizing function, purposes that the hearer also purpose that function, and finds a comprehending and cooperative hearer. Consider this example. I say, "Take out a good life insurance policy before you try that!" I am using the imperative not with the intent to produce the action specified but to convey the information that would justify such a directive: to do that is to risk your life. I expect my hearer to grasp this, the use of imperatives to serve functions related to their stabilizing functions in this way being a conventional medium of expression. If my intention carries, the imperative mood has served a parasitic function. Such usages are usually conventional, being copied by each generation from the last. (Children have to *learn* to use and understand such media as sarcasm, metaphor, metonymy, hyperbole, even joking and fictive uses, etc., this occurring, in most of these cases, relatively late in language development.) But sometimes they are improvised uses. (Improvised uses of things as signs are discussed in Chapter 7.)

4. Cases in which both the speaker and the hearer purpose the standardizing function but this function nonetheless is not performed include cases in which the imperative mood produces only a failing attempt at conformity on the part of the hearer, and cases in which, unbeknownst to the speaker, the indicative mood conveys misinformation.

Notice that, with the exception of parasitic use, every example that I have suggested of an indicative or imperative that fails to perform its stabilizing function is still a literal use. Now let us try to demonstrate that producing compliance *is* the stabilizing function of the imperative mood and that conveying information *is* the stabilizing function of the indicative mood. Begin with the imperative mood.

The stabilizing function of a language device is a function that helps to explain both why speakers continue to reproduce the device and why hearers continue to react to it in a standard way. We must look, then, for some characteristic contribution made by the imperative mood that can be understood as useful to both speaker and hearer. Or, if there are many such functions that the imperative mood performs, we are to look for a focused function. This will be the last function that all stabilizing imperatives perform before their stabilizing functions diverge, being from that point on only alternative, or simultaneous and unrelated functions, rather than serial functions. (See Chapter 1, "Focused Proper Functions.")

It seems clear at least that *speakers* are encouraged to reproduce tokens of the imperative mood mainly insofar as hearers comply with these imperatives. Mature speakers may also be reinforced in their use of imperatives when they perceive that their hearers attempt compliance or form intentions to comply. But on the large scale this is true only because such attempts and intentions are correlated with or understood to be necessary steps toward actual compliance. If no token of the imperative mood ever effected more than an abortive attempt or intention to comply with it, it is clear that speakers would soon cease to use the imperative forms at all or to use them as they now do. The various ways that hearer compliance contributes to satisfying *further* interests or goals of speakers, various further reasons that speakers may have for issuing imperatives, are very diverse, differing from occasion to occasion. Thus, further functions beyond producing hearer compliance that account for proliferation of the imperative mood by speakers could only be *alternative* functions, not focused functions, of the imperative mood. But how are we to understand the *hearer's* way of responding to imperatives as having compliance as a proper function?

The standard hearer of an imperative responds to the imperative first by forming an intention in accordance with certain rules of interpretation. The intention is then carried out. What perpetuates or reinforces the hearer's response—the use of *these* rules of interpretation, the forming of an intention, the carrying out of the intention? Clearly, hearers are reinforced when they comply with imperatives in a variety of different ways on different occasions. But presumably hearers often are reinforced in one way or another for compliance, or they would not continue the practice of complying. These reinforcements reinforce also their use of the rules of interpretation, their dispositions to form intentions and to carry them out. The focused function of the imperative sentence, viewed from the standpoint of the hearer, is only to occasion compliance, further functions being essential but alternative. The focused stabilizing function of the imperative mood, then, is to produce an act of compliance on the part of the hearer.

It is worth specifically noting some common alternative further functions of the imperative that directly but alternatively reinforce hearer acts of interpretation and compliance. Most of these functions are of interest to the speaker too, the speaker and the hearer both aiming, as it were, to get the same thing out of the imperative. This usually happens because one of these partners takes an interest in the interests of the other. In such cases, these functions count as further alternative *stabilizing* functions of the imperative, since the performance of these functions helps to account both for the proliferation of speaker uses and for the proliferation of cooperative hearer responses to imperatives. Alternative hearer motivations for complying with imperatives, when viewed as purposed or as ostensibly purposed by *speakers*, correspond to certain so-called "illocutionary acts" that may be performed by speakers uttering imperative mood sentences. Not all of these functions are stabilizing functions. But three out of the four that come most readily to mind are. Described as "illocutionary acts," these four are *giving orders, making requests, giving advice,* and *giving directions* ("turn left here," "add the sugar slowly," etc.).

In the case of Normally and properly functioning orders, it is within the speaker's control to invoke or apply sanctions to be sought or avoided by the hearer. This kind of hearer motivation is the one that does not correspond to a stabilizing function of the imperative, for the speaker's reasons for wanting the hearer to comply are not the same as the hearer's reasons for complying. The speaker does not issue the imperative in order to help the hearer to receive or avoid sanctions, but for some independent reason.

In the case of Normally and properly functioning requests, the hearer must already be motivated to further the speaker's interests as such, either as an end or as a means to further ends. Furthering of the speaker's interests is an alternative stabilizing function of the imperative, since it is a function or end that often motivates both the speaker and the hearer.

When advice is delivered in the imperative mood—that is, in the sort of cases that account for the survival of advice giving and taking as an institution—the speaker purposefully advocates ends that the hearer does well to adopt in the hearer's own interests. Furthering the hearer's interests in this manner is an alternative stabilizing function of imperatives.

When directions are given in the imperative mood ("turn left here," "this side up," "disconnect this appliance before changing filter"), the hearer is, Normally, already motivated toward a goal for which the imperative supplies a means. The speaker (or writer) is also motivated to help the hearer (or to help hearers or readers generally) to reach this goal. Otherwise he would not bother to speak. Furthering the hearer's interests in this manner is thus another alternative stabilizing function of the imperative mood.

Now consider indicative sentences. It seems clear that speakers proliferate tokens of the indicative mood mainly insofar as these tokens produce, at any rate, *beliefs* in hearers—either new beliefs or occurrent tokens of old dispositional beliefs (reminding). For this to be true it is not necessary that speakers should explicitly "intend" that their hearers believe what they say in a sense of "intend" that would require thinking of these beliefs or even having concepts of beliefs. Speakers are rewarded for speaking the *truth*, at least, in a wide variety of ways, one of the most common being friendly interest shown by the hearer rather than skepticism, blame, or annoyance. A proper function of speakers' acts in speaking could be to produce true beliefs in hearers even if the speakers had no concepts of mental states and no understanding of the hidden mechanisms whereby rewards result from speaking the truth.

Clearly, the hearer listens, then uses a certain rule of interpretation in forming a belief only because these acts have correlated in the past with the formation of *true* beliefs. Sometimes hearers may be reinforced in their acts of using certain rules to form beliefs from indicative sentences merely insofar as these acts produce beliefs that accord with the speaker's or the community's beliefs. But on the large scale this is surely so because what speakers or the community believes is highly correlated with the truth. Briefly, if no true beliefs ever resulted from hearer interpretations of indicative sentences, it is clear that indicative syntactic patterns would soon cease to be used first by hearers and, as a result, by speakers in the ways they now are. A closer look suggests that the production of a *true* belief in the hearer is also the dominant purpose of speaker use of the indicative mood. For nearly all of the kinds of further aims that speakers have in using indicatives can be achieved only if the hearer belief produced is true. Lying is not the rule, in part because it usually would not serve the speaker's purpose. The focused stabilizing function of the indicative mood is thus the production of a *true* hearer belief. "The function" of the indicative mood is to convey information.

Between the production of a true belief in the hearer and whatever final rewards a *speaker* achieves via producing it lie various alternative stabilizing functions of the indicative. Again, certain "illocutionary acts" that can be performed via use of the indicative provide us with a rough classification of these—reminding, informing, warning, etc. The latter functions are alternative stabilizing functions of the indicative because in these cases hearers' cooperative acts in listening, interpreting, and believing are typically reinforced by an end (though perhaps only an intermediate end) that motivates the speaker in speaking. For example, speakers typically remind, inform, or warn because they take it that the hearer has an interest in being reminded, informed, or warned.

Whether the use of a language device is literal or not depends upon the speaker's purpose. It is not necessary however that the speaker should purpose that its stabilizing function actually be performed. For example, when a speaker uses the indicative mood in lying, he may speak literally but he does not purpose that it fulfill its stabilizing function of producing a true belief. And a speaker who uses an imperative intending that his hearer should try to comply but fail may still use that imperative literally. A literal use is a use that is intended to be *taken* literally. The literal speaker proposes that his hearer's reaction should be to purpose, or that his hearer's reaction should have as a proper function, the function that is the stabilizing function of the words the speaker utters. In literal use of the imperative the speaker purposes that the hearer form an intention that corresponds to (that has the same proper function as—see Chapter 8) the sentence he utters. In literal use of the indicative, the speaker purposes that the hearer correctly interpret and believe the sentence uttered, even though the speaker may know that this interpreting and believing will not result in performance of the full proper function of the indicative mood—in the production of a *true* belief.

Perhaps there is another kind of case that counts as "literal" use of a language device. Suppose that, though having no hope that you will believe what I say or try to do what I say, still I tell you something or tell you to do something, as it were, "for the record." If I have no hope of your trying to do or of your believing what I say, surely I cannot be purposing that you will believe or that you will form an intention to do what I say. Notice that it will not help here to add more layers of Gricean intentions to my act of saying. For it may be that I do not expect you to believe that I expect you to believe or do what I say either. Both of us may be aware that my saying or telling to is only "for the record," and each may be aware that the other is aware of this. Such a use would count as "literal use," I believe, because its function is to keep up the pretense that the speaker intends stabilizing function, and this pretense can *be* kept up only insofar as the token counts as literal. An act of levitation makes such uses literal.

In order to define the notion "literal use," then, we must first have the notion that a language device has its own function independently of what a speaker happens to purpose in using it. And this function is not of course just an average use of the language device. Compare: the average use of ginger root is for flavoring food. It is used that way every day in innumerable households. But this does not lend ginger root a function that is its own function, such that if I were to use ginger root, say, for cleansing my teeth, I would be using it in a *secondary* way. In order to define "literal use" as opposed to "nonliteral use" we must first have a notion such as "proper function" or some *other* way of describing language-device function or meaning that makes this different from, just, average speaker meaning.

There is of course a movement, initiated by Grice, Lewis, and Bennett, that is also trying to do that.[1] I will speak to this movement in just a moment, when examining the status of "Gricean intentions." It is important to notice a crucial difference between the program of that movement and the thesis on language offered here. The Gricean theorists have assumed that one must either elucidate the notion "what a speaker means by language element x" in terms of the notion "what language element x means" *or* elucidate the notion "what language element x means" in terms of the notion "what a speaker means by language element x,"[2] and they have then argued that the latter is the more reasonable approach. I am proposing that we do neither. Rather, we can elucidate these notions quite separately and also understand the intimate relation between them by showing how each is derived by a separate route from a notion more general and fundamental than either—the notion "proper function."

One difference between Alan's bouquet of cross, button, and twigs and a public language device then is that a language device has its own or proper function quite independently of what it happens to be used for on this or on that occasion, whereas Alan's bouquet had no function at all of its own but only a function that Alan intended for it. Is there also another difference? Alan engaged in a very explicit process of speculation about the effects his bouquet would have upon the bouman's beliefs concerning Alan's intentions in making the bouquet. Further, if he had not engaged in this process of speculation, clearly he would not have produced that bouquet. And unless the bouman had also engaged in a process of speculation roughly of the kind Alan intended, he certainly would not have ended by honoring Alan's "request." Thus Alan's thoughts about the bouman's thoughts and the bouman's thoughts about Alan's thoughts were part of the *causal* mechanism through which communication was achieved. But when a natural language device serves its proper function, is it generally true that the speaker intends that the hearer should believe that the speaker intends this function, and is it generally true that the hearer cooperates *as a result* of believing that the speaker intends this?

There is an argument that has been used to support the view even that *limitlessly* nested intentional structure must underlie all normally communicative uses of language.[3] Taking the case of an imperative mood device "Do A," the argument might be isolated and brought to bear here as follows: If hearer H of "Do A" were to believe that speaker S did not intend that H do A, (normally) he would not do A; therefore, when H complies with "Do A," he must believe that S intends that H do A. And if S expected that H would believe that S did not intend H to do A, S could not rationally intend H to do A. So S, in intending that H do A, must also intend that H believe that S intends that H do A. Moreover, if the rational H were to believe that S intended that H should believe that S did not intend H to do A, (if H takes S to be rational) H would take it that S did not intend H to do A, hence would not do A. Hence the rational speaker must intend . . . and so on *ad infinitum*. (Nested intentions of this sort are called "Gricean intentions.")

The argument is fallacious. It does not follow from the fact that having the belief *that P* would interfere with or be incompatible with doing a thing, that in doing that thing one must have the belief *that not-P*. Analogous remarks apply to intentions, expectations, etc. If I believed that Jack the Ripper was under my bed, I would not crawl into bed and instantly fall asleep. In crawling so into bed, I clearly do not believe "Jack is under my bed." But it does not follow that I believe "Jack is not under my bed." Indeed, I may never have heard of Jack. Likewise, from the fact that if I had reason to believe that a speaker did not intend that I comply with an imperative then likely I would not comply, it does not follow that in normal cases of compliance with imperatives I believe that the speaker intends compliance. If the sergeant says to the well-trained infantry private, "This time when I say 'halt!' I will intend that you *not* halt," if the private concentrates *very* hard he *may* succeed in not halting when he hears "halt!". It does not follow that under normal circumstances the private does more than simply react when he hears "halt."

But that the argument is invalid does not show that its conclusion is false. And, indeed, it will pay to go very slowly here. First there is the problem just what it *is* to have a certain belief or intention. Then there is the problem what it is to *use* a belief in doing something as opposed, for example, to merely having it *while* doing something. And we must also ask whether there is any need to interpret Gricean intentions and beliefs as things actually used while speaking and understanding, or whether they may have another status entirely yet still do the work the Gricean theorists wish them to do of distinguishing a kind of "meaning" that all nonnatural signs have.

Later I will develop a theory about what it is to have a belief or intention, distinguishing between having beliefs and intentions and merely having certain things as proper functions of or Normal conditions for or Normal causes of one's activities. I will propose that this distinction is a distinction not of degree but of kind: acting from an explicit intention requires that one *represent* the act to be performed as a guide to performing it. Any act that is purposive has, as such, a proper function, but relatively few of our purposive acts, I will claim, are backed by explicit intentions. For example, when walking we do not usually place one foot in front of another in accordance with explicit intentions to do so, and yet this placing of one foot after the other is surely purposeful. A large proportion of one's purposeful acts, especially of those that lie as it were close in, are not first represented by intentions; only acts that lie *beyond* these acts are represented by intentions. And surely nothing lies any closer in than those acts involved in candidly speaking one's mind. In such speaking the speaker does "purpose" that the hearer acquire certain beliefs or intentions; but all that means is that it is a proper function of the speaker's behavior in speaking to *cause* these beliefs or intentions. It does not mean that the speaker *thinks of* these beliefs and intentions. As for what a hearer must do in order to understand what a speaker says, I will ultimately argue that in the most usual cases understanding speech is a form of direct perception of whatever speech is *about*. Interpreting speech does not require making any inferences or having any beliefs even about words, let alone about speaker intentions. But clearly I cannot use this theory before developing it. Here I will have to use rougher tools in order to clarify the status of Gricean intentions.

I will have to make two assumptions that it is conceivable someone might deny. I will assume, first, that when a person comes to have a particular belief, this is effected in part by some portion and only some portion of his insides, probably of his nervous system, undergoing alteration. (It is not implied that for two people to come to have the same belief is for their nervous systems to undergo identical alterations.) For example, coming to believe that smoking causes cancer did not involve that my entire nervous system underwent alteration, but only that some parts of it did. Second, I will assume that in helping to produce a particular action, such as the uttering of a sentence on a certain occasion, it is not always so that every channel and part of the nervous system is activated or used. The same is true when coming to understand and believe what a speaker says on a certain occasion. From these two assumptions it follows that it makes *sense* at least to speak of a belief that I have but do not use on a certain occasion of action or of coming to believe. For example, I suspect that I do not use my belief that Columbus discovered America *in* the process of brushing my teeth (though I might sometimes think of Columbus's discovery *while* brushing my teeth).

Now it may be objected that thinking of a person's beliefs as things he came to have at some time or other (or came to have slowly over time) and thinking of these comings to have as necessarily involving modifications of or occurrences of specific events in his nervous system (e.g., energy flowings might correspond to occurrent beliefs) is to ignore a large category of things we call beliefs. For example, Dennett has pointed out[4] that there are innumerable trivial beliefs that every person has, such as that New York is not on the moon, that salt is not sugar and not green and not oily, that tweed coats are not made of salt, that a grain of salt is smaller than an elephant, etc., which beliefs it is very implausible to suppose correspond each to a special little facet of the brain. Rather, some things we call "beliefs" must correspond to capacities to produce further modifications of or events within the brain, say, by inference. At the same time we should note that it is not plausible to count just any belief a person might come up with if he thought hard enough as a belief he now has. A mathematician who lies awake nights wondering whether a certain mathematical proposition is true or not and finally hits on a proof for it cannot be said to have believed that proposition all along. Nor is it sensible to say of someone who, had he just taken a moment to reflect, would have known that he couldn't thin epoxy with turpentine, that he tried to thin epoxy with turpentine while believing all along that it wouldn't work. But it is true that anything a speaker comes up with quite immediately when asked *is* something we are inclined to say he knew or believed before he was asked.

Now it is true that if you ask an adult who has just obeyed an order, or just come to believe something because he has just been told it, whether he thought that the speaker intended him to obey or believe this, he will likely say "yes," and say so quite immediately. But if his saying "yes" is only the result of his now quickly manufacturing the belief that the speaker intended him to comply or to believe and in no sense did he actually use any such belief during the process of coming to comply or to believe, it is hard to see what all the fuss about Gricean intentions is for. To say that, qua speaker, if I reflected I would always know that if my hearer reflected he would know that I purposed that he comply or believe, and that if he reflected he would know that if I reflected I would know that if he reflected he would know that I so purposed, etc., is no more than to say that he and I, like most adult speakers, have concepts of beliefs and intentions and some comprehension of the mechanisms in accordance with which speech Normally serves its functions. That is, it Normally works via the speaker saying something a proper function of which act of saying is to produce a hearer action or belief.

Interpreted this thinly, having Gricean intentions as one produces a sign is something quite other than having active intentions of the sort Alan had when producing his bouquet. Alan's intentions concerning John Breck Maccoll's beliefs were part of the direct causal mechanism that resulted in production of Alan's sign.

Interpreted this thinly, Gricean intentions also become useless as aids in distinguishing (nonnatural) *meaning* from less interesting things. Suppose that you pass on the pickles to me as they circle around the table during dinner. You do this purposing that I take the pickle dish from your hand. If I reflected, I would know that you purpose this. And if you reflected, you would know that if I reflected I would know that you purpose this, etc. Are we to conclude that there is something very special about acts of handing people things—a special "mechanism"—that puts these acts in a category deserving a large philosophical literature? Possibly. But if this were *all* that Gricean expectings, believings, and intendings amounted to, then in accordance with Grice's description of "meaning$_{nn}$" (nonnatural meaning), acts of handing people things would be acts of signing something and meaning$_{nn}$ it. For if A holds out something for B to take, he purposes that B will see him holding it out and move *from this* to taking it, and he expects (in the thin sense) that B will know (in the thin sense) that A intends B to take it, and to know (in the thin sense) that A expects (in the thin sense) B to know (in the thin sense) that A intends B to take it, etc. But in passing the pickles surely I am not signing something and meaning it in the sense that I sign something and mean it when I say "Please take the pickles."

I conclude that we need not consider any Gricean beliefs that correspond only to potential and not to actual modifications of the nervous system during speech and understanding. Only Gricean beliefs that were actually used in the process of speaking and understanding could be of any interest to the theory of meaning.

But now it will be objected that surely a person can have a certain *reason* for doing something or for reacting so without this reason's having to correspond to some presently activated part of his anatomy. For example, I may have a reason for brushing my teeth in the direction I do. My dentist told me to brush this way and why. But it is not plausible to suppose that my belief in the proposition that corresponds to this reason is activated every time I brush my teeth. Rather, I am in the habit of brushing in a certain way, and I maintain that habit for certain reasons. If I should stop believing that these were good reasons for brushing my teeth this way, I might very well drop my habit. And if I were to come to believe that the reasons were good ones most days but not on Christmas (bacteria get into the Christmas spirit too), I might not brush my teeth in the usual way on Christmas. Reasons, then, can *support* an activity without the structures in one that correspond to belief in these reasons being used during the activity.

Is that the way it is with Gricean intentions? Is my habit of usually believing what others say supported by a belief that others usually intend me to believe what they say? Perhaps we can imagine someone's becoming paranoiac and dropping the belief that others usually purpose that he believe what they say. But if such a person had any rationality left at all, wouldn't he wonder how it *does* happen that most of the things people say still seem to turn out true? And even if he were to come up with no theory on this subject, shouldn't he keep right on usually believing what people say anyhow? Further, what he once took as symptoms of parasitic usage will still serve him as good signs of when to inhibit the habit of believing what he hears, even though he no longer has a theory about the deeper things of which these signs are symptoms. There are surely lots of ways of disambiguating ambiguous sentences and interpreting parasitic usages that do not depend in any way upon having thoughts of speaker intentions—like considering what makes sense or what would obviously be false. Indeed, how could one *divine* a speaker's intention in cases of parasitic and ambiguous usage, in the average case, if one did not first pay attention to these *other* things?

So the only interesting question does seem to be whether Gricean intentions and beliefs are actually *in* there and operating causally *as* one speaks and understands.

Consider the private whose sergeant has told him *not* to halt the next time he hears "halt!". Suppose that the private's training is just too strong; he halts anyway, out of habit. Here is Bennett, considering a parallel case. A "careless" or "slow-witted" hearer A thinks that this time the utterer U does *not* intend to communicate a proposition P by uttering a sentence S, yet still mistakenly comes to believe P on hearing S on the strength of the well-established generalization "whenever S is uttered, P is true."

> Given time to reflect he will no doubt realize that he ought not to infer P's truth unless he thinks U intended to communicate P; but in the heat of the communicative moment A might blunder, and fall back on (i) [whenever S is uttered P is true] as though it were basic, thus inferring P's truth in a non-Gricean manner.[5]

Notice that Bennett assimilates A's "carelessness" in allowing himself to move from hearing S to believing that P *despite* knowledge that U did *not* intend to communicate P, to a supposed "carelessness" that would be involved if A allowed himself to move from hearing S to believing P without first thinking *positively* that S *does* intend to communicate P. The rational man, it seems, should take no shortcuts. It is not enough that he should take account of negative evidence about intentions; he should gather positive evidence.

Having raised the question of shortcuts (given "slow-witted" hearers), might not a hearer who believed both "whenever S is uttered P is true" and "P is true whenever S is uttered *because* whoever utters S intends to communicate P" still ignore all this erudition he has and merely *react* by translating the sentence, in accordance with rules he has learned to conform to, into a belief? More radically, might it not be true that anyone who *failed* in the average case to take this shortcut would thereby end up a slow-witted hearer? Would it even be rational to fail to take this shortcut in the average case?

The structure of the problem here is quite general; so let me speak to it generally (also omitting all niceties of expression in order to cut through). Suppose that John believes "usually when A then B." (Cf. "usually when S is uttered P is true.") He also believes "not-(usually when A-and-not-C then B)." (Cf. "it's not so that usually when S is uttered and U does not intend to communicate P then P is true.") If rational, John must also believe "usually when A then C" and "usually when A-and-C then B." Now consider these possible cases.

1. The only evidence John ever gets concerning whether C is true comes from his knowing that usually when A then C. (Cf. A only knows that U intends him to believe P via hearing S). In this case there would surely be no use in his ever bothering to think about C when he encounters A. He had better just move from A to B.

2. John has independent ways of coming, on evidence, to believe C vs. not-C. And he encounters A while already believing on such in-

dependent grounds that not-C. In this case John should certainly use his belief that not-C (or, more directly, use the evidence that led to this belief?) to inhibit the inference from A to B.

3. John has independent ways of coming, on evidence, to believe C vs. not-C. But on this occasion of encountering A he has no prior knowledge whether C. Is it possible that John, in order to be rational, should now independently check out whether C before jumping to the conclusion that B? Let us *try* answering "yes."

But now suppose that John's only way of finding out, in case 3, whether or not C, depends upon his belief "usually when D then C." But he also believes "not-(usually when D-and-not-E then C)." Should he then begin his task of being rational in moving from A to B by independently checking out not only whether D is true but whether E is true? And suppose that John's usual ways of checking on whether E is true are also fallible. (Did we expect there to be *infallible* methods for a hearer to discover whether to believe P on hearing S?) If John should come to discover more than he now knows about the conditions under which his fallible ways of deciding whether E are more vs. less likely to work, must he now begin by checking on these conditions too every time he wishes to know whether to believe B given that A? Poor John! The more knowledge he acquires of his world and of how it works, the more work he must do in order to be rational, until one can imagine him coming to a grinding halt, overwhelmed each time by the task of trying to decide "in accordance with reason" whether to believe B after encountering A. (The reader familiar with the various problems that AI people lump under the heading "frame problem" will recognize this as a relative.)

Wouldn't John in fact be more rational if he omitted all this checking out, reserving use of his knowledge "not-(usually when A-and-not-C then B)" for just those occasions when he *already* believes, or strongly suspects, or stumbles upon evidence that not-C? How would making an inference through thinking about the speaker's intentions do more than slow down the hearer in the usual case—the case in which there is no evidence of insincerity, and ambiguities or parasitic usages are easily resolved or grasped by what makes sense in the context?

If the most usual way that people understand the speech of others were by translating directly, without inference, into beliefs, then the most usual way that people derive beliefs via hearing what others say would be akin to forming beliefs on the basis of direct observation. In Chapters 18 and 19 I will argue that in the usual case, believing what one hears *is* making observation judgments. But background information that might inhibit the making of an observation judgment is not necessarily information the denial of which is *used* in the normal case of fixing beliefs on the basis of observation. This principle will be used against the Quinean doctrine that observation and theory are entwined in such a way as to force epistemological holism upon us.

There seems to be good reason not to interpret Gricean intentions and beliefs as a kind of "mechanism" that drives ordinary language use and understanding in the way that Alan's and the bouman's nested beliefs and intentions drove them toward a common understanding.

We creatures who possess language have a very long evolutionary history during which one after another of vastly many adaptive changes occurred. More sophisticated biological systems tend of course to develop not out of whole cloth but by modification of and superimposition upon more primitive systems. In particular, it makes sense to suppose that sophisticated motor-cognitive systems may be hierarchical systems, higher levels of the system being able to interrupt or inhibit lower motor systems and to use or discard the products of perceptual systems; hence to control the activities of older, somewhat blinder, more mechanical, but still extremely complex systems below. Similarly, a great deal of what a person does "automatically" or "with the mind on other things" may be done by systems that produce very complex prearranged patterns of behavior that are not put together or prescribed step by step on the spot but simply, habitually, "run off." It seems likely that the development of higher-order control is, largely, the development of systems that can start and stop and use pieces of the complicated performances of lower-level systems as appropriate and, in some cases, "train" or "program" them appropriately.[6]

Now this seems to me to be at least *plausible*. In starting my car, usually I simply react to my desire that it be started, do what I do automatically, meanwhile expecting the car to start. I make no inferences. I am usually using the higher parts of my brain in thinking about something else. But it is true that I know a certain amount about the insides of my car and what mediates between ignition-key-turning and motor-starting. Hence it is true that *if* I should look under the hood and see no battery or see that the distributor wires are not connected, I would become inhibited and not try to start my car—or I would do something else first. This does nothing to show that I normally make inferences of the form, "my battery is charged and in place, good wires lead from it to such and such places in the starter motor and to the distributor, etc., etc.; hence if I turn this key clockwise the car will start; and I want the car to start; so I will turn this key clockwise." Similarly, it does nothing to show that I *intend* the current to flow through the wires to the distributor, etc., as I start my car (though it is, of course, a proper function of my action to cause this flowing). My knowing how to start my car is prior to and quite independent of my knowledge of what is under my hood, even though the latter knowledge can affect my ignition-switch behavior.

Similarly, it seems reasonable to me that humans learn first how to talk and how to understand—a fairly automatic business of expressing and forming beliefs and intentions. Indeed, if there is anything to the reflections of such philosophers as Wittgenstein and Wilfrid Sellars, *concepts* of mental states such as believing and intending are not that easy to come by. It is very likely that small children speak and understand long before they have any such concepts. Later, however, they do learn something about the mechanics of *how* and *why* talking and believing- or doing-on-the-basis-of-what-they-hear produces results they want *when* it produces results they want. This requires developing concepts of beliefs and intentions. Thus they learn something about the conditions under which their automatic talking and believing mechanisms will succeed in doing good work for them and the conditions under which these automatic mechanisms will not. They develop sensitivities to the presences of certain conditions that are *not* conducive to the success of these devices, and when thus alerted, inhibit their automatic talking and believing mechanisms. They also devise ways in which the use of these equipments, in themselves and in others, can be turned to other tasks, and ways to make other people's equipment malfunction—ways to deceive. The truth in Grice's model is that we have the ability to interrupt and prevent the automatic running on of our talking and our doing-and-believing-what-we-are-told equipment, and assume others have this ability too. We interrupt, for example, when we have happened to look under the hood and discovered evidence that the conditions for normally *effective* talking or for *correct* believing-on-the-basis-of-what-we-hear are not met.

If this sort of model should be correct, then the genuine communicator is not a creature that, in the process of every speech act, intends that his hearer believe that he intends him to—etc. How inefficient that would be, if we take having intentions and beliefs to be real modifications of the nervous system! Rather he is a creature that, upon reflection, has some understanding of how and why language works when it works and, on reflection, takes it that his hearer, on reflection, has a similar understanding. Hence the true communicator is in a position to tinker with the mechanisms of normal language flow, is sensitive to symptoms that the other is tinkering with these mechanisms, and can rise above these automatic mechanisms if necessary.

Conventional signs, then, do not work *at all* in the same way that improvised signs such as Alan's bouquet do. Usually they work the way handing you the pickles works. What makes conventional signs special is that they have their very *own* proper functions, quite apart from how they happen to be handled by particular speakers and hearers on particular occasions.

Chapter 4
Language Device Types; Dictionary Senses; Stabilizing Proper Function as the First Aspect of Meaning

More exciting than questions about the stabilizing functions of the various grammatical moods is the question of the stabilizing function of denotative and/or referential terms. Alas, this question is also far more complex. First we need to ask a prior question. Is it in fact true that classification of terms into the category "denotative" and/or "referential" is classification in accordance with *function*? Or is it some other kind of classification? Later I will propose that the first distinguishing characteristic common to all denotative and referential terms is *not* function. It is intentionality. And an intentional device is not always such because of any particular function that it performs. Intentionality has more to do with the *way* a device Normally performs its proper functions than with its proper functions per se. Indeed, there is nothing whatever in common to the proper functions of all devices exhibiting intentionality.

But a second distinguishing characteristic of denotative and referential terms that separates these from other devices exhibiting intentionality *is* a matter of function. These terms function properly when they precipitate acts of identification of the variants in the world to which they correspond. Roughly, they function properly when an interpreter identifies or recognizes what their referents are. Because they have this kind of function they are *representations*. In contrast, bee dances, though (as I will argue) these are intentional items, do *not* contain denotative elements, because interpreter bees (presumably) do not identify the referents of these devices but merely react to them appropriately. Bee dances are not representations. But the act of identifying the referents of a representation cannot be understood until what it is for a device to have a mapping value at all is thoroughly understood. Before the stabilizing functions of denotative and referential terms are described, it will be necessary to give an account of intentionality. Indeed, although I will describe the stabilizing functions of a number of kinds of language elements other than the various grammatical moods before I am done, an understanding of nearly all of these depends upon understanding intentionality.

In this chapter I will have to ask the reader to assume that words usually have *some* kind of stabilizing and standardizing functions toward which, for the moment, I will merely wave my hands. It will still be helpful to indicate something of how the hypothesis that words of various kinds are members of reproductively established families having standardizing proper functions can be put to use in the theory of language.

We classify word tokens into types in several ways but never by reference to physical form (sound, shape) alone. For example, neither "the word 'seal' " nor "the English word 'seal' " unambiguously describes a unique language-device type. Under any normal interpretation there are *several* English words "seal."

Sometimes we classify words into types merely by reference to reproductively established families. Call such types "genetic types." Thus word tokens may count as examples of "the same word" even though the family of which these are members has undergone slow changes in form, say, from Early to Middle to Modern English, and even though the family has become divided by reference to function and form into many distinct branches. For example, if one looks in a dictionary, one can ascertain that "mean" as in "no mean city" is the same word as "mean" in "he was mean to me" but a different word from "mean" in "I didn't mean to" and that "mean" in "I didn't mean to" is the same word as "moan" in "he moaned and groaned." Because word tokens normally are copied because they serve a certain function and in order to serve the same or a related function, for the most part word tokens of the same genetic type serve at least related functions. But the parrot that mimics tokens of the English word "hello" tokens *the English word "hello"* and the child who uncomprehendingly copies out "il pleut" writes down *the French word "il,"* which shows that these categories are not here *defined* by reference to function. Furthermore, the Martian who due to historical accident utters what sounds just like the French "il pleut," even though he may happen to mean just what the Frenchman typically means when he uses this sound, does not utter the French but rather the Martian word "il." Contrast here, for example, Donald Davidson: "For languages (as Quine remarks in a similar context in *Word and Object*) are at least as badly individuated, and for much the same reasons, as propositions. Indeed, an obvious proposal linking them is this: languages are identical when identical sentences express identical propositions."[1] Many other examples might be cited of the failure to note that what makes tokens of a word or sentence tokens of the *same* word or sentence (in the same language) is, in the first instance, *history*, not form or function.

For other purposes, we divide such sprawling genetic families into smaller families or branches paying closer attention to function and form. Thus types corresponding to separate *main* dictionary entries are determined according to family *and* form in accordance with modern spelling. They are also very roughly divided in accordance with function under the headings "noun," "verb," etc.

Finally, word tokens falling under the same main dictionary entry are again divided according to whether they have the "same sense" or "different senses" labeled "a,b,c" or "1,2,3," etc. (These "dictionary senses" are not Frege's "*Sinne*"; "sense" here is not the complement of "reference." For example, several such "senses" are listed for "off," for "or," and for the adverb "still." Nor are they "senses" as I will usually use that term.) Call such (sub-sub-) types "least types." Upon what kind of *feature* is this classification into least types based?

I propose that the several dictionary senses of a word or genetic language-device type, its several least types, are *not* distinguished merely according to the actual functions performed, or according to the functions intended to be performed, by the tokens to be so classified. For example, the dictionary does not attribute several senses to a word merely because it can be used by extension, metaphorically, loosely, sarcastically, playfully, deceitfully. Rather the least types correspond to independently sufficient stabilizing functions of the word's tokens, hence to independent branches of the reproductively established families of which these are members. Each of these functions is capable *by itself* of accounting for continued proliferation of tokens of the word. Each accounts for the survival of an independent branch of the word's genetic family, tokens of each branch being currently copied, most frequently, from earlier tokens of the same branch rather than derived again from tokens of other branches or from earlier (often obsolete) branches. Each such function is entirely capable of continuing to stabilize and standardize the use of the word that performs it even if all the other branches of the family should die out. Each such standardizing function must also be capable of surviving failing and manipulative uses and possibly supporting parasitic uses such as metaphoric use, sarcastic use. Such secondary uses differ from the stabilizing functions from which they are derived in that their success or that they happen (e.g., failing uses) does not, indeed usually could not, *taken alone*, account for or encourage sustained proliferation of that word serving that function.

The picture that emerges is a new sketch of a familiar landscape. Word tokens usually have a stacked series of stabilizing functions (see Chapter 1, "A Note on Changes in Proper Functions"). These range from the historically very remote—those uncovered only by the work of etymologists—to the historically most proximate—those that are currently accounting for reproductions of the immediate family or least type of the word token. The meanings of a word token or of a word root token are accordingly divided into more historically remote and more historically proximate meanings. For example, the meaning of "cap" in "capitulation" and the meaning of "chief" in "handkerchief" is, by one way of reckoning, the same. Both mean "head" by reference to the historically most remote stabilizing functions known for them. Indeed, "cap" and "chief" are, by one way of reckoning, "the same word," both having been derived by successive reproduction from the Indo-European "Kaput." On the other hand, there are three current or historically most proximate dictionary senses that tokens of "capitulation" may have and two that tokens of "handkerchief" may have, and these five are distinct, each corresponding to a separate least type.

Consider "capitulation." "Capitulation" now means (1) the act of capitulating, (2) the instrument containing the terms of surrender, and (3) an enumeration of the main parts of a subject. Any given modern token of the genetic family "capitulation" has *one* of these meanings as its literal meaning—belongs to *one* of these least types. This is *not* because one of these meanings is what is meant by the *person* who utters the token. The person who utters the token may not fully or correctly understand the word he utters, or he may use it metaphorically or in some other secondary way. The token has *one* of these meanings or stabilizing functions because it has been reproduced on the model of but *one* of the modern "capitulation" families. It is not likely that a person who has heard "capitulation" used only in dictionary sense (1) above will reproduce it intending that it should serve the function that happens to be the function of sense (2) or of sense (3) tokens. But even if he did, he would be using a sense (1) token analogically rather than using a sense (2) or (3) token literally. A person who is acquainted with all three senses of "capitulation" uses each of these independently. For each current branch—each least type—of the genetic "capitulation" family it is independently true that if the members of that branch were sounded or spelled otherwise, their progeny would also be sounded or spelled otherwise.

The most useful kind of word type to consider for purposes of semantic analysis is the kind that corresponds to such a current independent branch of a genetic family. Unless I say otherwise, I will always mean by "word type" just such a "least" type. Members of independent branches of the same genetic family, though they may sound the same and have ancestors in common, are *not* tokens of the same type in this usage. For example, if there are seventeen boys called "John" at the high school, there are seventeen different name types in everyday use at the high school that happen (though not by complete accident) to sound the same. These various "Johns" are different least types because speakers do not reproduce tokens of any on the model of tokens of any others. Tokens of each boy's name proliferate independently.

Meaning, in the sense of historically proximate stabilizing proper function, attaches in the first instance to least types and in the second instance to all tokens belonging to these types. Assume that we will later be able to spell out how the referent or denotation of a term hangs upon its stabilizing function. Then we can understand how it is possible that a person can use a kind term or a proper name, reproducing it on the model of a certain least type, to talk about the kind of person that the word family or branch denotes, yet not himself fully understand the function of the word he uses or be able to give an identifying description of its referent or denotation. For example, I can talk about elm trees without myself having the ability to distinguish an elm from an oak or a birch. I can talk about molybdenum without myself knowing even that it is a chemical element, let alone that it is a metal or that it has the atomic number 42.[2] Similarly, to ask or talk about a person, I need only know his name. That is, I need only have acquired his name on the model of a member or members of the least type that *is* his name—the branch the independent stabilizing function of which determines *him* as referent. So I can ask or talk about a person without having the ability to identify him, and without being able to give any identifying description of him. These things are possible because as members of least types, the word tokens that I use have meanings—stabilizing proper functions—that are quite independent of anything that I do or don't do with these tokens. (This point will be explored more carefully in Chapter 9.)

What makes two word tokens tokens of the same word—e.g., same genetic type or same least type—is a matter of the history of these tokens. Word tokens are classified into types by reference to reproductively established families and branches of these rather than by reference merely to physical form or to actual or possible function. If syntactic forms are, at root, members of reproductively established families having proper functions, then what makes two sentence tokens tokens that display the same syntactic form should likewise be a matter of history, rather than mere physical form or actual function. In Chapter 1, I argued that embodiments of specific syntactic structures or forms are reproductively established characters of sentences. In the modern context it would perhaps have been more definite to say that embodiments of specific *surface* syntactic forms are reproductively established characters of sentences. Yet this is true only if we understand the notion "surface syntactic form" in our own rather special way—a way, indeed, that makes the proposition that surface syntactic forms are reproduced characters analytic. I think that this is the only coherent way, in the end, to understand the notion "surface syntactic form." But it is not the usual way; so I must explain and defend my usage.

What we must do is to put the same sort of gloss on "same surface syntactic form" that is put by common usage on "same word." According to the common way of using "same word," it is possible that two identical sentence tokens having the same shape or sound and exemplifying exactly the same surface syntactic structure may nonetheless contain tokens of different words and have different meanings. For example, which word "seal" a token of "He damaged the seal" contains (the animal, or that which seals something up?) depends upon which reproductively established "seal" family the token was in fact, via the inner psychological history of the speaker, etc., modeled on. Likewise, we must use "same surface syntactic form" such that it is possible that two identical sentence tokens having the same shape or sound, and containing the same words, might still display different surface syntactic forms. For example, consider "He cooked the meat dry." What surface syntactic structure a given token of "He cooked the meat dry" has depends upon its history. Was it reproduced on the model of sentences like "He washed the dishes clean"? Or was it reproduced on the model of sentences like "He ate the chicken raw"? Similarly, if two sentences such as the famous pair "John is easy to please" and "John is eager to please" in fact get produced on the model of members of different reproductively established families of sentences (as seems highly likely), then they have different *surface* structures.

If my way of glossing "same surface syntactic form" seems odd, reflect that any description of surface form must refer at some point either to *categories* or else to *lists* of words that count as of the same coarse-or fine-grained lexical type. If this reference is to categories, then the relevant categories must be described in terms of *function*, not of sound or shape. But the function of a word has to do with its history—what reproductively established family it came from, what proper function this family has. If this reference is to a list of words, then what is to count as "the same word again" must be clarified. And again, this cannot be done by reference to shape or sound but must be done by reference to history and to the reproductively established families word tokens are members of. The ubiquity of homonyms in natural languages would make this clear if nothing else did. Granted this, "same surface syntactic form" is itself most reasonably described directly in terms of history too, i.e., in terms of reproductively established families of sentences the forms of which have been copied from common ancestors. If it is objected that the history here is impossible to document, certainly impossible to document in detail, I agree. Word types and surface syntactic forms are theoretical entities in a way not that different from the way in which forces and genes are theoretical entities. Their reality is not "given" to perception.

Surface syntactic forms, too, can have both historically more proximate and historically more remote stabilizing functions. Consider the form in which orders are routinely delivered in the armed services: "You will proceed to . . . "; "You will report to . . . ", etc. Is this form indicative or imperative? Insofar as this form is now being reproduced in the armed services to serve the imperative function because it has been serving that function in the immediate past, the historically most proximate function of the form (of its least type) is imperative. The form is one among other imperative forms in English. But insofar as this form was, at some earlier point in history, modeled upon an English indicative form, it has also a historically less proximate *indicative* function. Moreover, it might well be argued that one reason this form is presently proliferated in the armed services is, exactly, that the form *is* indicative also. The suggestion in using an indicative form for giving orders is that the one who receives the orders is being presented with a *fait accompli* rather than with a choice. He is being told the *facts* about his future. To the degree that this is so, a historically proximate as well as a more remote function of the form in question is indicative. It *is* the ordinary indicative form put to a special (parasitic) purpose. It is *also* a special imperative form. Similar remarks apply to the use of the interrogative and indicative moods in making requests: "Could you . . . ?", "Would you . . . ?", "I would like . . . please," etc. These forms are imperative *as well as* interrogative or indicative. Their status is rather like that of trite but not yet dead metaphors.

The stabilizing function of a language device is part of its public meaning. Only because language devices have stabilizing functions is it possible to distinguish what such a device itself means from what a speaker means by it. Thus, because it has no stabilizing function, Alan Breck's bouquet of gold button and twigs does not itself mean "Meet Alan Breck in the Heugh of Corrynakiegh." It is only Alan who means this, intends to convey this, with the bouquet. The difference between saying and merely meaning something, and also the distinction between truth and falsity, are defined in relation to the stabilizing functions of language devices. That a person says what is true vs. what is false depends not upon that person's intent but upon the stabilizing functions of the language devices he uses. Try to imagine Alan contriving not just a bouquet that intentionally or unintentionally misleads John Breck Maccoll, but a *false* bouquet! No matter how deeply nested the Gricean intentions Alan manages to muster when presenting his bouquet, he cannot *say* anything with it or make *it* true or false. For *it* doesn't mean anything. (There are of course, other senses (least types) of "means," e.g., that in which smoke "means" fire and that in which the angry look on big John's face "means" that little Johnny had better watch his manners.)

The sense of "meaning" that is explicated by the notion "stabilizing function" is the "means" of what Wilfrid Sellars, in an early paper, calls the "translation rubric":

_____ (in L) means. . . .[3]

The translation rubric accommodates any kind of word or phrase or sentence as a value for its blank space, provided that the dot space is filled in appropriately. Thus, "und" (in German) means *and*; "rouge" (in French) means *red*; "Ach weh!" (in German) means *alas*! and "Chicago est grande" (in French) means *Chicago is large*. The "means" of the translation rubric does not then correspond to the "meaning" that is Frege's own *Sinn* or to the "meaning" that is intension, or reference or denotation (nor does it correspond to what I will later call *Fregean sense*). For the translation rubric can be used with expressions that have no *Sinn* and no intension and no referents or denotation.[4]

According to Sellars, "The expression 'means' as a translation rubric is easily confused with its other uses. The essential feature of this use is that whether the translation be from one language to another, or from one expression to another in the same language, the translated expression and the expression into which it translates must have the same use."[5] My first suggestion is that we substitute "stabilizing proper function" for "use" in the last phrase above. Second, we can clear up the vagueness of the expression "essential feature of this use" by saying that the translation rubric performs *its* stabilizing function in accordance with a Normal explanation only when the expressions that fill in the blank and the dots have the same stabilizing or direct proper functions as one another. Sellars adds a footnote: "To speak of two expressions as having the same use is to presuppose a criterion of sameness of use which separates relevant from irrelevant differences in use. Clearly, differences which are irrelevant to one context of inquiry may be relevant to another." Change "use" to "stabilizing proper function" and retain this footnote.

Last, we can eliminate the parenthetical phrase "(in L)" from our rendering of the translation rubric. The word to be translated names its *own* reproductively established family, not a sign design. As a member of its own reproductively established family it is, of course, a word in a certain language. Mentioning this language may sometimes be a help to an interpreter, enabling him to identify more easily the reproductively established family from which the token comes. But the fact that an interpreter may find it ambiguous which reproductively established family is named by a token in quotes does not make that token itself ambiguous. It names what it names, regardless of how the interpreter gets on. Similar remarks apply to tokens of proper names such as "John" or "Betty." The fact that an interpreter may not know or even have a clue about which Betty or John is named by such a token does not imply that no definite John or Betty *is* named. The one that is named is the one that corresponds to the least type of the name token used. Except in freakish cases this is, of course, also the one the speaker means.

If it is then asked, what *is* the stabilizing function of the translation rubric, Sellars's early answer is again helpful. With regard to " 'und' means *and*," Sellars says, "[the speaker] mentions the German vocable 'und' but *uses* the English vocable 'and.' He uses the latter, however, in a peculiar way, a way which is characteristic of *semantical* discourse. He presents us with an instance of the word itself, not a name of it, and, making use of the fact that we belong to the same language community, indicates to us that we have only to rehearse our use of 'and' to appreciate the role of 'und' on the other side of the Rhine."[6] Sellars is interested in denying that the way "and" is used in the rubric fits the hackneyed use-mention dichotomy. Neither is "and" mentioned nor is "and" used in the *ordinary* way of using "and." It is used in a special way. I am not yet ready to discuss reference, hence cannot here reject or defend Sellars's view on the latter matter.[7] The interest of Sellars's early account for us is that he seems to be describing something like the focused stabilizing function of the translation rubric. Namely, no matter how it does it in detail, no matter what earlier stages are gone through first, " '*x*' means *y*" has as its focused stabilizing function to bring a hearer to be able to use "*x*" in accordance with its stabilizing function. It does this Normally by presenting the hearer with a token from the reproductively established family "*y*", the stabilizing function of which the hearer is already in command, and causing the hearer to adopt the same posture toward the reproductively established family "*x*".

If this is what the "means" in " '*x*' means *y*" does, then it is natural to take "meaning" in one of its senses to denote stabilizing function. My suggestion is not that the notion "stabilizing function" can be used in giving a conceptual analysis of "meaning" in the translation-rubric sense. Rather, I suggest that the proposal that meaning is stabilizing function is a good *theory* about the natural nature or status of one aspect of meaning.

Appendix A: How the Functions of Significant Sentence Aspects Are Integrated

Every sentence token exhibits a variety of superimposed reproductively established characters derived from different models, each having its own stabilizing function. The sentence itself thus has a stabilizing function that is derived from the stabilizing functions of each of its significant elements or aspects. However, if we look at all closely we see that the stabilizing proper function of each significant element or aspect of a sentence is a *relational* proper function. What each part is supposed to do is something that can be described only by telling what relation this doing is to have to other parts of the sentence—specifically, what relation it is to bear to the stabilizing functions of other parts of the sentence. (Whatever has a relation to the proper function of a device has, as such, a definite relation to the device itself. Hence it is not sloppy to say that the stabilizing function of one part of a sentence can be described as doing something that bears a certain relation to other parts of the sentence, though not, of course, to these other parts qua mere sign designs.) For example, the aspect of an imperative sentence that makes it imperative does not have as its stabilizing function merely to produce an action on the part of the hearer. It must produce an action that bears a certain relation to the functions of other parts of the sentence—those parts that express the "propositional content" of the sentence. And what the parts that express the propositional content of the sentence are supposed to do depends in turn upon the grammatical mood of the sentence. Similarly, if it is the focused stabilizing function of a proper name to precipitate an act of identification of its referent, still, as I will later argue, acts of identification can occur in the context of various different kinds of mental activities. The kind of context in which the act of identification is supposed to occur depends upon the rest of the sentence.

Being a part of a sentence is a Normal condition for proper performance of every elementary sentence part. But it is also more than a Normal condition. It is a necessary condition. For just what each element is supposed to do cannot be defined except in relation to the rest of the sentence. Any description of the meaning in the sense of stabilizing function of any elementary language part thus necessarily involves reference to the Normal condition of being in the context of a sentence containing elements of other kinds. Although the stabilizing function of a language element can be described relationally, hence without making reference to any *particular* sentence context, there is still good reason to espouse the view that the basic unit of meaning is not, say, the word, but the sentence as a whole. The stabilizing functions of the elements of a sentence are not just added together to produce the direct proper function of the whole. Each element needs the other elements to have a determinate function at all. (In Chapter 6 I will reinforce this point, arguing that one key to understanding how sentences map onto the world lies in seeing that in the first instance it is the entire sentence that maps, the mapping of its parts following after.)

Appendix B: New Words

The theory of direct proper functions showed only how a word that has a history of reproductions behind it can have a proper function that is independent of the speaker's intention. To explain how a word that is just being introduced can also have a proper function that is independent of a speaker's intention requires, in one important kind of case, the theory of adapted and derived proper functions.

Sometimes a new word is introduced just by being used. The introduction of nicknames, for example, is often unaccompanied by any explanation or introducing device. Someone simply begins calling George-the-cat "Muffin" or begins calling the baby "Poof." Such a word has no stabilizing function and no function that is independent of a speaker's intentions until it is true that it is being reproduced because it has correlated with the serving of a certain function. This, however, can happen very swiftly. The very second use of a nickname often illustrates such reproduction. The first use is often understood by the hearer in the way the speaker intends. The hearer identifies the referent for the name that the speaker intends. If a communication that is of value to the speaker and/or the hearer results—e.g., information is imparted or amusement results—then each may note or infer the correlation and causal connection (correlation by a form of Mill's method of difference) of word with function (i.e., identification of a certain referent), and either may reproduce the word on other occasions precisely because of that connection. As early as the second occasion of use, then, a word that is introduced merely by being used can already be a member of a reproductively established family (containing only two members—an original and a copy) that already has a proper function.

Often, however, words are not introduced merely by being used, nor would such a method of introduction be effective. It would be too hard for a hearer to figure out, using context only, the rest of the sentence, etc., what the speaker intends the function or mapping value of the word to be. Instead, the originator of the term employs a conventional introducing device such as "I christen this child ____ " or "Let us call *such and such* ' ____ '." The conventional introducing device has a relational stabilizing function such that, given for its adaptor a new word or name filled in its blank, and given the context, say, of a christening ceremony complete with baby or of explanatory words filled in the "such and such" blank, it acquires an *adapted* proper function to cause the new word or name-family to perform a certain linguistic function. Performance of this function is then a *derived* proper function of the new word. It will not remain merely a derived proper function for long, of course. As soon as it becomes true that those who are using and understanding the new word as they are *continue* to do so in part because using and understanding it this way is working for them with partner hearers and speakers, the word has acquired a direct proper function. That is, as soon as the word is reproduced because its use in fact correlates with a function of interest to speakers and hearers, that function is its direct proper function. But before this time, the word that is introduced by a conventional introducing device still has a proper function that is derived not merely from speaker intentions but from the public stabilizing function of a public introducing device. As such it has a *public* meaning.

Appendix C: Conventional Drawings, Charts, etc.

Besides spoken and written words and sentences there are of course other conventional communication media. For example, one must learn to interpret ancient Egyptian paintings and ancient Roman paintings and even perspective paintings correctly. (Unless one has learned how to interpret ancient Egyptian paintings, one is liable to think that these represent awkwardly contorted figures of animals and people; unless one has learned how to interpret Roman paintings, one is liable to understand them as representing strangely surrealistic spaces.) Also, there are numerous kinds of conventional maps and diagrams and graphs and charts that one must learn, kind by kind, to make and to interpret. Conventional charts, diagrams, graphs, drawings, etc., presumably have describable syntactic structures as well. The drawings of impossible spaces that modern artists and experimental psychologists sometimes play with could surely be described as breaking the syntactic rules of perspective drawing. It is very easy to break the syntactic rules of electric circuit diagramming or of flow charting, etc. The basic significant elements or aspects of all such conventional devices are reproduced elements, the devices themselves being members of reproductively established families. All these devices, too, have direct proper functions that are independent of the intents of the individuals that produce them. As Alan put it, one sometimes has to "go to the school for two-three years" before one learns how to use and interpret them.

PART II

A General Theory of Signs

Chapter 5
Intentionality as a Natural Phenomenon

Natural signs, animals' signs, people's signs, indexes, signals, indicators, symbols, representations, sentences, maps, charts, pictures—there is no generic term in English that naturally covers all of these. Yet it has been felt by many philosophers that these are all related, and it is the term "sign" that has most often been used to cover them all, or all that were felt to be related (e.g., C. S. Peirce). What is it that a road-curve sign, a stoplight, the poised indicator on a voltmeter, storm clouds (signs of rain), false sentences, cookbook directions, Alan's bouquet, bee dances, beaver-tail splashes (danger signal), beliefs (if these are inner representations), the map on the cover of *Treasure Island*, and the *Mona Lisa* all have in common? Nothing whatever—that is clear. But the question how these are all related, as they intuitively seem to be, such as to fall naturally under a single heading, is perhaps answerable.

There are natural signs, conventional signs, improvised signs (such as Alan's bouquet), genetically determined signs (bee dances, beaver splashes), and if beliefs and intentions are inner representations, there are inner signs, which are none of the above. There are articulate signs (sentences, maps, bee dances) and inarticulate signs (stoplights, storm clouds). There are indicative signs (signs that say what *is*) and imperative signs (signs that tell what to *do*) and signs whose functions ride piggyback on these. I will argue that articulate conventional signs, indicative and imperative, are the *paradigm* cases of signs. All other signs are "signs" by virtue of one or another striking resemblance to these paradigms. To run down the major characteristics of articulate conventional signs, then, will be to see why one after another of the various other kinds of signs is felt to be related or naturally called "sign" too.

Most signs mean. But "mean" has various senses. Storm clouds mean rain; John means well; *Hund* means dog. Some but not others of these senses of "means," it is easy to assume, are intentional senses. Likewise, some signs but not others, it is easy to assume, display intentionality. Intentional signs are clearly distinguishable, though peculiar and puzzling, in that what they mean need not exist or be actual. A particular storm cloud cannot actually mean rain unless it soon rains. But I can mean to go but not actually go, and a sentence can mean snow is black, but snow is not actually black. Intentionality itself seems to be a clean-cut phenomenon, even though one that is exceedingly hard to understand. Indeed, the notion "intentionality" was reintroduced and brought into our modern philosophical vocabulary by Brentano exactly for the purpose of cleaving a *clean* gap between the mental and the physical.

But intentionality, I will argue, is not a clean-cut phenomenon. There is no clean distinction between intentional and nonintentional signs or between intentional and nonintentional senses of "means." Intentionality does have to do, very generally, with what is Normal or proper rather than with what is merely actual. It also has to do with mapping relations—ones that are Normal or proper rather than merely actual or average. But the notion "intentionality," like the notion "sign," is unified not by a definition but by a paradigm. Indeed, there are *two* paradigms of intentionality, an indicative paradigm and an imperative paradigm. And these display important differences as well as striking similarities between the ways "the sign" is properly and Normally related to "the signed." Intentionality is not of a piece.

In Chapter 6 I will give a description of those properties of indicative and imperative sentences that combine to produce their characteristic kinds of intentionality, in Chapter 7 I will show how various overt signs exhibit this or that kind of analogy, and in Chapter 8 I will discuss *inner* signs. In this chapter I wish only to make it initially plausible that the intentionality of sentences *might* be a phenomenon that has to do with mapping relations that are Normal or proper (though by no means with just *any* of these).

We can begin by noting that a theory that paradigm intentionality has to do with Normal and/or proper mapping rules between signs and things is, of course, some kind of correspondence theory. Correspondence theories are not exactly out of fashion, but at this time in history they need careful introduction.

If any certainty has emerged from the last thirty years of philosophy, it is that a *pure* correspondence theory of truth is vacuous. By a *pure* correspondence theory I mean a theory that signs or representations, when true or correct, are true or correct *merely* by virtue of there being a, some, mapping function that maps these representations onto parts of the world or reality. Following in the wake of Quine, Wittgenstein of *Philosophical Investigations*, and many others it is now easy to remind ourselves why a pure correspondence theory will not work. It is because mathematical mapping relations are infinitely numerous and ubiquitous whereas representation-represented relations are not. If any correspondence theory of truth is to avoid vacuousness, it must be a theory that tells what is *different* or *special* about the mapping relations that map representations onto representeds.

This difference or specialness cannot be merely a formal specialness, say, a special kind of simplicity required for those mapping functions that correlate representations with representeds. No kind of formal specialness is logically more special than any other; special formal complexities are as special, logically, as special simplicities. The specialness that turns a mathematical mapping function into a representation-represented relation in a given case must have to be some kind of special status that this function has in the real, the natural, or the *causal* order rather than the logical order. Thus, any coherent correspondence theory of truth must be part of our total theory of the world.

That our theory of the world has to be a totally naturalist theory I am not prepared to argue. But I am prepared to argue that a naturalist account of the specialness (or various kinds of specialness) of the mapping relation between a representation and its represented can be given—an account that places this specialness in the realm of natural science, that is, of physics, physiology, biology, and evolutionary theory. The job of creating such a theory, like the job of creating any good naturalist theory, is not of course a task of analysis but a task of *construction*, the phenomena to be explained rather than the concepts with which we have traditionally dealt with these phenomena taking center stage. Also, no proofs can be offered that will demonstrate the truth of a naturalist theory; naturalist answers cannot ward off Cartesian skepticism. Qua naturalist, it is not my business to *prove* that a correspondence theory is the only possible theory of truth or that truth *is* a natural property. My business is only to give a coherent account in which such items as signs, inner representations, meaning, truth, and knowledge appear and their peculiarities are understood *within* the natural world.

That sentences are in the natural world and that the world affairs they correspond to are, at least often, in the natural world too, nobody doubts, unless they have given up on correspondence theories generally. That the "correspondence" involved has something to do with mapping rules or rules of projection is less clear. It is not at all clear how to describe an ontology that will support this view or how to articulate the kinds of rules involved. In Chapter 6 I will introduce the most general principle in accordance with which, I believe, language maps onto the world. And the whole of Part III is an attempt to show how a variety of traditionally perplexing language devices do or don't map onto the world. The relevant ontological problems will be discussed in Chapters 16 and 17. Let us suppose that these problems can be solved. Problems of apparently larger proportion remain—problems more explicitly associated with intentionality.

Let us grant that when a sentence is true, often both it and the world affair to which it corresponds are in the natural world. Grant at least that this is so for some kinds of sentences, given the *kind* of truth they have. (The truths of mathematical equations, sentences containing value terms, etc., are probably of different kinds.) Let us grant also that the truth of a sentence has to do with there being a mapping rule with some special status that in fact correlates the sentence with what it represents. Several lines of argument suggest that this special status could not possibly be a special *natural* status—a status in the world of natural science. I will start with the easiest and most naive of these arguments.

Consider false sentences. They do not map onto the actual world. But they have "meaning" in the same sense that true sentences do. If they have meaning, they must mean something. So there must be something for them to mean. But what they mean is not something *actual*, hence not something in the natural world. So what a *true* sentence means must also be something not in the natural world. The relation of a true sentence to its actual represented in the natural world is clearly *mediated* by a relation to something not present in the natural world. It is mediated by the "meaning of the sentence." Hence this relation is not any sort of natural-world or causal-order relation.

The obvious reply that false sentences do not map onto nonnatural things called "meanings" but merely *fail* to map onto the world is not enough. Suppose that meanings are *not* strange nonnatural *objects* that mediate between sentences and the world. Still, it appears, meaning or representing something cannot be grounded in an *actual* relation between *true* sentences and the world. Whatever actual-world relation you attempt to specify that makes true sentences true, you won't find it in the case of false sentences. And certainly mere talk of the absence of this truth relation will not help us to understand false sentences. Apparently, what we need to understand is *meaning*—something common to both true and false sentences. And meaning appears to be something irrelevant to any *actual* mapping relations.

This sort of problem is immediately illuminated by introducing some such notions as "proper" and "Normal." Turn the problem this way. The true and the false sentence have in common that both are "supposed to" correspond to affairs in the actual world in accordance with certain mapping rules. The task is to give a naturalist account of "supposed to" in this context. This will be accomplished if we can show that "supposed to" can be unpacked in terms of proper or Normal rather than actual relations. For the categories "proper" and "Normal" have been defined as straightforward, causal-order, natural-history categories. If we can accomplish this, then a false sentence will prove to be no more problematic than, say, the color pattern of a chameleon that is "supposed to" match what it sits on, but doesn't.

A second kind of argument begins as follows. Sounds or scratch marks are or become sentences with meanings by virtue of relations to people who use and interpret them. The intentionality of a sentence is thus a dependent intentionality. If it were not for the intentionality of people's thoughts, which get communicated via sentences, sentences would not be intentional but would be quite ordinary objects. Clearly then, the intentionality of thoughts—say, beliefs or intentions—cannot be interpreted as like that of sentences. To attempt to interpret the intentionality of thoughts by analogy to that of sentences would lead to regress. Philosophers who take thoughts to be inner representations— inner pictures, mental sentences—are forgetting that sentences and pictures are intentional only in a derivative sense, making essential reference to an interpreter. They will have to postulate an inner interpreter of inner representations to close the analogical explanation. And if this interpreter is again analogous to an ordinary sentence interpreter, they will have to postulate an even more inner interpreter to interpret *his* inner representations, etc. Briefly, sentences are intentional in a *derivative* sense, requiring reference to something other that is intentional per se; so whatever is intentional per se cannot be understood on analogy with sentences. The sensible conclusion is that *basic* intentionality is something had directly by beliefs and intentions. For to proceed further with the regress could serve no purpose.

Now a new theme emerges. Sentences are in the ordinary natural world. But beliefs and intentions are mental things. Apparently basic intentionality is something that only mental things have. Indeed, it must be the involvement of the mental that *produces* the peculiarities that cause our puzzlement about intentionality. To explain intentionality in naturalist terms would thus be to explain the mental in naturalist terms. So if the mental cannot be understood in naturalist terms, neither can intentionality. Compatibly, those who believe that the mental *can* be explained in naturalist terms often take it that the same sorts of principles that will show how the intentionality of beliefs, intentions, fears and hopes, etc., resides in the natural world will show how pains, itches, tickles, and *consciousness* really reside in the natural world.

Of course, the last step in this argument is weak. Surely, even if sentences were not basic intentional entities whereas beliefs and intentions were, it would not follow that everything with basic intentionality is mental. Nor would it follow that intentionality is puzzling *because* it is a mental phenomenon. But the starting point of the argument is problematic in a more interesting way.

It does seem pretty clear that if we stopped having ideas, beliefs, and intentions, etc., we would stop uttering sentences with meanings. But *why* is this true? Does it have to be true because the intentionality of sentences is *derived* from the intentionality of ideas, beliefs, and intentions? An argument by explanation is best countered by offering another explanation just as plausible. In the next few chapters, I will propose an alternative explanation.

I will propose that a sentence, and every other typically intentional device, is intentional in part by virtue of certain proper and Normal relations that it bears to a "producer" or "producers" and to an "interpreter" or "interpreters." "Producers" and "interpreters" are cooperating devices that produce and use the intentional device and *that sometimes are and sometimes are not* contained within the same individual organism. The Normal and proper relations that obtain among intentional devices, their producers and their interpreters will be described such that it is neither necessary nor typical that the interpreter of an intentional device should interpret by producing *another* intentional device. This just *happens* to be how it works in the case of public-language sentences. Thus the intentionality of a public-language sentence is not derived from the *intentionality* of the inner representations that it Normally produces or expresses. Sentences are *basic* intentional items. And they are intentional for reasons that can be described without raising or answering any questions about what the mental is as such. That, at least, is what I shall argue.

But there is another argument that connects intentionality with the mental, suggesting that any analysis of the intentionality of thoughts or of *inner* representations, at least, would have to proceed in accordance with principles by which the mental or consciousness *itself* would then have been analyzed.

Offer whatever account you like, says my adversary, of interesting natural relations between sentences and the world. Offer whatever account you like even of the relations between inner representations, conceived as natural-world objects (say, brain states) and the world outside. Whatever these interesting relations are, they are merely *external* relations. At the very most, they might somehow ground connections that, in accordance with natural necessity, *correlate* alterations of consciousness, if this hangs upon brain states, with alterations of the world outside. Such correlations, and the relations of natural necessity upon which they rest, would lie totally outside of the mind, totally outside of consciousness. But in being aware or conscious of the world we are not conscious merely of alterations in consciousness or merely of our inner representations themselves. We *experience* the *intentionality* of our consciousness or of its content representations. Or at least we *can* experience this when we move to a reflective consciousness. We can be *conscious* of the intentionality of our thinkings or thoughts. The basic and interesting kind of intentionality is that which we *experience* in consciously knowing, believing, intending, etc., and this cannot possibly be the same as the external "intentionality" of which you, the naturalist, propose to offer an analysis. The basic and interesting kind of intentionality is somehow "in" consciousness, not outside it or externally between it and the world.

What exactly is the force here of the notion that we *experience* the intentionality of our thoughts or consciousness—that intentionality is somehow "in" consciousness? That is, what force does it have to have for the argument to go through? It is important to see that the force must be both epistemic and *rationalistically* so. The sense of "experience" here is a supposed sense in which one's "experience" infallibly attests to the being-there of *what* one seems to experience. Or, if we take it that intentionality is discovered first by reflective consciousness, in this consciousness one must necessarily and immediately know the *nature* of the experience reflected upon—have an automatic *understanding* of it taken as object. The idea that intentionality is somehow "in" consciousness carries the same weight. What is "in" consciousness is "in" in such a way that its being-there is *part* of, hence inseparable from, the act of consciousness and inseparable not merely in accordance with *natural* necessity but in accordance with rational necessity. The consciousness *could* not—in accordance with rational possibility—be thus or thus if what is "in" it were not there. The view of my adversary, then, is the view that consciousness is transparently and *infallibly* epistemic. Consciousness is or essentially involves an infallible kind of direct knowing—a knowing that is guaranteed as such from within consciousness itself. Specifically, the claim is that consciousness grasps its own intentionality, or that of its inner representations, with infallibility. Intentionality is a "given." Hence this intentionality cannot consist of mere matter-of-fact, even of naturally necessary, external relations to the world.

Suppose that we were to refuse to adopt this rationalist epistemic view of consciousness. That is, suppose we were *consistently* to deny that there are any epistemological "givens." We could admit that people are (sometimes) aware of the intentionality of their thoughts, just as they are sometimes aware of others looking at them or aware that it is raining. But we would maintain that this kind of *awareness of*, indeed every kind of *awareness of*, is in part an external relation, the inside of the awareness—that feeling part—giving no absolute guarantee that it *is* the inside of a genuine *awareness of* relation. Consciousness, that is, does not contain *within* it or directly before it any *objects* of consciousness. Even an awareness of an awareness does not have the object awareness as an *unmediated* object. There is nothing diaphanous about consciousness.

An unsettling possibility! One implication would be that we are no more in a position to know *merely via Cartesian reflection* that we are truly *thinking*, i.e., that we or our thoughts intend anything, than that we are thinking truly. Absolutely *nothing* is guaranteed directly from within an act of consciousness. This is the most ultimate form that an attack upon "the given" or upon rationalism could possibly take.

That is the position that I will adopt in this essay. It is a necessary consequence of the description I will give of intentionality. But that is not *why* I will adopt it. I adopt it because I believe that it must be true. I believe that it must be true because the most perplexing problems in epistemology, in the philosophy of mind and in the philosophy of language—problems that have led philosophers to one dead end after another, produced one paradoxical view after another and one kind of implicit or explicit nihilism after another—seem, one after another, to depend upon the prior explicit or implicit adoption of a *rationalist* view of intentionality. Later—mainly in Chapters 16 and the Epilogue—I will make some strenuous efforts to show exactly that and how this is so. But in one form or another, meaning rationalism permeates nearly every nook and cranny of our philosophical tradition. In order even to come to *comprehend* what meaning rationalism *is*, what various forms it can take, it is necessary forcefully to fling down on the table something with which to contrast it. The description of intentionality that I will offer is designed to serve that purpose. I also think that *it* is true. But if nothing else comes of it, may it at least leave behind it this question and, by the end of this book, leave this question in a relatively clear form: what if any grounds do we have for continuing blindly to bet on meaning rationalism, given its monotonous no-show track record?

Just as the negative thesis of this book—that something is very wrong with meaning rationalism—will be argued for indirectly by constructing an alternative positive thesis, the positive thesis will also be argued, for the most part, indirectly. I will argue my thesis by laying it out and then by showing how it bypasses certain traditional perplexities and unworldly worlds and goes on to solve many problems, rather than by deductive argument from currently acceptable premises. Its defense rests almost entirely on its power to unravel paradox and produce understanding. So that power will come out, if it does come out, only as this essay proceeds to the end. In the few paragraphs that remain in this chapter, let me clarify the direction that this positive thesis will take.

The position is that intentionality is grounded in external natural relations, Normal and/or proper relations, between representations and representeds, the notions "Normal" and "proper" being defined in terms of evolutionary *history*—of either the species or the evolving individual or both. Hence nothing that is either merely in consciousness or merely "in the head" displays intentionality *as such*.

On the one hand, this means that there is no way of looking just at a present-moment person, e.g., at his speech dispositions or at his neural network patterns, that will reveal even the intentional nature of his uttered sentences or inner representations, let alone reveal *what* these represent. On the other hand, it means that we do not have a priori knowledge, certain knowledge via Cartesian reflection, even of the fact *that* we mean, let alone knowledge of *what* we mean or knowledge that what we mean is true.

Let me put the position starkly—so starkly that the reader may simply close the book! Suppose that by some cosmic accident a collection of molecules formerly in random motion were to coalesce to form your exact physical double. Though possibly that being would be and even would *have* to be in a state of consciousness exactly like yours, that being would have no ideas, no beliefs, no intentions, no aspirations, no fears, and no hopes. (His *non*-intentional states, like being in pain or itching, may of course be another matter.) This because the evolutionary *history* of the being would be wrong. For only in virtue of one's evolutionary history do one's intentional mental states have proper functions, hence does one mean or intend at all, let alone mean anything determinate.[2] To the utterances of *that* being, Quine's theory of the indeterminacy of translation would apply—and with a vengeance never envisioned by Quine. That being would also have *no liver, no heart, no eyes, no brain*, etc. This, again, because the history of the being would be wrong. For the categories "heart," "liver," "eye," "brain," and also "idea," "belief," and "intention" are proper function categories, defined in the end by reference to long-term and short-term evolutionary history, not present constitution or disposition. Were this not so, there could not be *malformed* hearts or *nonfunctioning* hearts nor could there be *confused* ideas or *empty* ideas or *false* beliefs, etc. Ideas, beliefs, and intentions are not such because of what they do or could do. They are such because of what they are, given the context of their history, *supposed* to do and of how they are supposed to do it.

Why do I think that ideas and beliefs and intentions are, as such, members of biological or proper-function categories? First, because we acquired the ability to have them through a long evolutionary process and they are useful things to have; that is, they have survival value. But far more important, they display the characteristic mark that all things defined by proper-function categories display. It makes sense to speak of their being *defective*. Nothing that can be said to be defective is *what* it is merely by virtue of what it is actually like or what it actually does or would do if. What is defective is, just, that which is *not* what it *should* be or can*not* do what it *should* do, hence is something defined by its "shoulds" rather than by its "coulds" and "woulds." And I can see no way of unpacking the "should" in this sort of context by reference to present structure or disposition. How could any "should"s or "supposed to"s be applied to the inner arrangements of your newly arrived, randomly created double? How could anything in him be defective? Beliefs, on the other hand, are *essentially* things that can be true or false, correct or defective.

The thesis that Cartesian reflection does not by itself reveal even the intentionality of our ideas and beliefs has numerous corollaries and numerous implications, not all of which will digest easily. From this thesis it follows that whether our ideas and the terms we use to express them are clear and univocal is never determinable in the end by mere philosophical reflection. Corollaries are that knowledge of synonymy of terms even in one's own idiolect is not had a priori and that knowledge of "logical possibility," insofar as this knowledge cuts ice of any kind, is not a priori knowledge. It also follows that totally senseless or meaningless thoughts do not necessarily show themselves to be such even to those most intelligent and persevering in armchair work. In a nutshell, it follows that *all* of the rationalist positions on meaning are wrong.

Chapter 6

Intentional Icons: Fregean Sense, Reference, and Real Value Introduced

In the broadest possible sense of "intentionality," any device with a proper function might be said to display "intentionality." For the traditional earmark of the intentional is the puzzle that what is intentional apparently stands in relation to something else—that which it *intends* or *means* or *means to do* or *is meant to do*—which something can be described, yet which something may or may not *be*. The general solution to the puzzle, I have suggested, is to see that intentionality is at root properness or Normalness. The intentional is "supposed to" stand in a certain relation to something else; for example, it may be its proper function to produce such a something else. Every device with a proper function is *meant* to do something or other and as such displays intentionality in a very broad sense.

In a narrower and more usual sense of "intentionality"[1] not everything that is meant to perform a certain function displays intentionality. For example, the heart does not display intentionality, nor do screwdrivers nor do conditioned responses. Do bee dances display intentionality in the narrower sense? Does the exclamation "help!"? Does the carefully adjusted indicator on a voltmeter? Does Alan's bouquet?

In Chapter 5 I asserted that "intentionality is not of a piece." There is no single feature or set of features that characterizes everything we are sometimes tempted to say exhibits "intentionality." Rather there are various features that things can share with sentences that may inspire us, in different moods, to see these things too as "intentional." In this chapter I will define a category of devices, among which are sentences, which I will call "intentional icons." ("Icon" is C. S. Peirce's term. I use it because it remains fairly fresh as a technical term, not having been much muddied over.) Intentional icons exhibit a number of the most striking features of sentences. Intentional icons are devices that are "supposed to" map *thusly* onto the world in order to serve their direct proper functions; that is, Normally they do map so when serving these functions. And they are devices that are supposed to be used or "interpreted" by cooperating devices. Thus they exhibit a sort

of "ofness" or "aboutness" that one usually associates with intentionality. There are a great many things in the world that are intentional
icons. And *all* of the things that we are tempted to call "signs" exhibit
very striking analogies to intentional icons. Hence I believe that the
category of intentional icons is an important one to demarcate.

But not all of the most striking features of sentences are exhibited
by other intentional icons. One of the most striking features of sentences
is exhibited *only* by sentences. That is subject-predicate structure. A
second striking feature of sentences is the characteristic or defining
property of a most interesting category of things that I shall call "representations." *Representations are intentional icons the mapping values
of the referents of elements of which are supposed to be identified by the
cooperating interpreter.* Bee dances seem to have something in common
with sentences, but it is hard to suppose that interpreter bees actually
identify—roughly, understand the reference of—the mapping aspects
of the dance-maps they observe.[2] The act of identifying the referent
of an element of an intentional icon is, I will argue, a very special act
that requires a special analysis. But it will be best to work first with
the notion *intentional icon* for a good while in order to see just what
that notion can explain and what it cannot explain before introducing
the complications that representations bring with them.

Now there may be readers who will object to my calling intentional
icons that are not representations "intentional." Some may feel strongly
that being supposed to precipitate an act of identification of its referents
should be made central to the notion of an "intentional" device. If
what a sign signs is not supposed to be identified or recognized—if
the interpreter is not supposed to understand *what* the sign signs—
then, it may well be said, the sign is not "intentional." I propose to
ignore any such complaint. In the end this is merely a question of
terminology, and I think I can speak more plainly by ignoring it.

"Intentional Icon" Defined

I will abbreviate "when performing its proper functions in accordance
with a Normal explanation" as "Normally." There are four characteristics that an indicative or imperative sentence Normally has that contribute to its being an intentional icon. I will first name these, then
discuss each in turn.

(1)   A sentence is a member of a reproductively established family
having direct proper functions. (Which family is most relevant here will be explained below.)

(2)   Normally a sentence stands midway between two cooper-

ating devices, a producer device and an interpreter device, which are designed or standardized to fit one another, the presence and cooperation of each being a Normal condition for the proper performance of the other.

(3)   Normally the sentence serves to adapt the cooperating interpreter device to conditions such that proper functions of that device can be performed under those conditions.

(4a)   In the case of imperative sentences, it is a proper function of the interpreter device, as adapted* by the sentence, to produce conditions onto which the sentence will map in accordance with a specific mapping function of a kind to be described below.

(4b)   In the case of indicative sentences, the Normal explanation of how the sentence adapts* the interpreter device such that it can perform its proper functions makes reference to the fact that the sentence maps conditions in the world in accordance with a specific mapping function of a kind to be described below.

These four characteristics define the paradigm of what I will call an "intentional icon." The fourth characteristic concerns the mapping of intentional icons onto the world. Almost this entire chapter must go to explaining *how* intentional icons map onto the world, for it is here that we must part company with some traditional views of language.

1. *An intentional icon is a member of a reproductively established family having direct proper functions.* Most relevantly, a sentence is a member of a family of sentences having the same gross *overall* surface form. Given a Chomskian perspective, this basic form may be the reproductively established character that is conforming with the syntactic rules by which the root sentence or main clause is generated taking into account the lexical categories of the elements of this main clause. Other significant aspects of the sentence—the concrete words, the syntactic forms of embedded items—are members of other reproductively established families. The Normal reproductively established character of the sentence that is its basic form is a relational character, a relation among elements as having specified *kinds* of direct proper functions. The proper functions of the whole sentence, as exhibiting its overall surface form, are adapted proper functions, adapted most proximately to the specific functional character of its elements—the specific words and phrases in it (see Chapter 4, Appendix A). In a simpler but similar way, bee dances also fulfill condition (1) for being intentional icons.

* "Adapt" and "adapted" are technical terms, defined in Chapter 2.

That which is invariant in all well-formed bee dances is the overall syntactic form or Normal functioning character of the reproductively established family of bee dances. That which is variant is the content, to which the function of this invariant syntactic form is immediately adapted. (See Chapter 2, "Derived Proper Functions".)

2. *An intentional icon Normally stands midway between two cooperating devices, a producer device and an interpreting device, which are designed or standardized to fit one another, the presence and cooperation of each being a Normal condition for the proper performance of the other.*

Compare bee dances to sentences. Since bees do not have to learn how to dance, the mechanisms that (1) produce and (2) interpret bee dances are members of reproductively established families that are standardized via an evolutionary process to cooperate with one another in the performance of common invariant functions—getting in honey, etc. The presence and cooperation of some member of the reproductively established family of each is a Normal condition for the proper performance of any member of the other. Thus bee dances fulfill condition (2) for being intentional icons.

The mechanisms that produce and interpret sentences, on the other hand, are not members of reproductively established families.[3] The ability to speak and understand a particular human language is not built into the human but is learned. The devices that produce and interpret sentences are adapted devices or "programs," adapted to a particular linguistic environment. The relevant aspect of the language environment to which such speaker and hearer programs are each adapted is the correlation of various language device types with specifiable functions in the language community. Thus when a random speaker talks to a random hearer, the speaker and hearer programs involved have been standardized to fit one another. And it is a Normal condition for the proper performance of a standard speaker program that it is helped by a cooperating standard hearer program that has been standardized to fit it in this manner, and vice versa.

3. *Normally an intentional icon serves to adapt the cooperating interpreter device to conditions such that proper functions of that device can be performed under those conditions.*

The original adaptor to which the bee dance adapts the interpreter mechanisms in watching bees is, of course, the condition that is a current location of nectar. The proper functions that the interpreter devices then perform are the production of an appropriate direction of flight and the bringing in of nectar.

The original adaptor to which an imperative sentence Normally adapts the hearer's interpreting program (or adapts the hearer, if you prefer) is the existence of conditions under which compliance with the imperative will effect the fulfillment of some want or need of the hearer. The original adaptor to which the indicative sentence Normally adapts the hearer's interpreting program is the condition that makes the sentence true, thus aiding the production of a true belief.

4a. *In the case of imperative intentional icons, it is a proper function of the interpreter device, as adapted to the icon, to produce something onto which the icon will map in accordance with a specific mapping function of a kind to be described below.*

4b. *In the case of indicative intentional icons, the Normal explanation of how the icon adapts the interpreter device such that it can perform its proper functions makes reference to the fact that the icon maps onto something else in accordance with a specific mapping function of a kind to be described below.*

Intuitively it is clear that in some sense of "mapping," the bee dance that causes watching bees to find nectar in accordance with a historically Normal explanation is one that maps in accordance with certain rules onto a real configuration involving nectar, sun, and hive. As such it is an indicative intentional icon. The bee dance also maps onto a configuration that it is supposed to produce, namely, bees being (later) in a certain relation to hive and sun—that is, where the nectar is. So the bee dance is also an imperative intentional icon.

As for sentences, my claim will be that imperative sentences map in accordance with historically Normal mapping rules onto the configurations or world affairs that they produce when obeyed. And indicative sentences map in accordance with historically Normal mapping rules onto configurations or world affairs whenever they cause *true* beliefs in hearers *in accordance with Normal explanations.* Of course different hearers, unlike different bees, do not have identically structured interpreter mechanisms for words and sentences. What is a Normal explanation for one hearer's stabilizing response to a sentence may not be a Normal explanation for the next hearer's stabilizing response to that sentence. My claim is only that for every comprehending hearer who has come to comprehend in accordance with a Normal explanation for proper performance of his or her inborn language learning equipments, the Normal explanation for proper performance of his or her stabilizing response to an indicative or imperative sentence makes reference at some point to the same mapping rules as for every other comprehending hearer. These are rules in accordance with which a critical mass of sentences have mapped onto affairs in the world in the past, thus producing correlation patterns between certain kinds of configurations of sentence elements and certain kinds of configurations in the world, to which correlation patterns Normally functioning hearer interpreter devices are adapted, this adaptation *explaining* their successes. (Individual hearer programs function Normally in accordance with the description of Normal explanations for proper performance of adapted devices and derived proper functions given in Chapter 2.)

Conditions (1) through (4) tell us when something is an intentional icon. They do not, however, tell us what a given intentional icon is an intentional icon *of*. Assuming that the reader understands in a rough intuitive way what sort of thing I mean by "mapping," consider the pattern of impulses that passes through some particular cross section of an animal's optic nerve. Possibly this pattern P Normally maps (1) onto a pattern of retinal stimulations that caused P, (2) onto a pattern of optic nerve outputs to the brain that P causes, and (3) onto various patterns occurring in other cross sections of the optic nerve, some of which are causes of P and some of which are caused by P. Now let us lay this down:

(1) P is an imperative intentional icon *of* the *last* member of the series of things it is supposed to map onto and to produce.

(2) P is an indicative intentional icon *of* whatever it maps onto that must be mentioned in giving the *most proximate* Normal explanation for full proper performance of its interpreting device as adapted to the icon.

1. It follows that P is an imperative intentional icon either of the optic nerve's output pattern or, more likely, of something beyond this, for example, of a certain aspect of a visual percept (if visual percepts exist) that it is P's job finally to produce and onto which P should map. Similarly, although an imperative sentence may have as a proper function to produce an intention in the hearer, and although it may be that intentions are little things in the brain that sentences can map onto, what the Normally functioning imperative sentence is an imperative intentional icon *of* would be the conditions that were the hearer's having complied, not the hearer's intention to comply.

2. It follows that P is, most likely, an indicative intentional icon not of a retinal stimulation pattern but of an aspect of the world—of the animal's environment—to which it adapts its interpreter device (and the interpreter device's interpreter devices, etc.). For in giving the most *proximate* Normal explanation of how P's interpreter device serves its full set of proper functions, only the fact that some (perhaps very abstract) variable in the animal's environment is mapped by P needs to be mentioned. The most proximate explanation need make no reference to how the Normal condition that is P's mapping so onto the environment came about, any more than the most proximate Normal explanation of how the heart circulates the blood must tell how the Normal condition that is the presence of oxygen in the blood supplying

the heart muscles came about. Similarly, an indicative sentence is not an indicative intentional icon of the belief that it expresses, even though beliefs may turn out to be sorts of things that are mapped by sentences. The interpreter mechanisms that interpret an indicative sentence perform properly in accordance with the most proximate Normal explanation if the indicative sentence maps onto some affair in the *world*, regardless of how that mapping historically came about, for example, regardless of whether it came about via a true belief and its subsequent expression.

What an intentional icon is "of" I will call its "real value." The mapping function in accordance with which it is supposed to map onto a real value is its "Fregean sense." Imperative intentional icons that do not in fact produce the last item onto which they are supposed to map do not have real values; they are not icons "of" anything. For example, imperative sentences that are not obeyed have no real values. Similarly, indicative intentional icons that do not map onto anything in such a way that proper functions of their cooperating interpreter devices could be performed in accordance with a proximate Normal explanation do not have real values. They are not icons "of" anything. Indicative sentences that are false have no real values.

To describe the general kind of mapping function in accordance with which intentional icons map onto the world and to begin to defend this description for the case of language will require the rest of this chapter, and all of Part III will be needed in order to flesh out these claims about mapping. But first let me draw attention to one important feature of the characterization of sentences as intentional icons. Notice that the device that interprets an intentional icon does *not* always do this by producing *another* intentional icon. For example, although the mechanisms that interpret bee dances "translate" these dances into a direction of flight of the bee, they do this only in the physicist's sense of "translate." The result of this "translation" is a bee flying in a certain direction. But a bee-flying-in-a-certain-direction is not an intentional icon, for there is no cooperating device that interprets it. If sentences are intentional icons, this is not *because* they translate into beliefs and intentions which are themselves intentional icons—although, I will claim, they do so translate. It is because they display the four characteristics of intentional icons I have laid down. Because intentional icons are not, in general, interpreted by devices that produce new intentional icons from them, we will later be able to describe beliefs and intentions as species of intentional icons without inviting regress. Further, when I discuss representations—intentional icons the referents of which are supposed to be identified—I will not interpret the act of identifying a referent as an act of translation either (although I will temporarily *model* the act of identifying as an act of translation in Part

III). If the reader wishes to reserve the term "intentionality" for characterizing representations, it will still be true that the "intentionality" of beliefs will have been described without inviting regress.

Reinterpreting the Relation of Sense to Reference

Now consider the problem of mapping. Traditional views about how language does or why it doesn't map onto the world all seem to begin with the same assumption. The assumption is that any description of the mapping functions that correlate sentences with world affairs would, of course, begin by coordinating at least some words with some objects, that the kind of coordination involved is reference (or denoting), and that coordinations of sentences with world affairs must be built up out of these basic reference relations plus, perhaps, some added paraphernalia. The idea that coordinations of sentences with world affairs must be built up out of basic reference relations suggests at the start that the way in which words correspond to their referents is *similar* to the way in which true sentences correspond to world affairs. Hence the same term, say, "corresponds," can be used in speaking either of the relation of a word to its referent or of the relation of a true sentence to the world affair it maps. The problem then arises how words, each of which "corresponds" to something real, can be put together in such a way as to yield a sentence that does *not* "correspond" to anything real. Let me put this traditional problem in the simplest and most ancient terms.

We start with the simple notion that words correspond to things in the world; hence sentences composed of these words correspond to world affairs composed of these things. We put some words together: "Theaetetus flies." "Theaetetus" corresponds to Theaetetus; "flies" corresponds to flies (flying). Everything seems to correspond. So what is wrong with the sentence? Unfortunately, "Theaetetus flies" does not correspond to anything. For Theaetetus does not fly. One might suppose that we need only see that the *relation* between "Theaetetus" and "flies" also corresponds to something—to the sort of relation that obtains, say, between Theaetetus and speaking and between Theaetetus and walking. But this does not solve the problem. "Theaetetus" corresponds to Theaetetus; "flies" corresponds to flies (flying); the relation between "Theaetetus" and "flies" corresponds to a real or instantiated relation (instantiated, e.g., between Theaetetus and walking). Again, everything corresponds—*except* "Theaetetus flies."

Frege's solution to this problem was elegant. The gist of it was this. He correlated singular terms with "values" that were objects in the world: "Jane" with Jane; "the Taj Mahal" with the Taj Mahal, etc.

Then he took logical predicates (roughly, expressions for properties and relations) to express functions (mathematical sense) that took the values of singular terms upon which they operated over to other values, these values being either other objects or the values *the true* or *the false*. For example, "father of . . . " expresses a function which takes the value of "Jane" in "father of Jane" over to Jane's father, say, Alfred; " . . . is tall" expresses another function which takes the value Alfred in "The father of Jane is tall" over either to the value *the true* or to the value *the false*. Thus he interpreted sentences as being like *names*—complex signs that ended up naming either *the true* or *the false*. But how, if at all, this resulted in mapping different *sentences* onto different parts of or different aspects of *the world* is problematic.

Wittgenstein's solution to the Theaetetus problem is a better starting point for us. It is capsulized in the well-known passage ' . . . we must say, "That 'a' stands in the relation R to 'b' says *that aRb*".' (*Tractatus Logico Philosophicus*, 3.1432.) If we were to tolerate the notion that predicates correspond to properties or characters in the world (which Wittgenstein probably didn't), we should say that it is *that* "Theaetetus" stands in a certain relation to "flies" that would have to correspond to *that* Theaetetus stands in a certain relation to flying if the whole sentence "Theaetetus flies" is to correspond to a world affair. But this correspondence is absent; hence "Theaetetus flies" does not correspond to a world affair.

Note that this analysis gives up the notion that words correspond to their referents in the same sense of "correspond" in which sentences correspond to world affairs:

"2.15   That the elements of the picture are combined with one another in a definite way, represents that the things are so combined with one another."

"2.202   The picture represents a possible state of affairs in logical space."

"2.221   What the picture represents is its sense."

"2.222   In the agreement or disagreement of its sense with reality, its truth or falsity consists."[4]

The sentence represents a possibility or sense which may or may not correspond to the world. But "Theaetetus" simply corresponds to Theaetetus. *"Theaetetus" has no sense.*

But if having a sense has to do with intentionality and intentionality has to do with being supposed to map onto something, surely Wittgenstein has it upside down. To be sure, referential terms, simply as such, do not "correspond" to their referents in the same way that true sentences "correspond" to world affairs. But rather than displaying *no* intentionality, referential terms display an even more complex kind of intentionality than sentences. First, a referential term is supposed to appear in the context of a sentence. That is, this condition is a Normal condition for its proper performance. Second, qua in the context of a sentence, it is supposed to correspond to or map onto something—its referent. For this is another Normal condition for its proper performance. It maps onto its referent in the context of a sentence if and only if the sentence is *true*. (A word, taken by itself, does not map or fail to map onto anything. If this isn't intuitively true, at least it will follow from the description that I will soon give of the kinds of mapping functions that correlate intentional icons with the things they are icons of.) The most basic or most direct kind of correspondence, then, is the correspondence between a true sentence and a world affair.[5] When this correspondence occurs, we say that the sentence has a "real value"— namely, the affair it maps onto. A less direct, more mediated, kind of correspondence is the correspondence between a referential term *in the context of a true sentence* and its referent. When this correspondence occurs, let us say that the *term* has a "real value"—namely, its referent. And riding piggyback upon this second kind of correspondence is an even more derivative kind of correspondence—the correspondence of a lone term to its referent or of a term in a false sentence to its referent. Indeed, this last kind of correspondence is of a *totally* different kind— so different that from now on I will refuse to call it "correspondence" at all. It is, roughly, the relation that one thing has to another qua being, only, *supposed* to correspond to it. To mix corresponding with being *supposed* to correspond is an error of large proportion. All tokens of a referential term have a referent. That is, for all such tokens there is something to which they are *supposed* to correspond. But only those tokens that occur in true sentences have this referent as a real value. Only those tokens that occur in true sentences *do* correspond.

If being *supposed* to correspond to something is having a sense— and that is how I am defining, in the rough, the term "sense" or "Fregean sense"—then names are paradigm cases of words that have sense. Further, although the *referent* of a term is certainly not its mean*ing* or sense (Is the thing hit the same as the hitt*ing*?), its *referring is* its having a *certain kind* of meaning or sense.

What caused the illusion that simple referential terms do not have sense? Why should being supposed to correspond and actually corresponding be so easy to confuse in this case? Compare the way in which sentences have a sense with the way referential terms have a sense.

That the elements of a sentence are combined in a certain way does not necessarily correspond to *anything*, and certainly not to some *entity* called a "sense" or a "possibility." A sentence's sense is its being supposed to correspond to something, not something it is supposed to correspond to. From the fact that the sentence has a sense, it does not follow that there *is* anything to which it is supposed to correspond. For all its having a sense boils down to is that *when* sentences of this sentence's reproductively established family perform properly and Normally, these correspond to world affairs in accordance with certain mapping rules.

"Theaetetus" does not necessarily correspond to anything either. It is only supposed to correspond to something. That is, "Theaetetus" is supposed to be placed in an appropriate spot in the context of one or another of certain kinds of sentences and *then* it is supposed to correspond to something. And this just boils down to saying that tokens of syntactic forms that take "Theaetetus" as part of their content function Normally only when they correspond to world affairs in accordance with certain mapping rules such that "Theaetetus" corresponds to Theaetetus—such that "Theaetetus" has Theaetetus as a *real* value. Where, then, is the supposed difference between the way the combined elements of the sentence have a sense and the way "Theaetetus" has a sense?

There is a difference. From the fact that the sentence is supposed to correspond to something it does not follow that there is something to which the sentence is supposed to correspond. If s is the sentence and R the correspondence relation, then what is true of the sentence is only this:

Normally, $(Ex)\ sRx$.

But from the fact that a simple referential term—say, a name—is supposed to correspond to something, it *does* follow that there is something to which it is supposed to correspond. (Indexicals and complex referential terms will be discussed in Chapters 10 and 11.) For this "supposed to" depends upon the fact that the reproductively established family of the term has a history involving *actual* correspondences with the referent. If w is a simple referential term, r its referent, and R the correspondence relation, then what is true of the term w is this: Normally, wRr. Hence

$(Ex)(\text{Normally } wRx)$

(Note that the reference relation is not R but the relation between w and r that is satisfied in virtue of the fact that Normally, wRr—quite a different relation.) It is because the referent of a simple term exists, indeed qua referent necessarily exists, whereas what the sentence is supposed to correspond to may not exist, that "Theaetetus" is not obviously like a sentence in its way of being supposed to correspond.

Because the subject at hand is difficult, it may help to turn the whole matter another way.

Traditional views concerning how we must understand language as mapping began with the notion "refers to" or "denotes" or "has as a value" as an unanalyzed notion. This was the notion in terms of which the mapping of sentences was ultimately to be analyzed. But this was rather like beginning with the notion "weight" as an unanalyzed notion, then trying to analyze "mass" in terms of "weight." My claim is that if we analyze the notion "reference" correctly, we see that it depends upon more fundamental kinds of relations, such as the relation of a true sentence to the world affair it maps, which relations cannot be analyzed in terms of reference for the same sort of reason that "pumping blood" cannot be analyzed in terms of "being designed to pump blood."

Traditionally, *having the referent Theaetetus* was a property attributed to the (least) *type* "Theaetetus" in such a way as to imply that every *token* of "Theaetetus" also has the referent Theaetetus. What kind of analysis must we give of " 'Theaetetus' refers to Theaetetus" in order to be in accord with this usage? What kind of relation is there between *every* token of (the least type) "Theaetetus" and Theaetetus?

The relation is very complex. First it is mediated by the relation that obtains between the token of "Theaetetus" and the reproductively established family "Theaetetus"—the relation that connects the token with its least type. Then it is mediated by the relation between this reproductively established family "Theaetetus" and those tokens of the family that have, historically, performed its proper functions Normally. From here on, it might be thought, the analysis is simple. All of the *stabilizing* tokens of "Theaetetus"—those that perform properly in accordance with a Normal explanation—"correspond" to Theaetetus. That is, they *actually* correspond rather than merely being "supposed" to correspond to Theaetetus. The more fundamental kind of relation in terms of which "reference" must be analyzed is merely *actual* as opposed to "supposed" correspondence. Certainly it is clear that the former could not be analyzed taking the latter as a beginning.

But what is *"actual* correspondence"? Is it a direct relation between a stabilizing token of "Theaetetus" and Theaetetus? Clearly it is not. It is mediated by the relation of "Theaetetus" to the rest of the sentence in which "Theaetetus" occurs. It is, in the *first* instance, the *sentence* that corresponds, *hence* "Theaetetus." The sentence "corresponds" by mapping in accordance with rules that are Normal for such a sentence. "Theaetetus," by itself, could not possibly map anything. "Theaetetus" is just as incomplete a sign—just as much a sentence with gaps in it— as any predicate or sentence form. "Theaetetus," in fact, is so gappy that the sentence form itself needs to be filled in.

Somehow, we must begin by correlating *sentences* with world affairs, correspondence of words with things coming after. The articulation of the sentence into elements that are supposed to correspond must result from this analysis rather than being the basis of it—and so with the articulation of the world affair that the sentence maps.

How Intentional Icons Map onto the World

What I will describe is the correspondence relation between an *indicative* intentional icon and its real value. Description of the correspondence relation for imperative intentional icons is exactly parallel.

When an indicative intentional icon has a real value, it is related to that real value as follows: (1) The real value is a Normal condition for performance of the icon's direct proper functions. (2) There are operations upon or transformations (in the mathematical sense) of the icon that correspond one-to-one to operations upon or transformations of the real value such that (3) any transform of the icon resulting from one of these operations has as a Normal condition for proper performance the corresponding transform of the real value.

The governing idea here is that, in the first instance at least, it is *transformations* of the icon that correspond to *transformations* of the real value—*operations* upon the icon that correspond to *operations* upon the real value—not elements of the icon that correspond to elements of the real value.

Whatever is considered as subject to a set of transformations is as such "articulate" in a certain way. It is not articulated into parts but into invariant and variant aspects. What remains unchanged under all transformations in a transformation set is the invariant aspect of a thing relative to that set; what changes under these transformations are variant aspects. If it is transformations of an intentional icon that correspond to transformations of its real value, thus yielding correspondence between icons and world affairs, an intentional icon is always "articulate" in the above sense, and so is the affair to which it corresponds. But neither the articulation of the icon nor of the affair is an articulation into *parts*. Neither the icon nor the iconed is originally articulated as a configuration or concatenation of *objects* or of elements and relations.

In the case of bee dances, transformations of the dance (say, *increase the number of loops by one, rotate the angle of the axis of the figure eight 20° clockwise*) correspond to transformations of the sun-hive-nectar relation that is mapped. I do not know what is invariant in the bee dance. But invariant in the real value is the *relata* of the relation mapped—sun, hive, nectar. For example, there is no transformation of the bee dance that corresponds to replacing the sun with the moon such that the resulting dance maps the relation of moon, hive, and nectar.

In the case of *sentences* that map, the significant transformations of the icon are mostly substitution transformations, with the enormously important exception of the negation transformation. (Discussion of negation will be postponed to Chapter 14.) A sentence admits of transformations that replace its most basic parts with parts having direct proper functions of the same type (this is an aspect of the invariance of the sentence form) yet that are different. The transformations are of this sort: *replace the subject with "Theaetetus," replace the direct object with "fish," replace the verb with "eats," replace the predicate adjective with "red."* I will later show how a phrase like "the man who lives next door" or an indexical like "this" has, qua adapted to a context, the same *sort* of proper function that "Theaetetus" has. Namely, each is supposed to precipitate an act of identification of a given variant in the world. Hence the same basic sentence may be subject to such transformations as *replace the subject with "Theaetetus," replace the subject with "the man who lives next door" (with appropriate context),* and *replace the subject with "this" (with appropriate context).* Each of these transformations corresponds to a possible transformation of the world affair that is being mapped.

Taking the articulation of a world affair, qua mapped by a sentence, to be determined by a group of possible transformations or operations upon it rather than as the way the affair is built out of prior parts and relations has two advantages for ontology. First, consider the regress that produces "Bradley's paradox": if world affairs consist of objects (e.g., substances and properties) tied together by relations, then we must postulate further relations that tie these objects to these relations and then still further relations that tie the latter relations down, *ad infinitum.* (This regress, which led Bradley to deny the reality of relations, is the flip side of the problem discussed above concerning the failure of "Theaetetus flies" to correspond to how things are.) But if the mapping of language onto the world is as we have described it, this regress has no footing. World affairs are not torn apart into *sets* of objects by the mapping rules for intentional icons, hence do not have to be put together again.

Second, if the articulation of a world affair for the purpose of mapping it is determined by those transformations of it that correspond to significant transformations of the icon that maps it, then an affair that can be understood as subject to one set of transformations relative to one icon of it may be understood as subject to alternative sets of transformations relative to other icons of it. Each of these sets of transformations may articulate the same affair in a different way, and there is no reason to suppose in advance that any of these articulations would have to be *the* elemental or ideal articulation of that affair. For example, perhaps there is no reason to suppose that "Theaetetus swims" is any more or less perspicuous a rendering of an affair than is "Theaetetus exemplifies swimming," although the latter but not the former is subject to transformations that yield sentences and corresponding affairs such as "Theaetetus hates swimming" and "Theaetetus practices swimming." The assumption that there must be *one* ideal or final articulation of a world affair, and ultimately of the world as a whole, that gets things ontologically *right*, that shows what the affair or the world is really composed of, has driven great philosophical engines in its time. But it may be that ontology can ultimately be made simpler by dropping this assumption. Interesting transformations and corresponding invariances, structure rather than kinds of *things*, would be left as the basic subject matter of ontology, things and their properties being derived from structure rather than vice versa. As I understand it, this is the sort of ontology that is the implicit ontology of group theory in mathematics, a tool that has enormously simplified one branch of mathematics after another in this century. But I am not prepared to follow this rather vague suggestion through very far. The one place that I will make reference to it is in Chapter 16. There I will propose that the basic ontological categories "substance" and "property" are categories that are carved out relative to one another and relative to the negation transformation. "Properties" are variants in world affairs that become articulated when these affairs are considered *as* sensitive to negation transformations of various kinds; "substances" are variants that are articulated in relation to other kinds of transformations. Hence the categories "substance" and "property" are not mutually exclusive categories.

Clearly, enormously more needs to be said about the way in which language maps onto the world. In Part III I will talk about the sense and reference of definite descriptions and indexicals, about universal description and indefinite description, about negation, about statements of identity and existence, etc., and in Part IV I will say more about the ontology presupposed here. Many other problems I will not tackle. For my purpose is only to defend a certain *approach* to problems of this sort.

Aristotelian Realism Introduced

Perhaps the most controversial result of the approach is this. As I am interpreting the mapping functions that map language onto the world, there is no difference between the way in which logical subjects of sentences map and the way logical predicates of sentences map. There are two traditional anxieties that this should not arouse and one traditional anxiety that it should arouse.

The first anxiety is that understanding logical subjects and logical predicates as mapping in the same sort of way will turn predicates into things that stand for *objects*. I hope that this anxiety has already been quieted. Consider "Theaetetus walks." Various operations that can significantly be performed upon "Theaetetus walks," such as *replace the verb with "talks"* and *replace the verb with "swims,"* correspond to transformations performed upon the world affair that is mapped if all goes Normally. Understand these transformations of or operations upon world affairs however you like. There is certainly nothing in what has been said that dictates understanding them as *replacements of objects* with other *objects*.

The second anxiety is that in treating logical subjects and logical predicates as mapping in the same sort of way, one must attribute the same sort of existence or ontological status to "universals" as to "particulars." If the relation between a predicate transformation and the property transformation to which it corresponds is just like the relation between a subject transformation and the transformation to which *that* corresponds, isn't the relation between predicate and property just like the reference relation? If so, properties—"universals"—must *exist*, and they must exist in the same sort of way or in the same realm that referents—"particulars," "individuals"—do. But, it is traditionally thought, if universals exist at all, surely they need not exist, as particulars or individuals must, in *nature*. Universals are, in essence, objects of *thought* or, if independent of thought, *possibilities*.

Universals as objects of thought that need not be in nature? Universals as possibilities? A main point of the theory of intentionality we have been developing is to rid ourselves of the impulse to reify or make real those "objects of thought" that are *merely* subjective "intentional objects," that correspond only to seeming meanings—the impulse to reify subjective "possibilities." Every *simple* predicate, if it is truly meaningful, if it truly has a sense (and this, I am proposing, is not a matter that the bright light of conscious awareness directly and infallibly reveals to us), *has* to reflect a corresponding variant that is firmly entrenched as a *historical* variant *in nature*. Otherwise the elementary predicate could not have had the historical connection with the variant in nature that is required to ground a Normal explanation making reference to that variant. Complex predicates are *supposed* to correspond in sentences to something—to variants in nature—but there need not *be* any somethings (any complex universals) to which they are supposed to correspond. Properties and kinds have only one habitat, and that is Nature.

The last anxiety is this. We are talking about properties, relations, etc., as being variants in world affairs that, owing to their historical causal or explanatory connections with predicate terms, lend these predicate terms meaning or sense—intentionality. Properties and relations then must be in the natural world in such a way that their selfsameness or *identity* is there too. The identity of properties and relations must be *objective* identity, not identity or sameness that depends upon language. It must be an identity upon which the univocity or equivocity, meaningfulness or emptiness, of our actual language categories depends, not one that is created by these categories. And how are we to make this thesis out? This anxiety is well founded, and I am delighted if the reader is strongly affected by it. For then the reader may be motivated to continue through Part IV where a matching theory of the ontology of identity, of the act of identifying, and of the epistemology of identity is offered.

In introducing intentional icons, three very central notions—sense, real value, and reference—have also been introduced. Let me say a bit more about each of these notions before moving on to the next chapter.

Sense
Intentional icons have sense, and each of the various significant variant or invariant mapping elements or aspects of an intentional icon has sense, and every member of the reproductively established family of such an element has sense. This having of a sense is the icon's or the element's having as a Normal condition for performance of its direct proper functions that it map onto something else in accordance with mapping rules of the sort I have described. More briefly, the "sense" of a language element is its Normal mapping rule. We have indicated how simple denotative language elements, such as proper names and elementary predicates, have sense and how sentences have sense. How other garden-variety language parts have sense will be discussed in Part III, where it will also come out why I have called this notion of sense "Fregean."

It should be evident that sense, as I have described it, is totally other than intension (note the "s"). The sense of a certain icon or icon element is the rules, or better, mapping functions, in accordance with which it is supposed to map. The intension of a language element has traditionally been equated with a criterion for its application, this criterion being "known" in some way to speakers and applied by them. A term's intension is found by inspecting the mechanisms in speakers that are responsible for the term's use, or by looking at speakers' dispositions to apply terms or to justify their applications on the basis of beliefs or sensory stimulations. Crudely, the intension of a term has to do with the causes of or justification for its utterance. The sense of an intentional icon has nothing whatever to do with its causes, with the mechanisms that have produced it, or with any justification for its use. To know its sense one need know only what it would have to map onto in order to perform properly and Normally. One does not need to know how it *comes* to map so or to fail to map so or how speakers justify themselves in applying it. In Chapter 8 I will discuss the relation between senses and intensions in detail, comparing these also with Quine's "stimulus meanings."

That sense and intension are quite different things is especially evident in the case of simple terms that are vacuous. Consider, for example, a vacuous proper name—"Pegasus." It undoubtedly has an intension. But a vacuous proper name cannot have a sense. For it cannot have a history of having performed its proper functions *due* to having mapped onto something in the context of sentences. Similarly, simple adjectives and verbs sometimes lack sense; e.g., "bewitch," "bewitched," and "dephlogistonated" lack sense. Because our theory is a sort of "correspondence theory" of (one aspect of) "meaning," it raises epistemological problems that are new. These will be explored in Chapters 18 and 19.

Real Value
An intentional icon has a real value only when it in fact maps onto something of the kind it is supposed to map onto. Then this something is its real value. Further, each significant variant of this something to which a variant (an element or aspect) of the icon then corresponds is the real value of that variant token. "Theaetetus," taken out of context, has a sense but no real value. When placed in the context of a true sentence, however, a token of "Theaetetus" has Theaetetus as a real value.

But real value must not be simply equated with reference come to roost in the context of a true intentional icon. Later we will discover that certain sentence elements can have real value without having referents. These are elements that must map onto something or other of a certain *sort* in order to serve their functions Normally, but that need not map onto one rather than another of this sort in order to do so. Whatever such a sentence element does in fact map onto in the context of a given true sentence is, in the context of that sentence, its real value. But this real value is not a referent. Such sentence elements have "indefinite sense." For example, I will later argue that indefinite descriptions, universal descriptions, and the predicates of most negative sentences have real values when they are parts of true sentences, but they have no referents. Failure to draw a distinction such as that between reference and real value has, I believe, caused the philosophies of language and of mind much grief, and I cannot urge too strongly that the reader accept "real value" as itself and not another thing.

Referents

In Part III we will discover that the notion of reference is quite complex. First, there are indexical terms, the referents of tokens of which are determined by context (Chapter 10, and also 11). Second, there are contexts in which the usual referent of a term is displaced by another referent, as in the context of mention quotation marks and in intentional contexts (Chapter 13). Third, we will discover that there are two kinds of referents, "protoreferents" and "represented referents," that must be distinguished in certain contexts such as that of sentences asserting identities (Chapter 12). But amidst all these complexities, the root definition of a referent remains the same: *if there is something definite and real (existent) onto which a term or term token is supposed to map, this something is its referent.* When a term or token has a referent, there exists an *x* such that the term or token is supposed to map onto *x*. This situation contrasts with that in which a term or token is supposed to map onto something or other of a certain kind but where there is no *particular* thing of that kind onto which it must map in order to serve its proper functions Normally (e.g., indefinite description). And it contrasts with the situation of a term that is supposed to map onto whatever bears a certain relation to it but where nothing in fact bears that relation to it (e.g., empty indexicals and empty definite descriptions). These contrasts will be discussed in later chapters.

As I have described "referents," elementary predicates have referents (if they have sense). They map in the same sort of way that proper names do. (There is no reason that I can see why a "referent" has to be an "object.") Simple predicates (if they have sense) refer not to sets but to real variants in the world.

Chapter 7
Kinds of Signs

The philosopher's cover-all notion "sign" is not univocal but is unified by a paradigm. The paradigm is the intentional icon or, more specifically, the sentence. Yet the notion "intentional icon" is not univocal either.

Indicative and imperative intentional icons are not intentional icons in accordance with the same definition. That the indicative intentional icon should map so is a *Normal condition* for proper performance of its cooperating interpreting devices. To cause the imperative intentional icon to *come* to map so is a *proper function* of its Normal interpreting devices. What makes an item an imperative intentional icon is what it *does*. What makes an item an indicative intentional icon has nothing to do with what it does; it has to do only with the *conditions under which* it Normally does whatever it does. True, in the case of imperative intentional icons, that the icon should come to map so is a Normal condition for performance of those proper functions of its interpreting devices that lie *beyond* compliance with the imperative icon. But this seems a slender similarity upon which to argue the strict univocity of the notion "intentional icon."

Yet there is a connection between indicative and imperative intentional icons that should not be overlooked. As I will show immediately below, many of the most primitive of intentional icons—many "intentional signals"—are at once indicative *and* imperative. One might look at the unity of the notion "intentional icon," hence "sign," as pivoting about this original paradigm. Or consider bee dances, which are not "intentional signals" but still are quite primitive compared with sentences. The bee dance is an indicative intentional icon of the relation of nectar to hive and sun. At the same time it is an imperative intentional icon, determining the direction of flight of watching bees relative to hive and sun. Surely nothing could be simpler than an intentional icon that adapts its interpreting devices to do something that is a straightforward function (mathematical sense) of some relevant variable in the environment and does this by itself mapping the value of that variable. Any such icon is both indicative and imperative.

Intentional Signals

The description given in Chapter 6 of how an intentional icon maps onto its real value requires that every intentional icon is articulate. The intentional icon must contain at least one significant variant aspect and an invariant aspect. It is "articulate" in that it is "articulated"; it divides into significant aspects, its significant variant or variants and its invariant aspect. Also it is "articulate" in the sense that it "says" something: qua intentional icon it *contrasts* with other icons of the same family that are significant transforms of it. But if the intentional icon, intrinsically articulate, is the paradigm case of a sign, then how can a stop sign or a road-curve sign or the order "Halt!" be a sign? How can the red light on the car dash that signals when the engine needs oil be a sign? Or, looking at more primitive signs, how can the beaver's tail splash or the stickleback fish's mating dance be a sign? How can the multitude of chemical "messengers," such as adrenalin, that abound in every organism be "messengers" carrying "information" or be "signs of" what is happening in or outside the organism's body? These signs appear to be utterly inarticulate. I will call such signs "intentional signals." What we must show is that despite appearances, intentional signals are not entirely inarticulate—that they are a species of intentional icons.

More precisely, an intentional signal—the stop sign, the flowing adrenalin—is a significant *aspect* of an intentional icon. The whole of the icon is the signal's occurring *at a time* or *at a place* (or both). Let us take adrenalin as our example and, starting at the very beginning, show exactly why and how it is so that the running of adrenalin in the bloodstream *at a certain time* is an intentional icon in accordance with definitions we have laid down.

The proper function of flowing adrenalin, I suppose, is to ready various parts of the body for strenuous activity. The flowing adrenalin is a member of a higher-order reproductively established family. For it is a proper function of certain glands, themselves members of higher-order reproductively established families, to produce and release adrenalin. More specifically, these glands have the *relational* proper function of releasing adrenalin *when* there is something threatening in the immediate vicinity of the organism. The flowing of adrenalin *at a particular time* is thus an adapted device. It is a properly adapted device if the adrenalin flows at the same time that there exists a threat in the immediate vicinity of the organism, otherwise not. But whether or not a specific token of adrenalin-flowing-at-a-time is properly adapted, if it has been produced in accordance with an explanation that approximates to a Normal explanation of how adrenalin is caused to flow-at-a-time in the organism, it is a member of a reproductively established family not merely of tokens of adrenalin but also of tokens of adrenalin-flowing-at-a-time. That is, if we abstract the *specific* time at which the adrenalin flows from the character adrenalin-flowing-at-time-t_1, we have left a more abstract character Normal for all tokens of a certain reproductively established family—the family of adrenalin tokens-occurring-at-times.

A token of adrenalin-flowing-at-a-time is a member of a reproductively established family. This family has the proper function of readying the various parts of the organism for strenuous-activity-at-a-time and of helping to save the organism from danger. Hence condition (1) for being an intentional icon (see Chapter 6, " 'Intentional Icon' Defined") is satisfied in the case of adrenalin-flowing-at-a-time. Normally, the adrenalin-flowing-at-a-time stands midway between a producing device (glands) and an "interpreting device" (the other organs that react to the flow of adrenalin) which devices Normally cooperate via the adrenalin in the performance of certain proper functions (saving the organism from danger). The presence and cooperation of each of these devices is a Normal condition for the proper performance of each of the other(s) vis-à-vis the adrenalin. Hence condition (2) for intentional icons is satisfied by adrenalin-flowing-at-a-time. Normally, adrenalin-flowing-at-a-time serves to adapt the "interpreting devices" to conditions (presence of a threat) such that certain of their proper functions (saving the organism from danger) can be performed Normally. Hence condition (3) for intentional icons is satisfied by adrenalin-flowing-at-a-time.

Now consider condition (4)—the mapping condition for intentional icons. As adapted to the *specific* time at which it flows, a member of the reproductively established family adrenalin-flowing-at-a-time has as an adapted proper function to ready the organism for strenuous activity at a specific time—namely, the same time. (Think of adrenalin-flowing-at-a-time as like a sentence *form*, needing to have a blank—a specific time—filled in to which its proper function is then immediately adapted.) Further, time-change transformations of the adrenalin-flowing-at-*this*-time (transformations such as *move ahead 30 minutes in time*) correspond to identical time-change transformations of the readyings of the organism for strenuous activity that are supposed to be produced by the adrenalin. Hence, the adrenalin-flowing-at-a-time is an imperative intentional icon. It is also an indicative intentional icon. For the icon can perform its proper function of helping to save the organism from danger in accordance with a Normal explanation only if the time of the flowing adrenalin maps the time of a threat to the organism in accordance with the kind of time-change transformations suggested above.

Intentional signals, then, are limiting cases of intentional icons. The most primitive of these—chemical messengers in the body, genetically determined signals between animals of the same species such as danger signals and mating displays—are, I believe, always both indicative and imperative. Some intentional signals are articulated into an invariant signal device and a variant time, others into an invariant signal device and a variant place, and some have both time and place as significant variants. A stop sign is an imperative (perhaps also an indicative) intentional signal with place as a significant variant. A red light traffic signal is an imperative intentional signal having both time and place as significant variants. "Theaetetus!" when used to *call* Theaetetus is an imperative intentional signal having both time and place (place of the caller) as significant variants. Used this way, "Theaetetus" is, as usual, a referential term. It has a real value if Theaetetus comes.

Natural Signs

The notion of a sign makes intrinsic reference to a possible interpreter. Because it lacks an interpreter, the chameleon's color pattern, though it maps, is in no sense a "sign." (Caveat: Of course you or I might interpret it. We might use it as a natural sign of the color pattern that lies under the chameleon.) There are no signs without potential interpreters. Also, there are no signs without significant articulation—at least of the minimal sort that intentional signals have. All signs are signs only in relation to what might be signed instead by relevant transforms of these signs. But things that are called "signs" may fail to be intentional icons in other ways. For example, in the case of some signs, although the sign may be used by an interpreter in exactly the same way that intentional icons are used, it is neither a direct nor an indirect proper function of the sign itself that it should adapt any interpreting device.

Signs that have the adapting of an interpreter device neither as a direct nor as an indirect proper function are usually called "natural signs." A natural sign is analogous to an intentional icon in that it is the kind of thing that could be used by an interpreter in exactly the same way that interpreters use intentional icons. Consider indicative intentional icons first. It is a Normal condition for the proper performance of an interpreting device as adapted to an indicative intentional icon that the icon maps something else in accordance with certain definite rules. A natural sign that can be used by an interpreter as if it were an indicative icon maps something else in accordance with natural laws operating in situ. It does not do this Normally in the biological or medical sense. But is must do so relatively reliably or normally in the statistical sense. That is, the kind of situation in which or conditions under which the sign is determined by natural laws to map onto what it signifies must be a situation or conditions that are statistically usual or normal. The interpreter of a natural sign may be genetically programmed to interpret the sign. Many small mammals are genetically programmed to interpret a small shadow moving on the ground at-a-time by taking precautions against being spotted by the predator concurrently flying overhead, of which the shadow is likely to be a natural sign. Or the interpreter of a natural sign may have *learned* to interpret the sign. In either case, it is a Normal condition for the proper performance of the interpreting device (or programming of the interpreting device) as adapted to the natural sign that the sign map something else in accordance with definite rules (condition (4) for being an intentional icon). Natural signs are often used as imperative signs also. Thus, the time of the shadow on the ground "tells" the small mammal *when* to freeze or seek cover; the time of a certain position of the sun in the heavens has, for many peoples at many times, "told" them when to start the planting.

Some natural signs are articulate with respect to variables other than place and/or time. An animal's track may show not only where it walked but in what direction, how fast it was moving, its species (by substitution transformations), its sex and size as well, of course, as showing the shape of its foot. The relative sizes of the rings of a tree show the relative lengths of the growing seasons over past years, and so forth.

Natural signs are never false. If they mislead it is not because *they* are abNormal. Rather, the interpreter is at fault or operating under abNormal conditions relative to the interpreter's proper functions, not relative to any proper functions of the sign.

The analogy between natural signs and intentional icons rests in part upon the analogy between what is Normal and what is, merely, normal in the sense of usual or average. The intentional icon occurs Normally only and always in conjunction with certain conditions; the natural sign occurs usually, possibly always, in conjunction with certain conditions. But what is usual fades into what is not unusual, and what is not unusual fades into what is not altogether unexpected, etc. What we call "natural signs" are, in the paradigm cases, things the like of which almost never occur except in conjunction with the conditions they sign (e.g., rabbity tracks in the snow). Such natural signs bear a striking analogy to intentional icons. But paradigm cases of natural signs fade into less clear cases, until symptoms are called "signs" and, in the end, any manifestation of another thing can be called a "sign" of it.

One thing can be a symptom of another without there being much correlation at all between the two—as sore throats can be symptoms of many different kinds of diseases. Symptoms can be used *somewhat* as more paradigm cases of natural signs can be used. The major difference is that it is not the symptom taken alone that can be used to adapt an interpreter to conditions, say, causing belief in the existence of that of which the symptom is a symptom. Rather, symptoms taken together with *other* symptoms and, in general, with other information, can be used in this way. The paradigm natural sign merges into the symptom as more outside evidence is needed to interpret it. And symptoms fade into mere manifestations. It is possible that, in the case of a particular man, his giving away his ski boots should manifest his belief that he will soon die. Perhaps one can even say, in the case of *this* man, that his giving away his ski boots is a "sign" that he thinks he is dying. But the giving away of ski boots is not in the slenderest way correlated with owners of such boots having thoughts of dying. In the case of *this* man, the gift may be a "sign" of or may manifest his belief only because it is possible for astute others who know, say, this man's ungenerous nature, what his ski boots mean to him and that he is ill, etc., to discover via the gift that he believes he is dying. They can discover this by using knowledge of the fact of the gift and inferring, by the method of best explanation, to the cause of this. Such a "sign" has very little in common with an intentional icon.

Improvised Signs

Improvised signs (e.g., Alan's bouquet) are not members of reproductively established families, hence do not have direct proper functions (condition (1) for being an intentional icon). An improvised sign has only a derived proper function, derived from the intention or purpose of the producer in producing it. Such signs are not standardized. (Granted, Alan's bouquet contained the "crosstarrie," but it was not used to sign a gathering of the clan. And Duncan Stewart's button had no emblem on it.) They do not fall midway between a producer and an interpreter that have been standardized to fit one another in use of the sign in the performance of common proper functions, the participation of each being a Normal condition for proper performance of the other (condition (2) for intentional icons). But they are in a way more like intentional icons than natural signs, for they do have as proper functions, albeit merely derived ones, to adapt (or maladapt) an interpreter in the same sort of way as intentional icons do.

An improvised sign is designed with an interpreter in mind who will have such and such capacities. (Alan Breck was not too sure of John

Breck Maccoll's capacities.) The sign is designed to fit the mechanism that is to interpret it. That is, if the sign is designed *properly*, if the sign-producing devices or programs perform properly, the sign *will* fit the mechanism that is to interpret it in accordance with a Normal explanation. But the mechanisms that interpret the sign are general mechanisms—mechanisms *not* specifically designed or programmed to interpret *this* sign or significant transforms of this sign. Usually, they are the general mechanisms that interpret symptoms and manifestations. But there are all kinds of cases. I will examine only three.

The presence of a person's coat and hat is, usually, a natural sign that the person is close at hand or, at least, has been here. Suppose that Susan, arriving home from college unexpectedly, finds no one home. She conspicuously leaves her coat and hat in the entry hall and hides downstairs. She intends her younger brother and sister to recognize the hat and coat as a natural sign of her presence, and expects them excitedly to search for her. She may or she may not expect her brother and sister to realize that she left the hat and coat here *in order* that they should take these as a sign of her presence. In either case, the presence of the coat and hat is, first, a *natural* sign of Susan's presence in the house. At the same time, Susan has *designed* this sign to fit the natural-sign interpreting capacities of her siblings. Thus the sign is *more* than a natural sign. It has as a derived proper function to adapt the behavior of her siblings to the condition of her presence. If Susan intends her siblings to take the sign as one purposefully improvised by her, then her sign is even more like a sentence. For it is at least *characteristic* of sentences that those who interpret them recognize, at least on reflection, that they have been purposefully produced as signs and that the sentence producer assumes the interpreter would be able to recognize this.

But Susan's sign also differs from a sentence, and not only because it is merely a signal (time and place being the significant variants). Her sign is not a member of a reproductively established family having proper functions. It is not part of the (wider) Normal explanation for proper performance of the programs that interpret Susan's sign that these are helped in performance of their proper functions by a producing device such as Susan's. Susan's sign is itself neither true nor false. Suppose that rather than hiding downstairs, Susan purposefully leaves the hat and coat, then goes back to college in a huff at finding no one home. Her sign, though intended to mislead and frustrate, is not false. It is, however, very much like a false sign. For the natural sign that Susan uses is a paradigm one, one that normally corresponds. It is not *merely* a symptom or manifestation. And the interpreting mechanisms that Susan relies upon have already been programmed to interpret just *this* kind of natural sign. (Surely Susan's siblings have long ago discovered that where people's hats and coats are tends to sign where they are.)

More commonly, an improvised sign is not a paradigm natural sign but merely a *manifestation* of the conditions to which it adapts an interpreter. The interpreter is intended to observe the sign, then infer, or go through a process something like inference by the method of best explanation, what the sign signs. Typically, this inference or process is supposed to be mediated by recognition of the sign as an item designed to be used as a sign—i.e., used as intentional icons are used. Crudely, the interpreter is supposed, first, to think to himself, "This could only be here because someone is trying to tell me something," and proceed from there.

I was once stranded overnight, for the moment sans passport and sans *geld*, in the Köln train station. In the station "mission" (where they sober up the drunks with free black coffee) I met a (sober) Greek who spoke no English, French, or German. However, she was remarkably inventive with gestures—as in the silent movies—and we spent a very friendly evening together. How did I understand her? First, it had to be apparent to me that her motions were intended as signs. But then hand wavings and pantomine in the right context is surely a paradigm *natural* sign—a pretty reliable one—of someone's intention to communicate something. After that, the puzzle was to move to more specific explanations of her signs: the most likely explanation for the occurrence of this sign would be the intention to convey *what*? Unlike Susan's sign, such signs are not natural signs of their specific *content*. They are analogous to intentional icons in other ways. They have, though not direct proper functions, the same sort of derived proper functions that intentional icons have as direct proper functions. And they are like sentences insofar as it is characteristic of sentences that the hearer understands (on reflection would know) that the speaker intends them as signs, and is expected by the speaker to understand this. But such signs are not themselves either true or false.

Last, consider Alan's bouquet. This bouquet was surely not a paradigm natural sign even of someone's wanting to convey something. But anything so obviously an artifact would lead John Maccoll to wonder what it was for. Further, Alan's sign contained the crosstarrie, or something very like it, which would aid John Maccoll in the inference that it was meant as a sign. Alan's button was a natural sign of connection with Alan. Alan himself explained how the rest of John Maccoll's inference to an explanation was to proceed. Alan's sign was both like and unlike an intentional icon in exactly the same ways as my Greek friend's pantomimes.

In Chapter 2 I remarked concerning a bee dance that is maladapted to the actual place of the nectar that inspired the dance—a dance that is "mistaken"—that what we most naturally take to be represented by the dance hangs upon the dance's *direct* proper functions rather than upon its derived proper functions. The "mistaken" or "false" dance "represents" what would have to be its real value if it were to perform its direct proper functions Normally. It does not "represent" the actual place of honey from which its derived adapted proper functions are derived even though it was, of course, "supposed" to represent this. The same is true of every intentional icon that is maladapted to the conditions to which it is supposed to adapt its interpreter. Suppose that I observe John performing amusing acrobatics out on the lawn and, intending to call attention to this, mistakenly call out "listen to John!" My sentence is maladapted to the conditions to which it is intended to adapt my interpreter, for these conditions are not conditions under which listening to John will be rewarding. My *sentence* is about listening, not about looking. On the other hand, there is some tendency to think of my *exclamation*—the sentence *as* uttered *now* by *me*—as being about looking. For its derived proper function—derived from my intention—is to adapt my hearer to a situation by causing the hearer to look at John. An *improvised* sign has no direct proper function. So there is nothing for it to be about except as derived from the maker's intention. Its meaning is nothing more or less than what its maker intends it to map and to do.

Works of art that are intended to be representational or symbolic but that do not employ conventional signs or conventional methods of representation are improvised signs. Accordingly, what these "mean" is entirely a matter of the intent of the artist. These, and improvised signs generally, "have meaning" in a different sense from that in which intentional icons "have meaning." Their mode of "intentionality," if you wish to employ that term here, is different from the mode of intentionality of sentences.

Signs Produced by Instruments[1]

Consider the signs produced by meters, gauges, TV sets, phonographs, geiger counters, etc. Are these more than mere natural signs? How are these like and unlike intentional icons?

Consider an indicator poised on a car's gas gauge. Is this configuration of indicator-poised-on-gauge a member of a reproductively established family having proper functions? (Condition (1) for intentional icons.) Certainly this configuration is not a member of a first-order reproductively established family. It is not a reproduction of any previous gas-gauge readings. Higher-order reproductively established families must have members that have been produced by members of a common lower-order reproductively established family. Are gas *gauges* members of reproductively established families?

Undoubtedly many of them are—those that have been reproduced following the design of earlier gauges that have stood up well over the years. If we look at what is invariant from one poised indicator event to another produced by the same gauge or by gauges of the same family, this invariant is the Normal character of a reproductively established family of gauge readings. Think of this invariant as the syntactic form of the gauge reading. The particular place of the indicator is the variant of the icon. The poised indicator sign is thus a member of a reproductively established family, and certainly it has a proper function. It is supposed to adapt an interpreter to conditions, namely, to how full the gas tank is.

But even if the gas gauge is not a member of a reproductively established family, although the poised indicator sign is not strictly speaking a member of a reproductively established family either, still it is very much *like* a member of such a family in this way. It is one of a family of poised indicator events all produced by the same *gauge* in accordance with Normal explanations. A *derived* rather than a direct proper function (derived from the maker's intention) of this gauge is to produce such events—configurations having just this invariant form in common. And the poised indicator event has as a derived proper function that it should adapt an interpreter to certain conditions (how full the gas tank is) by adapting these interpreting devices, first, to the specific content of the sign—the position of the indicator. (Similarly, the bee-dance interpreters become adapted to the specific content of the bee dance, hence to the place of nectar.) The poised gas-gauge indicator comes very close to fulfilling condition (1) for being an intentional icon. Indeed, any sign produced by a man-made instrument, a proper function of which instrument is to produce such signs in order that they may be interpreted, is a device that comes at least close to fulfilling condition (1).

Is the poised gas-gauge indicator an item that stands midway between two devices, a producing device and an interpreter device that have been designed or standardized to fit one another in the performance of common functions, the cooperation of each being a Normal condition for the proper performance of the other? (Condition (2) for being an intentional icon.) How did it come about that I can read my gas gauge? A designer designed the gauge so that it could be read by a Normal adult. He did this in one of these two senses.

1. He designed the gauge such that any Normal adult could *learn*

to read it. Then people did learn to read it. We gas-gauge readers developed interpreter techniques, programs, to fit these gauges. The gauges, though not designed to fit ready-made interpreter programs, were designed to fit the interpreters' capacities to develop programs that would fit the gauges. Surely this case is very much like a case in which sign producer and sign interpreter have evolved to fit one another or been standardized to fit one another. Proper operation of the gauge is certainly a Normal condition for proper operation of its corresponding interpreter programs and vice versa. Electrocardiograms, echograms, the sounds that a geiger counter makes, etc., are all very similar to intentional icons in this way.

2. On the other hand, perhaps the gas-gauge designer designed the gauge to fit interpreter programs already present on the scene, these programs having been developed by people who needed to read other kinds of gauges or, in general, other kinds of signs. That is, the gauge was designed such that it could be read in a way already standard for other gauges or for other kinds of signs. In this case, the indicator-poised-on-gauge definitely has a reproductively established character or characters and is as such a member of a reproductively established family or families. Perhaps the pointer is a member of one such family, and the words "full" and "empty" and "gas" written in appropriate spots on the gauge are members of other reproductively established families. If *all* of the significant aspects of the poised indicator sign are characteristics reproduced on the model of aspects of prior intentional icon families, then this configuration is itself an intentional icon. The gas gauges placed on contemporary cars usually fit this description. One indication of this is that it is immediately obvious to any experienced driver getting into a new car which is the gas gauge and how to read it. Another indication is that we speak of such gauges as sometimes giving "false" readings. But being false is a characteristic that only an intentional icon or something very like it can have. Household thermometers and barometers, and, in general, dozens of kinds of dials and indicators that are common in the home are like these gas gauges in this way.

Suppose, however, that not all or that none of the significant aspects of the signs produced by a certain instrument are reproductively established characteristics taking prior intentional icons as models, nor is the interpreter expected to learn to interpret the sign. Rather, the instrument is designed to produce signs on the model of familiar *natural* signs. The TV set, for example, seems to be such an instrument. The signs that it produces are designed to be interpreted not by programs developed for reading intentional icons, but mainly by programs either inborn or already developed for reading natural signs—for making sense out of light patterns impinging on the eye. Light patterns that the microscope produces are like this, as are the (nonlinguistic) sounds that come out of loudspeakers. These are not as much like intentional icons as the signs produced by gauges. They are more reminiscent of *improvised* signs. For example, the cooperation of a TV set or of a loudspeaker is not a Normal condition for proper performance of the devices in people that interpret the signs these produce. Accordingly, it is not at all natural to speak of a distorted TV picture or distorted microscope image or distorted sound produced by a phonograph as being "false." Moreover, as in the case of improvised signs, what the TV picture is a picture *of*, what the recording heard is a recording *of*, is not what the *interpreter*, if performing Normally, would take it to be of, but that in the world to which it was *supposed* to be adapted. What it is "of" hangs upon its derived proper functions.

And yet, that is not an entirely adequate analysis of TV, loudspeaker, and microscope signs either. The TV picture is not correctly read in *exactly* the same way that normal visual data are read, nor is the microscope image read this way. A very small friend of mine once asked her father, who had appeared that afternoon on local TV, "Daddy, how did you get *in* there?" Similarly, the microscope image and the loudspeaker sounds must be interpreted *somewhat* in the usual way for sights and sounds, yet with a difference. To the degree that adjustments must be made in one's natural sign-interpreting programs in order to interpret the signs produced by instruments, these signs begin to look a bit more like intentional icons. For the sign producers and the sign-interpreting programs begin to look more like cooperative devices, the cooperation of each of which is a Normal condition for the proper performance of the other. Simultaneously, these signs begin to look more as if they might be true vs. false.

My purpose here, the reader will surely have divined, is to shake the impulse to insist of every sign that it either is or is not "intentional," e.g., that it either is or is not itself "true" vs. "false." Intentionality, I maintain, is not of a piece. It admits of degrees.

Chapter 8

Hubots, Rumans, and Others: Case Studies of Intensions, Senses, and "Stimulus Meanings"

The mythical hubots and their relatives that inhabit this chapter are here to serve as subjects for several preliminary studies. In the last part of the chapter I will propose that human beliefs and intentions may well be inner intentional icons, possibly inner sentences. Hubots and their kin harbor inner intentional icons, both indicative and imperative, that are like inner sentences. These inner sentences are in important ways *not* like human beliefs and intentions. For example, all hubots "think" in the same inner language, whereas it is very unlikely that all humans think in the same inner language. And hubots never develop *new* terms or concepts—except via lengthy evolutionary processes. But hubots will help us to bridge the rather large gap between understanding, say, the intentionality of bee dances and understanding the intentionality of human thought, assuming that human thought does or sometimes does take the form of inner language.

Hubots and their kin will also provide us with simple cases that will help us to drive a wedge between what I am calling *Fregean sense* and *intension.* I have promised to dissect the traditional sense-intension amalgam into two distinct elements. I have offered a preliminary description of the element I have chosen to call "sense" for certain kinds of single words and for certain kinds of complete sentences. In this chapter I will first contrast the "senses" of simple hubot terms with their "stimulus meanings" (à la Quine).[1] "Stimulus meanings" are *not* intensions in any traditional sense. But there are important connections between Quine's notion of "stimulus meaning" and the traditional notion of intension insofar as intensions are understood as criteria for application of terms. One way to begin straightening out the tangle that is the traditional sense-intension web is to show that the extremes of this web are not strands of one and the same thing. One strand of the tangle, I suggest, is "stimulus meaning"; another is what I have called "sense." Hubots and their kin provide us with simple examples of the contrast between sense and "stimulus meaning."

Next, the languages of hubots and their kin will provide us with simple examples of inner and outer terms that are ambiguous in sense and of terms that lack sense altogether—vacuous terms. These simple examples will provide paradigms for understanding ambiguity and vacuousness in the senses of human terms, inner and outer.

Last, we will allow our hubots to evolve until certain of their terms have, besides "stimulus meanings" and senses, also intensions of various kinds. They can then provide us with terms that, although vacuous or ambiguous in sense, are not ambiguous or vacuous in intension. They will help us to understand the sorts of relations there are and are not between senses and intensions.

A hubot is a kind of organism, as much like us as possible, but genetically programmed to manufacture inner "sentences" in a predetermined inner language or representational system in response to certain patterns of sensory stimulations and programmed to use these sentences in predetermined ways. The hubot is born knowing how to do this, and no learning processes affect the methods by which it is done. Hubots are born having a set inner vocabulary that each is programmed to use in inner sentences and with an inborn capacity to use sentences couched in this vocabulary in set ways. The hubot is not capable of adding to this inborn vocabulary. It is not capable of forming new concepts.

Some of the hubots' inner sentences, we suppose, are indicative intentional icons. They are members of (higher-order) reproductively established families in accordance with their syntax. They have direct relational proper functions, each sentence's adapted proper function being adapted to its content. The devices in hubots that produce inner indicative sentences have been tailored through an evolutionary process to fit other devices in these same hubots that use these sentences. The inner sentences serve to adapt the inner devices that interpret them to conditions in the world, and it is a Normal condition for the proper performance of these sentences and of the inner devices that use them that these sentences map certain kinds of affairs in the world in accordance with definite mapping rules of the sort described in Chapter 6. Compare hubots to bees. The bee-dance choreographers in one bee cooperate with interpreting devices in another bee. Hubots are different only in that the devices that make and interpret hubot inner sentences are both in the same hubot.

Of course hubots sometimes harbor inner sentences that are false, just as bees may sometimes dance maladapted dances. This is not just because hubots sometimes "break" or malfunction. Sometimes the external conditions under which the hubots' sentence-producing devices labor are not Normal for them. Then the hubots, through no fault of their own, produce false inner sentences.

In the case of hubots, surely there is nothing incoherent in the idea of inner sentences that are indicative intentional icons. Similarly we can coherently suppose that hubots harbor inner imperative sentences that are intentional icons. Hubots are born with the disposition to produce certain inner sentences in response to certain needs or in response to certain combinations of needs-plus-inner-indicative-sentences. The proper function of these inner sentences is to produce hubot actions, hence world affairs, which affairs map onto the inner imperative sentences in accordance with definite rules. The interpreting devices for these inner imperative sentences are devices that use these icons in combination with inner indicative sentences and/or with sensory input in predetermined ways, thus producing actions that are adapted (in the technical sense introduced in Chapter 2) simultaneously to the hubots' needs and to their environments.

Again, sometimes the external conditions under which the hubots' inner imperative icons are formed or used are not Normal for them. The hubots not only are not designed for every possible world, they are not ready for many contingencies in this world. Hence, their "intentions" sometimes fail to be carried out or, when carried out, sometimes fail to satisfy their needs.

Now hubots also have an outer language that they are programmed to use and to understand. Hubots are continually and automatically rehearsing their stores of beliefs out loud, their inner language mapping onto their outer language in accordance with simple rules. They "understand" what is said to them by automatically translating into their inner language. They "believe" everything they hear. Unlike humans' outer sentences, which are members of first-order reproductively established families, the hubots' outer sentences are members of higher-order reproductively established families. But these sentences are indicative intentional icons. (We could furnish our hubots with outer imperative sentences too, but it would serve no purpose for our studies and would complicate matters unnecessarily.)

The first thing of interest about hubots is that the *senses* of hubot terms, inner and outer, neither determine nor are determined by the "stimulus meanings" of these terms.

There is no need to be rigid or even very precise in defining "stimulus meanings" in order to see this. Think of "stimulus meanings" simply as input-output dispositions taking sensory stimulations as input, yielding indicative sentences, inner or outer, as output. Roughly, "stimulus meanings" of hubot terms are determined by the "programming in the head" of the hubot that is responsible for iterating inner and outer tokens of the term in indicative inner and outer sentences.

Imagine *two* species of organism, hubots and rubots, each genetically wired to produce inner and outer sentences in accordance with set programs in the manner we have described. But these organisms have completely different sensory apparatuses. Hubots are sensitive to light in the human visual range, sensitive to touch, temperature, and smells. Rubots are sensitive to a different portion of the radiation spectrum, to tastes, to sound, to lower-wavelength vibrations, and like bats, they use a sort of radar. Hubots and rubots might still have inner vocabularies that coincided perfectly with regard to the *senses* of terms. Sense is determined only by the mapping rules that say what a term must map onto in order that its Normal interpreting devices can operate Normally. These mapping rules determine neither the methods by which these terms must be iterated nor the Normal conditions for their correct iteration. Hubots and rubots might come to "know" and might knowledgeably "say" (in different languages) many of the same things. That is, the real values of many of their sentences might correspond. For example, each might come to "know" that the sun was shining or that it was raining or that there was a large square solid object just to the left. On the other hand, hubots and rubots would be capable of "finding out" and "knowing" the same truths under quite different external conditions, the Normal conditions for proper operation of their respective inner sentence-producing systems being quite different. Also, they would make mistakes under different conditions.

It is clear that the senses of hubot or rubot terms do not determine any particular "stimulus meanings" that must correspond. Similarly, the "stimulus meanings" of their terms do not determine the senses of these terms. Imagine that besides hubots and rubots, there are rumans. Hubots and rumans both employ "color terms." Rumans live in an environment very similar to that of hubots, but an important difference is that whereas hubots live under a sun like ours, rumans live under a sun that emits light that is considerably redder than our sun's light. Suppose that hubots and rumans are, with respect to their sentence-producing mechanisms, identical to one another. The stimulus meanings of their respective terms correspond perfectly. Suppose, further, that these organisms do not have built into them any way of adapting to lighting conditions so as to take account of these conditions when making color judgments. The only way the hubot or ruman has of telling the color of an object is to take it out directly under his sun and then respond with a color term. We should also make explicit that in the cases of both hubots and rumans the inner terms we are calling their "color terms" perform their proper functions Normally only when they map in sentences onto those variants in world affairs that are the colors of those *things* to which, when these are out under the shining sun, hubots or rumans typically respond by using these color terms.

Then the hubots' term "orange" will translate, say, as the rumans' term "yellow," and so on across color space. It is true that if a ruman were to be transported to hubot land, he would call "orange" just those things that the hubot calls "orange." But he would be wrong! For these things would not be the same color as things he correctly calls "orange" at home. Indeed, these very same things he would say were *not* orange if he were under his own sun again.

There is another kind of case that illustrates the detachment of "stimulus meaning" from sense in the case of hubots and their kin. Suppose that hubots and rumans both live on this earth but in a place where gold and copper are encountered with roughly the same frequency. The stimulus meanings for all hubot and ruman terms are identical for identical terms. But not all of the rest of their insides matches. What hubots call "golper" they are programmed to (try to) put to certain uses that require a noncorrosive metal. What rumans call "golper" they are programmed to (try to) put to a use that requires something that produces a green flame when thrown into the fire. The hubot-ruman "golper" iterating mechanisms do not distinguish between gold and copper. But the programs in hubots that produce tokens of "golper" have survived over the generations because, roughly half the time, the sentences they produced mapped onto affairs involving gold. (Many many biological mechanisms, reflexes, etc., seem to have survived only because *once in a while* they proved useful.) The programs in rumans that iterate tokens of "golper" have survived over the generations because, roughly half the time, the sentences they produced mapped onto affairs involving copper. The hubot term "golper" then has the sense "gold," whereas the ruman term "golper" has the sense "copper." The hubots and the rumans just make mistakes in applying their respective terms "golper" on different occasions.

Now let us suppose that hubots evolve for another million years. They change in no way except that now, like the rumans, they are programmed under certain need conditions to (try to) put what they call "golper" to a use that requires a substance that produces a green flame when thrown into the fire. Under other need conditions, they still (try to) use what they call "golper" in a way that requires a noncorrosive metal. "Golper" still has its old stimulus meaning. What is the sense of "golper" now?

The sense of "golper" in hubotese has become *ambiguous*. The reason for this is not that there is no objective *category* into which both gold and copper fall that could count as delimiting the extension of "golper" given its "stimulus meaning." There may well be such a category, say, *metal*. The reason is that the *explanation* for the survival of the "golper"-iterating program is disjunctive. The program has not survived because sentences containing "golper" mapped onto samples falling in some category C which happens to encompass both copper and gold. Rather, just as the feathers of waterfowl sometimes help them in accordance with one explanation and sometimes in accordance with another, so the "golper"-iterating programs have sometimes helped the hubots in accordance with one explanation and sometimes in accordance with another—indeed, in accordance with incompatible explanations. Sometimes they have helped because "golper" mapped onto gold, and sometimes they have helped because "golper" mapped onto copper.

It is very important not to confuse the sort of ambiguity that characterizes the hubots' term "golper" with another sort of ambiguity. Words in human languages often have more than one *dictionary* sense. That is, often a single genetic family of word tokens has several distinct branches each of which least types has an independent stabilizing function. Having several dictionary senses is not being ambiguous. On the other hand, there are contexts in which a hearer or a reader is given no clue as to which of several least types is the least type of a certain word token. We do call such a token "ambiguous," for one cannot tell from the context to which least type it belongs, hence what is stabilizing function is. The hubots' term "golper" is not ambiguous in *that* way, but in a more fundamental way. There is only *one* branch of the "golper" (higher-order) reproductively established family. "Golper" corresponds to only *one* least type. But the Fregean sense of that type is ambiguous. There are two incompatible things onto which "golper" is, equally, supposed to map in order that its Normal interpreting devices should peform their proper functions in accordance with a Normal explanation. "Golper" has only one dictionary sense, but it has *two* "Fregean senses" between which it hovers. Call this kind of ambiguity "ambiguity in Fregean sense" as opposed to "ambiguity in dictionary sense." If the analogy that I will soon press between hubot inner language and human inner language is sound, the ambiguous hubotese term "golper" is a paradigm for understanding ambiguity in human *thought*. And where there has been ambiguity in the Fregean senses of human thoughts, there is likely to be ambiguity in the Fregean senses of human outer terms—in least types—as well.

The next experiment we need to try on hubots may not take quite a million years. Let us suppose that hubots suddenly produce a mutant variety that couples better eyesight with the development of a new program for producing a new term "flogiston" in response to certain patterns of sensory stimulations. Gradually, because of their better eyesight, the mutant hubots edge out the old-style hubots until only the mutants remain. The program for producing "flogiston" in sentences in response to certain sensory stimulation patterns is of no value whatever to hubots. On the other hand, it doesn't seem to hurt anything. Alternatively, let the program have the function of frightening away rubots, who are unreasonably afraid of three-syllable words; hence rubots often leave hubots the food when hubots (automatically) utter sentences containing "flogiston." In either case, the hubots' new term "flogiston" has not survived because it has helped any cooperative interpreter devices to perform proper functions that depended upon "flogiston"'s mapping onto anything. "Flogiston" is a term with a *vacuous* sense. Indeed, is it a term at all? It is a standard response to certain sensory stimulations. But then so are sneezes and knee jerks, and we don't call *them* terms. Having a "stimulus meaning" does not even entail being a term, let alone having a sense.

Now let us introduce "intension" in a carefully restricted sense.

Classical intensions had a number of functions. These functions are all packed into the notion that intensions are "criteria for application" of terms. Traditionally, a "criterion for application" of a term was supposed to be, first, a set of properties or characters "associated" in the minds of term users with the term. Second, this "criterion" was supposed to determine that to which the term could be correctly applied—the term's extension. That is, the connection of a term having an intension with that term's extension was routed *through* the mind's grasp of the term's intension. It was only because people applied a term, or there was a norm that said they *should* apply the term, when and only when they believed the criterion for its application was satisfied that the term had an extension at all. That was how terms got together with their extensions. The word "criterion," which means a standard or measure, aptly expresses this view of intensions. The intension of a term was *the* standard by which its extension was determined or measured.

Now the theory of sense that I am offering is *another* theory about the way terms get together with their extensions, or with their referents. According to this theory, the connection between a term and its extension or referent is not routed through any particular methods that people have for determining when to use the term. Rather, it is routed through the *history* of the term which determines the proximate Normal explanation for proper functioning of its interpreter devices or programs. The connection between a term and its referent, which connection determines how the term is "supposed to" map in sentences onto that referent, lends the term a "sense," in my terminology. Need anything then be salvaged from the classical notion of intension?

One thing that needs to be salvaged is the notion that we do, sometimes at least, apply terms after having applied certain tests, the results of which we explicitly formulate in beliefs. *From* these prior beliefs we move *to* term applications or term productions. For example, the chemist has tests for the presence of each of the various elements. The results of these tests are explicitly formulated in such beliefs as, say, "when mixed with starch it turned blue" from which the chemist moves to "there's iodine in it." Moreover, there are occasions when, in talking about meaning, we apparently make reference to the existence of standard movements of this sort lying behind term uses. I will say that a term has an "explicit intension" relative, in the first instance, to a given *user* of that term, when there is a way or there are ways that the user is disposed to move in this manner from prior explicit beliefs to production of the term in inner or outer sentences.

How common is it for us to use such explicit methods of term application or production? Do members of the same language community all use the same explicit methods when producing the same term? Does a person sometimes use several alternative methods of this explicit kind for applying the *same* term? Is there an absolute difference or only a relative difference in the confidence we have in various explicit methods for production of the same term—a sharp deduction-induction or symptom-criterion distinction? Do we change our explicit methods of term production sometimes? If so, when and why and how?

Hubots are simple creatures and creatures of our will. We can supply *them* with whatever methods of term production we like. It will be best, as before, to keep our hubots relatively simpleminded. So that they get ready before the next ice age, we will only ask them to acquire three new terms with explicit intensions, "apple," "purvine," and "man." And we will ask them to add an explicit intension to "golper."

1. "apple"

One of the staples of the hubots' diet is apples. Other round red objects of apple size are infrequently encountered in hubot land. Let us suppose that hubots, when we left them last, had no term with the sense *apple*. They did, however, have a term "red" and a term "sphere" having roughly the same senses as our corresponding terms. And they had a third term "fisise," which we can translate roughly as *fist-sized*. The hubots, on seeing any fist-sized object, used to respond by taking it out into the sun (muttering "fisise, fisise" all the way). If it showed red and spherical, the hubot was disposed to produce inner and then outer sentences containing the string "fisise red sphere," if green and cubical, then containing the string "fisise green cube," etc. As time went by hubots mutated. Now, occurrence of the inner string "fisise red sphere" in any inner sentence causes production of a new inner sentence in which "apple" is substituted for "fisise red sphere." The hubot then (automatically) says the sentence containing "apple" out loud. Mechanisms that respond to inner and outer sentences containing "apple" have also developed. The hubots' "apple" sentences adapt certain activities of the hubot such that these effect the gathering, storage, and eating of apples. The hubots' term "apple" has an explicit intension, namely, "fisise red sphere." And, we suppose, it also has a sense— the sense *apple*. Let us compare hubotese "apple" with hubotese "fisise red sphere."

The string "fisise red sphere," we are supposing, does not have an explicit intension nor do any of its elements. It appears in direct response to sensory stimulations. For example, the hubot does not move from a prior string such as "the size of a fist" to "fisise." He just responds, under the relevant Normal conditions, to things of the right size with "fisise." The string "fisise red sphere" does have a sense. For there are mapping rules, making reference to such possible transformations as, say, *replace whatever is in the such and such syntactic place with "blue"* and *replace whatever is in the such and such syntactic place with "cube"* that must be referred to in giving a proximate Normal explanation of how tokens of "fisise red sphere" and the various transformations of this string significant to hubots have historically served their proper functions. The term "apple" has both an explicit intension and a sense. But the term "apple" does not have the same sense as its intension "fisise red sphere." The mapping rules for "apple" do not make reference to any possible transformations of sentences containing "apple" by substituting other things for parts of "apple." They make reference only to possible transformations of sentences containing "apple" by substituting other terms into the place "apple" holds. Moreover, some fist-sized red spheres are not "apples," even in hubotese. For they are not the kind of thing "apple" is supposed to map onto. "Fisise red sphere" is the only explicit intension that "apple" has in hubotese. And yet this intension is not entirely reliable.

Whereas hubotese "apple" has both a sense and an explicit intension, its having the sense it does is not contingent upon its having the explicit intension it does—indeed upon its having any explicit intension at all. Perhaps the rubots have now developed a term "apple" having the same sense as does the hubots' term "apple" but produced only as a direct result of stimulations to their radar sensors. Yet the fact that the hubot term "apple" has an explicit intension *is* dependent upon the fact that "fisise red sphere" has a sense. Sense, then, is more basic than explicit intension. Explicit intensions can exist only insofar as there exist prior terms that already have sense.

2. "purvine"

The hubots' new term "purvine" also has an explicit intension. It is produced as a replacement for or inference from the string "purple bovine." But "purvine" has no sense. There is no Normal explanation for proper performance of sentences containing "purvine" that makes reference to mapping rules mapping "purvine" onto affairs containing purple cows or anything else. How are we to imagine this situation to have developed?

Suppose that the mechanism that transforms "purple bovine" into "purvine" was an accidental by-product of the development of some other mechanism of use to the hubot, as the mechanism that produced "flogiston" was an accidental by-product of the genes that gave them better eyesight, but that the "purvine"-producing mechanism has no proper functions of its own. Perhaps there are purple cows in hubot land, or perhaps there are not and hubots utter "purvine" only under abNormal conditions that cause them to mistake bovines for being purple or mistake purple things for being bovine. In either event, if the term "purvine" has no proper functions, then clearly there can be no Normal explanation for performance of these functions and "purvine" can have no sense. Alternatively, we might suppose that "purvine" does have a proper function of a sort. Say, it too scares rumans away from the food supply, or, for some obscure reason, attracts honey-producing bees to hubot land. Still "purvine" has no sense because it does not need to map onto anything in sentences in order to perform its proper functions Normally. "Purvine" might have such a proper function even if there are no purple bovines in hubot land—supposing that hubots are exceedingly apt to mistake things for purple cows, hence often utter "purvine." But, of course, if there *are* no purple cows in hubot land there is no way that "purvine," regardless of the fact that its *intension* has a perfectly good sense, could ever *itself* acquire a sense in hubotese.

Does "purvine" have a *meaning*? "Purvine" is not an intentional device. In no way is it like an intentional icon element. But it is backed up with an explicit intension—by terms that are intentional, have sense. In the case of *human* terms such explicit intension-having but sense-lacking terms are always produced by devices whose proper functions are to manufacture mapping terms. Hence such terms are always "supposed to" have had senses. We tend to say of them that they have meanings. For example, "phlogiston" is not usually thought of as meaningless, for its explicit intension was at one time relatively uniform from naturalist to naturalist and relatively public. But here we are leaping ahead of our story.

3. "man"

The hubots' new term "man" has both sense and explicit intension. Indeed, it has two independent intensions. It has the explicit intension "rational animal" and it has the explicit intension "featherless biped." It has the sense *Homo sapiens*. We must suppose then that hubots live in our world, encounter us sometimes, and that being able to recognize members of our species serves some useful function for them. Occasionally hubots encounter plucked chickens. Then they utter sentences containing "man," and they behave (or try to behave) with regard to these chickens as with men. And sometimes they encounter irrational men and fail to recognize these creatures as members of the species *Homo sapiens*—fail to utter sentences containing "man." Such incidents have not of course helped to account for the survival of the hubots or of their "man"-producing mechanisms. But for the most part, having two ways of recognizing man is a help to hubots. Because they can recognize man either by looks or by actions, they are able to recognize man on a larger variety of occasions. The hubot's term "man" has two explicit intensions but only one sense. And, of course, neither of the explicit intensions of the hubot's term "man" is completely reliable or infallible, let alone "criterial" of its sense or meaning.

4. "golper"

Finally, there is the hubot term "golper." It used to have no explicit intension, but let us suppose that it acquires one. It acquires the intension "orange-yellow shiny hard malleable stuff." The hubots never utter "golper" anymore merely in response to stimulations. They always first determine that what they have is "orange-yellow shiny hard malleable stuff" and *then* produce the term "golper" in place of that phrase. This phrase, we assume, has the same sense as our corresponding phrase. Using this method of producing "golper" tokens, the hubots, as before, are unable to distinguish copper from gold. And, we suppose, their term "golper" is still supposed to map onto gold in order to serve certain of its proper functions but supposed to map onto copper in order to serve others. The hubots' term "golper" now has a single explicit intension the sense of which intension is unambiguous. Yet "golper" itself remains ambiguous in Fregean sense.

Now let us try one last experiment on our hubots. If hubots and rubots can harbor inner terms having the same senses yet having "stimulus meanings"—and even explicit intensions—that are completely different, surely hubots themselves might well harbor pairs of terms having the same senses yet having "stimulus meanings"—and even explicit intensions—that were completely different. Perhaps hubots recognize whippoorwills by day using sight and call them "whips"; they recognize whippoorwills at night by hearing their songs and call them "wills." (I won't speculate about what need hubots might have to recognize whippoorwills either by day or by night.) Without pausing to wonder what it would *be* for a hubot to "know" that his terms "whip" and "will" had the same sense, still it seems clear that the hubot might not know this. He might not identify whips with wills. There seems to be no reason to suppose, in the case of hubots, that knowledge of sameness or difference of *sense* for two terms would be knowledge he necessarily has.

But what relevance has all this to the case of humans—to the case of the "others" mentioned in the title of this chapter?

Although I strongly suspect that a good deal of human thought does not take the form of inner *sentences*, I suspect that it does always take the form of inner intentional icons and of operations we perform upon these. But these suspicions are about how the empirical details would turn out if we had an adequate grasp of the way the human brain functions, hence certainly cannot be validated by an essay of this kind. What I *will* do is to try to show that the hypothesis that human thoughts are intentional icons is coherent and fruitful. In particular, I will try to explain how the theory that humans sometimes think in inner sentences can be worked out and how such a theory would cast light upon certain problems in the philosophy of mind and of language—a project to which much of the rest of this book is devoted. In this chapter I wish only to contrast this hypothesis with more traditional "functionalist" approaches to thought and to explain, on this hypothesis, the relevance of our adventures into hubot land to an understanding of human thought.

To take human beliefs to be intentional icons is to postulate that beliefs (explicit occurrent ones, at least) correspond to something physiological—neural structures, energy-transfer patterns, or whatever—these physiological devices having their own jobs to do. The performance of these jobs, when coupled with the performance of other jobs by devices that cooperate with beliefs, leads to performance of further jobs, etc., all eventually contributing to the proliferation or survival of the species that believes. In this respect we take beliefs to be similar to the various other smaller and larger parts and systems that make up the human body. Of course, to say that a belief "is" a physiological device does not mean here that being a belief is the same as having a certain physiological structure. Rather, to be a belief involves having certain kinds of proper functions, and it is physiological structures or activities that *have* these proper functions. Compare: being a can opener or a mating display is not having a certain physical constitution (these constitutions vary enormously) but having been designed to open cans or to attract mates. Yet any given can opener or mating display *is* a thing with a certain physical constitution or physical description.

That *belief* is a "function" category and that differently constituted devices may have the same "function," hence that there is no reason to postulate a type-type identity between belief types and physical or physiological types, is a thesis that lies at the core of all contemporary functionalist accounts of belief. That sums up *and exhausts* the similarities between these accounts and the view that beliefs are intentional icons. Let us then turn to the differences.

First, the term "function" or "proper function," through which we have defined the notion "intentional icon," has been given a completely different construal than within standard functionalist accounts. According to our account, "the function" of a device is not what it does or what it has a disposition to do—e.g., not how its "possible states are counterfactually related to each other, input and output."[2] The bulk of what a biological device is actually disposed to do—say, to fall if dropped, to bleed if cut, to squash if sufficiently pressured, to hallucinate if under sufficient stress or if drugged, to stop metabolizing in the absence of water or of oxygen or in the presence of such and such poisonous chemicals, to bruise if pinched, to explode if placed in a vacuum, to cook if heated to 200°F, etc.—has nothing whatever to do with its proper functions. (I believe that it is a strength of my position that it distinguishes those dispositions—those possible "inputs" and "outputs"—that are relevant to "the function" of a device from those that are not—a distinction that has, for the most part, been neglected in the literature.[3]) Moreover, not every proper function of every device is something that it *is* disposed to do. Devices can be defective, hence fail to have capacities and dispositions that accord with their functions. (This entails that intentional psychology could never be an exact predictive science in the sense that the physical sciences are predictive. Nothing about dispositions to behave strictly follows from any intentional characterization of a person, no matter how complete.)

Second, if beliefs are *indicative* intentional icons, the *intentionality* of a belief has nothing whatever to do with its role in inference or indeed with anything that it is supposed to *do*. Indicative intentional icons are such because *whatever* they may ultimately be supposed to do, they cannot do it in accordance with a *Normal explanation* unless they map onto something else in accordance with certain rules. True, it does seem clear that human beliefs *are* supposed to participate in inference processes. Later I will propose that inference is a process involving acts of identification of the referents of terms in the premises of inference. Because it is a proper function of every belief to precipitate acts of identification of the referents of its elements, e.g., to serve as a premise for inferences, beliefs are *more* than mere intentional icons; they are representations. But their status as representations, which is coordinate with their having as proper functions to participate in inference, *presupposes* their intentionality rather than helping to define it. What a belief does or should do does not determine what it is *about*.

As for explicit desires, supposing these to be *imperative* intentional icons, of course they *are* defined as intentional in accordance with their proper functions. It is the focused proper function of an explicit desire to produce a state of affairs onto which it maps in accordance with certain mapping rules. (This is not to say that explicit desires are usually fulfilled. Many desires, like sperm, emerge in a world that does not permit their proper functions to be performed. But surely desires have proliferated in part because they are *sometimes* fulfilled. What use to have them otherwise?) Further, one Normal *way* that explicit desires manage to get fulfilled surely involves practical inference. But again, although that one of its proper functions is to become involved in inference is part of what makes an explicit desire a *representation*, and part of what makes it an explicit *desire*, it is not part of what makes it *intentional*. Intentionality and rationality are *not* two sides of a coin.

Third, the specific content of a belief is determined neither by the stimuli that might, under these or those conditions, even *Normally*, give rise to it, nor by its intension or intensions. The sense of an intentional icon is its Normal mapping rules, not its Normal causes or (except in the case of imperative icons) its Normal effects. (This is another reason why intentional psychology could never become an exact predictive science. A full intentional characterization of a person would not tell under what conditions that person would be prone to *acquire* these or those specific beliefs.)

Indeed, *if* human beliefs are intentional icons, then all the discoveries that we made about the relations among "stimulus meanings," explicit intensions, and Fregean senses in the case of the inner and outer terms of hubots and their kin apply *mutatis mutandis* to the inner and outer terms of humans. True, humans probably do not inherit mechanisms that produce and use specific inner terms in inner sentences any more than they inherit mechanisms that produce specific outer words in outer sentences. Rather, each individual human must develop his or her own programs by a process probably involving trial and error. But these programs must govern the production of inner terms at least many or most of which match terms in the public language of the community in which the individual lives—that have the same Fregean senses as these public terms. (How this matching comes about will be discussed in Chapters 9 and 18.) So the sorts of ways that hubot inner and outer language programs might differ from rubot and ruman programs for terms that still had the same *senses* parallel the ways that one *person's* inner language programs might differ from another *person's* inner language programs corresponding to the same public language terms. On the assumption that human beliefs *are* intentional icons, we can summarize the findings of our studies of hubots and their kin as these apply to humans as follows:

1. Neither the "stimulus meaning" of a term nor its explicit intension (if it has one) determines its sense.

2. The sense of a term determines neither its "stimulus meaning" nor its explicit intension (if it has one).

3. Hence people can have idiolect terms that have different "stimulus meanings" and/or intensions yet that have the same sense. It is even possible that they might have idiolect terms having the same "stimulus meaning" and/or intension but different senses.

4. Neither the "stimulus meaning" nor any explicit intension for an idiolect term is in principle infallible. "Stimulus meanings" and explicit intensions do not need to be infallible because they are not "criterial" of sense or meaning—because they are not what hooks a term onto its referent.

5. Senses—even the senses of thoughts—can be ambiguous and they (or the purported thoughts) can be vacuous.

6. A person can harbor a term in his or her idiolect that has multiple explicit intensions yet that has a univocal sense.

7. The sense of a term is not the same as the sense of any of its explicit intensions.

8. The sense of a term can be ambiguous or vacuous, and yet the term may have an explicit intension or intensions that have unambiguous sense.

9. If a vacuous term can be said to have a meaning in any way relating to intentionality, that can only be because it has an explicit intension that has *sense*. Lacking an explicit intension that has sense, a vacuous term is no more intentional than a sneeze. Sense, not intension, is the root of all intentionality; intension is "meaning" only in a secondary usage of "meaning."

10. A person can have two terms in his or her idiolect that have the same sense yet not know that they have the same sense (e.g., the proper names "Hesperus" and "Phosphorus"). That is, knowledge of synonymy of terms in one's idiolect is not a priori knowledge. And, although I did not demonstrate this with a hubotian case study, clearly knowledge

of ambiguity in the Fregean sense of terms is not a priori knowledge either.

But all of this presupposes that it can be shown how human beliefs could be inner intentional icons having Normal mapping rules. Here comparison with hubots and rubots serves again—serves this time to cast the difficulties in bold relief.

The beliefs of hubots, like the dances of bees, acquired Normal explanations for proper performance via lengthy evolutionary processes. For each hubot term there must have been past occasions—very very many of them—on which a token of that term in a sentence bore a certain mapping relation to conditions in the world and in fact adapted some activity of a hubot to those conditions such as to help the hubot survive or reproduce. But if our beliefs are like inner sentences, it is clear that the inner vocabulary we use is not genetically wired in—certainly not all of it. The inner term "mass," the inner term "civilization," the inner term "inflation," for example, are certainly not terms the human is hard-wired to produce in response to stimulations. We develop and teach each other *new* concepts. Perhaps we also develop and teach each other new methods of concept formation. Thus individual humans must somehow be capable of "coining" brand new *inner* terms for themselves and of developing programs in accordance with which to iterate these in inner sentences such that they consistently map onto elements of the outer world. Now it might be tempting to try to understand humans as like hubots except for the fact that we develop concepts—methods for iterating inner terms in sentences—by trial and error as individuals whereas hubots develop concepts by trial and error only via evolution. But any such attempt must fail.

It must fail, first, because it is clear that developing iteration programs for terms by wide-open trial and error—as evolution does such things—would take eons, whereas maturing individual humans acquire new concepts in very large numbers very quickly. If our concepts are developed by generate and test procedures, there must be considerable *method* in our ways of making trials. Second, notice that no hubot sentence could possibly have a sense unless all its terms had histories of involvement in *practical* activities of hubots. But humans do not develop new concepts only by trying to use these concepts in the production of *actions* and then succeeding or failing. That would be much too dangerous; an individual human cannot die a million deaths, as the hubots did, in the attempt to develop each new concept. Third, if beliefs Normally accomplish their practical functions via processes of practical and theoretical inference, then every practical test of a concept would be at the same time a test of dozens of other concepts—of all the concepts involved in producing those *other* beliefs, desires, and intentions that mediated the inference. And if the concept rested upon explicit intensions, and these in turn upon other explicit intensions (consider here Quine's worries about the role of "intrusive information" in the application of concepts) ultimately one's entire theory of the world as well as all of one's other concepts would seem to be tested in a lump with every test of a concept. But to be efficient, a generate and test procedure would have to test concepts either one by one or in small groups, so as to determine where the cause of the trouble lay when tests turned out negatively.

What I must argue then is that in fact we *have* methods of learning how to map the world with beliefs, which methods are (1) methodical, (2) disengaged from practical activities—disengaged, that is, from the test that is helping one to survive or to fulfill one's desires—and (3) such that concepts are tested in very small groups. And I must show that if a program for iterating a new inner term in inner sentences passes the appropriate tests, Normally the term will have acquired a mapping rule.

In Chapter 9 coupled with 18 I will argue that human outer language effects the generation of concepts in new individual humans in a straightforward and methodical way so that the rate at which children acquire concepts of things already named in their native languages is understandable. And in Chapter 18 I will also claim that there is much evidence that evolution has built into the human various perceptual abilities that are naturally harnessed during the process of concept formation. Thus the methodical nature of routine concept formation in individual humans will be explained.

As for our ways of testing new concepts, I will use a very familiar notion in a somewhat new way. In Chapters 16 through 19 I will build a case that the law of noncontradiction is, in the first instance, a *concept* tester rather than a judgment tester. I will argue that lack of contradiction in beliefs is an indicator (not infallible, of course) that these beliefs are mapping onto the world by determinate mapping rules in accordance with uniform hence Normal explanations. That is, the concepts or inner-term iterating programs that govern the production of terms in these beliefs are producing term tokens that are corresponding to things in the world and corresponding *for a reason*—necessarily corresponding given natural laws and the conditions under which these programs have usually been operating. I will argue that it is possible for the law of noncontradiction to have this function, first, because of the ontological structure of the world (Chapters 16 and 17). It is possible, second, because, contra Quinean themes, it is possible for the law of noncontradiction to be applied in testing very small groups of concepts in complete isolation from all other concepts—in isolation *even* from concepts that figure in the explicit intensions of the concepts to be tested (Chapter 19). It is possible, third, because inner terms characteristically have multiple ways of being iterated in inner sentences so that it is very very common for the same judgment to be made and remade multiple times (Chapter 18). For this reason there is abundant opportunity for contradictions to arise—a fact that we are not keenly aware of only because our everyday concepts tend to be extremely reliable when applied in accordance with the methods we trust most.

Relying (in good Sellarsian style) upon these promisory notes, in Chapter 9 I will complete the task of roughing out the three dimensions of public-language meaning with an examination of the intensions of public-language terms.

Appendix: Why Beliefs Are Intentional Icons

I have promised to construct a theory to explain how it can be true that, by using the test of noncontradiction, we can adjust our inner-term iterating programs until they are regularly producing tokens in sentences which sentences are mapping onto the world in accordance with standard mapping rules for standard reasons (Chapters 16 through 19). But would inner sentences containing coined or invented terms governed by term-iterating programs that had been fashioned in this way actually be intentional icons? Here are my reasons for thinking that such sentences would fulfill the four conditions laid down in Chapter 6 for being intentional icons.

We begin with these assumptions: (1) Humans contain mechanisms— call them "consistency testers"—that test for consistency among sentences. When the consistency tester finds that both a sentence and its negation have been produced, it monitors the various sentence-element-producing programs that participated in producing the offending sentence tokens, seeking to adjust or if necessary to scrap one or more of these programs so that contradictions will not continue to arise. (2) Syntactic forms of inner sentences may be thought of either as genetically determined or as produced by programs that are tested in the same way that term producing programs are tested—tested by the consistency tester.

The problem is to show why a sentence containing significant aspects (terms, syntactic forms) that have been produced by programs that have already survived the consistency tester's monitoring activities numerous times would be an intentional icon (granted the consistency tester was operating under conditions Normal for it, e.g., not confronting a long series of regularities that in fact had occurred by accident). The key will be to note that one proper function of every inner sentence token is to be used by the consistency tester as a standard against which to test programs *other* than those that in fact produced it— programs that are capable of producing sentences of the same *type* (or negations of these) by other means or methods.

First consider a token of an invented inner *term* that occurs in an inner sentence token and that has been produced by a program that has survived the consistency tester's inspections numerous times. The term token is a member of a reproductively established family, for a proper function of its producer is to produce term tokens that *match* one another so they will all be recognized, for example, by the devices that perform inferences, as tokens-of-the-same-type-again. The members of this reproductively established family have a direct proper function, for they have proliferated as a direct result of correlating with a function: they have, qua parts of inner sentence tokens, helped these sentence tokens to pass the test of consistency with other sentence tokens, hence helped to stabilize, or cause to be retained, their own producing programs.[4] (A tight circle, to be sure!) Hence such terms accord with condition (1) (Chapter 6, " 'Intentional Icon' Defined") for being elements of intentional icons. If all of the significant aspects of an inner sentence are members of reproductively established families having direct proper functions in this way, the sentence as a whole must accord with condition (1).

In order to meet condition (2) for being an intentional icon, the intentional icon's Normal interpreting device must be a mechanism designed or standardized to fit the icon that adapts it. Now the first job of the sentence-consistency-tester is to differentiate among (1) pairs of sentence tokens that are contradictories, (2) pairs of sentence tokens that say the same, and (3) pairs of sentence tokens that are neither contradictories nor say the same. In order to do this, the consistency-tester must be able to recognize two tokens of the same inner term *as* tokens of the same, be able to recognize two tokens of the same grammatical form—or tokens of equivalent grammatical forms—*as* tokens of the same, and be able to recognize the negation of a sentence *as* its negation. Consider the role that the phonetic structure of an outer language plays. Surely the major reason that outer languages all have definite phonetic structures, all words being made up out of a rather small number of phonemes strung together, is in order that what is the same word again vs. what is a different word should be immediately recognizable even when the word is new to a hearer. The phonetic structure of a language dictates identity vs. difference for its words. Similarly, either the devices that invent inner terms must be genetically determined to invent terms within a certain identity-difference scheme that the consistency-tester is genetically determined to recognize, or they must program the consistency-tester to recognize various tokens of the same invented terms *as* tokens of the same, simultaneously with the invention of these terms. Hence the invented terms and the consistency-tester are designed to fit one another. Similarly, the consistency-tester would have to be designed to recognize equivalence vs. nonequivalence among grammatical forms, whether these were or were not invented forms. And it would have to be designed to recognize the negation of any sentence, whether or not the sentence's form was an invented form. Hence inner sentences containing invented terms would meet condition (2) for intentional icons.

In order to meet conditions (3) and (4) for being an intentional icon, the belief token containing invented terms must have as a proper function to adapt an interpreter device to conditions in the world so that this device can perform proper functions, and it must be part of the most proximate Normal explanation for the interpreter's proper performance that the belief—the inner sentence—maps conditions in the world in accordance with some definite mapping rule. Begin with an inner sentence token S. S's relevant interpreter is the consistency tester qua tester of *other* programs that can produce tokens of the same type as S or negations of these. These other programs are good programs and should pass muster only if they are helping to produce sentences that map onto the world in accordance with some definite rules *for a reason*—a reason mentioning conditions under which the programs often operate and mentioning laws of nature which, under these conditions, *connect* these sentences with what they map. (That is, these sentences must bear *information* concerning what they map onto roughly in the sense that Dretske defines in *Knowledge and the Flow of Information*.[5]) These programs are then associated with definite mapping rules. But one of the jobs of the consistency-tester is to check on whether these programs *are* in fact helping to produce maps in this sort of regular way. The consistency-tester does this by comparing the sentences these other programs produce with, for example, S. Only if S in fact maps onto conditions in the world in accordance with the same mapping functions that these other programs are associated with can the consistency-tester, using S, do its job right in accordance with a proximate Normal explanation. S then adapts the consistency-tester to conditions in the world so that it can test these other programs. (Simultaneously, of course, the sentences produced by these other programs adapt the consistency-tester so that it can check on S's producing programs.) So S is an intentional icon.

Chapter 9

Intension: The Third Aspect of Meaning

We have now on the table all the elements needed in order to complete a theory of the meaning of public-language devices.

The meaning of any public-language device is, first, its stabilizing function. Words like "or" and "oh" and "please," syntactic forms, punctuations, etc., have meanings only in the sense that they have stabilizing functions. The meaning of denotative and referential idioms[1] has more dimensions. Besides their stabilizing functions (to precipitate acts of identification of their referents), referential idioms have, first, Fregean sense. Translation that preserves both stabilizing function and sense is literal translation. Literal translation, when it is possible at all, is completely determinate translation so long as the language devices that are correlated by the translation have clean-cut stabilizing functions and senses. Of course, they do not always. But the main problems that the literal translator runs into are the familiar ones of vagueness, ambiguity, and the simple failure of one language to have terms that correspond to those in another—nasty problems that can plague the literal translator but that do not touch the basic theory of meaning.

The meaning of referential terms includes also intension. Intension is the third part of meaning, and a complicated part indeed!

Intension is complicated because, with important exceptions to be noted presently, it is not at root a public phenomenon. It has to do in the first instance with what goes on inside individual speakers and hearers of a language. A public-language term is like a tool. It has its *own* proper function, but each individual who wishes to use it has to develop a program, a know-how, of his own in order to be able to use it in accordance with its function. And, as in the case of tools, the precise method of handling or of operating with a referential term may vary from individual to individual even though the end results of use are the same.

When a speaker takes over a public-language term, he must develop an inner program that matches the public function of that term. He must learn to translate the outer term into an inner term that has the same sense as the outer and vice versa. In order to do this he must either have on hand or else fashion an inner term that matches the outer term in sense. This inner term must be governed by a concept—by some method or methods whereby its tokens are introduced into inner sentences such that, under conditions Normal for operation of these methods, these inner sentences will map onto the world such that the inner term maps as the outer one does.

The concept that governs an inner term I will call its "intension" or its "set of intensions." Intensions are of two kinds, "explicit intensions" and "implicit intensions." *Explicit* intensions are the sort of intensions we discussed in Chapter 8. An inner term has an explicit intension if it is iterated in accordance with a rule from prior sentences that do not contain the term. An inner term has as many explicit intensions as there are distinct rules by which such iterations may occur. Explicit intensions often correspond to definite descriptions of the referent of the term such as "the (current) president of the United States," "my eldest daughter," or "the metal with atomic number seventy-nine." *Implicit* intensions correspond to methods by which a term is iterated by programs that work directly from perceptual data. Implicit intensions are not, however, "stimulus meanings." First, perception is not a passive but an active affair. In perceiving one does things, such as focusing the eyes, turning the head, touching and manipulating objects, moving closer to them, etc., in order to discover what they yield for perception. Second, implicit intensions, unlike stimulus meanings, are not large inclusive sets of stimulation patterns that might produce utterance of an inner term or of its negation. They are discrete abilities. A term in a person's idiolect has one stimulus meaning but may have many implicit intensions, each learned separately from the others, each corresponding to a separate method of observation. For example, I may tell a lemon by taste alone or by looks alone, by touch alone or by smell alone. I may tell it by looking at the outside or by seeing a section from the inside, etc.

Assuming that Chapters 16 through 19 will be successful, all of the points made in Chapter 8 concerning the relations of "stimulus meanings" and explicit intensions to the senses of hubot terms carry over to the case of terms in human inner languages. Exchanging the notion of "stimulus meanings" for that of "implicit intension(s)" the following, especially, should be true.

First, there would seem to be no reason to assume either that intensions, explicit or implicit, determine the senses of our inner terms or that the senses of these terms determine what their implicit and explicit intensions must be. For the sense of an inner term is a matter of its Normal mapping rules, not of its Normal method of iteration (and certainly not of possible causes of its inner utterance—"stimulus meanings"). Likely it is common for different people to employ inner terms that have the same senses but that are governed by different iterating programs—different intensions. For example, it may be that you and I have different methods of recognizing gold or of recognizing sugar maples. Of course, the conditions under which we are able to make correct judgments about gold and about sugar maples will then differ as well.

Second, there would seem to be no reason to suppose that to an unambiguous inner term there must correspond only *one* method of iteration—only *one* intension. Univocity in Fregean sense does not depend upon singleness of intension. Perhaps the chemist has a dozen independent ways of identifying the presence of sulfur. Surely I have many dozens of ways of identifying each member of my immediate family—by looks, behavior, body stance, voice, clothing, footstep, characteristic mess left in the bathroom, etc.

Third, having a definite and univocal sense does not depend upon there being any intension or method of iteration for an inner term that is infallible—that works under all conditions. The methods of inner term iteration that are implicit intensions characteristically work only under conditions that are Normal for them. And explicit intensions too can be intensions that work only for the most part. Some of the methods that I use for identifying the members of my family are more reliable than others and none can be known with Cartesian certainty to be infallible, yet, I trust, my inner names for these people have definite and univocal senses. Also, some of the intensions even of a nonvacuous inner term may be, simply, incorrect, there being no conditions under which these could produce correct iterations of the term in accordance with a Normal explanation. For example, if I believe that John, whom I know quite well, is Bill's oldest brother but there is in fact an older brother still of whom I have not heard, then I possess the intension "Bill's oldest brother" for "John," but this intension will never help me to produce sentences containing "John" that map correctly, unless via an abNormal explanation.

Thus, Quine's remarks about the "diversity of connections between words and experience" among individuals that yet yield "uniformity where it matters socially" aptly express the relation between private intensions and public *sense*: "Different persons growing up in the same language are like different bushes trimmed and trained to take the shape of identical elephants. The anatomical details of twigs and branches will fulfill the elephantine form differently from bush to bush, but the overall outward results are alike."[2] (The trimming and training, however, is not done with the tools Quine envisions—as I will argue in Chapters 18 and 19.)

Granted that all of this is so, what could be meant by "the" intension of a public-language term? Is there any intension for a public-language term that every person who understands the term must grasp or internalize?

Take any referential term in a language—say, the English word "red." Each person who understands the word "red" must have, corresponding to it, an inner term—a "thought"—into which he translates "red" and which he translates back into English by uttering "red." Consider, say, John's inner term that corresponds to "red." This inner term is governed by an intension or set of intensions—ways that John has of iterating his inner term in inner sentences. Perhaps it has explicit intensions such as *the color of blood* and *the color Grandfather thinks is too exciting to children for them to be allowed to wear.* Assuming that John is sighted, it also has implicit intensions—ways that John has of iterating his inner term on the basis of sensory input. Call the entire set of these intensions "the intension of the public term 'red' *in John's idiolect.*" (" 'Red' " refers here to the least type of the token inside the quotes. The reader knows what type that is, I assume.) Now, granted that John is a sophisticated language user—say, his mental development is beyond age four or five—one of the explicit intensions of "red" in John's idiolect will be *what "red" stands for* or *what is called "red."* Also, since John understands the word "red" and sometimes believes what people tell him, whether or not John is a sophisticated language user an implicit intension of "red" in John's idiolect is John's ability to translate tokens of "red" occurring in outer English sentences that he hears into his inner term for *red.* Further, the latter implicit intension and, for the sophisticated, the former explicit intension are intensions for "red" that are shared by all speakers who have the term "red" in their vocabularies.

Call these rather ephemeral intensions "language-bound intensions." If by the "public intension of a word" we would mean an intension that every person who understands that word *must* have for that word in his idiolect, then at least language-bound intensions are public intensions. That all words have public language-bound intensions is a truth that is obvious but, I will soon argue, not trivial.[3] Language-bound public intensions have the peculiarity that they never correspond for synonymous terms. The German "rot," the French "rouge," and the English "red" do not have the same language-bound public intensions. Speakers who speak more than one language, however, do of course harbor more than one set of language-bound intensions for many of their inner terms.

Now call all intensions that an inner term may have that are *not* language-bound "full-bodied intensions." Are there any full-bodied intensions that must be common to a public term in the idiolect of every person who uses it correctly?

I will argue that there are not. Then I will argue that it is nonetheless possible to define a notion, "public full-bodied intension," that accords roughly with the traditional notion of a public term's intension, although many terms do not have, on this definition, any clear-cut full-bodied public intensions. I will then argue that we do not in fact require of a person that he have mastered the public full-bodied intension of a term (that has one) in order to admit that he "knows what it means." And I will try to say what usually is required for a person to "know what a term means."

Learning a language involves acquiring, besides a specific vocabulary, a general grasp of the phonetic and syntactic structures of that language. Probably the reason that languages all have definite phonetic structures, words being comprised of combinations and permutations of a relatively small number of phonemes, is so that even when a word is brand-new to a hearer, it will still be clear what should count as the same-word-again. The phonetic structure of a language largely dictates identity vs. difference for its words. What this means is that if I know a language, I am in command of certain very general principles in accordance with which I can translate virtually any syntactically unambiguous set of sentences in that language, even though I may not understand many of the words in these sentences, at least into a set of inner *dummy* sentences in such a way as to preserve such relations as that between a sentence and its negation. The programs in me that are able to do this have a proper function, and any internalized sentence produced by these programs from an outer sentence has a proper function that is *derived* from this function. Any such inner sentence is supposed to end up being used to adapt my thinking processes or my behavior to whatever conditions the outer sentence mapped. The internalized sentence has this proper function as derived from a more direct source as well. For the outer sentence that has produced the inner sentence also has as a direct proper function to produce an inner sentence that will be used to adapt my thinking processes or my behaviors to the conditions that it maps.

Consider now a dummy inner sentence. Suppose that it is a dummy sentence because it contains an internalized token of "monotreme," a word I do not understand. My internalized "monotreme" token is not strictly an intentional icon element, for it is not yet a member of a reproductively established family having *direct* proper functions. But, given its derived proper functions, there is something onto which it is supposed to map in my inner sentence. It has, then, a kind of sense—

the same sense as the outer term "monotreme." We can call this kind of sense "derived sense," as opposed to "direct sense."

Now there is also at least one device in me that knows how to use any inner sentence that has been translated, even though quite blindly, from an outer sentence. That device is my "sentence-consistency tester." The purpose of having a sentence-consistency tester, I have promised to argue, is to monitor the programs in me that iterate inner terms in inner sentences to make sure they are producing sentences that map onto the world consistently in accordance with uniform reasons. Term-iterating programs that have survived audit by one's sentence-consistency tester have survived *due* to having helped to produce consistent sets of beliefs, hence have as direct proper functions to help to produce such consistent sets. And the programs pass the consistency tester's audit in accordance with a Normal explanation only if the term tokens they produce are mapping onto the world consistently in accordance with some sort of uniform explanation. Such tokens are intentional icon elements with ordinary or *direct* Fregean sense. (For more details here, see Appendix, Chapter 8.) So the first time I hear of "monotremes" I acquire an inner term that has only a derived proper function to adapt me to conditions involving monotremes and only a derived sense. But by the time I have read a chapter in a zoology text on monotremes, granted that the information given there is consistent, my inner term "monotreme" has become a genuine intentional icon element with direct rather than merely derived sense. It has, that is, assuming that the explanation for the consistency was Normal, this explanation reaching back through the sentences read in the book to a Normally explained connection of these, via the investigations of the experts on monotremes, with monotremes themselves. (Again, see Appendix, Chapter 8.) For if the information had *not* been consistent in the main, I would have stopped translating outer "monotreme" into an inner term in beliefs, figuring that what I was reading was nonsense. I would have scrapped this particular inner-term-iterating technique. (On the other hand, if I were to read a consistent eighteenth century treatise on phlogiston and believe what I read, I would acquire a vacuous inner term "phlogiston" from the vacuous outer term "phlogiston.")

In this manner, a layman's inner term is often completely parasitic upon its outer language counterpart, acquiring its derived and later its direct sense by a route that passes through the understanding of the experts. In "Meaning and Reference," Hilary Putnam, struck by the fact that most people use a variety of everyday terms like "gold" and "elm" without being able to produce any "criteria" that determine extensions for these terms, proposes the *"Hypothesis of the Universality of the Division of Linguistic Labor*: Every linguistic community . . .

posesses at least some terms whose associated "criteria" are known only to a subset of the speakers who acquire the terms, and whose use by the other speakers depends upon a structured cooperation between them and the speakers in the relevant subsets."[4] If my speculations are correct, then the relevant "structured cooperation" involves nothing more organized than that the experts sometimes *speak* to laymen about such things as gold and elms. Further, what is effected is not just that laymen are able to use terms like "gold" and "elm" such that these *terms* mean the same as when experts use them. That much is guaranteed by the mere fact that the laymen and the experts token terms that are tokens of the same least type. What is effected is that the layman is able to *think of* gold or of elms or, say, of monotremes, even though he may know little or nothing about them. Not only can I use the term "monotreme" such that *it* has *its* customary meaning without possessing any full-bodied intensions for "monotreme"; *I* can mean the same thing that the *expert* means when *he* says "monotreme." Hence there *are* no full-bodied intensions that are common to a public-language term in the idiolect of every person who uses it standardly.

But isn't there a paradox here? For surely, if I know nothing whatever about monotremes except their name, I do not know what "monotreme" means? So how can I mean what the *expert* means by "monotreme"? Imagine the following conversation:

Expert: I am going to spend the summer studying monotremes in Brazil.
Me: What are monotremes?
Expert: What do you mean, "monotremes"?
Me: I mean what *you* meant, of course.
Expert: Do you know what "monotreme" means?
Me: No. That's why I'm asking.
Expert: Then you can't have meant by "monotreme" what I meant because I *do* know what "monotreme" means.

Shades of Meno's paradox.

A Carnapian solution to this sort of puzzle would say that "What are monotremes?" is merely a shorthand version of "What does 'monotreme' mean?." But intuitively, "What are monotremes?" is a question about monotremes, not about words. Intuitively, asking "What are monotremes?" is an ordinary way of *using* the term "monotreme." And, if our analysis so far is correct, there would seem to be no reason why I can't ask a question about monotremes without knowing what they are. Even a parrot could utter a sentence that was a *question* about monotremes—by parroting the sentence. Further, there is no reason why I cannot myself *mean* this question *as* a question about monotremes.

(The parrot, of course, could not.) For, first, my inner term "monotreme" has a derived sense, hence constitutes a certain kind of thought of monotremes and, second, I can certainly purpose that my outer token of "monotreme" should function properly even though I cannot detail what proper function for "monotreme" tokens entails. The problem then is not that I cannot mean what the expert means by "monotreme." Rather, it is that there is a sense in which the expert "*knows* what 'monotreme' means" but in which I do not, hence, paradoxically, a sense in which the expert "knows what *he* means by 'monotreme' " but in which I do not "know what *I* mean by 'monotreme'." In the dialogue above, the expert assumes that in order to mean something by "monotreme" one must "know" in this sense, whatever this sense is, "what one means by 'monotreme'." It is this assumption that is in error. One thing we need to understand then is what it is to "know," in the sense in question, "what a word means," this kind of "knowing what a word means" being something *over and above* merely being able to mean something by the word.

Traditionally, "knowing the meaning of a word" has been equated with knowing a (the) public intension of the word. And, indeed, if I ask either "what are monotremes?" or "what does 'monotreme' mean?" it is initially plausible that I may be asking for some kind of standard intension to attach to my inner and outer terms "monotreme." What we have discovered so far is that a full-bodied public or standard intension for a public-language term cannot be, simply, an intension or set of intensions of which every correct user of the term is in command, for there are no such full-bodied intensions. Is there then some other way that we might define "full-bodied public intension"?

Among the various full-bodied intensions that a term has within a person's idiolect, there are usually some that are taken by that person to be more reliable than others. In some cases, there are intensions that the term user takes to be absolutely reliable—and he may be right. In other cases, a term user may be quite certain that none of *his* intentions for a term T (excepting the intension "what T stands for") are at all reliable. If asked, he will prefer to consult the experts before suggesting means of identifying the referent of the term. And it also sometimes happens that when one asks the experts, one discovers that there is a public tradition handed down from expert to expert of offering a certain intension for a term. The full-bodied public intension of a public term might then be sensibly calculated by averaging only over those full-bodied intensions that are deemed to be most reliable by laymen, or if laymen would ask experts, deemed reliable by experts or, when possible, traditionally handed down by experts. Indeed, so calculated, the full-bodied public intension of a term might be said to be one kind of "meaning" that it has. At least this fits with certain intuitions that philosophers have commonly had about "meaning."

In the case of proper names of ordinary people, one would expect there to be minimal or sometimes even no overlap among the full-bodied intensions that would confidently be assigned by all competent users of the name, and, usually, no recognized experts to appeal to on the question of intension. In the case of ordinary people, different speakers of their names recognize them by different descriptions. Being able to tell a person by his or her looks is probably as close as we can come to possessing a standard or public intension for that person's name, yet this sort of implicit intension most of us lack not only for Pythagoras's name but for the names of our own great-grandfathers. Names of famous persons excepted, proper names don't usually have clear public full-bodied intensions as we are calculating these. If "meaning" includes public full-bodied intension as well as stablizing function and sense, it is understandable that some should have denied that proper names have "meaning."

At another extreme are names of natural kinds that are studied by experts or specialists who have taught one another or communicated extensively with one another. One would expect there to be considerable agreement among such specialists on what were reliable intensions for such a term. And one would expect to find that laypersons would look to these experts, rather than to their own limited experience, if they wished to know what intensions were reliable for such terms. Such terms usually have very definite "meanings" in the sense of having quite definite full-bodied public intensions.

At a third extreme, there are terms for things that are familiar to almost everyone, almost everyone being in command of the same core of highly reliable means of identifying these things. Thus words like "apple" and "red" and "square" have highly public intensions, though these are liable to be implicit rather than explicit intensions. We all agree, for example, that the best way to be sure about the colors of things is to take these things into broad daylight and *look*. That is, it is the best way unless one is blind or color-blind, in which case one cannot learn the "meanings," in the sense of the public full-bodied intensions, of color terms.[5]

Granted that public full-bodied intension as we are calculating it, by averaging over full-bodied, ostensibly reliable, expert and/or traditional intensions, might be said to constitute one level of the "meaning" of a term, is grasping this public intension what it is to "know the meaning" of a word? We know that being able to use a word such that it has its standard sense and intending that very sense is not enough for "knowing the meaning." For I use "monotreme" *that* way when I ask "what are monotremes?" At the other extreme, we cannot insist that a person have an infallible means of identifying the referent of a term or even that he possess an infallible intension for the term[6] before he "knows its meaning." In principle, it can never be known with certainty that any particular intension for a term is infallible. Moreover, there are many terms that no one pretends to know any infallible intensions for, for example, the names of certain diseases of unknown etiology. It seems reasonable then that "knowing the meaning of a word" should be, just, knowing its full-bodied public intension.

But in fact we do *not* demand, say, that a person know what the experts think they know concerning reliable intensions for a term in order to "know its meaning." For example, I surely know what "nickel" (the metal) means, but I can't tell you much more than that nickel is the metal nickels are made of. Indeed, we do not always insist that a person know *any* reliable intensions for a term in order to "know its meaning." For example, it cannot be wrong to say of a person who knows and understands what a good dictionary says about the meaning of a term that he knows what the term means. Yet many dictionary definitions do not offer either synonyms or reliable intensions. In Thorndike-Barnhart's *Comprehensive Desk Dictionary*, 1967, I find on the first page to which I randomly open that myrtle is "an evergreen shrub of S. Europe with many shiny leaves, fragrant white flowers, and black berries." That is not enough to go on if one wishes to *identify* myrtle (the European variety) with assurance. But if I ask "what does 'myrtle' mean?" and you give Thorndike's answer, I certainly will not say "Oh, don't you know either?" Further, sometimes "knowing the meaning of word" has nothing to do with any intensions. Being able to give a literal translation of a word surely counts as knowing its meaning so long as one knows the meaning of the word into which one translates it. But consider our hubots and rumans from Chapter 8. These creatures had no sensory apparatuses in common. Yet surely a hubot might be said to know the meaning of a ruman term if he could translate it into his own language.

"Knowing the meaning of a word," I think we have to admit, is at best a vague affair. In the case of nonvacuous referential terms it is knowing *what* thing or kind the word refers to. Knowing this is exactly like knowing *who* the bearer of a certain proper name is. Depending on the setting, "knowing who" Bernard Shaw is can involve as little as knowing that he wrote plays or as much as being able to give an analysis of his character and impact on drama. Similarly, "knowing what 'malaria' means" can involve as little as knowing that malaria is a disease or as much as knowing what the average physician knows about malaria. Minimally, perhaps, "knowing the meaning" of a word is knowing enough about its referent that one can tell whether a good number of sentences employing the term make sense or not. For example, "monotremes are all voracious eaters" makes sense; "monotremes have a valence of two" does not. Or perhaps it is knowing enough to be able to "follow the conversation" in which the term is applied insofar as this depends upon knowledge about the term's referent. But whether one follows the conversation is a matter of degree, and conversations come in all degrees of difficulty. Whether or not one understands a term will then depend upon how sophisticated the people are with whom one is conversing.

Given these various reflections on intensions, why has the tradition been so insistent that intension is the basic stuff of meaning? This may have been due in part to the fact that same-language dictionaries often give reliable explicit intensions in lieu of "the meanings" of words. But I believe that a deeper cause of the insistence that intensions must be the real stuff of meaning is the deep-lying rationalism concerning intentionality and meaning with which our philosophical tradition is systemically infected.

Insistence that the knowledge that a term in one's idiolect has a meaning must be a priori knowledge leads directly to the view that meanings must be, or be determined by, intensions. Vacuous terms, the argument goes, are not known to be vacuous a priori. Hence whatever it is that a term lacks in being vacuous cannot be meaning. But the only kind of meaning that vacuous terms have is intension. Hence intension must be or must determine meaning.

A similar argument begins with the rationalist assumption that *what* a term in one's idiolect means must be knowable a priori. Synonymy must then be determined a priori. But all that one can tell a priori is whether or not two terms in one's idiolect have the same intension. So intensions must determine synonymy, hence meaning.

Further, according to the rationalist, ambiguity must be detectable a priori. But if a term had more than one intension, one could not be certain a priori that these intensions would converge upon the same when it came time to apply the term. So it must be that every unambiguous term has but *one* intension.

If we know all these things with a rationalist's certainty, then there is no point in examining the evidence. If univocal public terms do not superficially appear to have single public intensions that determine their meanings, that *must* be an illusion!

But if meaning is, at root, Fregean sense rather than intension, then vacuousness is the primary kind of meaninglessness, and neither ambiguity nor synonymy can be determined in the end merely by a priori reflection. The intension of a term is only a secondary kind of meaning.

Intension is meaning at all only insofar as intensions govern terms that have sense or insofar as intensions are explicit and themselves have sense.

The history of medicine contains public names for various diseases that later turned out each to be several diseases rather than one. Presumably each of these names once corresponded to a public full-bodied intension set handed down from physician to physician. But the fact that this intension governed an ambiguous term is not something the physicians should have known if they had only taken the time to *reflect*. The ambiguity was discovered through experience. Similarly, public terms are sometimes proliferated for reasons that have nothing to do with the mapping of these onto real-world variants. Then these terms are vacuous. Such a term might survive because it served a political or social or psychological function rather than a world-mapping function. (Compare hubotese "flogiston" which frightens rumans away from the food supply with the medieval terms "witch" and "possessed.") Or, when a vacuous public term has survived in purely theoretical contexts, perhaps the degree of consistency obtained in judgments using it is explained by reference to real-world phenomena with which the term's iterating programs are connected only obliquely. Such a term has no sense. Its only meaning is its intension. But *that* it has no sense must be discovered, if it is discovered, through experience, not by a priori reflection.

These remarks fairly cry out for support from a suitable epistemology. To supply one is the job of Part IV. But there will be more motivation for completing this task if it can be shown that the principles we have already laid down can actually be used for solving bread-and-butter problems in the philosophies of language and of mind. Then we will have very strong reason to wish to put a foundation under these principles. Part III discusses a number of such bread-and-butter problems.

But first a warning in connection with the conclusion reached above that "knowing the meaning of a public term" is a vague affair. In Chapter 15 I will discuss what I call "the act of identifying the referent of a term."In the Introduction to this book I informally equated the ability to identify the referent of a term with "knowing what the term represents." "Knowing the meaning of a public term" as I described this just above—and here I was doing something akin to ordinary language analysis—is *not* the same as "knowing what a term represents" as I am using the latter phrase—perhaps not in accordance with ordinary usage. The act of identifying the referent of a term or of coming to be able to identify it is not the same as the vague affair "coming to know what the term means."

PART III

A Short Lexicon for Philosophers

Chapter 10
Simple Indexicals

"Theaetetus flies" and "Fly, Theaetetus!" are good English sentences, but not exactly paradigms of the richness of which natural languages are capable. One purpose of the following five chapters is to examine a few of the principles that make this richness possible. These chapters contain preliminary studies of the stabilizing functions and senses of various kinds of language elements that have traditionally given philosophers trouble. Their purpose is in part to indicate the general methods available to a study of language and thought that understands these as biological categories. Their purpose is also to prepare the way for Part IV by filling in a number of details about how language maps onto the world that will be needed when we turn to the theory of identity. Yet because these studies move between the philosophy of language and the philosophy of mind, touching also upon important issues in ontology, much that I will say or suggest in these chapters will be better understood after a reading of Part IV. Unfortunately *something* has to come first in exposition even when it does not in thought.

The task of this chapter is to describe the kind of sense that indexical language elements have. That is, it is to characterize the kind of mapping rules that are Normal for indexicals, thus making them indexical. Indexicals, like other language parts, have relational proper functions that can be performed only given the presence of suitable adaptors. But unlike other language parts, the adaptors for indexicals are not just other parts of a sentence; they are also things outside the sentence. Our friend the chameleon from Chapter 2 (and, I suggest, a review of the early pages in Chapter 2) will help to make the situation of indexicals clear.

The pigment arrangers in a chameleon have as a relational proper function to rearrange pigmented matter in the chameleon's skin to match what the chameleon sits on. Depending upon what the chameleon is sitting on, these pigment arrangers acquire various adapted proper functions, the function of producing this or that color pattern. But consider a chameleon suspended in midair by a philosopher with an ax to grind. The relational proper function of the pigment arrangers is to produce a skin pattern that matches what is so-related to, namely, just under, the chameleon. But nothing is so-related to the chameleon. The pigment arrangers of such a chameleon have no adapted proper function. There is nothing that they are supposed to do given this predicament.

Every element in a sentence has a relational proper function. For exactly what any element is supposed to produce or effect is fully described only as a something bearing a certain relation to the functions of other parts of the sentence (see Appendix A, Chapter 4). Usually, a sentence element acquires an adapted proper function when placed in the context of a well-formed sentence. Outside the context of such a sentence, the element has no adapted proper function. There just is nothing in particular that it is supposed to do.

An indexical sentence element has as a relational proper function to produce something that bears a certain relation to something *outside* the sentence as well as to the rest of the sentence. It is supposed to produce an act of identification on the part of the hearer of something outside the sentence which something is so-related to it. For example, the pronoun "I" is supposed to produce an act of identification of a person bearing to it the relation *utterer of*. Pending discussion of the act of identifying in Chapter 15, we can take as our model for "identifying" in this context the act of translating "I" into an inner name, the referent of "I" being by this means "identified" with the referent of this inner name. If there is nothing outside a sentence containing an indexical that is appropriately related to the indexical, there simply is nothing particular that the indexical or that the sentence as a whole is supposed to do. For example, a token of "he" that has no antecedent (and that is not being used demonstratively) has no adapted proper function. It has as a relational proper function to translate into an inner name having the same referent as that of an antecedent term bearing a certain relation to it. (Grammarians are still investigating the rather complex rules that determine these relations for pronouns taking antecedents.) But given its actual situation in the world, there is nothing more specific that it is supposed to do.

Now consider a particular color pattern of a particular chameleon. The color pattern is supposed to match what the chameleon sits on. That is, that the color pattern should match what the chameleon sits on is a Normal condition for proper performance of that color pattern. This Normal condition can be considered as having two components. First, there must be something that the chameleon is sitting on. Second, the color pattern of this something must be (more or less) the same as the color pattern of the chameleon. If only chameleons were a bit more accurate in reproducing the patterns as well as the colors of what they sit on, we could say that, second, the color pattern of the chameleon must *map* (in accordance with the simplest sort of mapping rule) the color pattern of this something. Let us pretend that chameleons' color patterns are, Normally, maps of the patterns they sit on. Then we can draw a distinction between two types of Normal conditions for proper performance of a chameleon's color pattern which conditions reflect the Normal relation between this pattern and its adaptor.[1] First, there is an existential condition; second, there is a mapping condition. The color pattern Normally maps the color pattern of what the chameleon sits on. But it does not map the existential condition. The pattern maps the pattern of what is so-related to it; but it does not map this *relation* nor does it map that something is so related to it. For example, there are no transformations of color patterns of chameleons that Normally correspond to transformations in the worlds of chameleons yielding such world affairs as *nothing underneath* or *something to the left having this pattern.*

A language element that is indexical is like the chameleon's color pattern in that it is supposed to help map something that is so-related to it, but it does not map the relation of that something to it nor does it map that there exists something so-related to it. A sentence in which an indexical occurs can serve its proper functions Normally only if the indexical, in the context of the sentence, maps onto something that is so-related to it. In order to be true, it must map onto a world affair in accordance with certain Normal mapping rules. In order to map in accordance with these mapping rules there must *be* something that is so-related to its indexical element. Thus, there being something so-related to its indexical element and its mapping an affair involving this thing are both Normal conditions for its proper performance. But the sentence maps only the affair. It does not map either the relation between the indexical and its referent or the affair (if this could be called an "affair") that is the existence of this referent. Similarly, although singular indexicals function Normally only if there is only one thing that is so-related to them for them to map, *that* there is only one thing so-related to them is not mapped by them or by sentences containing them.

Insofar as every indexical is coordinate with a mapping rule that tells, *relationally*, what it is supposed to map onto, let us say that every indexical has a "relational sense." Its relational sense is described by telling what relation to it determines those things onto which tokens of it, when placed in sentences, are supposed to map. We can call this relation its "indexical adapting" relation. When a token of an indexical type bears its indexical adapting relation to something, let us say that the token has an "adapted sense." There is then something determinate onto which the token is supposed to map.

Now in order for a sentence to be true, first it must have a determinate proper function and a determinate sense. And in order for a sentence containing an indexical to have a determinate proper function and sense, the indexical must have an indexical adaptor. Hence, that there is one and, for singular indexicals, only one thing properly indexically related to an indexical is a condition that must be met in order that the sentence containing it be true. But it does not follow that *that* an indexical has one and only one thing so-related to it is a "truth condition" of sentences containing it. Compare: In order for the configuration "John sat on . . . " to have a determinate sense, some noun phrase must be filled in its blank space. It does not follow that *that* some noun phrase is filled in its blank space is a truth condition of the sentence "John sat on. . . ." A sentence containing an indexical that has no adaptor is like an incomplete sentence. Its indexical is only *half* of a member of a reproductively established family having proper functions. The reproductively established family that is an adapted indexical's family is like the reproductively established family of handshakes. My hand waving up and down may be a member of a reproductively established family, but only if you add the other person's hand do we have a member of a reproductively established family that has a proper function. What the indexical lacking an adaptor lacks is a complete *sense*, not truth. Having merely a relational sense is having a sense in the way isolated words and incomplete sentences have sense. They do not lack meaning, but they do lack truth value.

For a word to have a referent it must not only be supposed to map onto something; there must also *be* something determinate onto which it is supposed to map. Indexicals qua types do not have referents because there is no particular thing upon which these are, in the context of sentences, supposed to map. But tokens of indexicals that have indexical adaptors have these adaptors as referents. We can call such referents "adapted referents" to distinguish them from the kind of referents that proper names have. An indexical token that lacks an indexical adaptor has an incomplete or relational sense but no adapted sense and, of course, no referent.

It is obvious enough what the indexical adapting relations are for the English words "I," "you," "here," and "now." The indexical adapting relation for "then" points to the time at which what was just talked about occurs, or the time immediately following after that time, or the position of being next in logical order after what was just talked about. We can safely leave the description of the indexical adapting relations for third person personal pronouns, when these require specially located antecedents, to grammarians. But the indexical adapting relations for the demonstrative pronouns "this" and "that" are trickier. "There" means in or at *that* place or point, hence follows after "that" in analysis. Third person pronouns, when used demonstratively, are roughly equivalent to such forms as "*this* male," "*those* people," etc., hence also follow after "this" and "that" in analysis. Let us take "this" as our example, "that" obviously having a parallel analysis.

The dictionary tells us that "this" is "a demonstrative word referring particularly to what is present or near in place, time or thought, or to something just mentioned or to be mentioned" and that "it is applied to a person, thing or idea." "Near in thought" would seem to be logically connected or naturally associated with something present or something just mentioned or to be mentioned. We might add, although the above does imply it, that "this" sometimes refers to something a natural or improvised sign of which is near or present, not just to something that has been or will be explicitly mentioned. And we can add that "present or near" is present or near the speaker, often as opposed to the hearer. For example, what I have just said is "this"; what the hearer has just said is "that."

Let us also add that sometimes the referent of "this" is held up, pointed to, circled (say, on the blackboard as one speaks), or indicated by an arrow, etc. These particular ways of directing the hearer's attention to the referent of "this" may all be conventional devices, handed down from speaker to speaker and learned by, rather than just naturally understood by, hearers. Hence each may represent a different reproductively established family having as a direct proper function this directing of attention, and each may be understood or attended to because the hearer has in him a device or program that is standardized to fit this method. "This" coupled with each of these devices may be, accordingly, an indexical intentional icon element having, with each, a different indexical adapting relation—for pointing, what is in front of the finger, for circling, what is inside, etc. Is it possible that "this" has numerous other more subtle indexical adapting relations as well, so that *every* use of "this" corresponds to some conventional method used by speakers to indicate what "this" refers to?

First, notice that methods that at first seem indisputably to be conventional methods of drawing the hearer's attention by extralinguistic means to what is meant by "this" merge imperceptibly into methods that, at the other extreme, at first seem indisputably to be improvised. Some of the latter methods are very obvious techniques, hence commonly used, but this alone does not make them members of reproductively established families. Rather, they may be improvised again and again without having to be reproduced or copied by one speaker from another. They seem to be techniques that are "only natural" rather than conventional (cf. Chapter 1, "First-Order Reproductively Established Families"). Gesturing toward something, pointedly looking at it, nodding toward it, pointing with a toe, standing with one's back to it while an audience looks at it, rolling one's eyes toward it, or for "that," speaking while one's hearer is studying it or while he is looking at it or while he is holding it up or has it in his lap or hand—these are common ways to assure that one's hearer will think of the right thing. And there are less common ways. "This lady" the child says, mimicking her perfectly. Or someone says "this dog," showing the hugeness of it with outstretched arms. (Note that in the latter two cases what is near is an improvised sign of the referent.)

Second, there is the problem that whereas "I" and "you" name persons and "now" and "here" name times and places, "this" can refer to any kind of thing. When "this" is used with a category word—"this cat," "this color," "this thought," "this tune"—there is of course no problem of how "this" manages to convey the category of the thing to which it refers. But "this" is very commonly used bare. As has often been noted, even when an explicit act such as pointing resolves ambiguity about the general location of the referent of "this," the category of this referent (is the referent, say, a book? a book cover? a color? a shape? a kind of print?) is apparently left indeterminate by an unadorned "this." Is there in fact some kind of very subtle convention that determines an indexical adapting relation that in turn determines this category for each such instance? One that speakers copy from one another and to which hearers' interpreting mechanisms are specifically programmed to respond?

Consider this case. I hold out a book to you saying "This is more than a hundred years old." But by "this" I mean a pressed flower hidden between the book's leaves. And you understand me—because we have been looking at pressed flowers hidden in books all afternoon. Is there some kind of complex or subtle yet rigid convention, such as the rules that govern the relations of third person pronouns to their antecedents, that I have followed in order to convey my meaning? It seems unlikely.

Rather, "this" appears in such cases to be a peculiar sort of free variable—a place holder for something the speaker has in mind and that the hearer will easily gather from context as what the speaker means. A prominent part of the context from which the hearer gathers the referent is, of course, the rest of the sentence containing "this." If I suddenly look up from a book I have been reading in a peaceful place on a balmy day and say "this is beautifully written," "this" will be interpreted quite differently than if I say "this is how to live!" But the

fact that the rest of the sentence is usually an important cue in interpreting a value for "this" does not have to mean that the value of
"this" is determined as some definite function of the rest of the sentence
plus external context. Rather, "this" often holds a place for improvisation. As in the case of improvised signs (Chapter 7), the speaker has
the hearer's capacities, viewpoint, and dispositions in mind as he utters
"this" and utters it purposing that the hearer supply a certain referent
for it, that is, that he translate it into an inner term having a certain
referent. This referent is to be something proximate, or a sign or reminder
of which is proximate, but beyond that the hearer is often pretty much
on his own. He picks up his cues from the rest of the sentence and
from his knowledge of what he and the speaker both know of that it
would be reasonable for the speaker to expect him to think of first.
When all goes well, speaker and hearer thus achieve a coordination,
but not a coordination that results from the speaker's and the hearer's
speech-producing and understanding abilities having been *standardized*
to fit one another.

Improvised signs are not intentional icons or intentional icon elements.
They do not *themselves* have referents that can be distinguished from
what the maker of the sign proposes they should sign. What they mean
is, just, what the improviser intends them to mean. When "this" holds
a place for improvisation, it does of course have a direct proper function,
and it is an intentional icon element, but what it conventionally signs
is, only, that improvisation is occurring. It works rather as the fiery
cross worked in Alan's bouquet saying, crudely, "This is an improvised
sign," only it says this conventionally. (This signing of improvisation
is not, incidentally, what I will later call "representational referring"
but is "protoreferring." See Chapter 12, "The 'is' of Identity.") What
more "this" is to sign must be improvised. When "this" holds a place
for improvisation, then, it has no public referent (or, anticipating Chapter
12, no public *represented* referent, but only the public protoreferent
that is the occurrence of improvisation).

For example, very young children tend to have little grasp of the
points of view of other people. Thus they are very liable to use "this"
to refer to something that is on *their* minds and near but that the hearer
has no way of knowing is on their minds. (I cannot document this,
but I have often observed it.) Then you have to ask the child, "what
is it that you are talking about?" or "what's 'this'?" (Typically, the child
is puzzled by your stupidity.) But it does not seem right to say that
such a child does not yet grasp the sense of—the rules for—"this."
He is just inept at the business of improvising in an understandable
way. The only meaning that such a child's token of "this" has is *not*
what one may, perfectly reasonably, interpret the child to mean, but

what the child *does* mean with his "this." His "this" is just like his inept childish drawings, which portray whatever he means them to portray.

When "this" holds a place for improvisation, it is not a true indexical. As filling in informally to denote this *particular* thing or that *particular* thing it is not an intentional icon element. It can have no Normal indexical adapting relation because it is not an element that is produced and interpreted by devices that are standardized to fit one another. Rather, either the speaker adapts to the hearer's natural dispositions to think of such and such in the context, or the hearer adapts to the speaker's natural disposition to be thinking of such and such in the context, or speaker and hearer meet one another halfway—or a misunderstanding occurs. When a misunderstanding does occur, it is not because the speaker or hearer does not know how to use the language or how to interpret it.

But, it may be asked, how often *does* "this" merely hold a place for improvisation? Considering the frequency of its use and the infrequency of misunderstanding over its use, isn't it plausible to suppose that there are a lot more conventional pointing devices or rules used with "this" than we are conscious of or than meet the eye? The difficulty in trying to reply to this question is not just that the evidence is largely buried in social history but that the border between improvised coordination and standardized coordination has width. Standardization admits of degree.

If a certain method of getting the hearer to think of the right thing is half the time invented over again by those learning to use "this" and half the time copied by them, then there is no clean answer to the question whether use of that method corresponds to a single reproductively established family. And if a certain method of getting the hearer to think of the right thing just naturally works with a good proportion of very small and naive hearers, and yet other learners have to make some trials and errors before discovering how to understand similarly positioned tokens of "this," then there is no general answer to the question whether when that method of positioning occurs, it works because speaker and hearer doings and reactings have been standardized to fit one another. Moreover, if there are certain methods of getting the hearer to think of the right thing that nearly *always* just naturally work with anyone, the question can still be asked whether the built-in dispositions of hearers to attend to this or that under the influence of a fellow creature who does this or that may itself have evolved in the human nervous system precisely for purposes of communication. Human infants are born with a great many dispositions that, it seems extremely likely, are there precisely in order to make learning to communicate with language possible. For example, apparently they attend to human faces and to human speech sounds with a very special built-in interest. Putting things graphically, perhaps in part they *mature into* rather than merely learning to attend to what the pointing finger indicates? And perhaps they partly *mature into*, rather than either just copying or just inventing, the device of pointing to things they want others to attend to? The idea is not totally absurd. That we are designed to communicate surely must have a good number of rather specific manifestations of one kind of another in our natural ways of attending to one another and of drawing one another's attention to things.

However, except in those cases in which "this" is accompanied by some kind of very common and evident pointing device and adorned with an accompanying category word, we are inclined, I believe, to treat "this" as an improvised sign of its referent. Improvised signs differ from public-language signs in that they themselves are neither true nor false. Accordingly, if a hearer does not understand what a speaker means by a certain unadorned token of "this," the question of the truth or falsity of the *sentence* the speaker has uttered does not arise until the reference has been clarified. The speaker has not *said* the true or *said* the false, although of course he may have meant the true or meant the false. On the other hand, when the hearer does understand what the speaker intends by "this," the speaker's sentence is treated in the usual way as having itself a truth value. And this makes sense. For where coordination is actually achieved in a Normal way between speaker and hearer, i.e., it is not achieved by freak accident, then either their doings and respondings actually have been standardized to fit one another in some subtle or less subtle way, or they have been *sort of* standardized to fit one another—or they fit one another in accordance with the purposing of the speaker or the hearer or both, in which case these doings and respondings bear at least a close analogy to standardized devices.

When "this" is accompanied by both a category word and a well-recognized pointing device, the sentence containing it does count, I believe, as itself having a truth value so long as there exists something, and only one thing, that bears the appropriate indexical adapting relation to it. Of course "being accompanied by a well-recognized pointing device" must mean being *purposefully* so accompanied. More accurately, this pointing device must have been reproduced on the model of ancestors used for pointing, or produced again after such ancestors by a system or program that had producing-the-same-again as a proper function. For example, I may say "this" *while* holding out (offering) the sugar to you, my "this" meaning not the sugar but a suggestion I am about to make. But my token of "this" does not display ambiguity in *Fregean* sense so long as my holding out the sugar bowl was not a member of a reproductively established family of holding-outs used for pointers. Ambiguity in dictionary sense, however, is another thing (see Chapter 8). It may be that I confuse *you* by holding out the sugar bowl while saying, "this," how to read my token of "this" being unclear.

Again, consider "this" when it is used coupled with a supporting category word: "this book," "this color," "this idea." How does the *category* word map? Category words are common nouns or, as used to be said, "common names." Common names are just that. They are names that are held in common by all members of a certain class: "hey, waiter!" "go home, dog!" "baby, see the baby," "lady, do you have the time?" In English and related languages common names are for the most part preceded by the definite or indefinite article, a number or quantifier, a possessive or a demonstrative adjective. What is common to these various different uses is that the common name, if it is singular, is supposed to map in each sentence onto an individual member of this class, if plural (distributive plural), onto each of various individual members of this class. What differentiates among these uses is that only in some cases is there some designated individual or individuals of the class onto which the common name, given its context, is supposed to map. In other cases, the common name is merely supposed to map onto some individual or other or onto some individuals or other in the class. Examples of the latter kind are indefinite descriptions. "A dog bit me yesterday" maps in accordance with Normal rules if there is any dog involved in any affair corresponding to "dog bit me yesterday." Then it has real value. If more than one dog bit me yesterday, then both of these dogs lend real value to "dog" in "a dog bit me yesterday." For there is no particular dog that "a dog" is supposed to map onto more than another. "A dog bit me yesterday" can function Normally because of the one dog or because of the other—it doesn't matter. (Much more will be said about indefinite descriptions in the next chapter.) But what happens when "this dog" is used instead of "a dog"?

The proper function of "this" coupled with "dog" is to bring it about that the hearer indentifies some particular proximate dog as the referent of "dog." For the moment we are glossing "identifies some particular dog as the referent of 'dog' " as "translates 'this dog' into an inner name that stands for a particular dog." When someone says "this dog," placing it in a sentence, Normally there is something definite—a particular dog—onto which "this dog" is supposed to map. Thus it is that "this dog" has a referent (either public or improvised or something in between), whereas "a dog" does not.

Sentences containing simple indexicals accompanied by pointing devices and category words or descriptions can fail to be indexically adapted because there is nothing having the right relation to them fitting the description that is held out with them. Such sentences lack truth values. Suppose that I point and say, "These peaches are very sweet" but what I (purposefully) point to are not in fact peaches but nectarines. My sentence, having no adapted sense, lacks a truth value. If you know that these are not peaches but gather that these must be what I mean and then believe me that they are sweet, you are believing *me*, not my sentence. That is, the belief you form is one that it is only a *derived* proper function of my sentence, derived from my intention in use, to produce. And you interpret the sentence not in the Normal way but, first, as a symptom of my state of mind. If we suppose, on the other hand, that you too take the nectarines to be peaches, then you make a mistake during the process of interpreting the sentence I used rather than interpreting it correctly in accordance with *its* proper mapping rules. In both these cases "the reference goes through," but not in accordance with any Normal explanation.

Now if it is true, as I have claimed, that "this," when accompanied with an appropriate category word and pointed out with some well-recognized pointing device, has a determinate public referent, one might expect to be able to supply evidence by describing cases in which what the speaker means by "this" disagrees with what his public token of "this" means. That is, one might expect to be able to describe cases parallel to the sort of case in which I mean timidity by "temerity," but my word "temerity" actually means boldness. In fact it is very hard to describe such cases. Consider two candidates.

First, suppose that I intentionally point in the direction of a very small table on which there are both a very large modern ashtray that I have not recognized as an ashtray and an antique porringer that is of normal ashtray size and which I have mistaken for an ashtray. I say "This ashtray is beautiful" meaning the porringer, not the ashtray. Have I *said* that the ashtray was beautiful even though I meant otherwise? The problem is that either there was a vagueness about what I pointed to, or, if I actually touched the porringer, my sentence fails to be indexically adapted—as in the case described just above where nectarines were mistaken for peaches. In neither case is there a clean-cut opposition between what I said and what I meant. Rather, the case would have to be one in which there were *two* ashtrays on the table and I awkwardly, that is, through lack of muscular or eye-hand co-ordination, touched the wrong one.

Second, suppose that, holding out a book to the hearer, I say "this book belonged to my great-grandfather," but I have inadvertently picked up the wrong book. The book I "really mean" is still on the bookshelf.

Clearly, what I have *said* is false. What is not so clear is whether what I *meant* is in fact other than what I said. For, I will argue, the situation here is not really that I and my token of "this" mean different things. It is that what I mean by "this" is ambiguous in Fregean sense. That is, my mental term corresponding to "this" is temporarily ambiguous in Fregean sense. On the one hand I mean the book my great-grandfather once owned; on the other hand I mean the book in my hand, having taken these to be the same.

The example is an especially interesting one because it brings to our attention a whole area that has been almost completely neglected in the philosophies of language and mind: analysis of the genesis and use of the *temporary* concepts with which we so often deal with items that are directly perceived or whose locations relative to items we directly perceive are temporarily known to us. Each of us possesses certain very general abilities—methods of temporary concept formation—these having either been programmed in or learned or most likely a mixture of both, that allow us to coin temporary inner terms for almost any item that we may perceive. The intensions attached to these temporary terms are for the most part implicit. They correspond to what we might call "tracking abilities." These abilities allow us to keep track of an object that remains in the environment for a time, sometimes literally by tracking it with eyes and head and even feet, while we gather various bits of information about it. That is, these abilities allow us to reidentify a thing that we are "tracking" as we compound information about it. Again, for the moment we can gloss "reidentifying" as reiterating the same inner term in inner sentences. (Or reiterating the same inner icon element in inner intentional icons. I really do not believe that all thought is in inner *sentences*, though it is convenient to talk that way.) These general abilities yield temporary concepts of individual things in the environment. But such concepts do not last longer than the tracking process. Indeed, the inner term types that these concepts govern typically do not last much longer than the tracking process. They do not last longer than this unless, while tracking, one either independently identifies the object being tracked as one for which one harbors a permanent inner term (Aha! my great-grandfather's book) or discovers and afterward remembers some permanent identifying characteristic that will allow this object to be re-identified later by some means other than tracking.

Consider, for example, the inner term that I temporarily possess, as I move about the kitchen, for a certain cup that I took out a moment ago intending to put my coffee in it. The cup is completely indistinguishable from a half dozen other cups we own. But for the moment, I do distinguish it. I keep track of the cup for a while (this is not as hard as keeping track of a bird I am trying to observe in the wild, but still I must keep track), and I may even express my inner term for it and part of the temporary concept that governs this term in outer language. Having lost track for the moment by one means of tracking, I may try another means: "Do you know what I did with the cup I took out for my coffee?" But the next day this cup has merged with its fellows again in my mind and become once more simply "one of our cups." Of course, it is theoretically possible that I might forever remember this cup as, say, *the cup I took out for my coffee about five in the evening on January twentieth, 1982.* But this would be unusual. First, I would not be likely to have a reason for bothering with such a memory. Second, even if I did happen to remember this cup under such a description, it is enormously unlikely that I should ever have a chance to reidentify this cup using this intension. Conceivably, someone else might remember the cup under the same description, and might even possess more usable intensions for the cup that could later be imparted to me—say, the cup is in fact distinguishable by a certain flaw in glazing. But this is unlikely enough that it is problematic whether retaining such a "concept" of that cup really counts as retaining an "ability" to iterate its inner name in new sentences, hence whether it counts as a "concept" at all.

Inner terms that are governed exclusively by tracking abilities or tracking intensions are indexical inner terms. The Normal explanations for their being able to serve their proper functions always involve at some point a reference to something that is perceived—either the referent itself or something that bears a known relation to the referent. And Normal mapping relations for percepts always have an indexical component. Indeed, one outstanding difference between perception and thought not mediated by concurrent perception is this. In perception one's contemporary temporal and spatial relation to the perceived is indexed; in unmediated thought it is not. But these reflections open up an enormous and complex area for investigation that it is not the purpose of this chapter to explore.

The programs that allow us to form temporary concepts and that correspond to applications of our tracking abilities have as proper functions to produce temporary inner terms that help map our immediate world for us. There are Normal explanations for how such programs work. And there are, derived from these, Normal explanations for how such inner maps serve their proper functions, these explanations lending these inner terms derived senses that become direct when the information gathered by tracking is consistent. Explicitly noticing anything in my immediate environment is coining a temporary inner term for it that is governed by my tracking abilities, even though I may not in fact bother to track the thing. (Even purposefully staring at a thing—keeping it in focus—is tracking it.) If, upon noticing or tracking a thing for a time I recognize it, then my tracking abilities come into play to provide temporary intensions to govern the inner term that I already possess for this thing.

But suppose that, rather than recognizing what I notice or track, I misidentify it. The result is that, temporarily at least, I possess an inner term that has two senses, hence is ambiguous in Fregean sense. The first sense is the sense that is derived from the application of my tracking abilities to what has been perceived and explicitly noticed. The second is the sense of the inner term that I already possessed. The case in which I hold out the wrong book saying "this was my great-grand-father's book" is an example of such temporary ambiguity in inner-term sense. In such a case what I mean by "this" is ambiguous. The case is not then like the case in which I say "temerity" meaning timidity but "temerity" really means boldness.[2]

I have tried to discuss "this" patiently. I have done so partly because "this" is an interesting word that has not commonly been treated with much subtlety by philosophers. But I have had an ulterior motive as well. The next chapter is about descriptions, and the little word "the" plays a central role in it. "The," as we will see, is not only etymologically connected with "that" the demonstrative; it is often very closely connected with "this" and "that" in function. A firm understanding of how the simpler and less confusing "this" works takes us a good way toward understanding the indexical and improvised uses of various kinds of definite descriptions.

Chapter 11
Descriptions

What are the stabilizing functions of definite and indefinite descriptions? In accordance with what kinds of rules do these map onto the world when serving their stabilizing functions Normally?

In order to answer these questions, we will have to strike out on our own. The only tradition that has talked about the way in which descriptions map is the Frege-Tarski tradition, from which we made a radical departure in Chapter 6. And the classical debate on descriptions among Russell,[1] Strawson,[2] and Donnellan,[3] insofar as it is a debate about the *functions* of descriptions, took place without benefit of the distinction we have drawn between speaker meaning or reference and public-language meaning or reference. " . . . 'referring' is not something an expression does," Strawson tells us, " . . . it is something that someone can use an expression to do."[4] But if the position of this book is correct, referring is *both* something a speaker does *and* something an expression does, and these two kinds of reference must be kept distinct. More recently Donnellan,[5] apparently following Kripke,[6] has introduced a distinction between "speaker reference" and "semantic reference," but this distinction is not the same as the one we have drawn, nor does it rest upon a general theory of language function. Although the analysis of definite descriptions that I propose in this chapter is heavily indebted to Russell's, Strawson's, and Donnellan's work, the purpose of the present chapter is not to enter into the Russell-Strawson-Donnellan dispute. It is to explain how definite and indefinite descriptions function, how they map onto the world, when definite descriptions are *indexical* and when they are not, and how the sense of a definite description determines its reference. It is because the sense, qua Normal mapping rule, of a definite description does determine its reference that I have called the Normal mapping rule for an expression its "sense" or "Fregean sense."

Individual objects do not usually have individual names. Instead, all objects of a given kind share a name. This shared or common name may be used in sentences to map any affair involving any of these individuals, mapping onto different individuals in different sentences. Of course, a common name also maps—i.e., its occurrences vary with— the attribute that is *being of that kind*, showing configurations in which this attribute stands as ingredient in world affairs. And this kind is always supposed to be identified by the hearer. For these reasons common names are always referential, always having at least kinds as referents. But sometimes the complex kind to which a common-name-plus-modifiers corresponds is supposed to be identified by the hearer *only* in order that a particular *individual* of this kind should then be identified as the referent of the whole expression, the kind and other properties mentioned of the individual being of no interest otherwise. That is, the hearer is supposed to translate the common-name-plus-modifiers (the description) into an inner proper name, whether he also remembers or marks the properties mentioned being immaterial: *"The girl in blue over there* dances well." In such cases I will say that the description taken as a whole is *"purely* referential." In other cases the hearer is not supposed to translate the description into an inner proper name at all—not supposed to identify an individual as referent for the whole: "Sally was talking to *a close friend* when I interrupted her." Then I will say that the description functions "purely descriptively." In a third kind of case the hearer is supposed both to identify an individual as referent for the description as a whole *and* to mark the description itself as relevant: "Why, *your youngest* is now taller than *your eldest!"* Such descriptions function both referentially and descriptively.

Indefinite Descriptions

In English, the article "a" or "an" placed before a common name has as a stabilizing function to cause the name plus its modifiers to function *purely* descriptively. For example, the purpose of *"a poisonous snake* bit Henry" is to adapt the hearer to a world affair involving only *the being of a poisonous snake* or, crudely, the ingredient poisonous-snakeness. True, if a poisonous snake bit Henry it is not poisonous-snakeness— not an attribute—that bit Henry. "A poisonous snake bit Henry," to be true, must map a world affair involving an individual snake, some individual snake being the real value of "snake" in the sentence. But *which* snake doesn't matter for the proper functioning of the sentence. What matters is only the disposition of poisonous-snakeness in the world in relation to Henry.

The individual that is the real value (or the individuals that are the real values) of a common name in an indefinite description is (or are) determined by the content of the *rest* of the sentence, not by the description alone. Consider "a chair" in "Adam made a chair." Whether or not the entire sentence "Adam made a chair" has real value, hence whether "a chair" has real value in this sentence, is of course determined by whether or not Adam made a chair. Further, which individual chair is the real value of "a chair," if any individual chair is that value, is entirely determined by the content of the *rest* of the sentence. Which chair this real value is depends only upon which chair Adam made. Further, if Adam made more than one chair, each of these chairs is equally a real value of "chair" in "Adam made a chair." A *definite* description, I will soon argue, is supposed to map onto an individual that is determined by it alone—determined *prior* to the mapping of the whole sentence. But the job of an indefinite description is only to map onto at least one individual *in the context of the whole sentence.* Indefinite descriptions do not then have individuals as referents.

Indefinite descriptions map onto individuals but without referring to them even when in predicate nominative position. Consider "I know a mother who is a professor and an active scholar and a lion tamer on the side." Here "a mother," "a professor," "an active scholar," and "a lion tamer" must have as real values the *same* individual, just as in "Xavier went skiing and he didn't like it," "Xavier" and "he" must have the same real value. In both cases this identity of value is indicated by the grammar. Similarly, in "Fido is *a dog*" the real value of "a dog," as indicated by the grammar, must be the same as the real value of the subject "Fido." The sentence "Fido is a dog" thus shows the disposition in the world of the property *being a dog* in relation to Fido— a disposition that differs, for example, from that shown in "Fido was bitten by a dog."

Although an indefinite description is of course supposed to have a real value and this value is always an individual or individuals, the job of an indefinite description is not to translate into an inner proper name for this individual or into inner names for these individuals. An indefinite description Normally translates into an inner *description*, containing, still, a *common* name. Such inner descriptions sometimes help to represent very complex configurations of properties. For example, consider the configuration mapped by "I met a child in the street trying to sell polished rocks" followed by several other sentences beginning with "he"—e.g., "He told me . . . ", " . . . then he went with me to . . . ," "He said that his mother and father . . . ," etc. Possibly the main history of a child is imparted this way—a tangled web of properties instantiated in various relations to one another. But the proper functions that account for the proliferation of such indefinite descriptions—and indefinite short stories—are functions for the performance of which it is immaterial which individuals lend the descriptions real value. Again, indefinite descriptions are not, taken as wholes, referential terms.

But it has sometimes been thought that indefinite descriptions *are* referential terms. Suppose, for example, that I show you a rubbing of a bas-relief, saying, "A friend of mine from India gave me this." Surely, in saying "a friend of mine from India" I am talking about a particular individual. Say, it is Rakesh. So, it is thought, Rakesh must be the referent of this token of "a friend of mine from India," even though I do not tell you exactly who this referent is but leave the matter indefinite. But to talk this way invites confusion. It is of course true that I know Rakesh to be the real value of "friend of mine" in my sentence. And it is true that I *intended* that Rakesh be the real value of "friend of mine." Hence *I* am referring to Rakesh in one perfectly good sense of "referring"—a sense in which *people* rather than terms refer. If you ask, "To whom do you refer?" after I have said "A friend of mine from India," I must reply "Rakesh." But if you do not ask me or if I fail to reply, then if Rakesh asks me afterward "Did you tell them that I gave this to you?" I must reply, "No, I did not mention you." For my words did not refer to Rakesh. It is neither a direct proper function nor, if mine is a stabilizing use of an indefinite description, is it a derived proper function of my token of "a friend of mine from India" to translate into an inner proper name for Rakesh. It is neither its direct nor its derived proper function to do anything requiring it to map, specifically, an affair involving Rakesh. (Of course I might say "a friend of mine from India" archly, in such a way that you will know that I intend you to know who this friend is. But that would be a whimsical use, not a stabilizing use of indefinite description.)[7]

Suppose that I have made a mistake. It was not in fact my Indian friend Rakesh but my Indian friend Ravi who gave the rubbing to me. My sentence "A friend of mine from India gave me this" would still be true. Surely it cannot be true yet not true of *its own subject's* referent! So Rakesh cannot be the referent of "friend of mine" in the sentence. Also, should you later explain to someone else in the room "An Indian friend of RM's gave her this rubbing," it is clear that Rakesh cannot be the referent of *your* token of "an Indian friend." There is not even anyone to whom *you* refer with this description, let alone anyone to whom the description refers.

On the other hand, if "A friend of mine from India gave me this" is true in accordance with a fully Normal explanation, it is a *natural* sign of an affair in the world with which it is causally connected. Intentional icons are not usually true by accident. There are Normal explanations for their truth, these explanations connecting the icons with what they icon in accordance with natural laws operating in situ (different ones, of course, for different speakers). The causal connection of intentional icon with real value makes it possible for a hearer to use an intentional icon as a natural indexical sign. Treating "A friend of mine from India gave me this" as a natural indexical sign of an affair in the world, it indexes some particular affair involving some particular person. That particular person, let us again suppose, is Rakesh. Granted this, the hearer of the sentence can coin an inner name for Rakesh, just as he might coin an inner name for any other thing encountered via a natural indexical sign that he knows how to interpret. At least he can always do this granted that he knows how to track the thing or how to supply a permanent intension with which to govern iteration of its name. And in this case, supplying a permanent intension is easy enough. The person in question is the person responsible for RM's utterance of "A friend of mine from India" and also the person who gave RM this rubbing.

Every indefinite description that has real value in accordance with a Normal explanation has in this way what might be called a "natural referent." Even indefinite descriptions of characters in stories or jokes that are passed on through hundreds of tellings sometimes have natural referents, though to track down these natural referents would often be quite impossible, the intension *person whom this story was originally about* being quite useless. But natural reference is not public reference. It is not qua cause of it that a name or description has a public referent but qua having Normal mapping rules that have accounted for inter-preters' past successes in using earlier members of its reproductively established family. Hence a name or description token can have a public referent without having a natural referent (e.g., definite descrip-tion tokens that refer by accident). And hence, as in the case of indefinite descriptions, a language device can have a natural referent without having that referent as a public referent.

Simple Descriptions with "The"

The Indo-European forebear of English "the" was "to," a demonstrative pronoun. The Old English form of "the" was "se" (masculine singular) which, according to the *Oxford English Dictionary*, served as an article and also as a demonstrative adjective, the modern English "that" being derived from another inflection of "se." This suggests that the oldest uses of "the" are probably demonstrative uses and that it may be useful to try to understand various modern uses in the light of this.

Consider, for example, the commonest of all occurrences of the definite article "the"—"the" followed only by a common name N. In these occurrences "the" functions in ways quite similar to the ways "this" functions when followed by a common name except that "the" does not necessarily point to something proximate. Sometimes "the N" has a clearly public referent, the rules in accordance with which it is supposed to map including a clear indexical adapting relation. But sometimes "the N" holds a place for improvisation. Then it is not, strictly speaking, indexical, and its referent is not, strictly speaking, public. It informally denotes what the speaker supposes will naturally come to the hearer's mind in the context. Further, as in the case of "this," the border between these two kinds of cases may well have width.

That "the N" sometimes has a clear indexical adapting relation is illustrated by uses of "the N" that function like third person pronouns, making reference to an N just mentioned or described. For example, I can say either "A man in town was bitten by a dog yesterday but luckily *it* didn't have rabies" or "A man in town was bitten by a dog yesterday but luckily *the dog* didn't have rabies." This particular use of "the N" can follow an indefinite introduction of "N," as in the illustration given. "The N" following upon the heels of "an N" is adapted by this relation and is supposed to have not a referent but a *real value* in common with its antecedent. (So far as I can make out, this is the only extremely common use of "the" that does not signal reference of some kind. Indeed, as we will see, to signal reference is the *main* function that "the" has in many contexts.) But, of course, where "the N" follows after a definite description or proper name rather than an indefinite description, it *is* referential. Its indexical adapting relation is *being the referent of its antecedent*, and it is supposed to translate into an inner singular term.

Examples of the second kind of case—cases in which "the N" has an improvised or perhaps half-improvised referent—are ubiquitous: "Where's the cat?" "Would you hand me the screwdriver?" "Pass the sugar" "Did you put gas in the car?" "We walked by the duck pond and saw the ducks." As in the case of an unadorned "this," the distinction between public meaning and speaker meaning partially breaks down in these cases of "the N." Of course, it is public that "the N" must have an N as a referent. But which N it (improvisationally) refers to may be entirely determined by the speaker's intentions. About this particular employment of "the," Strawson is right in blurring the distinction between what the speaker refers to and the reference of the description itself. Often it is indeed the "use" of the description "the N" that lends it a referent—an improvised referent. In these cases it is not so that the speaker strictly *says* what he means by "the N." Hence if the hearer does not grasp the speaker's meaning correctly, we do not think of a sentence containing such a token of "the N" as being either true or false until the speaker has clarified the reference.

In the case of "an N," the rest of the sentence determines which N or Ns are real values of "N." In the most common cases of "the N," the rest of the sentence determines whether "N" has a real value or not, but *which N* that real value would have to be is determined prior to the rest of the sentence. That is why "the N" is referential in these cases.

Prior Classification of Complex Descriptions

It will be a help when discussing more complex descriptions with "the" to have certain distinctions and terms with which to express these distinctions already on the table. First it will be helpful to distinguish among certain kinds of descriptions that are distinguishable *prior* to the definite-indefinite distinction.

Perhaps most important is a distinction between descriptions that are necessarily identifying, such as "eldest son of . . . ," and descriptions that are not necessarily identifying, such as "son of. . . ." Necessarily identifying descriptions are easily formed with the help of superlatives, for if a superlative description describes anything at all in a category, it describes just one. For example, perhaps no one in the room is tallest, best violinist, or first in line, but if someone is, necessarily no one *else* is.

Descriptions that attribute responsibility for a specific action are necessarily identifying descriptions. *Principia Mathematica* had two authors but, for just this reason, it is not true of Whitehead that he wrote *Principia Mathematica* or that he was *Principia Mathematica*'s author. Julius Caesar was murdered by a gang but, for just this reason, it is not true of Brutus that he killed Caesar or that he was Caesar's murderer. "Author of . . . ," "murderer of . . . " and other singular descriptions that attribute responsibility for an action are *empty* if more than one was responsible for the action, a plural description being required instead: "authors of . . . ," "murderers of. . . ." Correlatively, "one of *Principia*'s authors" and "one of Caesar's murderers" refer to parts of collectives, not to members of classes. Compare: from "Bill is one of John's sons," "Bill is John's son" follows; from "Brutus was one of Caesar's murderers," "Brutus was Caesar's murderer" does not follow. Similarly, "boy that delivers our paper" and "man that teaches Jane piano" are necessarily identifying descriptions. If various boys deliver our paper, "he delivers our paper" is not true of any one of these boys. Rather, "he sometimes delivers our paper" or "he often delivers our paper" or "he is one of the boys that deliver our paper" is true instead. If more than one boy delivers our paper, then no one falls under the description "boy that delivers our paper."

A third kind of description that is necessarily identifying is exemplified by "king of . . . ," "chairman of . . . ," "president of . . . ," "Duke of," "secretary of," "capital of . . . ," etc. An organization can have co-chairmen, occasionally two kings have shared a throne, and a country can have a summer capital and a winter capital. But "chairman of . . . " and "king of . . . " and "capital of . . . ," like "tallest of . . . ," all imply uniqueness when used bare. If the two tallest are equally tall, I cannot say of *each* that he is tallest. Similarly, I cannot say of one of the cochairmen simply that he is chairman, or of a king who shares his throne simply that he is king, or of the summer capital of C simply that it is "capital of C."

The distinction, prior to the definite-indefinite distinction, between necessarily identifying descriptions and descriptions that are not necessarily identifying is of some importance. For it is easy to think that it is the little word "the," as opposed to the little word "a," that turns descriptions such as "the King of France," "the author of Waverly," and "the boy that delivers our papers" into descriptions purporting to be identifying. But "Smith's murderer," an expression without "the," is identifying too, "a murderer of Smith" (as opposed to "one of Smith's murderers") being impossible. Similarly, "a (present) king of France" (as opposed to "one of the (present) kings of France"), "an author of Waverly," and "a boy that delivers our paper" are not possible, or at least not correct, any more than "a tallest person in the room" is possible.

Within the broad category of descriptions that are *not* necessarily identifying there are descriptions that happen, but only accidentally, to be identifying. We can call these "accidentally identifying descriptions." "Jack's sister" is accidentally identifying if it happens that Jack has just one sister. "Student that got an A last term in my introductory class" is accidentally identifying if I gave just one student in that class an A.

Within the broad category of descriptions that are not necessarily identifying there are also descriptions that have in fact multiple instances: "child that ate too much birthday cake," "man that ran a mile in less than four minutes," "dog that bit someone," "black and white dog." Call these descriptions "multivalued descriptions."

Last, we can divide *all* descriptions into those that are empty and those that are filled. Accidentally identifying descriptions and multivalued descriptions are, as such, always filled. For descriptions fall into these categories by virtue of happening to have exactly one or by virtue of happening to have multiple instances. But necessarily identifying descriptions may be empty or filled. Descriptions are necessarily identifying by virtue of their sense rather than the accidental number of their instances.

Two Kinds of Referent Introduction

A second kind of distinction that it will be helpful to have on the table before discussing complex definite descriptions is a distinction between two sorts of referent introduction.

A description that has a referential function is supposed to precipitate, in the hearer, an act of identification of its referent. For the moment we are modeling the act of identifying an individual as the referent of a description as the act of translating that description into an inner proper name. But does this inner proper name have to be one that is already in the hearer's inner vocabulary? Or will it be enough if he coins an inner name for the purpose, this name to be governed by an intension corresponding to the description the speaker supplies? For example, if the speaker says "tallest man in Toonerville" and the hearer does not know this man, will it be enough if he coins an inner name, say TMT, for this man and, pending the accumulation of more intensions to help govern its iteration, proceeds to govern the iteration of TMT with the intension "tallest man in Toonerville"?

In Part IV I will argue that the act of coining an inner name that has a sense and an intension, though not a full-fledged act of identifying, is an act of potential identification of the referent of that name. Here it will be enough simply to distinguish two cases in which a hearer translates a common name or description into an inner proper name— the case in which the proper name is an old one already in the hearer's inner vocabulary and the case in which the proper name is coined for the occasion, deriving its sense only from the adapted but direct proper function of the description that introduces it. In the latter case, the inner proper name will have, at first, only a derived sense, as does an inner term "monotreme" that has been derived from the outer public term "monotreme" but that has not been put to work enough times to have acquired a direct proper function (see Chapter 9). Descriptions that are translated into *old* proper names, I will say, serve the "old referent-" or "familiar-referent-introducing" function; those that are translated into newly coined proper names serve the "new-referent-introducing" function.

Having thus sharply divided the referring functions of descriptions into two—the new-referent-introducing function and the old-referent-introducing function—we should note that the various referring functions that descriptions perform can also be looked upon as falling on two continua.

A description that introduces a familiar referent refers to something for which the hearer already possesses an inner name. This inner name must be governed by a concept. And this concept may be very rich in intensions or very lean in intensions. For example, the concepts that I have of each of the members of my immediate family are very rich in both implicit and explicit intensions. There are dozens of ways that I know how to recognize (not, of course, infallibly) each of these people in the flesh, via various names and via dozens of descriptions. By comparison with these concepts, the concept that I have of the first degree-holding American woman doctor is very impoverished. I have forgotten her name; I cannot at the moment recall anything else that I know about her that would surely be identifying; I could not recognize her in a picture or recognize her handwriting or her voice. Indeed, my concept of her seems to include but one intension: *first degree-holding American woman doctor*. Yet my concept of the person that murdered Alma Rae is leaner still. In the case of the first degree-holding American woman doctor, I still remember a good number of facts about her that could help to distinguish her from others. But nobody knows who murdered Alma Rae or anything about that person (i.e., under that description). Then there is this case. I know that someone won the Boston Marathon last spring. And I know that this man must be the man that was presented the 1982 Boston Marathon trophy, for if he'd died on the spot or refused the trophy, I surely would have heard *that*. And he must be the man the *Hartford Courant* said, next day, won the race, or I'd have heard of that mistake. At least three intensions govern my concept of this man, but two of these are rather weak, i.e., not likely to find use. So there is a continuum of possible cases of old-referent introduction, beginning with the case in which a very familiar referent is introduced and proceeding to the case (e.g., the Alma Rae case) in which the concept the hearer already had of the referent consisted only of the intension that corresponds to the description itself.

The second continuum is this. When a description is used to introduce a new referent, an intension corresponding to the description itself will be the only intension that the hearer has at first for the inner term he coins. But it may be that, had the hearer bothered to think about it, he would have been dead certain of the existence of this referent without being told: "John's mother." Or it may be that he would have been fairly certain of its existence or not surprised to learn of its existence or, on the other hand, very surprised to learn of its existence. Compare: "conductor of the Cleveland Orchestra," "John's eldest brother," "woman that teaches the Queen of England karate."

Complex Descriptions in Ur

Before considering complex descriptions with "the" in English, we should note that not all languages force an article before common names as do English and related languages. Rather, common nouns in these languages occur for the most part bare or are sometimes accompanied by a demonstrative. We can get some feel for what a language that does not employ articles is like by thinking of Pidgin English. Try "tall white man has red hair comes today." Or consider the way possessives are used in Modern English. If I say "My brother is coming today," I use no definite or indefinite article. "My brother" is neither a definite nor an indefinite description. I can use it if I have seven brothers all unknown to you or if I have one brother well known to you. Indeed, what would I say instead of "my brother" if I wished to convey that I expected you to know exactly who I meant, "the brother of mine" not being exactly idiomatic?

Consider a hypothetical language that contains proper names, common names, and demonstratives corresponding to "this" and "that" but no articles and no way of embedding clauses that indicates whether these are or are not supposed to contain identifying information about their subjects. Call this language "Ur." Affairs involving things with proper names are mapped in Ur by sentences containing these proper names. Affairs involving things without proper names are mapped by sentences containing common names. If a speaker of Ur wishes the hearer to identify as an old referent the individual he has in mind when he uses a common name, he has two options. If the situation is right, he can use the demonstratives corresponding to "this" or "that" with the common name. Alternatively, he can make some introductory remarks about the individual he has in mind that will probably make it clear to a hearer familiar with this individual that he is purposefully mapping *this* individual with a certain common name before going on to say something that is new to the hearer about this individual. That is, he can begin with a description of this individual, not with the intention of conveying information about *it* or with the intention of conveying information about the disposition of a complex kind as ingredient in world affairs but with the intention of getting the hearer to translate the common name he uses into an inner *proper* name for that individual. He can use an introductory description with the intention that it serve a merely referring function. Or he can use such a description intending that it serve both a referring and a descriptive function. For example, if a speaker of Ur says "*Queen of Ur* sometimes goes barefoot," it is possible that he should intend this both as a comment on the character of a well-known person to be identified by the hearer *and* as a comment on the stature of some who go barefoot (or on the humility of some in high places). The information contained in "Queen of Ur" (as expressed in the embedded sentence "[a] Queen is of Ur") may not be intended to be new to the hearer, but the information that *a queen* goes barefoot may be intended to be new.

Keeping this in mind, let us inquire which of the various kinds of descriptions that we have distinguished might be used by a speaker of Ur to introduce a referent. And let us generalize the question to include the problem of introducing new as well as old referents to hearers of Ur.

Clearly only a necessarily identifying description could be used to introduce a new referent to a hearer of Ur. If the referent is brand new to the hearer, he being supposed to coin an inner name for it, he must be supplied with an intension of some sort by which to govern iteration of that inner name. True, a description that was only accidentally identifying could supply a perfectly good intension by which to govern the new inner name. However, the bare use of such a description (say, "RGM's sister," this description happening in fact to be identifying) will not convey to the hearer *that* it is identifying; yet to indicate *that* it is identifying (say, "RGM's only sister") is, simply, to use a necessarily identifying description instead.

Either a necessarily identifying description or an accidentally identifying description could be used by a speaker of Ur to introduce a familiar referent so long as the hearer already knew that the description applied to this familiar thing and, in the case of accidentally identifying descriptions, so long as the hearer already knew that it applied *uniquely* to the familiar thing.

But it is not always easy, given a particular object or person, to come up with a ready and brief description of it that is identifying, that one is sure the hearer knows is identifying, and that one is sure the hearer already knows applies to that object or person. Often it is more natural to employ a description that does not discriminate among all objects in the world but discriminates only among objects likely to be uppermost in the hearer's mind. That is, often it is more natural to employ a nonidentifying description or one you don't know whether is identifying and to rely upon the hearer's limits of acquaintance, his special perspective on the world, and his grasp of your perspective to finish the job of distinguishing. For example, the speaker of Ur might introduce a familiar referent and then inform his hearer about it in this manner: "Dog is black; it bit man yesterday; I killed it." And he might do this despite having no opinion about whether or not more than one black dog in the world was the biter of a man yesterday and despite having no expectation that his hearer should have such an opinion either. That is, he might use a nonidentifying description to improvise communication. Then, if all goes according to plan, the hearer understands which dog was killed, translating "Dog is black; it bit man yesterday" not into an inner description but into an inner proper name. But let us look at "Dog is black; it bit man yesterday; I killed it" from the standpoint of the hearer.

On hearing "Dog is black; it bit man yesterday; I killed it," the hearer of Ur has to figure out, on the basis of external evidence, whether the speaker does or does not expect him to identify the dog in question. If there are no external cues about this available (facial expression, tone of voice?), then either he will happen or he will not happen to identify the dog, that is all. The hearer of such a set of clauses is given no guides by which to monitor whether he is fully following the speaker or not—whether he is ending up with what the speaker intends. It is as though the speaker handed the hearer a sketchy picture of certain entwined affairs and left it completely up to him to figure out if he was expected to recognize anything or anyone in particular in the picture.

Given this ambiguity, wouldn't it be quite natural for a speaker of Ur to try to help his hearer by indicating when he expects him to identify a familiar referent? And might not a demonstrative such as "this" or "that" quite easily be turned to this purpose? "This" and "that" are often used for improvised reference. Abstracting from the requirement that the referent of "this" or "that" should be *near*, such an extension of the use of demonstratives would be natural. It is easy to understand how Modern English "the" and Modern English "that" came to be derived from the same Old English demonstrative. But before turning to complex descriptions as they appear in Modern English, let us summarize the functions in Ur of the various kinds of descriptions we have distinguished.

In Ur, necessarily identifying descriptions have three alternative stabilizing functions. First, they are used to introduce familiar referents into conversations. In order to serve this purpose, it is necessary of course that the hearer already know that the description is true of the referent. Second, they are used to introduce new referents into conversations. When used to introduce either old or new referents, these descriptions may or may not have a describing function as well. For example, if a speaker says pointedly to his littlest child, "littlest girl in family has taken biggest piece again!" "littlest girl in family" plays both a referring and a describing role. Third, necessarily identifying descriptions are sometimes used purely descriptively, the point being merely to *characterize* or to map interesting relations among attributes as ingredients in world affairs. For example, in "Johnny is tallest boy in family," used *not* to express an identity (judgments of identity will be discussed in Chapter 12), the referent Johnny is already introduced by "Johnny," "tallest boy in family" having a descriptive function only.

Or consider *"First woman medicine man in Urland* came to no good end," the interest lying not at all in this person but only in the connection between being a medicine woman or first medicine woman and coming to no good end.

Descriptions that are not necessarily identifying have just two alternative functions in Ur. They can function purely descriptively: *"Man I met at market* said hard winter comes" (reading "a man"). Or they can serve to introduce familiar referents, either with or without simultaneous descriptive force. Which of these two functions a description that is not necessarily identifying is supposed to serve, the hearer must guess or gather from context.

Complex Descriptions in English

In Modern English the article "the" is used routinely with *all* necessarily identifying singular descriptions that are built upon common nouns. Of course, one can say "He was king of England at that time" just as one can say "He was tallest in his class," but here "king" functions as "tallest" functions—as an adjective, not as a common noun. One cannot say "King of France at that time was wise" or "He admired tallest boy in his class." Nor can one say "a tallest boy in his class" or "a king of France at that time," the latter not even if there were two kings of France at that time. (See above, "Prior Classification of Complex Descriptions.") Because "the" is forced with all necessarily identifying singular descriptions in English, all three of the functions that necessarily identifying descriptions in Ur could serve are served by necessarily identifying descriptions plus "the" in English. For example, one can imagine the italicized part of *"the first degree-holding American woman doctor* graduated from medical school in 1849" serving a purely descriptive function, the date of entrance of women into the field of medicine being the point rather than the iteration of an old inner name or the coining of a new inner name preliminary to collecting more information about this woman. One can imagine it serving the new-referent-introducing function, the speaker then going on to impart considerable information about this interesting person. And one can imagine "the first degree-holding American woman doctor" (especially if one has forgotten her name) being used to introduce a completely familiar referent. "The" used with necessarily identifying descriptions is thus superfluous. It neither signals that the description is to serve a particular function nor is it needed to signal that the description is identifying, for necessarily identifying descriptions are necessarily identifying without "the." "The" used with necessarily identifying descriptions is merely *idiomatic* English, not functional English. "The" has *powers* only when used with other kinds of descriptions.

Used with singular descriptions that are not necessarily identifying, "the" almost invariably signals the familiar-referent-introducing function. If such a description is in fact multivalued, performance of the new-referent-introducing function is obviously impossible for it, for the description does not offer any intension by which to govern iteration of a new term. And it is mandatory to signal the purely descriptive function by "a" or "an" in the case of all but necessarily identifying descriptions. Very occasionally "the," used with emphasis, signals that a description is accidentally identifying. Thus I might say, with emphasis, "*The* student that got an A in my introductory class this term was a freshman." But I cannot use it to introduce a new referent without this emphasis. If I tried to, you would suppose that I expected you *already* to know of the student I meant, and to know of him under that description. You would be left racking your brains trying to remember which A student I might recently have mentioned or would expect you to think of in the context.

Contra Russell, the primary function of "the" with complex singular descriptions then is not to indicate uniqueness. It is to indicate that the description is referential. The exception is the necessarily identifying description that functions purely descriptively. But even here, translation of the description into an inner proper name is always possible, and it cannot hurt if it occurs. For example, though the point of "The first degree-holding American woman doctor graduated from medical school in 1849" may be only to comment on how early or how late it was when women entered the medical profession, still it cannot hurt communication if the hearer happens to know who this woman is and registers the date 1849 as *her* date of graduation.

How Referring Descriptions Map onto the World

Multivalued descriptions with "the," unless these are functioning pronominally (see above, "Simple Descriptions with 'the' ") are invariably referential, but unless there are more unconscious standardized rules for their use than meet the eye, their referents seem to be informal or improvised. Accidentally identifying descriptions with "the," however, are indexical. And relative to a referring function, necessarily identifying definite descriptions are also indexical. In order to see exactly how the indexicality works in these cases, let us take descriptions of the form "the _____ N that . . . ," e.g., "the black dog that bit Bill," as our example, other forms of description that can perform a referring function indexically having analyses that are parallel in obvious ways.

In indexically referring descriptions of the form "the _____ N that . . . ," "the" coupled with "that" shows that the hearer is to identify a specific individual as the value of the common name "N" and that he is to use the embedded sentence represented by " _____ N" (i.e., the embedded sentence "N is _____ ") and the embedded sentence represented by "that . . . " to this end. The indexical adaptor for such a description must be a real value of "N" in the embedded sentence "N is _____ " and a real value of "that" in the embedded sentence "that . . . ," which value is unique. If no such value exists, then the description is like the pigment arrangers of a floating chameleon. There is nothing in particular that it is supposed to do; the description has no adapted sense. If properly adapted, the entire description has as a focused proper function to translate into an inner proper name denoting an individual N.

"The _____ N that . . . " thus contains within itself two embedded icons or maps of world affairs. But the purpose of these icons—of these embedded sentences—is quite different from the purpose of an independent clause or sentence taken as a whole. The embedded sentence does not map in order to or merely in order to adapt the hearer to the affair it maps. It maps in order to show to which complex category belongs that to which its subject is supposed to correspond in the context of the *independent* clause containing it. The rest of the indexical adapting relation for the description (i.e., being unique), *taken with the actual world*, then determines a referent. The independent clause in which the description occurs then adapts the hearer to an affair involving this referent. Thus it is that the *sense* of a referring definite description— the mapping rules that determine the kinds of affairs its *embedded* icons are supposed to map onto—determines the *referent* of the description— the thing onto which the description as a whole is supposed to map in the context of the sentence entire.

It should now be clear why I have chosen to call the rules for how a language element is supposed to map onto the world its "sense." For it is with respect to these rules that different definite descriptions characteristically differ even though having the same referent, and the latter difference is what Frege called a difference in "*Sinn*," or sense. Contrary to Frege's view, however, it is our view that having a referent is, merely, having a sense of a special kind. A term or description that has a referent is distinguished by the fact that there *is* something definite onto which it is supposed to map in a sentence, this something being determined prior to the content of the rest of the sentence. Other descriptions are such that they are supposed to map onto something of a certain kind but *without* there being something definite of that kind onto which they are supposed to map. But having a referent and having a sense are clearly very similar kinds of havings.

The indexical adapting relation for an indexical referring description of the form "the ____ N that . . . " is, then, *being the only real value of both "N" and "that."* This relation is not mediated by time, place, or relation to a speaker. Hence, in those cases in which no indexicals appear *within* the embedded sentences "N is ____ " and "that . . . ," it does not matter where, when, or by whom a token of such a description is uttered; like a proper name, it has always the same referent. It thus appears to have a referent qua type. The appearance is misleading, for as in the case of any other indexical, its referent is not determined by the senses of its combined elements alone but by the relational proper functions of these as adapted to the context in which it is uttered, namely, the actual world.

Descriptions of Properties

There are two kinds of descriptions that still need to be discussed. One kind are such universal descriptions as "All A's," "All A's that are ø," "Every A," and "No A's." It will be easiest to discuss universal descriptions after discussing negation. I will do this at the end of Chapter 14 under the heading "All." The second kind of description is description of properties.

That definite descriptions of properties are possible, indeed common, is seldom discussed by philosophers. Definite descriptions, it is generally supposed, have *referents*, and very few feel comfortable speaking of properties as referents. That there are definite descriptions of properties has thus been a source of more embarrassment than enlightenment in the tradition. But in the context of this essay there is no reason for embarrassment in speaking of properties as referents. Properties are real-world variants just as individuals are.

Descriptions of properties sometimes occur with an indefinite article ("a somber color," "a distance measured in light-years") and sometimes with the definite article ("the color of cranberries," "the length of my arm"). They function just as descriptions of individuals do, being either indefinite or definite and, when definite, serving either a referential function or a descriptive function or both. But descriptions of properties also occur without an article. This is because they can occur without a noun, and only nouns take articles. Indeed, most descriptions of properties occur in this way, bare. It is these bare descriptions of properties that deserve discussion, not so much because they are remarkable in any way, but because they never seem to *be* discussed.

Compare "John is the same height as Bill" with "John is (just) as tall as Bill." The first of these sentences contains a description with the definite article: "the same height as Bill." "Same height as Bill" is a necessarily identifying description, and the use of "the" with necessarily identifying descriptions, we have noted, is mandatory in English. It does not always indicate that a referent for the description is supposed to be identified by the hearer. Accordingly, "the same height as Bill" might function purely descriptively in the sentence "John is the same height as Bill," conveying to the hearer only that Bill and John are equivalent in height, i.e., that a certain relation obtains between them. Or it might function referentially, the hearer being supposed to identify the height in question. That is, it might be that the hearer is presumed to know *how* tall Bill is—not necessarily in feet and inches, but to have some prior idea of Bill's height. But "John is the same height as Bill" is equivalent to "John is (just) as tall as Bill" Accordingly, one who says "John is as tall as Bill" also may or may not purpose that the hearer will identify the height in question. "As tall as Bill," like all necessarily identifying descriptions, whether in English or in Ur, has both a referential function and a descriptive function.

Necessarily identifying descriptions of properties are not usually built upon common nouns but upon terms for relations: "He is *as tall as* Bill," "He is *just behind* Bill," "He is *with* Bill," "He is *at* home," "That is *colder than* ice," "It *feels like* falling," "She slept *later than* Susan did," etc. All such descriptions function exactly as do necessarily identifying descriptions with "the." Sometimes they have a referential function, sometimes a purely descriptive function, and sometimes both a referential and a descriptive function, these being alternative stabilizing functions of these descriptions.

Chapter 12

"Is" and "Exists": Represented Referents and Protoreferents

Paradoxes associated with sentences such as "Pegasus does not exist" and "Cicero is Tully" are well known. If one takes the realist position that the usual job of an indicative sentence is to represent an affair in the world by mapping it, to what world-affair element does "Pegasus" correspond if Pegasus doesn't exist? And if Cicero *is* Tully, what world affair is there for "Cicero is Tully" to represent beyond the affair that Cicero is Cicero? To what do "Cicero" and "Tully" correspond such that "Cicero is Tully" might be informative, which, under some circumstances, it surely might be? Realists' responses to these paradoxes have mainly been of one kind. Realists have looked for entities other than Pegasus in the flesh or Cicero himself for "Pegasus" and "Cicero" and "Tully" to correspond to. Meinong introduced "objects" some of which do not exist into his ontology, and Moore[1] introduced "concepts" in much the same spirit so that "Pegasus" and other empty names would have something to correspond to. Frege introduced "senses" so that referentially equivalent terms might correspond to different senses while still having the same referent. Panayot Butchvarov has recently introduced "objects" alongside ordinary "entities" for these words to correspond (in part) to.[2] Following Carnap, others have maintained that in one way or another it is really the *words* "Pegasus" and "Cicero" and "Tully" that are talked about in such sentences.

Rather than looking for novel objects for "Pegasus" and "Cicero" and "Tully" to represent in these puzzling contexts, I will propose that referential terms do not always serve a referential or representing function. There are certain kinds of sentences that are not representations, nor are terms these sentences contain. In this chapter I will argue that neither sentences containing the "is" of identity nor sentences containing "exists" are sentences that represent. On the other hand, I will argue that such sentences *are* intentional icons. They are intentional icons of a more primitive kind than representations. Although they must map in accordance with definite mapping rules if they are to serve their proper functions in accordance with Normal explanations, the variants of the world affairs they map are not supposed to be identified. I will argue that these sentences are icons of the relations of *words* to each other or to the world. But the hearer has no need to apply concepts of words or concepts of word-world relations in order to process them Normally. He does not process them by translating them into inner icons of affairs involving words.

The "Is" of Identity

That there is a difference between the "is" in "Cicero is Roman" and the "is" in "Cicero is Tully" is generally believed, although exactly what the difference is remains a matter of dispute. The first kind of "is" is sometimes called the "is" of predication, the second the "is" of identity. The "is" of identity has the limelight in this chapter. But toward the end I will argue that these two "is"'s do not correspond to different dictionary senses of "is" but to two alternative stabilizing functions of the same least type "is," which functions are inevitably joined together.

The question has sometimes been raised whether the "is" of identity expresses a relation and, if so, between what and what. A relation between a thing and itself? Or a relation between expressions? Or between senses or intensions? Suppose that we tackle the problem by asking first about the focused stabilizing function of sentences containing the "is" of identity. If we can describe this function, perhaps we will be able to discern what, if anything, such sentences must map onto in order to perform Normally. If it should turn out that they could perform Normally without mapping at all, as, for example, the word "or" performs normally without mapping at all, then we could conclude that the "*A*" and the "*B*" in sentences of the form "*A* is *B*" have nonreferential functions. The results of our inquiry will not turn out to be quite so simple as this, but let us begin and see what happens.

At first we restrict our attention to the simplest sorts of equations where "is" is flanked on both sides with simple terms: "Cicero is Tully," "Hesperus is Phosphorus," "the Greeks are the Hellenes." Consider "Cicero is Tully." If Cicero is in fact Tully, then not only the usual referents but the *senses* of the least types "Cicero" and "Tully" must be the same, for these names are supposed to map onto the same person. But, of course, senses can be the same without concepts— either idiolect intensions or public intensions—being the same. Indeed, if we look at the most strictly public intensions of "Cicero" and of "Tully"—to intensions that *must* be common to *all* competent users of these terms—there is one necessary difference between these. Every person's set of intensions for "Cicero" must include the implicit intension that corresponds to a program for iterating an inner name with the sense of "Cicero" upon hearing the outer term "Cicero" in sentences. But this inner name may or may not be iterated via hearing the outer term "Tully." And the converse is true, exchanging "Cicero" and "Tully." (Cf.: the language-bound intensions common to all users of the German "rot" necessarily differ from those for the English "red"—see Chapter 9). Only if an individual believes that Cicero is Tully will his idiolect terms "Cicero" and "Tully" have *all* the same intensions.

Turn this last observation around, and an answer to the question we are asking suggests itself. For what *is* believing that Cicero is Tully beyond, exactly, that one's idiolect terms "Cicero" and "Tully" have all the same intensions? Better, what is it beyond that one translates outer tokens of "Cicero" and of "Tully" into the same inner name? And surely the focused stabilizing function of "Cicero is Tully" is to produce in the hearer a (true) belief that Cicero is Tully.

In Chapter 15 I will develop a theory of the act of identifying. In the meanwhile, it will not be wrong but merely incomplete to think of the act of identifying-as-the-same the referents of two outer terms as the act, merely, of translating these two outer terms into the same inner term. The suggestion on the table then is that the focused stabilizing function of the form "*A* is *B*", where "*A*" and "*B* are simple terms, is to bring it about that the hearer should identify the values of "*A*" and of "*B*" as the same, henceforth translating members of the reproductively established family "*A*" and members of the reproductively established family "*B*" into the same inner term, this inner term being univocal in sense. Sentences of the form "*A* is *B*" that do not produce this result or that produce translation of "*A*" and of "*B*" into an inner term that has, as a result, an equivocal sense do not perform the function upon which the proliferation of the "*A* is *B*" family has historically depended.

An equivalent but possibly more graphic way to characterize the "is" of identity when placed between single words is this. "*A* is *B*" is supposed to cause the hearer to merge the concept he associates with "*A*" *with* the concept he associates with "*B*" so as to produce one univocal concept. By "the concept he associates with '*A* '" I mean the concept that governs iteration of the inner term into which he translates "*A*." By the "merging" of two concepts, I mean that the joint set composed of all the intensions formerly governing two inner terms comes to govern just one inner term. The merging of concepts governing inner terms having the same sense produces a concept governing an inner term that has this same sense. The merging of concepts governing inner terms having different senses produces a concept governing an inner term that is ambiguous in Fregean sense. The form "*A* is *B*" performs properly, of course, only when it effects the first kind of merging. (Compare: the stabilizing function of sentences in the indicative mood is to produce *true* beliefs.)

But if this is what "*A* is *B*" is supposed to do, won't the form be essentially resistant to translation? Its stabilizing function is, roughly, to cause the hearer to treat members of two particular least types in the same way—the least types that "*A*" and "*B*" are members of. But "*A*" and "*B*" are always terms in some *given* language. How then could any sentence of the form "*A* is *B*", where "*A*" and "*B*" are simple terms, be translated into another language?

Well, *does* "Cicero is Tully" translate into other languages? Yes it does. But this seems to be possible only because names of people do not, in general, have to be translated. One simply carries them over as is into another language when translating the rest of the sentence containing them. Or, when names of famous historical figures (or names of anything, for that matter) have taken somewhat different forms in different languages but these forms are still easily recognizable as members of the same genetic family, there is no problem about translating the "*A* is *B*" form. But try translating "spigots are faucets" into German!

On the other hand, consider "Hesperus" (the evening star) and "Phosphorus" (the morning star). Suppose that, in deepest Africa, there is a tribe that has named the heavenly bodies quite independently of our classical tradition. They have a name "Morven" that they attach to Venus when they see it in the morning and another name "Even" that they attach to Venus when they see it in the evening. They are not aware that Morven is Even. Surely we could translate "Hesperus is Phosphorus" into their language as "Even is Morven" (supposing that their "is" meant the same as our "is")? But if correct translation preserves stabilizing function, and the stabilizing function of "*A* is *B*" is, merely, to cause the hearer to change his habits with regard to members of the reproductively established families of "*A*" and of "*B*", then the "Morven is Even" translation would be incorrect. How are we to square this?

The full-bodied public intension of "Morven" and the full-bodied public intension of "Phosphorus" bear a striking resemblance. And so for "Even" and "Hesperus." Hence "Hesperus is Phosphorus" and "Morven is Even" have as stabilizing functions to produce mergings of pairs of concepts that are, for those who grasp the full-bodied public intensions of the terms used, similar in a striking way. Thus "Morven is Even" would perform the bulk of the stabilizing function of "Hesperus is Phosphorus."

Now let us ask, is there anything onto which a sentence of the form

"*A* is *B*", "*A*" and "*B*" being single words, must *map* in order for its stabilizing function to be performed Normally?

In accordance with the stabilizing functions of the least types "*A*" and "*B*", "*A*" and "*B*" are referential terms. And "*A* is *B*" performs Normally, is true, only when these referential types have the same referent. Call this referent "*R*." But in the context of the sentence "*A* is *B*" do "*A*" and "*B*" have their ordinary referents? Does "*A* is *B*," when true, map onto a world affair having *R* as a variant? "*A* is *B*," if it is an intentional icon, contains two variants "*A*" and "*B*" and the invariant " _____ is _____ ." If it is an intentional icon of a world affair, this world affair must likewise be articulated into a triad of two variants and an invariant in accordance with transformations that define its correspondence to "*A* is *B*." But to what triadic world affair containing *R* as a variant could "*A* is *B*" correspond?

Identity is sometimes thought of as a diadic relation that a thing has to itself but to no other thing. To think of identity as a diadic relation is to think of it as a variant in triadic world affairs. Thus, it is thought, just as "loves" is a diadic relation that a thing sometimes has to itself— say, when Narcissus loves Narcissus—so identity is a diadic relation that a thing always has to itself and only to itself. *R*'s being identical with *R* would then be a triadic world affair mapped by "*A* is *B*." But this view is a terrible muddle! Clearly, what *makes* "loves" or any other diadic relation *diadic* is that it *can* take relata that are genuinely two— that are different. A relation that necessarily has but one relatum is, simply, *monadic*—is a simple property. If identity is a variant in world affairs, it must be the simple property *self-identity* that has this status. But "*A* is *B*" has two variants and an invariant. Clearly it cannot be an intentional icon of the diadic affair that is, merely, *R*'s being self-identical.

In Chapter 16 I will argue that every property is a property only by virtue of having *contrary* properties—properties that exclude it or are incompatible with it. According to this analysis, self-identity cannot even be a simple property. What would its contraries be? Self-otherness? Other-identity? What would it be for a thing *not* to be self-identical? Identity is no more a property or relation than "or-ness" or "and-ness" is a property or relation. Identity is not a variant in world affairs. The identity of a thing with itself is reflected in representations of the thing not via the articulateness of these representations but only insofar as the same is represented by the same.

If sentences of the form "*A* is *B*" are intentional icons, they are not then intentional icons real values of which are affairs involving the usual referents of "*A*" and "*B*." But "*A* is *B*" does seem to be an intentional icon of another kind of world affair. For every true sentence of the form "*A is B*" there must be least types to which "*A*" and "*B*" belong, and these types must have the same referent. Transformations of the sort *replace the A-place term with X* and/or *replace the B-place term with Y* will produce a new true sentence from an old true sentence of the "*A is B*" kind only when these transformations correspond to transformations upon the real values of these sentences of this sort: *replace the first least type with the X least type* and/or *replace the second least type with the Y least type*. "*A is B*" maps that something is the referent of both "*A*" and "*B*."

But from the fact that "*A is B*" is an intentional icon it does not follow that it is a representation. A representation must have as its focused proper function to precipitate acts of identification of the referents of its elements. I have not yet offered a description of the act of identifying the referent of an intentional icon element, but this much we can anticipate. In order for an outer term to precipitate an act of identification of its referent, it must be translated into an inner term that has the same referent, for the act of identification of the referent is an inner act. And if the inner term is to have the same referent as the outer term, it must have the same sense as the outer. Now as we have described the situation, the sense—the mapping rule—for the sentence "*A is B*" requires that "*A*" and "*B*" map onto least *word* types—smallest branches of reproductively established families of words—that bear a certain relation to one another, namely, that have the same referent. But the focused stabilizing function of "*A is B*" is not to produce in hearers any inner terms that are supposed to map onto *words*. The hearer is not to merge the concepts he has of two *word* types, but the concepts that govern the inner terms he translates these word types into. Certainly he is not supposed to produce an inner sentence that is about words. Of course, he may in fact do this. It may even be that, idiosyncratically, the effect that "*A is B*" always has upon him (when he believes it) is that he first thinks to himself " '*A*' and '*B*' refer to the same" and then proceeds to merge his concepts associated with "*A*" and "*B*." But there is no reason to think that this is the usual reaction of people to sentences of the "*A is B*" form. And even if it were, to produce the inner sentence " '*A*' and '*B*' refer to the same" would not be the *focused* stabilizing function of "*A is B*." Hence, although "*A is B*" is an intentional icon and has a sense, it is not a representation. Call the sense that a representation has qua representation its "representational sense." Then we can say that "*A is B*" has a sense, but not a representational sense.

Do "*A*" and "*B*" in "*A is B*" have referents? So far we have spoken of the "referent" of an intentional icon element or sentence element simply as something existent which must be its real value if it is to perform Normally, which something is determined prior to the content of the rest of the icon or sentence. The real value of "A" when "A is B" performs Normally is the word type "A"; the real value of "B" is the word type "B." And that these must be the values of "A" and "B" is determined not by the content but only by the *form* of the rest of the sentence. Yet no unbiased person (no person not schooled in the tradition of Carnap) would suggest that "A" in "A is B" refers to the *word* "A." Two distinct kinds of reference or kins of reference need to be distinguished.

First consider the mapping of the tokens "A" and "B" in the context of the nonrepresentational sentence "A is B." If the sentence is true, "A" and "B" are related to their real values in exactly the same way that the elements (variants) of a correctly executed bee dance are related to their real values. But in neither case are the values of these icon elements supposed to be identified. Call this kind of reference "protoreference." Although it is not yet fully developed reference, all fully developed reference presupposes protoreference. Protoreferents of "A" and "B" in "A is B" are the least types "A" and "B."

Second, consider "John" and "tall" in the sentence "John is tall." "John is tall" is an intentional icon the real values of the elements of which are supposed to be identified. "John is tall" is supposed to map an affair in the world, and the hearer of "John is tall" is supposed to identify the variants of this world affair that are mapped by "John" and "tall." (For the moment we are modeling these acts of identifying as acts of translating "John" and "tall" into inner terms that have the same real values as "John" and "tall.") "John is tall" is thus a representation. Let us call the relation between "John" and John, the person who is supposed to be the real value of "John," "representational reference" or for short just "reference," this being the common meaning of "reference." John is the represented referent of "John," and the variant "tall" is the represented referent of "tall." The tokens "John" and "tall" in "John is tall" are representationally referential. In "Cicero is Tully" the word types "Cicero" and "Tully" are not represented referents of the tokens "Cicero" and "Tully" but *only* protoreferents of these.

Closer inspection suggests that not only is the word type "Cicero" a protoreferent of the token "Cicero" in "Cicero is Tully," Cicero himself is also a protoreferent of "Cicero." For "Cicero is Tully" maps that "Tully" *names* Cicero. Sometimes intentional icons can be considered to be icons of more than one world affair. For the notion "most proximate Normal explanation," from which the notion "real value of an intentional icon" is derived, is not a precise notion. Is it, most proximately, because (1) "Tully" and "Cicero" name the same or because (2) "Tully" names Cicero and "Cicero" names Cicero that "Cicero is Tully" can perform its proper functions Normally? Perhaps (1) is a less detailed explanation than (2). But neither is a less proximate explanation than the other in the sense that it spells out Normal causes of Normal conditions that the other mentions bald.

Though Cicero may be treated as a protoreferent of "Cicero" in the context "Cicero is Tully," it is not, as we have noted, a represented referent. Sentences of the form "A is B" are not representations. But "A" and "B" are still representationally referential *terms, in the sense that* the stabilizing functions of their respective families is to figure as elements of representations and to have their referents identified. The use of these terms in the context "A is B" is a *parasitic* use. The function of "A" in "A is B" is not to translate into an inner term in an inner sentence but to bring about a change in the concept that governs the inner term it would usually translate into—i.e., would translate into in the case of a *stabilizing* use of it. For a sentence of the form "A is B" has a function at all only insofar as "A" and "B" have prior stabilizing functions that are representationally referential. Thus the "A" and the "B" in "A is B" both are and are not (representationally) referential in somewhat the same way that "vixen" in "the lady is a real vixen" both does and does not mean "female fox." The representationally referential functions of these terms are displaced, given the proper function of the syntactic form of the sentence in which they are placed. (I will have more to say about the phenomenon of displaced reference in Chapter 13.)

Now consider the "is" of identity when it is flanked on one or both sides with definite descriptions: "Scott is the author of *Waverley*," "The woman in blue is the Queen of England."

The function of the "is" of identity is parasitic upon the stabilizing representationally *referential* functions of the terms that flank it. When flanked by definite descriptions it must be upon the potential referring functions of these two descriptions that the "is" of identity is parasitic. But the referential function of any definite description is only one of its alternative stabilizing functions. Even definite descriptions that are not necessarily identifying, although these always have a referential function, often serve a descriptive function as well. The "is" of identity, flanked on one or both sides with definite descriptions, is never then *merely* the "is" of identity; it is undifferentiated between being the "is" of identity and being the "is" of predication, for it has the stabilizing functions of both. Consider: if I say, "my daughter is the smallest child on the block" and "the smallest child on the block" serves a purely descriptive function, my "is" does not function as an "is" of identity but as an "is" of predication. That is, "the smallest child" functions as a predicate nominative functions—as, e.g., "a small child" functions. But it does not follow that the "is" in my sentence simply *is* the "is" of predication. For my intention and my hearer's use of a sentence token do not affect the meaning or the stabilizing function of the sentence itself, and the sentence has another stabilizing function too.

This suggests that what we have been calling "the 'is' of identity" and "the 'is' of predication" do not represent two distinct reproductively established families or two least types. The "is" in "Cicero is Tully" is joined to the "is" in "Cicero is Roman" via intermediate cases involving descriptions such as "Cicero is the author of the *Philippics*," in which the stabilizing function of "is" is to serve both a predicative and an identifying function or to serve these alternately.

Yet it is of the utmost importance to distinguish these alternative functions of "is." In relation to one of these functions, "is" forms part of a representation; in relation to the other it does not. If we mistakenly conflate "is" in its role of producing concept mergings with "is" in its role as an element in representations, we end by having to supply an entity for the "is" of identity to *map*. We end by reifying something called "identity," thinking of it as a property or relation, as an element in world affairs, as a puzzling ingredient of reality. And this way of thinking is an error of consequence. The nonentity *identity* will be a subject of discussion throughout Part IV.

"Exists"

Consider first "exists" as predicated of or denied of a simple subject: "aardvarks exist," "Alice B. Toklas existed," "Santa Claus does not exist," "phlogiston does not exist." Surely the stabilizing function of such sentences is not to produce in the hearer a representation of a world affair. It is to produce alteration in a concept, that is, in the programs that govern iteration and use of an inner term—the inner term into which the hearer translates the grammatical subject of the exists sentence. If I come to believe that x does not exist, then either "x" is simply eliminated from my inner and outer vocabulary, or I disengage inner and outer sentences containing "x" from the ordinary referential uses whereby sentences adapt me to world affairs, reserving them for one or another kind of special use. If I suddenly come to believe that x does exist after all, then I begin to engage inner and outer tokens of the term "x" for the ordinary referential uses from which they had previously been withheld.

One kind of disengaged use of inner and outer terms is fictional use. It is not easy to describe the kind of disengagement that characterizes one's use of a term for a character or thing from myth or fiction. To understand it we should have to know exactly what *pretending* is. Pretending, unlike just imagining, is a way of being actively engaged with the world. It involves treating or reacting to things or situations in the world as if they were other than they are, but in limited ways and within some kind of frame, say, of time or context. Terms like "Santa Claus" and "Winnie-the-Pooh" are pretend names. That is, they are words we pretend are names. Part of this pretense involves translating outer tokens of these names into pretend inner names and vice versa. We pretend to hear about, to *think* about, and to talk about something, and this pretending involves inner and outer *sayings* of "Santa Claus" or "Winnie-the-Pooh." But what we are actually disposed to *do* with sentences containing these inner and outer terms is severely limited, and occurs within some kind of frame. The child that believes in Santa Claus is confused in rather the same way as a child would be that believed that a doll is a real baby. The child takes the outer name "Santa Claus" to be a real name, and translates it into an inner name that he uses in the ordinary referential way. *His* inner name for Santa Claus is a *vacuous* name rather than merely a pretend name. But terms like "Santa Claus" and "Winnie-the-Pooh" are not vacuous terms for those who use them *as* fictional. They do not resemble the eighteenth century "phlogiston" at all. Such terms proliferate *not* because they are apparently serving a mapping function but because they are functioning as counters in amusing games.

A second kind of disengaged use of inner and outer terms is in modeling another person's thoughts. The inner representations in my head that map or model dogs do not, I suppose, much resemble dogs, nor is my inner term "blue" blue. But it seems reasonable that, having in my head an apparatus for thinking, I might use this apparatus to model your thinking. Thus, instead of modeling in my head the *relation* between your thoughts and the world that makes your thoughts thoughts *of* these things, I might simply utter inner sentences of my own which have the same senses as the representations in your head that I wish to model. I might even actively think with these models, modeling or attempting to model the inferences that you make, the reactions you have, and the intentions you form, by myself making inferences natural to me and allowing to develop reactions and intentions natural to me, given these thoughts in my head. That is, I might understand your thought by imitating it. Of course, this imitation could serve me as a model of *your thought*, rather than being only another icon of my world, only if dissociated and cut off from the normal sort of interaction with the rest of my thought and from my perception and action.

Perhaps it is by using this sort of technique that we understand best "what 'phlogiston' means," i.e., what it meant to eighteenth century naturalists, and "what witches are." In any event such terms as "phlogiston" and "witch" are not vacuous terms in our present-day vocabularies as they were for those who believed in phlogiston and witches. Nor are these terms merely counters in interesting games of fiction. Supplied with pretend intensions, but disengaged from other uses, they are turned exclusively to the purpose of speaking and thinking about the inner worlds of others.

The function of "x does not exist" where "x" is a simple subject term is either entirely to remove the inner term into which the hearer translates "x" from his inner vocabulary or to disengage it from ordinary referential use. The function of "x exists," where "x" is a simple subject term, is firmly to engage or reengage for ordinary referential use the inner term into which the hearer translates "x." Neither "x exists" nor "x does not exist" is a representation. The purpose of these forms is to alter concepts, not to produce inner icons of world affairs. However, "x exists" is an intentional icon. It is just that the real values of the significant elements of this icon are not supposed to be identified.

For example, if we take the true sentence "Alice B. Toklas exists" and perform upon it the operation *substitute "Mr. Olympus" into the subject place,* this operation corresponds to an operation upon the world affair that is "Alice B. Toklas" 's having a referent, which operation yields "Mt. Olympus" 's having a referent, the latter affair being what makes "Mt. Olympus exists" true. Thus "Alice B. Toklas exists" is an intentional icon having as its real value the affair that is "Alice B. Toklas" 's having a referent, and so for other simple "exists" sentences. The name type "Alice B. Toklas" is thus a protoreferent of the token "Alice B. Toklas" and the attribute *having a referent* is a protoreferent of "exists."

The problem of translating existence sentences with simple subjects is similar to the problem of translating simple identity sentences. If any other word, say "y," is substituted for "x" when translating "x exists," the resulting sentence will not icon what "x exists" icons; "y" does not have the same protoreferent as "x" in this context. And in describing the stabilizing function of "x exists," we have to mention "x": the function is *firmly to engage for active referential use the inner term into which the hearer translates "x."* So it looks as though the word "x" will itself have to appear in any correct translation of "x exists" that preserves stabilizing function. But in practice, often it is enough if the "x" in "x exists" or in "x doesn't exist" is translated by a term that has a full-bodied public intension similar in relevant ways to the full-bodied public intension of "x." Then "Unicorns exist" translates as "Einhornen existieren" and "Hesperus exists" might well translate into our mythical

African language as "Even exists" but not as "Morven exists." Or, considering that the most abstract function of "x exists" is simply to engage a mental term that has x as a referent for active referential use, "Tully exists" might be translated as "Cicero exists" for a hearer who is familiar with Cicero under the name "Cicero" but does not know he was also called "Tully."

Now consider "exists" sentences that have complex indefinite subject terms: "Albino snakes exist," "Tigers without stripes exist," "Girls that like math but not history exist," "Purple cows do not exist." The subject of each of these sentences contains an embedded sentence: *snakes are albino, tigers lack stripes, girls like math but not history, cows are purple.* Each of these sentences, taken just in itself, either has real value(s) or does not have real value(s). For example, the embedded sentence *snakes are albino* has as real values all world affairs that consist in an individual snake's being albino. When the phrase "albino snakes" occurs in an ordinary sentence, of course, it may no longer have any real value, for such phrases are indefinite descriptions, and both whether an indefinite description has a real value and what that real value is is determined by the rest of the sentence in which it occurs (see Chapter 11, "Indefinite Descriptions"). "Albino snakes exist" is an intentional icon that maps that the phrase type "albino snakes," taken alone, has real value; the phrase type "albino snakes" is a protoreferent of the token of "albino snakes" that occurs in "Albino snakes exist." But this protoreferent is not supposed to be identified. It is not a stabilizing function of "Albino snakes exist" to translate into an inner name for the expression "albino snakes" plus an inner descriptive predicate. The hearer need have no concepts of words or expressions and no concept of real value in order to understand "Albino snakes exist." Rather, the sentence translates into an inner belief of the form "(Some) snakes are albino," which *belief* the hearer engages for active use in real-world contexts as opposed to reserving it for the world of pretend. Qua representation, "Albino snakes exist" says what "Some snakes are albino" says. It is just that "Albino snakes exist" is *also* a nonrepresentational icon of an affair between the phrase "albino snakes" and the world, its transformation into, say, "Toads exist" corresponding to a parallel transformation of real value.

When "Albino snakes exist" is viewed merely as a representation, "exists" appears as what linguists call a "dummy" predicate. It serves to shift the entire burden of mapping onto the sentence embedded in the sentence's subject term. Similarly, "There are albino snakes" contains a dummy subject which serves to shift the entire burden of representational mapping onto the grammatical predicate of the sentence. "There are . . ." works exactly parallel to the way ". . . exists" works. It forms a sentence that is an intentional icon of an affair between its grammatical predicate *term* and the world, but only the predicate of the sentence functions as a representation.

Insofar as definite descriptions have a descriptive function as well as a referent-introducing function, the grammatical predicate "exists" turns these descriptions too into complete representations. For example, relative to the descriptive function of "the present King of France," "The present King of France exists" is a false *representation* as well as a false intentional icon; it is equivalent, qua representation, to "A king is presently of France." Relative to the referent-introducing function of "the present King of France," however, "The present King of France exists" is only a false intentional icon and not a representation at all. It is false because for it to perform its proper function in accordance with a Normal explanation it would have to correspond to an affair consisting in "The present King of France" having a referent, and there is no such affair. But it does not *say* that "the present King of France" has a referent. Like "Santa Claus exists," it does not *say* anything. But it has a function.

Chapter 13

Quotation Marks, "Says That" and "Believes That"

There is a way in which the sense of a referential term or expression always remains the same regardless of its context. All tokens of the familiar least type "Abe Lincoln" have the same stabilizing function and the same associated Normal explanation for proper performance qua tokens *of* that type. So whether a token of "Abe Lincoln" occurs in a historical treatise, out of the beak of a parrot, in quotation marks, in the context "Abe Lincoln existed," or in the context "John believes that Abe Lincoln was tall," its sense and its referent remain, in one way, always the same. On the other hand, there exist a number of overriding conventional contexts such as that of quotation marks that mention and "believes that . . . " and " . . . exists" into which referential and other kinds of expressions can be inserted, which contexts have their *own* stabilizing functions that conflict with the stabilizing functions of the terms inserted into them. There is nothing mysterious about this. It is not at all unusual for a thing to have conflicting proper functions as derived from several sources. This happens, for example, when a speaker's intention in speaking conflicts with the stabilizing function of the expression he uses. In the present case it happens because a term is reproduced on the model of a family having a certain proper function but is also reproduced as part of a bit of syntax, and this bit of syntax has a direct proper function requiring the term to function otherwise than in its own proper way. Such overriding contexts turn inserted expressions to *secondary* or *parasitic* uses. For example, it is not due to performance in such contexts as ' "Abe Lincoln" is a proper name' that the (least) reproductively established family of "Abe Lincoln" tokens *proliferates*. It has proliferated due to the performance of its tokens in the context of sentences in which these tokens have mapped onto Abe Lincoln, not onto the name "Abe Lincoln."

Overriding contexts that turn inserted expressions to secondary uses may or may not have stabilizing functions that are adapted to the stabilizing functions of the inserted expressions. Quotation marks that mention produce a configuration that has a stabilizing function that is *not* adapted to the stabilizing function of the expression that lies within; "believes that . . . " produces a configuration that has a stabilizing function that *is* adapted to the stabilizing function of the expression that lies within. In either sort of case I will say that the overriding context causes the expression within to have its usual function "displaced," and I will call this usual function a "displaced function." I will call the new function of the expression qua in the overriding context its "displacing function." If the function of an expression is displaced so that it no longer has its usual sense or usual referent, I will say that its usual sense and/or referent is displaced. And if the new—the displacing—function of an expression in a given context requires that it map but in accordance with *new* rules—that it take on a new Fregean sense—I will call its new sense and/or referent its displacing sense and/or referent.

In this chapter I will illustrate the phenomenon of displaced function by analyzing three function-displacing contexts that have traditionally puzzled philosophers: quotation marks that mention, "says that . . . ," and "believes that . . . ." The latter two contexts, along with such others as "wishes that . . . ," "intends that . . . ," "knows that . . . ," "deplores that . . . ," "suggested that," etc., are sometimes called "intentional contexts" (with a 't'); and it has been noted by a number of writers that there are ways in which these contexts differ systematically from other kinds of so-called intensional contexts (with an 's'), notably, from modal contexts—"necessarily . . . ," "probably . . . ," "because . . . ," etc. That the analysis I will give of "says that . . . " and "believes that . . . " is of a form that could easily be extended to cover all intentional contexts will be obvious, I hope. But I have no idea, yet, whether or not any light might be cast upon modal contexts using a similar approach.

Mention Quotes[1]

Because quotation marks have several other uses than turning an expression to the purpose of mentioning itself, let me dub the kind of quotation marks that serve this particular purpose "mention quotes."

It is true of every significant aspect of a sentence that its *complete* stabilizing function is determined only as adapted to the rest of the sentence in which it occurs. Mention quotes are no exception. Especially obvious is the fact that the stabilizing function of a pair of mention quotes is adapted to the expression—the "filling"—that lies in the middle. Count word tokens as tokens of the same type if they are tokens of the same least type, and count phrases and sentences as tokens of the same type if every one of their significant aspects matches in least type. Alternatively, group expressions into types by reference to reproductively established *genetic* families. Or count expressions as tokens of the same type if they are composed of spaces and of *letters* or of *phonemes* from the same reproductively established families arranged in the same order. These are genuinely alternative ways of counting types, and sometimes mention quotes are understood one way (the German *word* "rot") and sometimes another (the *syllable* "rot"). (Accordingly, it is possible that mention quotes themselves divide into several least types.) Mention quotes then have as a relational proper function to produce an act of identification of the *type* (one kind or another) of which their filling is a token. Given some particular filling, mention quotes acquire as an adapted proper function to produce identification of that particular language-device type. What falls between mention quotes has as a displacing function the *relational* proper function of producing an act of identification of its *own* type.

The mere fact that mention quotes must be supplied with an adaptor that occurs between them in order to have an adapted and hence fully determinate function does not of course make mention quotes *indexical* sentence elements. All words and all syntactic forms need to be supplied with adaptors from the rest of the sentence before their functions become fully determinate. But the expression token that occurs *between* mention quotes *is* an indexical element qua having a displacing function that is relational. It performs its displacing function Normally only if it maps onto something that bears a certain *relation* to it, this something being supposed to be identified by the hearer. This something is the reproductively established family or the type of the token. The indexical adapting relation for the token is the relation that any language-device token bears to its type. Thus the displacing referent of "Abe Lincoln" in the context ' "Abe Lincoln" is a proper name' is an *indexed* referent: the type "Abe Lincoln."

What has tended to confuse the issue here is our tradition that takes the word "this," the arrow " →," and the pointing index finger as its only paradigms of indexicality. We are then encouraged to suppose that all indexical adapting relations must be relations rather like next-to-ness—say, spatial or temporal relations. But the relation of token to type is a perfectly good relation too, and serves very well for the purpose of indexical adaptation.

In a paper called "Quotation"[2] Donald Davidson has recently argued that mention quotes are indexical or "demonstrative" devices. Davidson takes the quotation marks themselves to be complete demonstratives and takes their filling to fall, "from a semantical point of view," *outside* the sentence, as a fish to which he pointed while saying "I caught this fish today" would fall outside his sentence. And Davidson takes the mention quotes to mean something like, and I quote him, "the expression with the shape here pictured." Two comments about Davidson's analysis will help to clarify my view.

Suppose that we adopt the view that the quotation marks alone do the indexing and that their filling falls outside the sentence proper. Then the indexical adapting relation for quotation marks is the relation that a *type* of filling bears to a token of quotation marks by virtue of being the-type-of-the-token-that-falls-in-between them. There's nothing really wrong with that way of looking at the matter. But given that there is an equally sensible way of looking at the matter while treating the filling as part of the sentence proper, one would wonder what criterion was being used here, and to what purpose, in deciding where a sentence ends and its environment begins. Intuitively, "I caught this fish today" is a complete sentence whether accompanied by a fish or not. But intuitively "The word ' ' has five letters" is not a complete sentence. What should be *treated* as being in a sentence, one might feel, is whatever is spatially (or temporally) in the sentence, so long as that something got there via reproduction of elements and aspects of earlier sentence tokens and so long as it has a direct proper function. Surely the aspect that is containing-an-expression-token-in-quotes is a reproductively established aspect of a sentence and has a direct proper function.

The second portion of Davidson's analysis that needs comment is his view that the *shape* of the token between mention quotes is (transitionally) referred to by these marks. This view results from an inadequate view, indeed from the absence of any clear view, of the nature of an expression type. Surely everybody knows on reflection that expressions are never typed by shape. It is a strength of my view, I believe, that I have given a plausible characterization of some ways that language devices *are* grouped into types. But it should be noticed that if it is not the shape of an expression but its least type or its reproductively established genetic family or its arrangement of reproductively established aspects that is pointed to between mention quotes, then the token between mention quotes must have a reproductively established character or characters. It follows that it will not do to write

First little Noah drew "   " on the paper and then he drew "   " and also "   ."

And indeed, in such cases we do not use quotation marks but ordinary demonstratives:

First little Noah drew something like this on the paper and then . . .

When introducing a brand-new symbol with the use of mention

quotes, what is referred to is a reproductively established family that will follow *after* this ancestor token. Further, the introduced symbol had better be composed at least of *elements* or *aspects* that are already reproductively established in character in accordance with some conventions or other, consciously or unconsciously followed. Otherwise the token between quotes will not fall within any established same-different scheme, which it must do if the reader is to recognize its progeny *as* its progeny—as tokens of the same type. I cannot, for example, just introduce a symbol 〔symbol〕 and expect you to be able to identify other members of this budding reproductively established family when you meet them.

One last feature of the analysis of mention quotes advanced here should be noted. On this analysis some expressions, as occurring between mention quotes, are significantly articulate while others are not. The expression "c" in the context "the letter 'c' " is inarticulate—just as a proper name is inarticulate and an unadorned "this" is inarticulate. Also the expression "rot" in the context "the German word 'rot' " is inarticulate. But when the filling between mention quotes is typed in accordance with its membership in several reproductively established families and in accordance with the organization or ordering of these families in the filling—"the syllable 'rot'," "the phrase 'the king of France' "—the filling is significantly articulate. It is articulate in the sense that a sentence is articulate or that a complex description functioning descriptively is articulate: significant transformations of it correspond to transformations of its displacing real value when all goes Normally. If a singular term, quoting Davidson, is a term "without significant semantic structure,"[3] then the filling between mention quotes is not, in general, a singular term. It is, if you like, a description.

"Says That . . ." and "Believes That . . .": The Program

Having come this far, a promising analysis of such intentional contexts as "says that . . . " and "believes that . . . " is just around the corner. First we collect the following observations:

1. Placement in a special context can sometimes cause an expression to have a displacing function that is indexical and such that the expression refers to its own type.

2. Surely there is more than one way of typing expressions. Indeed, we have already mentioned three different ways of typing expressions just in the context of mention quotes. Might there not be a way or ways of typing public-language expressions such that these types cut across reproductively established families, hence across languages? Perhaps indicated by "says that . . . " rather than by mention quotes?

For example, Galileo said "Eppur si muove" and he did not say "the earth moves" (mention quotes), but Galileo *did* say *that* the earth moves. A simple comparison might be typing body organs in accordance with their most proximate proper functions, so that my heart and the fishes' hearts, though these are members of different reproductively established families, fall in the same category.

3. Public-language sentences are but one among other kinds of representations. Beliefs *that* and intentions *to* and wonderings *whether*, etc., are also representations—inner representations. Might there not be a way or ways of typing representations that would cut across the inner representation/outer representation boundary? Then an outer expression token might be used to index the type of an inner expression token. For example, "Galileo believed that the earth moves."

Perhaps our project is as simple as this. (1) Find the method or methods of typing expressions across reproductively established families and hence across languages that corresponds to "says that . . . ". (2) Find the method or methods of typing representations across the inner representation/outer representation boundary that corresponds to "believes that . . . ".

There is a complication in the case of "believes that . . . ". Such contexts are occasionally filled with outer sentences that are not representational, that do not correspond to any inner representations, indeed, that do not have to produce inner sentences in order to function properly. One can say "John believes that Cicero is Tully" or "John believes that there are no unicorns," but if the position sketched in Chapter 12 was correct, neither of those "believes that . . . " fillings is, in accordance with its *displaced* function, a representation, nor is it the displaced stabilizing function of either to produce a mental sentence. So we cannot say that the filling in an "S believes that . . . " context always indexes its own type as the type of some inner sentence that S harbors. Rather, what the filling does is to index the type of mental state that it is a focused proper function of the expression type of which it is a token to produce. That is, rather than indexing its own type, the filling indexes a mental-state-type that is so-related to, namely, properly caused by tokens of, its type.

But this complication leaves things pretty much as they were. We must inquire concerning the fillings in "believes that . . . " contexts as well as "says that . . . " contexts how these fillings—these outer language devices—are typed in these contexts in accordance with their *displaced* functions in order to serve their displacing functions.

If these expressions are not typed in accordance with reproductively established families, there are these obvious alternatives. First, there is stabilizing function. Surely we can assume that the stabilizing function, hence also the Fregean sense, of the most basic syntactic form of the whole sentence in intentional context is considered for purposes of typing it. But what about the referring expressions in the sentence? These expressions have Fregean sense. In the case of indexical expressions, there are two kinds of Fregean sense—relational sense and adapted sense (see Chapter 10). And these expressions have public intensions—two kinds: language-bound public intensions and full-bodied public intentions. Which of these four are considered when typing referring expressions in the context "says that . . . "? Which in the context "believes that . . . "?

The answer I will suggest is that in both of these kinds of intentional contexts different methods of typing and of cross-typing (part of the filling typed one way, part another) may occur. A full-scale examination of the various methods of typing and of how these are indicated by surrounding context would be an interesting study, but I will not undertake it here. I will merely give some examples that suggest that the general situation is this: there is a (single) *norm* for the typing of referring expressions in all intentional contexts, but there are also various kinds of special surroundings that indicate departure from this norm. The norm, I will claim, is that in intentional contexts *all* expressions are typed by reference (e.g., adapted sense) *only*, with the exception of referring descriptions that obviously would be functioning *descriptively* (as well, perhaps, as referentially) if they were functioning in accordance with their displaced functions.

Examples of Methods of Typing for Referring Expressions

One way to think about the typing of expressions that occur in intentional contexts is to ask what features of expressions have to be preserved when "translating," as it were, from direct to indirect discourse (from "John said '*p*' " to "John said that *q*") or from a mental state to a description of that mental state by use of an intentional context (from "John thinks in his heart '*p*' " to "John thinks that *q*"). Looked at this way, my claim is that when moving into intentional context the rule that expresses the norm is *preserve reference*, and for this purpose *employ whatever terms will most readily get this reference across to the present hearer*. The exception, special surroundings put aside, is the case in which a referring description that is also functioning descriptively needs to be translated. Then the rule is *preserve relational sense as well as reference* except that any *simple indexicals that occur in the description must still be translated preserving reference even at the cost of losing relational sense*.

In order to understand this rule, first we must see that behind it lies a second completely hard-and-fast rule: *any indexical expression token occurring in an intentional context is read as acquiring its displaced* (i.e., ordinary) *adapted referent from its PRESENT context*—not from the context of the original saying-that or the original belief that it helps to translate or describe. Ordinarily, simple indexicals shift their adapted senses—their referents—depending upon the contexts in which they are placed. Hence, for the most part, two simple indexical tokens having the same relational sense will have different adapted senses because of their different locations in the world. But what counts as the place in the world where a simple indexical token appearing in intentional context is, is the place in the world it *actually is*—i.e., being spoken by *this* speaker *now* to *this* hearer in *this* linguistic and *this* nonlinguistic context. Consider: "John thinks that *I* am a spy"; "John said that *he* [John] disliked clams"; "I like clams but John says that he hates *them*"; "John wants to make a painting of *this*"; "John once said of your father that *he* was a scoundrel." Because this rule is in force, clearly it is usually impossible to preserve both (displaced) relational and (displaced) adapted sense when moving a simple indexical over into intentional context.

Not only do demonstrative and personal pronouns in intentional contexts derive their (displaced) referents from their *present* contexts; so do those indexical elements that are the tenses of verbs, and so do nonidentifying descriptions that are being used referentially. From John's "I *am* going" we derive "John said he *was* going"; from John's "what *will* happen is this: . . . " we derive "John predicted that that *would* happen"; and from John's "*That character over there* is a spy" we may later derive "John said that *the woman* [*we* have just mentioned] was a spy."

Now my claim is not only that all indexicals appearing in intentional contexts, including all garnished indexicals (e.g., definite descriptions), are read in relation to their present context but that this rule is a sensible and appropriate rule. It is appropriate *because* the norm is that referring expressions are typed in intentional contexts by reference *only*, and not by relational sense or intension. The translation rule into intentional contexts, "let the relational sense go and preserve *reference* in whatever way the hearer will most easily understand" *dictates* that indexicals should be read relative to present context. For it is the present context that the hearer, who is the one that must understand the reference, is in.

Setting aside descriptions that describe as well as referring, that the rule "preserve reference only" is the norm is quite clear. Simple indexicals go over into descriptions and vice versa: from Jenny's "*She* is tall" we can get "Jenny said *your mother* is tall"; from Jenny's "*Johnny's mother* is tall" we can get "Jenny said *she* is tall" or "Jenny thinks *she* is tall." Names go over into descriptions and vice versa: from Jenny's "*Mrs. Jones* is ill" we can get "Jenny said *her boss* was ill"; from Jenny's belief "*Mrs. Jones* is ill" we can get "Jenny thinks *his mother* is ill," the latter with no implication that Jenny knows which child belongs to Mrs. Jones; from Jenny's "*The woman in red over there* dances well" we may get "Jenny thinks that *Mrs. Jones* dances well" with no implication that Jenny knows Mrs. Jones's name. And, of course, descriptions go over into other descriptions: from Jenny's "*That blond woman over there* dances well" we may get "Jenny thinks that *the woman in red over there* dances well" or we may get "Jenny says *your wife* dances well."

Now consider the norm for the exception to the "preserve reference only" rule: descriptions that would obviously be functioning descriptively if they had their displaced functions. In these cases, descriptions are typed by relational sense as well as by reference except for simple indexicals that these descriptions may contain. That is, in these cases, the relevant part of the sense *inside* the description is preserved in translation. Consider: "She thinks that *John's daughter* looks like him [John]"; "He said that *the first king of England* lived in the fourteenth Century!"; "He knows that *your father* is an important man." In each of these cases, the description in italics is obviously a relevant one— one that helps to map a relation among properties that is significant, or one that is obviously of interest to the hearer ("*your* father is important"). If one wished to avoid having one's hearer type the subject terms of the dependent clauses in these sentences in accordance with relational sense as well as reference, one would have to go to some pains, e.g., "She thinks that John's daughter looks like him and she doesn't even know they are related." Usually one would avoid the difficulty either by using another description that was not relevant in this way or by placing the describing description *outside* of the intentional context, then making a (displaced) reference back to its referent with a *pronoun* inside the intentional context: "She thinks of John's daughter that *she* looks like John"; "He said of the (man who was the) first King of England that *he* lived in the fourteenth century"; "He knows of your father that *he* is an important man."

Now let me give some examples of exceptions to these norms in typing within intentional contexts.

There is a simple way to force a description that would be functioning descriptively if it had merely its displaced function *into* typing by reference only. This is to give it a context such that no other reading makes plausible sense: "He said that (or thought that) *the winner* was the loser"; "I thought that your yacht was *larger than it is*" (Russell).

Here "the winner" and "larger than [your yacht] is" (see "Descriptions of Properties," Chapter 11) must be read as typed by *adapted* sense (reference) only, while "the loser" is probably read as having *only* a descriptive sense, "*your* yacht," as especially relevant, is read as typed by both adapted and relational sense, except that "your," the simple indexical, is typed by reference only. In this connection, Quine's classic sentence "Philip believes that the capital of Honduras is in Nicaragua," said when Philip believes that Tegucigalpa is in Nicaragua but does not know that Tegucigalpa is the capital of Honduras, is *not*, as Quine claims,[4] obviously false. It can perfectly well be read as true, given the implausibility of typing "the capital of Honduras" by relational sense in this context.

Now let me give some examples of exceptions to the main part of the rule for typing in intentional contexts—examples of terms that are not functioning descriptively yet are not typed by reference alone but also by relational sense or intension.

Suppose that both you and I know a certain John Winthrop very well, each of us knows his name very well, and each of us knows that the other knows, etc. I say to you "Jennifer says that the man who drove the two of you home the other night ought to meet her brother." Suppose that John Winthrop is that man, and both you and I know that and each knows the other knows, etc. From this you will infer at least that Jennifer did not refer to John by the name "John" and that she probably used some locution similar in relational sense to "the man who drove . . . and me home." Why? Because the *second* half of the rule for going over into intentional context is obviously being violated—the half that reads "employ whatever term will most simply get the reference across to the present hearer." Violation of this half of the rule is often a signal that the first half is being violated—a sign that not merely reference but sense or intension is being preserved. Why else use such an awkward locution in referring to John?

Occasionally a speaker will make reference to something *through the eyes* of a believer or sayer that he is describing. When this happens, and the reference is put in intentional context, obviously it will be typed by relational sense (simple indexicals excluded). Consider this classic example from Quine:

> There is a certain man in a brown hat whom Ralph has glimpsed several times under questionable circumstances on which we need not enter here; suffice it to say that Ralph suspects he is a spy.[5]

Consider the following sentences, taken in that context *only*:

(*a*)   Ralph believes that *the man he glimpsed* is a spy.

(*b*)   Ralph believes that *the man in the brown hat* is a spy.

Certainly the italicized part of sentence (*a*) and perhaps also of sentence (*b*) would be typed by the hearer in part by relational sense. (*b*) is more questionable than (*a*), for it has not been made absolutely explicit that Ralph noticed this man *as* one wearing a brown hat. But the minimum implication is that it is via some implicit or explicit intension derived from Ralph's glimpses that Ralph thinks of this man when attributing spyhood to him. Quine continues:

> Also there is a grey-haired man, vaguely known to Ralph as rather a pillar of the community, whom Ralph is not aware of having seen except once at the beach.

Given that context, the italicized part of the sentence

(*c*)   Ralph believes that *the man seen at the beach* is a spy.

would certainly be typed by relational sense. As such, it will count as definitely *not* following from (*a*) or from (*b*) and count this way even after Quine adds the punch line "Ralph does not know it, but the men are one and the same." However, adding this *last* bit of information to the context opens up an entirely new consideration that reinforces these readings. Apparently Ralph does not identify the man glimpsed in the brown hat with the man seen at the beach. Having now been carefully alerted that in describing Ralph's beliefs about this man it will be *essential* to type by relational sense, both (*c*) and

(*d*)   Ralph believes that *the man in the brown hat* is not a spy.

will now be read as plain *false*. No other interpretation is possible in the context.

But what about:

(*e*)   Ralph believes that *Ortcutt* is a spy.

(*f*)   Ralph believes that *Ortcutt* is not a spy.

For after all of this, Quine tells us that our man's name is "Ortcutt." Let us try another example first.

Suppose that Jennifer Jones, a contemporary and acquaintance of Samuel Clemens, does not know that Clemens's pen name is "Mark Twain." To a friend she confesses that she wishes very much to meet Mark Twain. Can we say of her that she confessed that she wished to meet Samuel Clemens?

Don't answer that question. Instead, reflect on the last two sentences of the paragraph above. You read "to a friend she confesses that she wishes to meet Mark Twain" to mean that she said something like "I really want to meet Mark Twain" *as opposed to* something like "I really want to meet Samuel Clemens." If you hadn't read it that way, the last sentence in the paragraph would have struck you as stupid or pointless, which I hope and trust it did not. This shows that in reading "She confesses that she wishes to meet Mark Twain" you typed "Mark Twain" in accordance with *language-bound intensions*. So even language-bound intensions are not always irrelevant to typing in intentional contexts. Why did you type "Mark Twain" in accordance with language-bound intensions? Because the context had been set up *both* to make it plain that what name Jennifer used for Samuel Clemens would be essential information to have *and* such that it would make no sense to suppose that she said something like "I really want to meet Samuel Clemens."

Now we can return to Ralph and Ortcutt. Quine implies, as the passage we were dissecting moves on, not only that Ralph harbors two separate inner names for Ortcutt but that only one of these—the one bound in part by the intension "man seen at the beach"—is bound also to the outer name "Ortcutt." That is, only one of these inner names is used by Ralph to translate outer tokens of "Bernard J. Ortcutt" into his inner language. And it is clear that it *matters* in the context, especially given the purposes of Quine and his readers, which inner name Ralph employs when he thinks this or that about Ortcutt. Hence "Ralph believes that Orcutt is a spy" will be read as false, "Ralph believes that Ortcutt is no spy" as true, "Ortcutt" being typed in these contexts by language-bound intensions. Change the scene. You and I are watching Ralph who is looking suspiciously at Ortcutt who is behind the bushes with a camera (photographing spider webs, no doubt). But Ralph obviously has not recognized Ortcutt. I say to you, "Good grief! Ralph believes that Ortcutt is a spy!" In this context, the sentence goes through as true; the typing of "Ortcutt" is by reference only. Compare: "Last Halloween Susy thought Rob [her brother] really was a ghost." And, contra Quine, so long as no one has raised or answered in the negative the question whether or not Tom knows that Cicero is Tully, "Tom believes that Cicero denounced Cataline" is equivalent to "Tom believes that Tully denounced Cataline." Compare: "Teacher believes that Mouse lied" can count as true, even though Teacher may not know that the child in question has the nickname "Mouse."

In general, language-bound intensions are preserved only when the context makes it clear that what public-language words were used or what public-language words a believer has in his vocabulary as implicit intensions for his terms is crucial in the context. The same is true of contexts in which full-bodied public intensions are purposefully preserved: "The natives think Hesperus [the Evening Star] is a god and they think Phosphorus [the Morning Star] is a devil."

But notice, in these connections, that the reason that a person who says or believes "Cicero is Tully" cannot ever be described merely as a person who has said or who believes that Cicero is Cicero is merely that the *proper function* of a sentence form must be preserved when going over into intentional context. The stabilizing functions of sentences of the form "*A* is *B*" where "*A*" and "*B*" are simple terms is to bring it about that the hearer should henceforth translate members of the reproductively established family "*A*" and of the reproductively established family "*B*" into the same inner term. Hence the proper function of "Cicero is Cicero" is different from that of "Cicero is Tully," so the one can *never* fill in for the other in intentional context. Similarly, the overall sentence form of "Ortcutt is and is not a spy" has as a *proper function* to translate into an inner sentence having one subject and two predicates (or a subject doubled, once with each of two predicates). No such inner sentence is (or sentences are) to be found in Ralph's head. It is for this reason that it cannot be said of Ralph, "Ralph believes that Ortcutt is and is not a spy."

Given the right context, however, "Ralph believes that Ortcutt is a spy yet Ralph believes that Ortcutt is not a spy" is true. Indeed, that is a good way of summing up Ralph's predicament.

A Note on Intentional Contexts with Indefinite and Universal Descriptions

The indefinite description "Ralph believes that *someone* is a spy" is of course ambiguous. The clause "someone is a spy" can be read straightforwardly as indexing through its own type to the type of belief that "someone is a spy" Normally produces in a hearer. That is, it can mean that Ralph says in his heart "Someone is a spy." On the other hand, the dependent clause "someone is a spy" can be read as indexing a belief *form*—a belief type with a gap in it. It can be read such that Ralph says in his heart " _____ is a spy," where the gap is to be filled in with a term that refers to somebody, we are not told whom. The gap is like a free variable, but not one that awaits being *bound*. On this reading, "Ralph believes of someone that *he* is a spy" would be a clearer way of speaking in that it places all and only the sentence form that is serving a displacing function *spatially* inside the intentional context, the indefinite "someone" being placed outside. The displaced function of "he" in this context is referential. But "he" dangles, because it has an indefinite rather than a definite antecedent in its present context. No matter which of these two ways we read "Ralph believes that someone is a spy," it maps *at least* a relation between Ralph and a belief type—on the second reading, a belief type that is not completely specified.

Similar remarks can be made about the sentence "Ralph believes that every member of our secret club is a spy." It can be read such that Ralph says in his heart "Every member of their secret club is a spy." Or it can be read such that Ralph says in his heart several sentences, each of the form " _____ is a spy," each time filling in the blank with an expression that refers to some member of our secret club, and such that Ralph's sentences cover all the members of our club. It must be read the latter way, for example, if Ralph does not know of our secret club. It then has the same sense as the more perspicuous "Of every member of our secret club Ralph thinks that *he* is a spy." But again, no matter which of these two ways we read "Ralph believes that every member of our secret club is a spy," it maps a relation between Ralph and a belief type, or else it maps each of a set of relations between Ralph and a gappy belief type. (How sentences containing universal descriptions map onto each of a set of real values will be discussed in the next chapter.)

Chapter 14

"Not" and "All": Two More Kinds of Indefinite Description

"Not": Introducing the Problem

Perhaps no one is tempted anymore to take the word "not" as a word that stands for something—as a word that maps a variant in world affairs. "Not," as Wittgenstein pointed out in the *Tractatus*, is an operator. It operates upon the rest of the sentence in which it occurs to change the sense of the whole sentence.

Wittgenstein thought that "not" "reversed the sense" of a sentence containing it so that rather than standing for what exists, the sentence stood for what does not exist. But this interpretation of the mapping rule for "not" involves just that reification of possibilities—possible but nonactual states of affairs—which it is our purpose to avoid. True negative sentences cannot have nonexistent world affairs as real values, for the real value of a sentence must figure in an explanation for proper functioning of that sentence. But nonexistent world affairs would surely have no powers in the causal order, hence could not play roles in Normal explanations. Either true negative sentences must map *real* world affairs or else they do not map world affairs at all, hence are not representations.

Suppose that we try to interpret negative sentences as sentences that are not representations. Perhaps we can do this by interpreting "not-*p*" as saying "the affair that-*p* does not exist." For I have argued (Chapter 12) that sentences of the form "*x* does not exist" do not map affairs out in the world beyond language and that they are not representations. Wittgenstein took it that "not-*p*" said roughly the same that "that-*p* does not exist" says. But he took sentences of the form "*x* does not exist" to be sentences that pictured nonexistent world affairs. Consonant with this, he thought that the "*x*" in the form "*x* does not exist" did not range over the names of elementary objects but only over representations of possible states of affairs and that ordinary names contained propositions representing possible states of affairs. Thus he was able to maintain that ordinary sentences of the form "*x* does not exist" have sense—are, in our terms, *representations*—and at the same time maintain that the most *elementary* elements of all propositions with sense correspond to real objects. The result was that he thought that "*x* does not exist" was always equivalent to some sentence of the form "not-*p*" as well as vice versa. But couldn't we retain just half of this thesis—just the half that says that "not-*p*" is equivalent to "that-*p* does not exist"? No, we could not.

If Wittgenstein were right that "not-*p*" says "that-*p* does not exist," the upshot for my position would be that negative sentences do not map world affairs that are out in the world beyond language and that they are not representations. Rather, they would map linguistic affairs. "Not-*p*" would then icon, but it would not represent, a world affair having the sentence type "*p*" as a variant. "*p*" would be not a represented referent of "not-*p*" but a protoreferent. Perhaps "not-*p*" would icon what " '*p*' is false" explicitly represents?

First notice that the "not" in "not-*p*" would not then be an operator. The mapping rule for "not-*p*" would not then be a function of the mapping rule for "*p*." Not understanding the sense of "*p*" would not then prohibit one's fully understanding "not-*p*"—and this seems wrong.

Second if "not-*p*" says "that-*p* does not exist," surely "not-*p*" will have to be true if *any* variant in "*p*" lacks fully determinate—e.g., lacks adapted—sense. Hence, "Pegasus was not a winged horse," "The present king of France is not wise," and "The slithy toves did not gyre and gimble in the wabe" would all be true sentences, and for the same *reason* that "snow is not black" is true. That does not seem right either.

Third, surely " '*p*' is false" at least *icons* that "*p*" does *not* have a real value. Similarly, "*x* does not exist" icons the affair that is "*x*" 's *not* having a mapping correlate or referent. So if "not-*p*" says "that-*p* does not exist," it still icons a negative state of affairs. Unless we can show that a negative state of affairs is other than the nonexistence of a positive state of affairs, we will only have come round in a circle. For a nonexistent state of affairs cannot be the real value of any kind of intentional icon any more than it can be the real value of a representation. But if we *can* show that a negative state of affairs is other than the nonexistence of a positive state of affairs, we will have no need to postulate that "not-*p*" says "that-*p* does not exist."

What I must argue then is that negative sentences map real or existent world affairs. How to give such a position rough underpinnings is well known. One argues that the negative operates in the end only upon the logical predicate of a sentence, reversing the sense of this predicate so that it maps a contrary of what it would normally map. For example, "John is not tall" says of John that he has an attribute that is contrary to or incompatible with being tall, hence is true if John is of medium height or if he is short. Supposing that simple singular negative sentences will yield to this sort of analysis, there seems to be no problem about reducing more complex sentences containing external negatives to sentences in which the negative appears only internally. For example, "No A's are ϕ" becomes "Every A is non-ϕ," "Not all A's are ϕ" becomes "Some A's are non-ϕ" and "It is not the case that a is ϕ and b is ϕ" becomes "a is non-ϕ or b is non-ϕ," etc. But various difficulties with the position that all simple singular negative sentences map positive world affairs are also well known.

First there is the problem of interpreting the function of "not" in supersimple sentences of the form "x is not"—for example, in "Pegasus is not (period)." Sentences of the form "x is not" do not have mapping predicates; hence "not" cannot be interpreted as operating upon their mapping predicates. Sentences of the form "x is not" are of course equivalent to sentences of the form "x does not exist." But I have argued that "exists" is not a representing predicate. Hence, "not" cannot be interpreted as *always* operating upon the predicate of a representing sentence. Similarly, the "not" in "Cicero is not Brutus" cannot operate upon the logical predicate of the sentence, for simple identity sentences have no logical predicates. So "not" must have other functions as well as that of operating upon the predicate of representing sentences. But if it has other functions as well—if it operates differently upon sentences that are not representations than upon sentences that are representations—then some account must be given showing the relation between these different functions of "not" so that we can see why it is that "not" does not strike us as having different *meanings* in different contexts.

The same problem is posed by the "not" in such sentences as "Gold is not square," "Ideas are not green," and "I do not have an atomic number of seventy-nine." Clearly "Gold is not square" is not true because gold is some contrary of square, nor is "I do not have an atomic number of seventy-nine" true because my atomic number is contrary to seventy-nine. These negative sentences have corresponding affirmatives that seem to lack sense—and shouldn't the denial of a sentence that lacks sense also lack sense? Yet "Gold is not square," etc., do seem to say things that are true. Again, if "not" has another function in these sentences than it has in representing sentences, this function and its connections with the usual use of "not" need to be explained.

Another and major problem concerns the mapping rules that correlate simple sentences of the form "x is not ϕ" with their real values. Suppose that "John is not tall" is true. Is its real value a *general* world affair—the affair of John's being non-tall? Or is its real value the precise affair that is John's being the exact height he is—say his being five feet six and three-eighths inches tall? I will argue that the latter is correct. Negative representations have indefinite sense. As in the case of in- definite descriptions, their real values are determinate when they occur in true sentences but do not need to be identified by hearers for their functions to be performed.

I will begin by offering several very general arguments to the effect that negative sentences the contradictories of which are ordinary rep- resenting sentences must themselves map positive states of affairs. Then I will explain how I believe they do this—what the mapping rules are for simple negative representational sentences. Last I will discuss the function of the negative in sentences that are not repre- sentations and the problem of the univocity of "not."

Negative Representations Correspond to Positive World Affairs

What is the stabilizing function of "not" when used in the context of quite ordinary representing sentences? One thing is perfectly clear: "not" is *not* used merely to cancel out the rest of the sentence containing it. "Not" is not an eraser. Sometimes we have need of an eraser when speaking, for sometimes we start to misspeak and need to cancel or correct our false starts. In such cases we say "sorry" or "no" or "that's not what I mean" and then produce a new sentence. We do not negate the sentence in order to accomplish this task, or if we do, that is sup- plying further information. Similarly, the function of "not" in a sentence cannot be to produce no belief. Merely producing no belief would be having no function at all.

"Not" does not cancel the sentence it appears within but operates upon that sentence. That is, the proper function of "not" is relational; i.e., it is a function (mathematical sense) of the proper function of the sentence without "not." An affirmative representing sentence has as a proper function to produce a particular true belief or a particular, consequently realized, intention. A corresponding sentence with "not" must be supposed to produce something too—something that can be described as so-related to what the affirmative sentence produces and something that we can understand to have possible uses.

Perhaps what the negative sentence does is this. It is used when the hearer has a wrong belief or intention or when it seems likely that the hearer may contract such a wrong belief or intention. Then what the negative sentence does is to eliminate the wrong belief or intention or inoculate the hearer against it. This at least would give the negative something to *do*, and something to do that would be related to the function of the corresponding positive sentence. If the negative func- tioned this way, it would function rather as "does not exist" functions.

"Does not exist" functions properly when it either simply eliminates the mental correlate of "x" from the hearer's mental vocabulary or relegates this term to a disengaged use. Does "John is not tall" say, roughly, "Chuck the belief that John is tall or at least disengage it from active use"? Does "Don't leave the door open" say, roughly, "Eliminate any intention you may have or acquire to leave the door open or else relegate it to your fantasy world rather than carrying it out"? Suppose that I say to my child, "Please, don't track mud into the house!" If the child has hitherto been tracking mud into the house on purpose, or if tracking mud into the house is something he might discover was fun to do, clearly the first function of my imperative *is* to cancel this destructive intention or to inoculate against it. If the child should continue to intend or if he should begin to intend to track mud in, clearly my imperative would not fulfill its proper function.

But surely "Don't track mud into the house!" has a positive function as well. It is supposed to produce in the child an intention *not* to track mud into the house and it is supposed to be followed by the carrying out of this intention—a positive act. Intending not to do something is something *more* than merely not intending to do it. For example, if the child continues to track mud in and then tries to excuse himself by saying, and saying honestly, "I didn't *mean* to do it," that will not be enough of an excuse. I will counter, "Not only must you not mean *to* do it; you must also mean *not* to do it!" And if he says "I did not know I was doing it," I will counter, "You must know that you are *not* doing it." My imperative "Don't track mud into the house" is not supposed to produce merely the absence of an intention to track mud in; nor is it supposed to produce merely the absence of a belief that mud is being tracked into the house. It is supposed to produce a fulfilled intention *not* to track mud in.

To carry out an intention *not* to track mud in requires positive action. It requires doing something contrary to or incompatible with tracking mud in. For example, the child must be sure that he either stays outside or stays inside, or that when he comes in his boots are clean, or that if they are muddy they will stay *off* the floor when he comes in—say, in his hand. The function of "Don't track mud into the house!" is surely to produce just as much of this sort of positive intentional behavior as is necessary to guarantee that the child does not track mud into the house.

The function of "not" in the context of a negative imperative is not then parallel to the function of "does not exist." True, "Don't do *A*!" does serve to shelve or inoculate against having an active intention to do *A*, but it does this only along the way to doing something else. This something else involves the production of positive acts that are contrary to or incompatible with doing *A*.

Now the imperative "Don't do *A*", when issued to *H*, has as its proper function to bring about the same state of affairs as would make the indicative sentence "*H* did not do *A*" true. Hence the proper function of the positive acts that the sentence "Don't do *A*" causes *H* to produce is to bring about a state of affairs that makes "*H* did not do *A*" true. But positive acts in the natural world have positive consequences in the natural world. They do produce not nonexistent things but existent things. The real value of "Don't do *A*" when obeyed, and the real value of "*H* did not do *A*" when it is true, must then be affairs that are real rather than affairs that are not real.

Consider the proper function of "John did not go to the office." It is supposed to produce in the hearer a belief that John did not go to the office, which is something different from having no opinion about whether John went to the office, and different from the state of being immune to a positive belief. (Inanimate objects are immune to all positive beliefs. They do not on this account have negative beliefs.) Rather, negative beliefs must serve some positive function of their own. And what this function is is really pretty obvious. Knowledge that John did not go to the office limits the options concerning what John *did* do. If he did not go to the office, he did something *else* than going to the office. Rather than going to the office, he did something or something happened to him that was *contrary* to his going to the office, and if what happened to him was other than his expiring (a positive happening), he is now somewhere *contrary* to being at the office. To know what John did not do is to have very slender yet positive information about what John did do. Combined with other information about what John didn't do, including that which results from knowing what John couldn't possibly do and what John wouldn't do, one may well be able to figure out what John *did* do under some description that is adequate for one's purposes. It is because John and his doings necessarily take place within a space of structured alternatives or of contrary doings or happenings, which alternatives can often be limited to a finite number given the large degree of inaccuracy of description that one's purposes usually tolerate, that knowing what John did not do may prove helpful.

I am claiming that what it is for one thing not to be the case is, always, for something or other *else* to be the case. Let me add another argument to this effect.

As we have seen, if I can cause something not to be the case by positive action, as when I obey a negative imperative, then its not being the case must be something that positive action can cause. But positive acts cause positive states of affairs. So one thing's not being the case must always correspond to something else's being the case. Otherwise we cannot explain how negative intentions are carried out. A parallel argument applies to beliefs. When all goes Normally, intentions cause their real values. Reciprocally, in the simplest cases at least, when all goes Normally the real values of beliefs cause the beliefs. It is because John's coat is brown that I believe John's coat is brown and it is because it is ten degrees below zero that I believe that it is ten degrees below zero. Negative beliefs too must have causes. Surely they too must be caused by their real values when all goes Normally. It is because John's coat is not red that I believe it is not red. But only real and positive affairs can be causes. So the real value of my belief that John's coat is not red must be the affair that is the coat's being nonred or perhaps, more specifically, brown. Certainly I *ascertain* that John's coat is not red *not* by failing to see that John's coat is red but by seeing that his coat is some other color. If I have not been able to see at all what color John's coat is, I will not judge that it is not red.

For one thing not to be the case is for some contrary thing or another to *be* the case. But it is, broadly speaking, only properties and relations that have contraries. And these are never contraries of one another absolutely. For example, both *ruddy* and *pale*, both *sitting* and *standing*, both *being on top of* and *being beside* are real variants in the world. Contrary properties and relations are contraries only upon given grounds, which grounds correspond to logical subjects of sentences. It is Johnny or it is Bill that cannot be at once ruddy and pale, sitting and standing, or one on top of and also beside the other. Thus the negative operates upon the logical predicate of a sentence only and does not affect the sense—the mapping rules for—its logical subject term or terms.

Indeed, the most customary job of the negative seems to be to operate only upon that part of the logical predicate of a sentence that is contained in the *grammatical* predicate of the sentence. Thus although "Painfully disappointed, Johnny did not return again" has the sentence "Johnny was painfully disappointed" embedded within its grammatical subject, the sentence will not be made true by the fact that Johnny was in fact pleased rather than disappointed. Similarly, although "Some diurnal bats are not herbivorous" has the sentence "some bats are diurnal" embedded within its grammatical subject, it is not made true by the fact that all bats are nocturnal. Since the function of a negative indicative sentence is to give positive information, a useful negative sentence should restrict rather than expand the domain of the possibilities it covers. Dividing a negative sentence into a grammatical subject that contains those parts of the logical predicate of the sentence that the negative is not operating upon and a grammatical predicate that contains those parts of the logical predicate that the negative is operating upon is an effective way to achieve this end. (It is true, however, that when "not" is placed externally, as in "It is not so that painfully disappointed, Johnny returned," it may affect more than the grammatical predicate of the "that" clause. Soon I will discuss this use of "not", calling it an "immunizing use of 'not.'")

How Negative Representations Map onto the World

The operator "not" customarily reverses the sense of that part of the logical predicate of a sentence that is contained in its grammatical predicate, so that this part now must correspond to a contrary of its ordinary *in re* value. But it is clear that there is no *particular* contrary of this *in re* value that the negative sentence must map. *"Not" turns a definite predicate into an indefinite one.* Consider the indefinite description "a dog." There is no particular dog that "a dog" has to correspond to in order for "a dog bit Johnny" to be true. Nor does "a dog" map an indefinite dog or, say, indefinite dogness. But if "a dog bit Johnny" is true, there must of course be some definite dog that makes the sentence true, and this dog is the real value of "a dog" in "a dog bit Johnny." Similarly, there are no particular herbivorous bats that "herbivorous bats" must correspond to for the sentence "Some herbivorous bats are blind" to be true. But if the sentence is true, there are some definite herbivorous bats that make it true and that are the real values of "some herbivorous bats" in that sentence. Likewise, if "John's coat is not red" is true, there must be some definite color that John's coat is, and this color is the real value of "not red" in the sentence. (I will discuss sentences like "Ideas are not red" soon.) But there is no particular color that John's coat must be in order for "John's coat is not red" to be true. And certainly, "not red" does not map a color that is indefinite or map indefinite coloredness. Also, just as the real value of "a dog" in "a dog bit Johnny" need not be identified in order that the sentence containing it should serve its proper functions Normally, so the real value of "not red" in the sentence "John's coat is not red" need not be identified in order for the sentence to serve its proper functions Normally. Negative outer sentences translate into negative inner sentences.

Consonant with this position on negation, in Chapter 16 I will argue that the ontological phenomenon of contrariety is more fundamental than the linguistic phenomenon of negation rather than the other way around. I will claim that the very identity of a property or relation is bound up with the identity of its contraries and that this is a truth of ontology not just logic.

Logical subjects do not as such have contraries, hence are unaffected by negation. Now it may be thought that in claiming that "not" customarily operates upon the logical predicates only of simple representing sentences I am claiming that the excluded middle does not apply to such sentences. For, it may be said, besides the possibility that the predicate of a sentence is true of its subject(s) and the possibility that some contrary of the predicate is true of its subject(s) there is the possibility that the supposed *in re* subject of a sentence does not exist and never did. But this third possibility, I am claiming, is just the possibility that the sentence has no determinate Fregean sense. It is the possibility that the subject term is a sham. Hence the sentence, too, is a sham. And the possibility that a sentence is a sham—that it is not fully determinate in sense, that it has in fact no proper function—is irrelevant to application of the law of the excluded middle. Obviously "*p* or not-*p*" has sense only if "*p*" has sense. My claim is merely that it is never a job of the negative, *in the context of a representational sentence*, to say that the sentence containing it lacks sense.

A difficulty is that whether or not a sentence has sense—and likewise, whether or not a belief is about anything—is not open to a priori inspection. Sentences can seem to have sense that do not—and beliefs can seem to be about something when they are not. Failure to appreciate this fact results in the impulse to believe, as early Wittgenstein and many others have believed, that if the "*x*" in "*x* does not exist" can *seem* to anyone to have a sense—e.g., if it has an intension—it must *really* have a sense, hence to view "*x* does not exist" as a negative *representation*. Then of course it is natural also to believe that a truly sweeping negative—one that will allow the law of excluded middle to hold—operates as does the negative in "*x* does not exist," substituting "that-*p*" for "*x*." The rationalist conviction that knowledge of the distinction between sense and non-sense must be a priori knowledge lies very deep in our tradition.

Other Uses of "Not"

The explanation that I have now given of the way "not" operates upon the Fregean sense of a simple representing sentence obviously casts no light upon how "not" functions in the context of nonrepresentational sentences. (More accurately, this explanation applies to nonrepresentational sentences, insofar as it applies, only at the level of protoreference.) But if the negative does something different in the context of nonrepresentational sentences than in the context of representational ones, what makes it always "the negative" in some unambiguous sense? For surely the "not," say, in "Cicero is not Brutus" must somehow be "the very same 'not'" as the "not" in "John did not go to the office"?

As we have seen, the "not" in "John did not go to the office" does more than merely inoculate a hearer against the belief that John went to the office. It inspires the belief that John did other than going to the office. Broadly speaking, it induces the hearer not just to leave his mind empty of the belief that John went to the office but to fill that void with an alternative mental attitude *of a certain kind* (this kind of belief, however, being indefinite belief). Similarly, the "not" in "Cicero is not Brutus" does more than leave the mind void of the disposition to identify Cicero with Brutus. It leaves the mind with the positive disposition to keep mental tokens of "Cicero" and of "Brutus" separate. And this attitude is other than the attitude that is having no opinion about whether Cicero was or was not Brutus—having a blank mind on the matter. Similarly, beyond believing that Homer existed and believing that he did not exist is a third alternative, excluded *both* by "Homer existed" *and* by "Homer did not exist," namely, not knowing whether Homer existed. It seems likely then that what is common to the function of "not" in the context of all kinds of sentence is to shunt the mental attitude of the hearer away from the attitude the corresponding affirmative would induce *toward* some definite *kind* of alternative. Putting this graphically, it is not a stabilizing response of hearers to *any* kind of negative sentence—not among the responses that will have helped account for proliferation of *any* kind of negative sentence— to turn the mind to jelly on the matter of the sentence. *Simply* not believing "*p*" is never the appropriate response to hearing "not-*p*." Rather, each kind of negative sentence shunts the mind toward its *own* kind of specific alternative to believing that *p*.

But if we now try to say more concretely what is the least common denominator of the functions of *all* kinds of negative sentences, what seems to be in common is just that in each case the negative shunts the mind *away* from the response the corresponding positive sentence would have produced. All that is in common to the function of all sentences of the form "not-*p*" is that all begin by surgically removing or inoculating against the belief that *p*. And this *abstracted* function of negation is occasionally recognized by speakers and hearers as they cooperatively turn the negative to a certain secondary or parasitic use:

> Sleepy child: "Has Santa come yet?"
> First adult: "No dear, he has not come yet."
> Second adult to first adult, laughing: "Very true, very very true! Santa has not been here yet."

It is possible that both of the adults in the dialogue would say that "Santa has not been here" was *literally* true, though misleading. But the adults would be mistaken. For what makes "Santa has not been here," in this usage, true is that there is no Santa. And it is perfectly clear that merely saying "Santa has not been here" will mislead *anyone* who does not *already* know that Santa does not exist. If "Santa has not been here" can be appreciated only by one who *already* knows that there is no Santa, clearly it cannot be a proper function of it to induce the belief that there is no Santa. The use of "not" in "Santa has not been here" has got to be a secondary use, not one that independently helps to proliferate tokens of "not." An indication of this is that, as in the case of all parasitic uses of language, a special context and a special understanding between speaker and hearer is needed to force "Santa has not been here" to join a *cooperative* speaker with a *cooperative* hearer in a *common* venture with language—in this case, a joke. Because the child does not have this special understanding, the joke goes over the child's head.

Similar remarks go for "My chauffeur is not picking me up tonight" when everyone present knows that I have no chauffeur, and for "None of *my* sons ever gets into mischief" when the company knows I have no sons. How do such jokes work? They work because there *is* a secondary or parasitic usage of "not" that extracts from usual uses of "not" only the common function that is removal of a belief or immunizing of the hearer against belief. Call this the "immunizing" use of the negative, for its function is only to inoculate against a belief—not to give information. Immunizing uses of the negative are parasitic. They always require a special context to make them work.

The immunizing use of "not" is found in response to a question that has been asked or a statement made but that is without fully determinate sense. If someone seriously asks me "Is your chauffeur coming for you tonight?" I may temporarily block with the reply "no" or say "My chauffeur is not coming." But then I must immediately force that sentence, in order that it not be in essence a lie, into the immunizing use by adding "I don't have a chauffeur." When the negative occurs externally unless it is operating upon a logical operator, it is, I believe, always an immunizing negative. Can you construct a situation in which someone would naturally say, "It is not so that, painfully disappointed, Johnny returned" or in which someone would say "It is not the case that the present king of France is wise" yet in which the reason for use of such a labored expression was not that the speaker had reason to believe that the hearer already believed or would otherwise believe the contrary?

Any sentence without determinate sense can be disposed of with an immunizing "not" so long as the context makes it clear that this immunizing use is what is intended. Thus gold is *not* square and *not* round, ideas are *not* green, light bulbs are *not* filled with dephlogistonated air, and indeed, the slithy toves did *not* gyre and gimble in the wabe in case you thought they did. (I used to think that God forthine-ested the kingdom, the power and the glory forever when He answered the last line of the Lord's Prayer. But He doesn't.)

We are tempted to take external or immunizing negation as the deep and true kind of negation, I believe, *because* this use of "not" abstracts what is common to all more specific functions of "not."

"All"

The "not" in "Not all *A*'s are ϕ" is not just an immunizing "not." If it were, then the fact that "All slithy toves gyre" lacks sense would entail that "Not all slithy toves gyre" was straightforwardly true. Because the "not" in "not all *A*'s are ϕ" is not merely an immunizing "not," it does not follow from the fact that a sentence of the form "Not all *A*'s are ϕ" is not true that the correlative sentence of the form "All *A*'s are ϕ" is true. From the fact that "Not all slithy toves gyre" is not true, it does not follow that "All slithy toves gyre" is true. So from the fact that "Not all unicorns are white" is not true, it *should* not follow that "All unicorns are white" is true. Indeed, if "unicorn" lacks sense (this not to be confused with lacking intension), then "All unicorns are white" *should* lack sense too—though it might still have "pretend" uses.

Indeed, if the "not" in "Not all *A*'s are ϕ" operated the way "not" operates in the context of other *representational* sentences, then "All *A*'s are ϕ" would *never* be true if there were no *A*'s. "All *A*'s are ϕ" would always imply "Some *A*'s are ϕ"; i.e., it would have existential import. First let me explain why this is so. Then let us tackle the prior question *whether* sentences of the form "All *A*'s are ϕ" *are* representations.

Consider the following negative representations: "Painfully disappointed, Johnny did not return again"; "The boy who delivers our paper is not very tall"; "Some diurnal bats are not herbivorous"; "No herbivorous bats are diurnal." In not one of these sentences does the negative operate upon any logical predicate contained in the sentence's grammatical subject. Suppose that it were true that the "not" in "Not all *A*'s are ϕ" also failed to operate upon or apply to any logical predicates contained in the sentence's grammatical subject. "Not all *A*'s are ϕ" is equivalent to "Some *A*'s are not ϕ." Hence if there were any positive sentence embedded in the grammatical subject "some *A*'s," this positive sentence would have *also* to be embedded in the grammatical subject "All *A*'s." For example, consider "All purple cows are gentle." Negated it becomes "Not all purple cows are gentle," which is equivalent to

"Some purple cows are not gentle." The grammatical subject of this last sentence contains the embedded sentence "(some) cows are purple." If negation has not affected any logical predicates embedded in the grammatical subject of the original sentence, then that original sentence, "All purple cows are gentle," must also have had embedded in its grammatical subject the sentence "(some) cows are purple." So, if sentences of the form "All A's are ϕ" *do* imply sentences of the form "Some A's are ϕ," as Aristotle said they did, *then the way that the negative operates upon them is perfectly consistent with the way the negative operates upon other representational sentences* and requires no special commentary.

Are sentences of the form "All A's are ϕ" then representations? I will answer that usually they are but that sometimes they are not. Let us begin as we have on other occasions by asking what the stabilizing functions of sentences of the form "All A's are ϕ" might be. Then we can go on to ask whether, in order to serve these proper functions, they would have to map onto the world.

Surely a stabilizing function of all sentences of the form "All A's are ϕ" is at *least* to produce in the hearer a disposition to make certain kinds of inferences yielding true conclusions. For example, one who believes that all A's are ϕ, if his thinking processes operate Normally, will at least move from beliefs of the form "x is an A" to beliefs of the form "x is ϕ" and from "x is not ϕ" to "x is not an A" and from "No B's are ϕ" to "No B's are A's," etc. But beyond these basic functions, the functions of "All A's are ϕ" seem to divide.

There is a use of "All A's are ϕ" that is what might be called "nomic." Then "All A's are ϕ" licenses subjunctive inferences of this sort: "Suppose x were an A; then x would be ϕ" and "Suppose x is not to be ϕ; then x had better not be an A." For example, consider the sentence "All students found cheating on examinations will be failed," suitably placed in a college catalogue or handbook. The student who draws appropriate theoretical and practical inferences with regard to himself upon reading this sentence may well become properly adapted to his world thereby, and this despite the fact that, perhaps, no student at his college is ever found cheating on an exam and he knows this. The student may become properly adapted to his world by the sentence simply because the inference dispositions produced in him by the sentence parallel or map dispositions in his world—e.g., map or parallel a certain causal law that is true in situ. For it may well be that the authorities are so disposed that they would fail any student found cheating. Thus one might say that his thinking *processes* or dispositions were correct intentional icons because they mirrored potential *processes* or dispositions in his world.

But so far as I can see, "All A's are ϕ," used merely nomically, is not a representation. It does not have to map onto anything in order to serve its proper functions Normally. Rather, it causes a disposition in the hearer that maps onto a disposition in the world. But the nomic use of "All A's are ϕ" is, I believe, a rather special use and is always flagged in one way or another, certainly in those cases in which there are not or may not be any A's. In the above example, it is flagged by the future tense and by its position among the regulations, say, in the handbook.

The more common and unflagged use of "All A's are ϕ" requires that there be some A's in order that it function Normally. For one of the functions that it performs is that of introducing the term "A's" to the hearer as a term that maps. Just as one alternative function of "the man who supplies our lab with white mice" is to introduce a hearer to a new referent, one of the functions of "All herbivorous bats" is to introduce the hearer to a new nonempty class of entities—the class of herbivorous bats. Barring a very special context of introduction or a very special understanding between speaker and hearer, no hearer and believer of the sentence "All herbivorous bats are nocturnal" will fail to believe that there are herbivorous bats and no speaker of such a sentence could fail to purpose that his hearer believe this. Moreover, if the hearer were to fail to believe this, in most cases the point of the speaker's utterance would be completely lost.

Granted this, two questions still need to be answered about "All." First, why is there a temptation to believe that "All A's are ϕ" may be true not just *despite* the fact that there are no A's but actually *because* of the fact that there are no A's? No one is tempted to believe that "The man who supplies white mice to our lab is tall" would be made true by the fact that no one supplies our lab with white mice. Why then should "All diurnal bats are herbivorous" be supposed to be true because there are no diurnal bats? Second, we still need to ask whether and how ordinary sentences of the form "All A's are ϕ" are supposed to map onto the world.

Notice that if we extract only what is common to the nomic and the ordinary uses of "All A's are ϕ," there is no common Normal explanation that explains proper performance of both but only a common focused proper function. This proper function is to produce certain inference dispositions in the hearer. When there are no A's, acquiring these inference dispositions certainly will not maladapt a hearer. The disposition to infer from "x is an A" to "x is ϕ" will never be activated in the hearer at all unless he mistakenly takes something to be an A, and then the mistaken conclusion will be attributable to the false premise "x is an A." Moreover, inferences from "x is not ϕ" to "x is not an A"

and from "No B's are ϕ" to "No B's are A's" will yield *true* conclusions if there are no A's (granted "A's" has a sense, hence, in this case, that "A" is a complex term). For example, from "All the bad apples have been removed from the bin" one can conclude that the bin contains, if any apples, only good apples, which may be just what one wants to know, whether there were any bad apples in the bin in the first place being of no consequence. Such inferences will yield true conclusions in accordance with a perfectly reliable, though not in accordance with a Normal, explanation. Hence, "All A's are ϕ" acquires a secondary use that is abstracted from what is in common to its primary uses, just as the immunizing "not" acquires such a use. But, as in the case of the immunizing "not," "All A's are ϕ" cannot be used *cooperatively* by speaker and hearer in this abstracted sense unless either a special context or a special mutual understanding is supplied. "All my violins are Stradivariuses," when I have no violins, is clearly not a stabilizing use of "All A's are ϕ."

These lengthy preliminaries over, now we can address what from our standpoint is the most important problem. Supposing that if and when "All A's are ϕ" is a representation there must be A's for it to map, in accordance with what rule does it map? What is its real value when true, and how is this real value determined in accordance with a rule?

Consider the subject term "all A's" as a description, as "the A" and "an A" and "some A's" are descriptions. Is "all A's" a definite description or an indefinite description? Definite descriptions, we have said, have a referential function. That is, when a definite description is properly indexically adapted, there *is* something definite onto which it is supposed to map in a sentence, which something is determined *prior* to completing the sentence. If "all A's are ϕ" is a mapping sentence and if there are A's, surely there *is* something definite onto which the "A" in "all A's" is supposed to map in the sentence which something is determined *prior* to completing the sentence. It is supposed to map onto *each* and every one of the A's. In this respect, "all A's" is like a definite description. It has an indexical adaptor, hence has determinate sense, if and only if there are A's for it to map onto. On the other hand, the referent of a definite description is supposed to be *identified* by the hearer, whereas the hearer of "All A's are ϕ" is *not* supposed to identify each of the A's. In this respect "all A's" is unlike a definite description but like an indefinite one. For although an indefinite description must have a real value, this value is not supposed to be identified by the hearer. "All A's" thus escapes the definite-and-referential vs. indefinite-and-non-referential dichotomy. When properly adapted, there is something definite onto which it is supposed to map, namely, onto each of the A's;

but this something—these somethings—are not supposed to be individually identified. (Necessarily identifying descriptions that are functioning purely descriptively also escape the dichotomy.)

"All A's are ϕ" maps onto the world as it should if every one of the A's is a real value of "A" in that sentence. That is, the real value of a true sentence of the form "All A's are ϕ" is the affair that is a's being ϕ plus the affair that is b's being ϕ plus the affair that is c's being ϕ, etc., where a, b, and c, etc., constitute all the A's. It does not follow that "All A's are ϕ" is equivalent to a sentence of the form "a is ϕ and b is ϕ and c is ϕ . . . " where "a" and "b" and "c", etc., name all the A's. A sentence naming all the A's by turn and saying of each that it is ϕ would have to have added to it "a is an A and b is an A and c is an A, etc.," and would also have to have added "and that is all the A's there are" in order even to *imply* "All A's are ϕ." Conversely, "All A's are ϕ" does not name or identify each of the A's, hence could not imply any sentence that did.

Compare: although the real value of "A dog bit Johnny" may be the affair that was *Fido's* biting Johnny, "A dog bit Johnny" is not equivalent to "Fido bit Johnny." To "Fido bit Johnny" there would have to be added "and Fido is a dog" in order for it to imply "a dog bit Johnny." And "A dog bit Johnny" does not identify any particular dog as a biter of Johnny, so cannot imply "Fido bit Johnny." The real value of "A dog bit Johnny" is determined by what there happens to be *in the world* that corresponds to that sentence in accordance with its particular mapping rules. Thus it is that the real value of "A dog bit Johnny" comes to be specific, although the sentence itself did no specifying.

In exactly parallel fashion, the real value of "All my students are unmarried," if true, is determined by what there happens to be *in the world* that corresponds to it in accordance with its Normal mapping rule. According to this mapping rule what must correspond to it for it to function Normally is a set of affairs each of which is constituted by an individual student's being unmarried, the set of these individual students being, precisely, the set of my students. The set of affairs that satisfies this requirement, supposing that the requirement is satisfied, consists of Mary's being unmarried, Bill's being unmarried, Sam's being unmarried, etc. So this set is the real value of "All my students are unmarried." The real value is thus specific, although the sentence, taken alone, does not specify this value. The *world*, coupled with the sentence, specifies this value.

Part IV
Theory of Identity

Chapter 15
The Act of Identifying

Any number of times in previous chapters we have run into problems pertaining to identity, only to brush them aside.

In Chapter 6 I drafted a sketch of how language maps onto the world. In Part III I added many details to that sketch. Yet the most important obstacle to a correspondence theory of meaning and truth has not been tackled. If language has its powers because it maps the world, then the identity or selfsameness of the significant variables of the affairs it maps must be an objective or thought-independent sameness—one that explains rather than being explained by the operations of language and thought. There must be objectively selfsame world affairs that different sentence tokens can map, objectively selfsame subject variants *in re* for subjects of sentences to map, and objectively selfsame predicate variants *in re* for predicates of sentences to map. A realist view needs support from a compatible ontology. I have to make it plausible that the world contains objective selfsames that are discovered rather than created by thought and language. I will do this in Chapters 16 and 17.

Besides sketching an ontology of identity, I must forge a link with the philosophy of mind, supplying a plausible description of the act of recognizing identity. Many times, especially in Part III, I have reiterated that what distinguishes representations from more primitive intentional icons is that the mapping values of the elements of representations are supposed to be identified. But the temporary model that I offered of the act of identifying the mapping value of an icon element was not adequate. I described the act of identifying the mapping value of an outer language element as the act of translating this into an inner language element having the same sense. But what is it for the mapping value of an *inner* icon element to be identified? What is it for me to know *what* I am thinking of as opposed merely to having an intentional icon element in my head—or body? Where, in the end, lies the difference between the inner adrenalin icon and a thought of something? I have vowed not to invoke the mystery of consciousness in order to explain this difference (Chapter 5). The purpose of the present chapter is to describe the act of identifying in naturalist terms.

Finally, to the ontology of identity and the philosophy of mind of identity must be added an epistemology of identity. In Chapter 5 I warned that I would take the position that the knowledge of what one is thinking of, indeed the very knowledge that one is thinking at all, is not a priori but a posteriori knowledge. But then it must be explained what a posteriori criterion is used in order to tell if one is thinking of something and whether one can identify the value of one's thought—and why this criterion works. This will be accomplished in Chapters 18 and 19.

The Act of Identifying

The act of identifying the real value of an intentional icon element is the act of knowing or cognizing *what* in the world that element maps or represents. Soon I will discuss the classical realist view that knowledge of what I am thinking of or representing to myself must, in the end, be grounded in a direct apprehension of that thing, or a direct apprehension of its nature as presented to mind by, for example, a likeness. I will also discuss the nominalist view of the act of identifying. But first let me present my own view quite baldly. I will start with some examples of acts of identifying and then move to a general characterization.

A primitive sort of act of identifying occurs whenever percepts originating in separate senses but representing something common are used jointly in guiding an activity. For example, in tying a clove hitch or a bowline, though probably not in tying your shoes, you may need to see as well as feel what you are doing. The way visual representations are joined with tactual representations to guide the movements that produce the knot is effective in part *because* certain aspects of the visual and tactual representations overlap in real value. For example, you first see and then feel the *same* end of the rope, the *same* loop, etc., and the success of the programs that guide your movements cannot be given a Normal explanation that does not make reference to this sameness in the mapping values of certain elements of the percepts that guide you. Thus the most ordinary manipulations of everyday objects often require abilities to identify these objects and their parts as common real values of different representations. It is reasonable to suppose that this often occurs without the mediation of explicit beliefs or intentions. Rather, one's most basic know-hows probably often involve abilities to identify the real values of various kinds of percepts with one another directly. After all, even quite lowly animals often exhibit quite sophisticated kinds of visual-tactual coordination.

Applications of what one has learned from past experience usually involve acts of identifying. These applications involve acts of identifying whenever it is true that inner icons of past affairs are joined with inner icons of present affairs to produce thoughts or actions in a way that presupposes that these icons overlap in real value. In applying my past experience with kittens to the training of Tabby, I identify the world-variant *kitten* as represented in my memory of certain past dealings with kittens with this same world-variant as represented in present perceptions of Tabby-as-a-kitten. Even if I have no explicit memories of my past experiences with training kittens, if the know-how that I use in training Tabby was learned, in part, via perceptions of kittens, still it is true that those past perceptions of kittens have been used jointly with my present perceptions of Tabby-as-a-kitten to produce my responses to Tabby. Hence acts of identification of the world-variant *kitten* are involved. On the other hand, it seems reasonable that much learning, even by people, is not mediated by perception or thought but occurs below the level of the formation of inner representations. Classical conditioning is probably this kind of learning. If you condition me to blink when a buzzer sounds by coupling the buzzer with puffs of air into my eye, it seems unlikely that representations of any kind are involved in this process, or that acts of identifying are required.

Perhaps the neatest examples of acts of identifying are acts of explicit mediate inference. Suppose that I move in thought from "John is taller than Bill" and "Bill is taller than Tom" to "John is taller than Tom." The two representations upon which the act of identifying operates are the inner representations "John is taller than Bill" and "Bill is taller than Tom." Each of these icons contains a different inner token of "Bill," and if the premises of my inference are true these have real values and values that are the same. The interpreting device that uses "John is taller than Bill" and "Bill is taller than Tom" such that in so using these it performs an act of identifying is the device that performs inferences of the general type "x is ϕer than y and y is ϕer than z, so x is ϕer than z." It performs properly when it produces a true conclusion. In this case, it performs properly in accordance with a Normal explanation rather than by accident in part because the tokens of "Bill" that occur in the two premises have the same real value. In so doing it performs an act of correct identification of the referent of "Bill" as appearing in *each* of the two premises, or correctly identifies the referent of the one token of "Bill" *with* that of the other.

In order to carry out an explicit intention, one must perform acts of identification of the referents of elements in the representation that is that intention. If I plan to take a certain bus and carry out this intention Normally, there must come a point at which I identify the bus as represented in perception with the bus of my intention and act accordingly. That is, there must come a time when my activities are guided jointly by my intention and my perception, the Normal explanation for how the relevant action-guiding mechanisms in me manage to perform their ultimate functions making a necessary reference to the fact that intention and perception contain elements that map onto the same.

The process of forming explicit intentions on the basis of desires and beliefs requires acts of identifying. Often long chains of practical mediate inference—the process of building model "bridges" from desires and beliefs to a future intended world—are involved. Or consider, for example, how many pieces of information about a child one may have to put together before making a responsible major decision affecting that child's life. Obviously, that all these bits of information are about the *same* child will figure in any explanation of how benefits result from this deliberation process if any benefits follow in accordance with a Normal explanation.

Speaking now quite generally, in order that a correct act of identification should be performed we need at least *two* intentional icons, one element of each of these icons having the same real value as one of the elements of the other. Then an act of correct identification is performed by any interpreting device that uses these icons *jointly* in order to perform a proper function where the Normal explanation for proper performance of this function makes reference to the fact that the real value of these two elements *is* the same. That is, the interpreting device will be able to accomplish what good it does Normally only *because* these elements map the same. The act of identifying operates upon pairs of intentional icons. But in so doing it identifies variants in the world.

Acts of incorrect identification are merely acts performed by devices the proper functions of which are to perform correct acts of identification, but where the conditions are not Normal for their performance (for example, the icons upon which they operate are maladapted) or where these devices are not working correctly.

Intentional icon elements Normally are manifestations—in a suitably broad sense of that word in which the present can also make manifest the future—of the world-variants that are their real values. Thus the fully Normal act of identifying is an act whereby manifestations of a thing, which manifestations have been dispersed via different causal chains, perhaps through diverse media, perhaps from different times and places, and which carry different information about the disposition of that thing in world affairs, are brought *together* to bear in the fashioning of a purposive act or process the outcome of which hangs upon the disposition of that thing in a variety of world affairs. The act of identifying an individual or a material (gold, water) bears the same description as does the act of identifying a kind, a property or a relation, all of these being possible real values of elements of representations.

In Part III I used the act of translating an outer term or representation into an inner term or representation as a temporary model of the act of identifying the referent of the outer term. And this act *is* an example of the act of identifying. First consider the case in which the referent of the inner term token into which the outer term is translated is later identified via this inner term's being joined with *another* inner term token during an act that identifies the referents of these inner tokens with one another. The mechanisms that did the translating of the outer term, combined with the mechanisms that later produced the inner act of identifying, will have served a cooperative proper function in accordance with a Normal explanation only if the outer term has in fact the same referent as the inner tokens do. Hence the referent of the outer term has been identified. Similarly, when one follows a map, one identifies the real values of various elements and aspects of the map by translating these into inner sentences or inner percepts, values of which are identified with real values of percepts derived directly from the world. One looks at the map, then looks at the world, then is guided by the two together, identifying certain places on the map with places as one sees them in the world. Following instructions also requires that the values of various terms in the instructions be identified with values of elements in one's percepts.

But suppose that an outer representation is translated into an inner representation but that the inner representation never happens to get used as a premise of inference or as a guide to practical activity. Have the referents of the outer representation still been identified?

It is reasonable to suppose that the systems that coin inner terms and the systems that use these terms employ some kind of scheme comparable with the phonetic schemes that all conventional languages employ. Even sign languages employ such schemes, as do all nonalphabetic systems of writing. We must suppose that what the inner language interpreter devices identify as the same inner term again vs. a different inner term is determined in accordance with some kind of same-difference scheme natural to the media of inner representation so that the term inventing and iterating programs and their corresponding interpreter programs can manage to coordinate. Iterating an inner term—producing new tokens of the same term type again in new inner sentences—is then preparation, specifically, for acts of identifying. The term-iterating programs determine when their interpreters will perform acts of identifying upon the representations they produce by producing these in accordance with a certain same-difference scheme.

Hence the act of iterating an inner term can be considered to be a secondary kind of act of *identification* of the term's value. To say an inner "red" or "Johnny" to oneself once again in the context of a new inner sentence is to identify, or potentially identify, the referent of this token of "red" or "Johnny" with the referent of earlier tokens of these types and of tokens to come in future. That is why we were able in Part III to model the act of identifying the referent of an outer language term as the act of translating this into an inner term having the same sense. Such an act of translation is always at least a preliminary act of identification. It is, as it were, a "first act" identification. Similarly, the act of coining a new inner name to be governed by some definite intension or method of iteration is a preliminary act of identification of the referent of that term.

The various media in which visual, auditory, and tactual, etc., representations occur also must be characterized by same-difference schemas that are read by the devices that identify the values of icons occurring in these media. Also, it seems that a *general* coordination among visual space, auditory space, kinesthetic space, and tactual space is achieved by normal people, transformations of each of these spaces mapping onto transformations of the others in accordance with general rules that are taken into account by the devices that guide our activities in space by joint use of the various senses. The formation of a percept— a seeing *as* or a hearing *as* or a feeling *as*—seems to be a preliminary act of identification of, at a minimum, the spatial values of its variants. Thus seeing something as a (real) duck or as a (real) rabbit is in part seeing it as a certain kind of three-dimensional object in space, having such and such a back side, top side, and side side. But it is reasonable to suppose that such a *seeing as* is a way of being prepared to identify the various values of aspects one's percept also with those of *prior* and *future* percepts and with those of mental sentences about rabbits or ducks as one applies one's previous experience to the present situation, hence that perception in general is first-act identification of what is perceived. (Seeing a duck or a rabbit *in a picture* (à la Wittgenstein) is, of course, only a pretend *seeing as.*)

How the Classical Realist Thinks, and How He Knows What He Thinks

I have distinguished three issues in talking about thoughts. First is the issue of intentionality. What is it for a thought to be of or about something? The theory of intentional icons addressed this question. More specifically, thoughts-of are special *kinds* of intentional icon elements or variants, the values of which are supposed to be identified. Second, there is the question what it is for a person to grasp *what* his thought is of. I have claimed that for him to grasp this is for him to have the ability correctly to identify the referents of this thought with referents of other intentional icon elements. Third, there is the question what test or measure is used to assess whether or not an apparent thought is in fact of something and whether it is of what one takes it to be of. That is, there is the question what standard we use when we throw out terms as being vacuous or throw out intensions as being wrong or too unreliable; what standard we use to determine whether the acts of identifying we are performing are acts of correct identification. This third question I have promised to discuss under the heading *epistemology of identity* in Chapters 18 and 19. Separation of these three issues, so crucial to the thesis of this book, is completely foreign to the world of the classical realist. (There are always exceptions, of course. In this case at least Leibniz, Spinoza, and in some moods Descartes are partial exceptions to what follows.)

According to the classical realist, to think of a thing is to bring it or its "nature"—that which makes it to be itself or to be what it is— before the aware or conscious mind. The thing's nature may come before or enter consciousness alone (e.g., Plato, Aristotle, Husserl) or as *in* the thing thought of which is thus itself directly before the mind (e.g., early Russell and Moore, phenomenalism) or as in some representation of the thing that embodies its nature by being a copy of it (e.g., Locke, Hume) or as in some mode or aspect of the thing that presents its nature to mind (e.g., Descartes, Whitehead). Thus to think of a thing is ipso facto to know *what* it is that one is thinking of. Indeed, for the classical realist there is no distinction among these four: seeming to oneself to be thinking of something; really thinking of something; seeming to oneself to know what one is thinking of; actually knowing what one is thinking of. Identifying the value of one's thought, knowing the identity of that of which one thinks, is not an act of identifying *with* or *re*identifying, but an act needing to involve only *one* encounter with the thing identified or with a representation of it. And, of course, the idea that there might be evidence gathered from outside of that compact drama occurring within the momentary act of thinking-of, which evidence bears on whether this act qua act of thinking of and qua act of identification is genuine, is utterly foreign to classical realist views. (True, Descartes, Spinoza, Leibniz, and even Hume[1] take it that ideas when indistinct may not correspond to anything real or possible. But whether the thing or nature present to mind is clear and distinct is either determined from within the act of thought or determined by armchair reflection, and if it is distinct, then one is necessarily really thinking of and knowing the nature or identity of that thing, real or possible.)

If some kind of act of mind or of awareness is required in order for consciousness to grasp or recognize the identity or nature of what is presented to it in thought, according to classical realist theories this act is in each instance exactly identical, regardless of the nature or identity that is recognized. The difference between acts of identification of different things or between thoughts of different things lies only in the difference of what is presented to mind on the occasions of these acts. Further, each instance of the act of identifying is understood to take place wholly within the confines of a single moment of time, making, of itself, no reference to past or future acts or thoughts. The classical thesis thus tends to place severe restrictions upon the kinds of things that can be admitted as possible objects for thought, or upon what the "natures" of things can be like. And the classical thesis tends to mystify the act of taking one thing to be the same thing as *another*. Let me take up these points in order.

Since thinking of something takes place at a single definite moment, the thing identified in thought, or its nature if that is what is present to mind in its stead, must be presented to mind at a single definite moment. But the mind recognizes only that which is presented to it and only *as* presented. It follows that the thing or nature should not be of an *enduring* temporal character. For how could an enduring entity be presented qua enduring in a single moment of time? Whatever it is that can come before mind must be either momentary, or outside of time entirely—eternal. Thus all things that can be thought of must be either momentary or eternal, or have natures that are either momentary or eternal. How can this be so?

From the time of Plato through that of Descartes and Locke, a fundamental distinction was drawn between perception and thought. Perception involved something's being before the mind, but nothing was known or identified in perception alone. Rather, recognition, an act of pure thought, took place as a result of encounter with the fleeting and momentary stuff of sense. Sense was thought of as managing somehow to turn the mind toward eternal entities that were only partially, distortedly, or impurely disclosed in sense. Thus the classical theories of recollection, illumination, and abstraction. According to these early realist theories, what came directly before the mind during *thought* was always an eternal entity of some kind. Hence, anything that could be thought of had to be either an eternal object or an object having a nature—a something that made it to be itself—that was eternal.

Now it was not too difficult to think of properties and kinds as being eternal objects, their ingression here or there into temporal affairs seeming accidental to their essential nature. So properties and kinds were generally taken to be thought of directly. They themselves could appear before or inform the mind; they could be their *own* natures. But thinking of properties and kinds as eternal objects did pose problems for ontology. It was hard to see how eternal objects stood in relation to temporal affairs—how they could have adventures in time and space. And no matter how these eternal objects were understood as managing to relate to the flux that is the ordinary world, it was very hard to see how involvement in the world could be essential to them. The idea that properties and kinds—forms, universals—do not really need the actual world at all but might perfectly well be without being exemplified was nearly irresistible.

Enduring objects, on the other hand, could not come directly before the mind. Yet they could not be thought of unless they had natures that *could* come before the mind. Hence the enduring object and its nature must be separated: one is temporal, the other eternal; one is only accidentally, the other necessarily. An obvious and simplifying move here was to suppose that the natures of temporal objects were sets of properties, properties being things that could be thought of directly. The nature of an ordinary spatial and temporal thing was a set of properties by which one might think of the thing. But this view again posed problems for ontology. How the nature—the itselfness, the very identity—of a concrete temporally located individual could be a set of eternal and essentially nonlocated properties is repeatedly puzzled over in the classical tradition. And the more basic and general question of how the nature of a thing—its itselfness, its identity—could be anything other than the-thing-itself-over-again surely *should* have puzzled the classical philosophers even when it did not. The notion that the identity or itselfness of a thing is a *thing* of some kind—a "nature"—is queer enough. The notion that its itselfness is something *other than it* is desperate.

Empiricism concerning the origin of ideas turned these classical problems upside down. What was revolutionary about the new empiricism was not, of course, the notion that ideas are not innate. What was revolutionary was the idea that nothing more than, less than, or other than what is first presented in sense constitutes the content of thoughts. Hume's thesis was revolutionary in insisting that the complete, undistorted, and pure nature of everything that can be thought of must first have been presented in sense. The crucial distinction that had previously been insisted upon between perception and thought thus collapsed. If one thinks of perception as the awareness of impressions, sense data or percepts, these being what are within or before the mind during perception, the natural result is an about-face from earlier realist positions: what is thought of is, in the first instance, always *momentary* rather than eternal. The problem becomes not how to construct the temporal out of the eternal, but how to construct enduring things and also properties and kinds out of momentary things. Thus both ordinary spatiotemporal objects and abstract entities came to be viewed as suspicious items needing to be explained or explained away. Various forms of phenomenalism and nominalism were the natural result.

Besides the tendency to view "natures" (properties or reified possibilities or meanings or essences) as eternal things that didn't need the actual world in order to be, the tendency to separate "natures" of ordinary objects from these objects themselves and the tendency toward various kinds of phenomenalism and nominalism, classical realist views showed a strong tendency to assimilate ordinary acts of thinking-of to acts of judgment. If it is the nature of an object rather than the object itself that comes before the mind in thought, and if the nature does not need the object in order to be, then the nature could come before the mind even though the object was not real or existent. To think of an object as existing rather than merely as possible must then require an act of mind over and above mere contemplation of the nature of the object. This more is then assimilated to an act of judgment. Engaged thinking-of (contrast pretend thinking-of—see Chapter 12, "Exists") is taken to be the act of thinking *that* something exists. This sort of move proved especially useful to the empiricists, who believed that the only things that can be thought of are things originally presented in sense. Now things that were not presented in sense so that one could not have, as Russell called it, "knowledge by acquaintance" of them could still be *judged* about. One judged about them by first judging *that* something existed having certain properties and relations to other things and then going on to assert what more was true of this something.

But turning thoughts-of into acts of judgment in this way raises new difficulties for ontology. "Exists" now appears to correspond to something that needs to be *added* to a thing's nature or to its identifying properties before one has an *actual* thing of that nature. Existence threatens to become an aspect of the world that must be taken separate account of by ontology. Moreover, instead of being perfectly simple or elementary variants in thoughts, ideas of objects now appear to be necessarily complex, articulate information about these objects being packed into mere thoughts *of* them. Applying a term is equated with judging *that* its intension is exemplified; simple ideas of ordinary objects are turned into judgments *about* the properties of and relations among simpler objects, for example, sense data. In brief, the classical realist view of the acts of thinking-of and identifying was what drove philosophers toward philosophical analysis in its various forms.

But the classical realist view that equates thinking-of with identifying has still another kind of consequence that seems to me to be even more telling. According to the classical thesis, an act of identifying is completely contained in a single moment of time and involves just one encounter with its object. This description makes the act of identifying appear to be nothing more than a sort of aesthetic experience—a moment in which consciousness is bathed in the awareness of a thing or of its nature. But what possible purpose could such an experience serve?

Let us begin the other way around, asking what kinds of purposes identifying usually does serve. What is the point of identifying things? Aside from such peculiar contexts as those of playing twenty questions or taking biology lab quizzes, the point of identifying is always the same. It is to enable one to bring one's prior knowledge or experience of the identified to bear in its present context or to ready one to take one's present knowledge or experience of the identified to future encounters with it. Or, it is to make it possible to bring one's experience of the identified that is gained via one medium of perception—say, one's experience of it as seen—to bear, during action or thought, along *with* experience of it that has been gained via other media—language, touch, hearing, inference, etc.

But this sort of purpose can be served only if the identifying is or makes possible *identifying-with*—identifying an object presently encountered with an object of prior or future knowledge, or identifying an object encountered in one way with itself as encountered another way. Any plausible description of the act of identifying must describe that act as intrinsically relational—as at root really an *identifying-with*—or at least describe it in such a way that we can understand how the act might lead to, aid, or make possible acts of identifying-with. But this, the classical realist theories do not do.

The classical realist takes thinking of a thing to include identifying it. Yet he takes thinking of a thing to be a momentary experience, having no necessary connections to anything or any time outside itself. Suppose that I am reading a biography of Kant. Now I think of him as a child in Königsberg. Now I think of him teaching, carrying thirteen lecture courses at one time. Now I think of him writing about physical geography. Now I think of him mixing a new bottle of ink before plunging into the "A Deduction," and so forth. Suppose that in this manner I think of Kant one hundred and thirteen times in an hour and, during the next day or two, twenty-three more times. Each time I think of him I identify him. That is, I know *who* I am thinking of. Yet, according to the classical realist, this knowing who I am thinking of has nothing to do with my *connecting* any of these one hundred and thirty-six thoughts together. Grasping that it is the *same* person who spent his childhood in Königsberg, wrote about physical geography, gave all those lecture courses at once, etc., has nothing to do with the matter of knowing who I am thinking of each of those hundred and thirty-six times. Thinking of Kant and knowing who I am thinking of one hundred and thirty-six times is merely having one hundred and thirty-six successive vivid flashes of Immanuel-Kant-awareness, nothing else. But, of course, the relation or relating involved in identifying a thing with itself cannot be constituted merely through the real or objective identity of the thing that appears to mind on separate occasions. In order to identify-with, a thinker must *recognize* the sameness of a thing as encountered or thought-of on separate occasions. Merely to think again of what is in fact the same thing is not to recognize it *as* the same again.

Let me now summarize what I take to be certain strengths of my position as against that of the classical realist.

The theory of intentionality and of the act of identifying that I have offered places no restrictions upon the sorts of things that can be thought of and identified, except that these things must be real and capable of figuring in explanations of natural events in time. The theory does not require a supporting ontology that admits real things (Platonic forms, meanings, reified possibilities, etc.) that don't need the actual world or natural order in order to be. The theory has no tendency to divorce a thing's identity or itselfness from the thing or to treat its itselfness as a thing. The theory does not tend to turn thoughts *of* things into judgments, to reify existence, or to pack *into* a thought *of* something what one knows *about* it. The theory allows simple thoughts to be of complex things and allows one to know what one is thinking of *while* one is finding out about its complexities. Also, the theory does not confuse having definite intentionality with having criterial intensions; hence it allows that one's concept of a thing may change over time without one's losing track of the thing's identity. Concepts can change while sense remains the same and while grasp of the identity of what is thought of becomes more and more firmly established.

How Nominalists Identify Things

Nominalists tend to view the act of identifying as involving a series of responses to the world of the same *kind*. For example, identifying *red* is applying the concept "red" again or applying or responding with the word "red" again or having the inner reaction "red" again. In brief, identifying is identifying-as-the-same-again, which is as it should be. Of course, the nominalist also believes that many of the things we identify-as-the-same-again are not really selfsames at all, or that their selfsameness is constituted only through their being identified as the same. Nominalists are especially suspicious about the objectivity of the identities of properties and kinds, which seems to raise the puzzle what it is for the *same* word or *same* mental reaction to occur again, hence a puzzle about what it is, at the end of the regress, for the act of identifying to occur. But there is no need even to mention nominalism itself in order to comment on the nominalist view of the act of identifying.

Notice that the nominalist description of the act of identifying as the act of applying or reacting with the same word or concept again needs to be supplemented with some kind of plausible description of what a word or a concept *is*. Having a sneezing fit is not identifying anything, but it is reacting with the same sound again and again to sensory stimulations. A flow of adrenalin in one's body is not an act of identifying, but it is reacting the same way again—and reacting the same way other people react—to the presence of danger. (Have we "agreement in judgments" if our adrenalin flows at the same time?) Hobbes thought that the difference between such things as sneezes and words was that words are conventional whereas sneezes are not. But whatever the nominalist comes up with, he has to supply *some* characterization of words or of ideas or of applications of concepts that differentiates these from other reactions that people can have to things. (I have argued that what makes a word such as "red" a representation and what makes a mental term a mental *term* is, in part, that the values of these icon elements are supposed to be identified. If I am right about this, then the nominalist description of the act of identifying is circular.)

Suppose then that the nominalist supplies us with a theory of what a word or a concept or a mental term is. And suppose that he is able to define the notion *same-word-again, same-concept-again,* or *same-mental-term-again* without regress. The problem that he still faces, I believe, is how to explain what reacting again in the same way to a thing contributes toward accomplishment of the most obvious purposes of identifying things. How does reacting again with the same word help us to learn from experience and to apply what we have learned? Indeed, reacting again in the same way as before is often a sign that one has *not* learned anything or that one has *not* identified something to which one's learning is applicable. Consider, for example, how you will tell whether or not a dog with which you have been friendly on a previous occasion has identified you or recognized you. If he responds in much the same way that he did when you met him first, you will assume that he does *not* recognize you. He treats you, once again, as he treats strangers. If, on the other hand, he responds quite differently, and in a manner appropriate to the way in which you treated him on the earlier occasion of meeting, you will assume that he does recognize you.

I have argued that mapping the same with the same inner term again does contribute to learning and to applying that learning. But that is because correctly iterating a term is preparation for more *primary* acts of identifying, these primary acts being quite other than iterated reactions.

(I will return to discuss the role of public agreement in the use of language as understood by the nominalists Wittgenstein and Quine in Chapter 18.)

Concepts

My claim is that correctly identifying the referent of an inner intentional icon element is *the* act that manifests one's knowledge of what that element represents. Crudely, knowing what one is thinking of is having the capacity correctly to identify the referents of the elements of one's thought tokens. To know what I am thinking of now I must have programs in me that have a Normal way in which they might perform correct acts of identification of the referents of my present thought token. But from this it follows that knowing what I am thinking of admits of degree.

My hold on what I am thinking of depends upon how versatile and how reliable I am in performing acts of correct identification of the referents of my thought. Knowing lots about a thing provides me with lots of true representations of it upon which to perform acts of correct identification, thus tending to increase my grasp of what this thing is that I am thinking of. Having lots of intensions by which to iterate a thing's inner name in inner sentences increases my capacity to form new inner sentences containing its name. Because such iterations of its name are preliminary acts of identification of it, having more intensions for its name tends to increase my grasp of what I am thinking of. Having the capacity to identify what I am thinking of via percepts as well as via thought and language is another way to increase my hold on what I am thinking of. This capacity normally goes along with a capacity to iterate my inner name for what I am thinking of via implicit intensions whereby percepts are translated into inner sentences. If I can recognize you on the street or recognize your voice on the phone as well as knowing your name and something about you, I have a better hold on who I am thinking of when I think of you than if I cannot. I am able to identify you across more kinds of inner icon elements.

On the other hand, having more intensions for an inner term increases my grasp of what the referent of this term is only so far as these intensions are reliable. Suppose that I can recognize mauve, but not with great reliability. Sometimes the lighting conditions fool me. I would know better what mauve is—know better what I am thinking of when I think of mauve—if I could learn to recognize those lighting conditions that tend to confuse me. Then I would make fewer errors, for I would not try to iterate "mauve" (vs. "not mauve") under these conditions, and a larger proportion of my iterations of "mauve" would be correct. Also, having more intensions for an inner term increases my grasp of its referent only so far as these intensions are likely to find application. Suppose that I think over and over of a beggar I once saw on the Paris streets, remembering not only the place but also the date and time of his passing. I thus possess an identifying description of him, even one that is perfectly reliable. But it is not likely that I will ever be able to put this reliable intension to work, for it is unlikely that either the beggar or anyone else remembers that he was there on that corner that hour of that day. If this is the only intension I possess for the beggar's inner name (suppose that I am very bad at remembering faces and anyway it has been years and people's appearances change), then I really have no hold on *who* I am thinking of when I think of him, despite the vividness of my memory and the reliability of my identifying description. Similarly, the intension "my hundredth-great-grandfather down the fathers' sides" is, for each of us, a perfectly reliable identifying description. But, for you I assume as well as for me, it finds no application and undoubtedly would find no application no matter how diligently we tried to research our family trees. We will never be able to use this intention to iterate this ancestor's inner name in any (nonanalytic) inner sentence. Hence we do not really know who we are thinking of if we think of this person.

In earlier chapters I used the word "concept" to denote the set of intensions that govern iteration of an inner referential term. But the notion "concept" might more naturally be used to mean something broader. One's concept of a thing might be described as one's ability to identify that thing and all that goes into that ability fleshed out. The intensions that govern iteration of the inner term for a thing are thus one part or aspect of the concept of it; all that one knows about that thing is another aspect. Depending upon how versatile and how reliable one's capacity to identify a thing is, the concept of that thing may be very rich or very lean, very clear and reliable or somewhat confused and unreliable. The concept of a thing may also divide into more central and more peripheral intensions and beliefs, depending upon the degree of confidence that one has in the reliability of these intentions and beliefs.

But if concepts correspond to abilities to identify things, then concepts display other dimensions besides beliefs and intensions associated with them. Specific world variants such as *Johnny, gold, red,* and *beside* fall into ontological categories. For example, *Johnny* is an enduring individual object, an animal and a person; *gold* is a material and a chemical element and a metal; *red* is a physical property and a color; *beside* is a relation and, more specifically, a spatial relation. To know into what category or categories a world-variant falls is to have a grasp of the *grammar* of its corresponding inner term. And to have a grasp of the grammar of an inner term is an essential part of understanding its value—an essential part of one's concept of it. Let me clarify this.

In Chapter 16 I will argue that the very identities of what I will call "substances" and "properties" are determined in relation to one another. A substance is what it is and the selfsame as itself relative to a set of property ranges from each of which, in accordance with natural necessity, it has one property to the exclusion of others in that range. Correlatively, a property is what it is and is the selfsame as itself relative to a range of contraries and to a set of substance categories members of which categories always have, in accordance with natural necessity, one property from this range to the exclusion of all others. (The problem of change will, of course, be addressed.) This ontological thesis entails that to have a grasp of the identity of any substance necessitates having some grasp of the contrary ranges in relation to which it is a selfsame substance. And to have a grasp of the identity of any property necessitates having a grasp of at least some substance categories in relation to which it is a selfsame property. A substance *category* corresponds to a set of substances that are identities relative to the same predicate contrary-ranges. Similarly, a predicate falls in a predicate *category* by virtue of being from a range that applies to members of certain substance categories. For example, gold, like other members of the category *chemical element,* has an atomic number, a valence, a melting point, a characteristic solid-state structure, a specific heat, a color. But it does not have a size, a weight, a shape, a mother, a birth date, a posture (sitting, standing), or any personality traits. Johnny, like other members of the category *persons,* has (at each time) a size, a weight, a posture. He also has a mother and a shape and a birth date and personality traits. But he has no atomic number, no valence, and no determinate melting point.

Now insofar as identifying a thing is accomplished by first iterating its name in true inner representations, grasp of the identity of a thing must involve having some grasp of the kind of grammatical place that name can hold in inner representations, including a knowledge of what categories of things it fits with in these representations. For example, in order for a sentence to have sense it is not sufficient that each of its referential terms have sense. Thus, "Gold is chemically inert" makes sense but "Gold is large" does not; "Johnny is tall" makes sense but "Johnny has an atomic number of seventy-nine" does not. In general, the more one knows about what ranges of predicates go with a term taken as subject in sentences and what categories of subjects go with a term taken as predicate in sentences, the better grasp one has of the identity of the referent of the term. That is why one knows better what "monotreme" means if one knows that "monotremes are voracious eaters" makes sense but that "monotremes have a valence of two" does not (see Chapter 9).

To believe that a thing falls in a certain ontological category is not to harbor another inner representation for it but to have a fuller concept of it. Correlatively, sentences such as "Gold has an atomic weight," "Gold is a chemical element," "Johnny is a physical object," "Johnny has a determinate position in space at each time," and "red is a color" are not representations any more than "Cicero is Tully" and "Unicorns don't exist" are representations. Their function is to alter concepts, not to map the world. On the other hand, many of our words that express categories are *also* mapping predicates. They are representations as well as showing category. For example, to know that a thing is a mineral or that it is an animal is to know something *about* it as well as to know what makes sense to *ask* about it. A mineral must have a certain *kind* of chemical composition, and an animal must exhibit respiration and have body cells, etc. Most common nouns indicate a substance category and a good deal of positive information as well.

Because substances and properties fall into ontological categories, there are besides concepts of particular world variants like *Johnny*, *gold*, and *red* also higher-order concepts. These higher-order concepts are not abilities to identify anything in particular but are generalized abilities to *acquire* concepts of particular variants that fall in certain categories. For example, one such higher-order concept, apparently programmed into humans at birth, is the ability to reidentify almost any three-dimensional form or shape when encountered again from another angle of observation. Whatever shape we are shown, if we are shown the same shape again from a different angle we can identify this as being the same shape again. This ability is a higher-order concept that can be used for iterating mental names for shapes. Similarly, we have higher-order concepts in accordance with which we can iterate mental names for colors as seen under a variety of lighting conditions. Usually we can recognize any color as the same again even though the lighting conditions have changed. Another higher-order concept, involving motor responses as well as cognitive responses, enables us to reidentify any medium-sized physical object—say, a squirrel or a man—as we continuously track it with our eyes, head, and feet, gaining first this and then that bit of information about it. This higher-order concept is a general mechanism for iterating either temporary or permanent names for physical objects (cf. remarks on temporary concepts, Chapter 10). Another higher-order concept enables us to reidentify people by remembering their faces, a skill that we seem to be designed to do especially well. Still another enables us to reidentify any variant via language icons of it by remembering its name—another skill we seem to be designed especially to have. The ability to recognize a necessarily identifying description *as* necessarily identifying (see Chapter 11, "Prior Classification of Complex Descriptions") is also a higher-order concept. Anything that is found to fit a necessarily identifying description, if one knows that this *is* a necessarily identifying description, can always be identified by that description.

Chapter 16

Notes on the Identity of Substances and Properties

I would like to put forth a rough and general principle that, if correct, helps us to see how the identity of a substance or of a property can be an objective affair, hence how the general theory of signs that I have proposed can be given a foundation in ontology. The central idea that I will defend is this. The identity or itselfness of a substance implies its *naturally necessary* refusal to admit properties, from each of a co-ordinate set of property ranges, that are contrary to one another; the identity or itselfness of a property implies its *naturally necessary* incompatibility with other properties from a certain range, upon the ground of all substances that admit of properties from that range. Hence the identities of substances, of properties, and of contraries of properties are identities only as in a natural nexus with one another. Identity is a structured natural phenomenon, just as natural law is a natural, rather than merely a "logical," phenomenon.

A representation that contains the negative, I have argued, maps not the absence of a world affair but the presence of a contrary world affair. Add that contrariety is at root a natural-order opposition (for dramatic effect, think of it as a "repulsion," although that of course is wildly metaphorical) among properties (or relations) that compete on the ground of substances (or ordered *n*-tuples of substances). Then the law of noncontradiction as applied to representations reflects a thoroughly natural structural principle rather than an a priori metaphysical or rational principle, or the workings of our language (or, say, the workings of a constructive Kantian understanding). If the law of noncontradiction is grasped "a priori," this is not the kind of "a priori" that is reason's grasp of eternal realities or necessities that are prior to actuality or to nature, nor is it the kind that is rooted in our ability to play language games we have freely fashioned (nor, say, the kind that grasps principles in accordance with which we construct a phenomenal world). If the law of noncontradiction is grasped "a priori," this must be so only in the sense that nature, *via evolution*, has built this grasp into us as a mirror or reflection (possibly only a sufficing reflection) of a structural principle in the natural world with which we must deal in order to survive.

I will support the ontology that I adopt with independent arguments. But the main support for this position is that it is needed in order to support, and that it *can* support, the theory of signs that I have offered and the epistemology that I will offer. If the ontology of identity is as I will describe it, then it is possible for us to discover objective self-sameness in the world, that is, to know when we are identifying *correctly*. It is possible for us to leave the flat plane at which the world impinges upon our senses and arrive at judgments that map world affairs at a remove from this plane—to leave the paradoxes of phenomenalism, verificationism, and various kinds of idealisms cleanly behind and to embrace instead a fully emancipated realism. If adopting such an ontology makes a coherent realist epistemology and coherent theory of intentionality possible, then I suggest we should adopt it.

Leibniz's Law of the Identity of Indiscernibles

In Chapter 12 I argued that identity is not a relation between a thing and itself. Sentences of the form "$A=B$," when "A" and "B" are simple terms, do not map world affairs having the ordinary referent(s) of "A" and of "B" as variants. Rather, such sentences are supposed to map a relation between the reproductively established families of "A" and of "B," these families being protoreferents rather than represented referents of "A" and of "B" in the context of the identity sentence. The grammatical predicate " . . . is A," like the grammatical predicate " . . . exists," has a completely different kind of function than does the garden variety of grammatical predicate, the garden variety being an element of a representation.

If the grammatical category "predicate" were a function category, then since the forms " . . . $= A$," " " . . . exists," and " . . . is blue," though these are all called "predicates," have no function in common, we would have to conclude that the grammarian's notion "predicate" was a seriously ambiguous notion. It is better to view the grammarian's categories "subject," "predicate," "verb," "noun," etc., as linguists generally do nowadays, as syntactic or surface-pattern categories, carved out not by reference to function only, but by reference to surface transformations that can be performed upon sentences while preserving meaningfulness. For example, putting matters very crudely, "Pegasus exists" is to "Pegasus existed yesterday" and to "Will Pegasus exist after tomorrow?" etc., as "John tries" is to "John tried yesterday" and to "Will John try after tomorrow?" etc.; hence "exists" and "tries" fall in a common grammatical category. Similarly, "There are books on the table" is to "Are there books on the table?" as "Cats are curious" is to "Are cats curious?" but "Here are books on the table" does not go over to "Are here books on the table?" Hence "There" in "There are books on the table" falls in a common grammatical category with "cats" in "Cats are curious" but in a different category than "here" in "Here are books on the table." But it is only on the level of surface pattern transformations that "exists" has anything in common with "tries" or that "there" in "There are books on the table" has anything in common with "cats" in "Cats are curious." It seems to follow that any attempt to make uncritical use of grammatical categories to foot serious work in ontology is likely to fail.

In line with the above, surely it is of no use to interpret Leibniz's principle of the identity of indiscernibles in such a way that it becomes, implicitly, a claim about grammatical predicates. Suppose that we formulate Leibniz's principle of the identity of indiscernibles this way:

$$(x)(y)[(F)(Fx \equiv Fy) \supset x = y]$$

To the question, what is the domain of the quantifier "(F)"? we must not give an answer that simply pairs members of this domain with grammatical predicates. The set of grammatical predicates does not pair off neatly with any set that might be of interest to the ontologist. For example, neither " . . . exists" nor " . . . $=A$" nor " . . . means red" is paired with anything in the same sense that " . . . is green" is paired with a variant in world affairs. Perhaps we can say that the quantifier "(F)" ranges over all "properties," but then we must have a way of marking off the domain of "properties" other than by blindly pairing "properties" with grammatical predicates. For example, Baruch Brody's recent attempt[1] to cut through the puzzles that surround Leibniz's law by treating *being identical with x* as a "property" of x in the domain of the quantifier "(F)" is misguided at the start. True, if *being identical with x* were a "property" of x, then anything that had all of x's properties would be x. But "property" is not a coherent ontological category under this interpretation.

Is there some way of characterizing the notion "property" so that it will correspond to a genuine ontological category, so that we may interpret and examine Leibniz's principle as a claim within ontology? We can begin by saying that a property is a variant in world affairs. Existence and self-identity are not variants in world affairs, hence are not properties. But Socrates and the Taj Mahal are variants in world affairs, and they are not properties in any ordinary sense. We need also to distinguish properties at least from things that *have* properties—from things that are, as I shall say, "substances." A "substance," as I will use this term, is, very roughly, a logical subject *in re*. What it is more precisely will emerge as we proceed. At the moment, let me just say that individual objects are examples of substances—and that individual objects are the only examples of substances that I will talk about for some pages.

Soon I will claim that the variants in world affairs that are properties are distinguished by the fact that they stand in opposition, in accord with something like natural law, to contrary properties as incompatible variants in world affairs. This incompatibility is relative, being, always, incompatibility upon the ground of certain *categories* of substance. But it will take me a little time to unfold this view, and the initial comments that I wish to make about Leibniz's principle of the identity of indiscernibles do not depend upon it. For the moment, let us work just from the ordinary intuition that there is an ontological distinction, potentially clarifiable, between properties and things that have properties. But we should keep in mind that grammar may not reflect this distinction in any simple way. For example, in the sentence "Tallness is exemplified by John," "is exemplified by John" is (grammatically) predicated of "tallness." Further, "tallness" is never predicated of a subject but is always something that other terms are predicated of. From these truths about grammar, I do not think we should hastily jump to the conclusion that *tallness*, unlike *tall*, is not a property but only a thing that has properties, or to the conclusion that *being exemplified by John* is a property. On the other hand, probably the predicates of most ordinary true sentences do correspond to property variants in world affairs.

In contexts other than discussions of Leibniz's own complex views, Leibniz's principle of the identity of indiscernibles is usually treated as a claim about the identity of individual substances—substances about which it makes sense to ask *where* they are at given times. That is, the "(x)" and the "(y)" in the formula $(x)(y)[(F)(Fx \equiv Fy) \supset x = y]$ range over individuals. The quantifier "(F)" is usually taken to range only over "general properties" or over "purely qualitative properties." Specifically, its domain does not include any properties that contain specific individuals as element variants. For example, the property of being taller than Mt. Washington is not included in the domain of "(F)," although the property of being taller than something that has such and such general properties, these being Mt. Washington's properties, is included. The reason that is commonly given for excluding relations to specific individuals is that this would allow inclusion of properties of the kind *being identical with x*, thus yielding an empty reading of Leibniz's law. I have argued that this is not so—that "is identical with x" does not correspond to a property of x on any reasonable interpretation of the notion "property." But Leibniz's law is usually examined in the context of questions concerning what relation the domain of general properties bears to the domain of things that have these properties—in the context of wondering, for example, whether we need to postulate a domain of things that have general properties over and above the domain of these general properties, or whether the itselfness of an individual can be defined in purely qualitative terms. In this sort of context, the property of bearing a certain relation to a specified individual thing appears to be impure or mixed in ontological category. This seems a legitimate reason for excluding such properties when exploring the role of Leibniz's law in ontology.

The classical way to challenge Leibniz's law is to point to the possibility that the universe might be perfectly symmetrical, so that for every individual in one portion of it there was an identical individual in some other portion or in numerous other portions having all of the same internal properties and bearing all of the same external relations to other exactly similar things. Bisymmetry, radial symmetry, and temporal symmetry—a cyclical universe that repeats itself eternally—have been suggested as well as more sophisticated symmetries.[2] The easiest to imagine is a universe containing just two identical drops of water or just two identical billiard balls situated some distance apart. Each such drop of water or billiard ball would seem to have all the properties the other had, so that no difference could be discerned between them. Thus, it is argued, Leibniz's law must be mistaken. (To see the point of these examples, one must of course make the Leibnizian assumption that being in a certain place or at a certain time is not a purely qualitative property but is to be analyzed, for example, in terms of bearing such and such spatial *relations* to such and such *individuals*. Otherwise, taking the billiard balls as our example, the balls do not have the same spatial properties as one another.)

As R. M. Adams has pointed out,[3] the principle used in constructing these symmetrical world examples is the principle that an individual cannot be separated from itself in space or disconnected from itself in time—hence the intuition that the two world halves or various temporally separated world phases could not be one and the same half or world phase. All such examples are thus open to the same objection, most recently put by Ian Hacking,[4] that they fail to take account of the possibility of geometries or chronometries other than Euclidean, in which the same thing turns up again within a space that is curved, or turns up both before and after itself.

On the other hand, to insist just because every such example *could* be interpreted as a case in which space or time is warped rather than as a case in which nonidentical things are indiscernible that every example *must* be so intrepreted would be to beg the question at issue. Rather than dogmatically insisting upon the metaphysical necessity of the identity of indiscernibles or, alternatively, dogmatically insisting upon the metaphysical necessity of Euclidean-like simplicity in space-time frameworks, there are two more interesting options available to us.

Option One is to affirm that in the case of a symmetrical world there simply would be no truth to the matter whether space was curved or the world was doubled. This would entail not only denying that the principle of the identity of indiscernibles is logically or metaphysically necessary but also affirming that whether the principle was in *fact* true might rest, in some possible worlds, *only on convention*.

Option Two is to deny that the symmetrical world problem admits of a *general* solution but to affirm that for any *given* symmetrical world there would in fact be a truth to the matter whether space was warped or the world was doubled. Thus, both Armstrong[5] and Adams[6] have recently suggested that *either* such a world would have warped space (or time) *or* it would contain indiscernible nonidenticals, *but not both*, and that these alternatives are ontologically different but equally coherent possibilities. Hence the principle of the identity of indiscernibles is neither logically nor metaphysically necessary. But whether it holds in our world is a matter of *fact*, not convention. Neither Armstrong nor Adams explains exactly what the difference between these two distinct kinds of possible worlds would amount to. And yet I think it is clear what it would have to amount to—and that a very exposed metaphysical position is built into Option Two.

The difference between an apparently symmetrical world that was actually double and one that was merely in a folded space would be a difference in what was naturally necessary vs. what was a matter of accident in these worlds. In the world with a folded space, if one "half" of the world *had* been different in any respect, the other "half" *would have had* to differ accordingly, because these "halves" are really the same thing over again. In the truly double world, there are respects in which one half *could* have differed without the other half differing accordingly. The double world is symmetrical only by accident. The world in a folded space only *appears* to be double, but this appearance of doubleness is in accordance with natural necessity.

Implicit in the above suggestion is the thesis that if individuals have all of the same properties as one another in accordance with a natural necessity, each determining the properties of the other, and if this necessity is not merely necessity in situ, then these individuals are really the selfsame individual. That is, it is denied that there could be a *basic* causal law or law of reciprocity that directly connects two different individuals, determining that these must be the same in all respects under all possible circumstances, unless this law were, precisely, a material law of identity. Individual identity, if we take Option Two, is in the same metaphysical boat as causality. Causality is a naturally necessary connection between naturally possible occurrences upon which counterfactual conditionals can be founded. Individual identity might be characterized by the formula $(x)(y)\{[NN(F)Fx \equiv Fy] \equiv x = y\}$, where NN means "naturally necessary under all naturally possible conditions." ("Under all naturally possible conditions" merely makes explicit that the natural necessity is a *basic* necessity, not merely a natural necessity in situ.)

This position, which I take to be the only plausible explication of Option Two, is, as I have said, an extremely exposed position. It is of a piece with the position of one who maintains that, should two non-equivalent sets of laws explain all the happenings of the world throughout all space and time, one of these sets and not the other would be *true*, even though there would be no way of finding out which set was true. Those counterfactual conditionals entailed by one set of laws but not the other would be either true or false, even though no evidence would be available, no matter how far and wide one looked, to tell which. Taking Option Two, that is just how it would be if one inhabited an apparently symmetrical world. *Either* it would be true that the "two halves" were really two *or* it would be true that they were really one, although one could never find out which.

It is hard for a generation that follows hard upon the heels of verificationism even to consider Option Two. Option One, on the other hand, seems to imply that a law of nature is merely a summary description of a uniformity in brute fact present throughout nature. From the point of view of Option One, the categories of natural necessity and empirical possibility are merely shadows cast by our conventional theories or ways of thinking about and representing things, and counterfactual conditionals are true or false only relative to such a theory.

I am forced to adopt Option Two in the context of this essay. For the theory of intentionality that I have offered depends upon the assumption that there is such a thing as a real Normal explanation for the proper function of any intentional icon or representation—a kind of explanation that is, as it were, out there in the world supporting rather than being supported by our ways of thinking and speaking. For this to be true, there must be natural laws that are *in* nature—principles that actually account for the patterns in nature rather than merely summing these patterns up. Happily, the theory of intentionality that I have proposed offers protection from the usual objections to views like Option Two. For if the theory is correct, verificationism in every form is simply wrong. In the final analysis both meaningfulness and truth lie with relations that are genuinely *between* thought and the world, and thought cannot internalize, hence cannot certify, these relations.

My initial suggestion then is that the itselfness of an individual can be viewed as constituted in part by the natural necessity that it have all the same properties as itself. This suggestion is not put forth as a "conceptual truth" but as a *theory* about the nature of identity. Call this a "naturalist" view (as opposed, say, to a "logician's view") of individual identity. This naturalist view of the itselfness of an individual does not of course *reduce* the identity of an individual to something else. For example, the identity of an individual qua the selfsame having a variety of *different* properties is not reduced or explained by this view—the identity of an individual with itself as represented in statements of the form "*Px* and *Sx* and *Rx*." Only if the category *individual* could be eliminated in favor of an ontology recognizing only properties would a reductive definition of the itselfness of an individual in terms of properties be possible.

If this naturalist view of individual identity is correct, then discovering that a certain individual exists is rather like discovering that a certain natural law holds. Where there is a natural law, there is a resulting uniformity observable in nature. But disovery of a uniformity throughout part or even throughout all of nature would not be enough to guarantee the presence of a natural law. Uniformities *might* happen by accident. Similarly, where a selfsame individual is found, there is a resulting uniformity or coincidence in the properties found. But discovering a coincidence of properties, even a coincidence of *all* properties, would not be enough to guarantee the presence of a selfsame individual. Coincidences of properties *might* happen by accident.

But this (extremely abstract) naturalist view of individual identity has few if any interesting consequences unless, first, coupled with a complementary view of the identity of properties and of what it is for a substance to *have* a property and second, generalized to apply to all substances. To generalize the view of individual identity will be to show how other things that have properties, such as natural kinds and materials, have a similar kind of identity to that of individuals. Hence they too are "substances" in a univocal sense. But in order to see how this is so, we must first examine the problem of the identity of properties.

Leibniz's Law Inverted: The Identity of Properties

Is there some way of describing the kind of selfsameness or itselfness that a property has? First, consider only properties that individuals can have.

Let us try turning Leibniz's principle of the identity of indiscernibles around, but adding, as we did when discussing the itselfness of individuals, a natural necessity operator:

$$(F)(G)\{[NN(x)Fx \equiv Gx] \equiv F=G\}$$

Let "x" range over all individuals. But over what domain should "F" and "G" range?

Since part of our purpose here is to define the sort of identity that a property has, hence to define the notion "property" itself, the range of "F" and of "G" should remain, for the moment, somewhat of an open question. But certainly we should like the notion "property" to correspond to an interesting and univocal *ontological* category. It seems reasonable then to begin by excluding from the range of "F" and "G" any property that has an individual or individuals as element variants, i.e., any "impure" property. Impure properties, such as . . . *is taller than John* (taken descriptively, not referentially—see Chapter 11, "Descriptions of Properties"), *hates Mary*, and *gave the kitten to Jane*, have certain characteristics in common with pure properties, we suppose, because they contain relations as element variants, and because relations are ontologically like pure properties. We must then make the sound and traditional move that drives a final wedge between the notion of a grammatical predicate and that of a property by recognizing relations as ontologically like properties even though no term for a relation ever stands alone as a grammatical predicate. In order to investigate the inverse of Leibniz's law as proposed above, we must generalize it so that it speaks about relations as well as about properties. Informally, we might represent such a generalization thus:

$$(F)(G)\{[NN(x_1 \ldots x_n)Fx_1 \ldots x_n \equiv Gx_1 \ldots x_n] \equiv F = G\}$$

"$(x_1 \ldots x_n)$" represents, of course, an ordered series. But perhaps the reader will excuse me if I call both pure properties and pure relations just "properties" (think of "properties of ordered pairs," "properties of ordered trios," etc.) in order to simplify expression of the following thoughts.

Let me make two initial observations about this proposed formula. First, even if this formula should turn out to be correct (I will try to show that it is not correct), it cannot pretend to be a full definition or analysis of property itselfness or identity. For just as our earlier description of the identity of an individual does not explain its identity qua the selfsame having a diversity of properties, this description of property identity does not explain or reduce the identity of a property as common to many individuals. That is, it says nothing about the identity of P with itself as represented in statements of the form "Px and Py." This I do not take to be a defect of the formula. Only if the category *property* could be eliminated in favor of an ontology recognizing only individuals would a reductive analysis of properties in terms of individuals be possible. Second, notice that the proposed formula describing property identity, when compared with the formula with which we described individual identity, tells us nothing about the *difference* between individuals and properties. If we consider only pure properties that are properties of single individuals (as opposed to being properties of ordered pairs or trios of individuals, that is, as opposed to being relations), the symmetry between the formula describing individual identity and the proposed formula describing property identity is exact. True, we could add to our description of properties that each has a definite "*n*-adicity." A monadic property always participates in at minimum a diadic world affair, a diadic property at minimum in a triadic world affair, etc., whereas individuals can participate in world affairs involving any number of element variants above one. But this description would not help to describe the difference between the kind of identity that an individual has and the kind of identity that a monadic property has. And, since we propose later to generalize the description of substance identity, showing how it applies to substances other than individuals, the traditional move that adds reference to space-time position in defining what an individual substance is will not help us here either. This failure, I hope to show, *is* a defect of the proposed formula describing property identity.

The usual objections to the suggestion that properties are the same when all of their instances are the same are of two kinds. First, there are objections raised by those who believe that properties correspond one-to-one to possible concepts. These are the people who are influenced by what Armstrong calls the "Argument from Meaning" " . . . which has so often, and so fatally, distorted the Problem of Universals. If universals are conceived of as meanings, and if a semantic criterion is accepted for the identity of predicates, then it follows at once that each predicate-type is associated with its own universal. Realists have put an inflationary, Nominalists a deflationary, interpretation on this situation."[7] The Argument from Meaning depends of course upon identifying meaning with intension—upon correlating meanings with the concepts one has of the things mapped or referred to by terms. Having distinguished between sense and intension, so that we can understand how there might be numerous concepts of what is in fact the same *in re* variant, we can ignore all objections from this quarter. For example, to suppose that the hubots' and the rubots' concepts of *square* were concepts of different variants in nature because these concepts were governed by different intensions would be as mistaken as to suppose that the ancients' concept of Hesperus and their concept of Phosphorus were concepts of different heavenly bodies because governed by different intensions.

The second objection to the view that properties are the same when their instances coincide is that counterexamples come so readily to mind. It is claimed, for example, that even though it might be the case that every creature with a kidney was a creature with a heart and vice versa, this does nothing to show that the property *having a kidney* might be the same property as the property *having a heart*. Of course, we are examining not the view that properties are the same when their instances happen to coincide but the view that properties are the same when their instances coincide in accordance with natural necessity. This view carries us at least a little distance beyond the traditional counterexamples. It is not so easy to suppose that it could be a matter of direct natural necessity not depending on laws in situ that all creatures with kidneys have hearts and vice versa. Taking another example, suppose that there were a very special shade of green that only one object in the world, from the world's beginning to its end, ever had. And suppose that this object also had a precise shape, describable if one was very careful and exact, that no other object ever had. Surely it would not follow that that special color of green and that special shape were the same property. And indeed we have good reason to suppose that there are no principles of natural necessity that directly correlate particular colors with particular shapes. However, not all counterexamples to our proposed inverse of Leibniz's law can be scouted so easily.

Consider the various identifying properties that any natural material may have. Consider, for example, gold's particular spectrum, its particular electrical conductivity, and its atomic number. Assuming that each of these properties is peculiar to gold and hence identifying, each of these properties coexists in samples of materials always with the others. If the conductivity and spectrum depend upon the atomic number of an element, then these three properties are always found together in accordance with natural necessity. But surely these properties are not one and the same property. How do we know that being composed of atoms having atomic number seventy-nine, having such and such an electrical conductivity, and exhibiting such and such a spectrum are different properties, even though these are always found together? How do we know that they are not like a shape that is seen and a shape that is felt which, though determined in different manners, are in fact the same objective property? This is a question in epistemology, not ontology. But if the question cannot be answered without making certain assumptions in ontology, surely it will be reasonable to make these assumptions.

The intuitive answer to our question is this. In order for, say, the particular spectrum of a piece of gold and the particular conductivity of a piece of gold to be the same property, the entire *range* of possible electrical conductivities would have to map onto the entire *range* of possible spectra, one-to-one. That is, it couldn't be that one exact electrical conductivity was the same as one spectrum without other electrical conductivities being the same as other spectra. Similarly, a particular color could not be the same as a particular shape unless every color was a shape and every shape was a color. By making this sort of assumption, the amount of play in deciding which properties can reasonably be identified with which other properties is immeasurably reduced. What are the implications of making this assumption?

Properties (monadic or n-adic) that fall into the same range are properties that are contraries of one another. For example, whatever is red cannot at the same time be green, what has only atoms with atomic number seventy-nine cannot also have only atoms with atomic number seventy-eight or atomic number sixty-five, and what is beside a thing cannot at the same time be on top of it. True, most of our property words correspond to property *areas* rather than to exact properties, and one property area can include or overlap another. Property words are usually somewhat indefinite, rather as common nouns with "a" are indefinite, their exact real values being determined by the rest of the sentence in which they occur plus the world. Thus "red" includes rather than being incompatible with "scarlet," and "being 2.00 inches plus or minus .1 inch" overlaps rather than being incompatible with "being 2.05 inches plus or minus .1 inch." But each such property area is carved out of a range of exact properties that are strict contraries of one another. The assumption that two properties can be the same only if the entire contrary ranges from which these come coincide, suggests that the very identity of a property or property area is bound to the identity of the wider range from which it comes, hence *bound to the identity of its contraries*.

Contrast Leibniz's view about contrary properties with that of Aristotle. Leibniz thought that all perfectly simple properties were intrinsically compatible. True, they might not be compatible in nature—because God created only the best of the possible worlds—but they were compatible in some prior way, Leibniz says "metaphysically compatible." Any properties that were *not* metaphysically compatible were complex properties containing within them negatives or absences of properties. They had the general form "A and not B." The property "A and not B" was, of course, incompatible with the property "A and B." Thus all metaphysical incompatibility rested on logical incompatibility—on contradiction. In the (metaphysical order) "beginning" there was only one kind of incompatibility and, in general, only one kind of necessity—formal logical incompatibility and formal logical necessity. Then God created natural necessity—or the appearance of it—as something more. What we take to be contrary properties, on Leibniz's view, are of two kinds. Either to assert that both contraries apply to the same thing is simply to contradict oneself, or the contrariety is between properties that are in their own natures—so far as their identity or itselfness is concerned—completely indifferent to one another but prevented by something external to them (God) from ever actually meeting on common ground. This is the view that I am rejecting.

Aristotle thought of contrary properties quite differently. He used them in order to explain change, a problem on the philosophical agenda at that time being to do this without allowing that something can come from nothing. Contrary properties are properties each of which is a privation of the other. The privation of a property *is* that property, but potentially rather than actually. When change occurs, substances acquire new properties that are contraries of their old properties, and they can do this because the contrary of a property *is* that property in potency. Change is something potential becoming actual, not a new nature coming from nothing. If Aristotle is right, Leibniz is completely mistaken. Contrary properties oppose one another, and their identities or natures are tied up with one another on the most fundamental level there is.

I do not wish to advocate any of the details of Aristotle's position. But I do wish to claim that he was right in tying properties to their contraries *in their inmost natures*. It is *not* that "in the beginning" there were properties that in their ownselves—in order to be what they were—*could* have been indifferent to all other properties and that then something else came along and made some of them enemies.

On the other hand, there is something right about Leibniz's idea that to assert that two contraries hold of the same substance can be to contradict oneself. Indeed, it is always to contradict oneself. But this is because negation, when applied to a representing thought or sentence, *is* an indefinite assertion of contrariety. It is not an assertion of absence. Or rather, absence is itself merely the presence of an incompatibility. (Empty space, zero force, zero acceleration, zero momentum, zero temperature, etc., are not nothings but rather somethings that are at the extremes. The discovery of zero and the slow realization that zero always represents a quantity and not just a nothing was the beginning of modern mathematics and science.) The law of noncontradiction, then, is a template of abstract natural-world structure—or it is something that suffices for such a template.

Observe this contrast between the Leibnizian and the Aristotelian views of the ontology of contrariety as it reappears on the level of epistemology. Consider the claim that "*x* is red" is *equivalent* to "*x* looks red to standard observers under standard conditions." It follows that "*x* is not red" is equivalent to "*x* does not look red to standard observers under standard conditions." This claim is parallel to the claim on the level of ontology that not being red is an emptiness—an absence of red—rather than being of some contrary color (or being in some range that is contrary to color, say, being white-transparent). But the idea that "*x* is not red" is equivalent to "*x* does not look red to standard observers under standard conditions" is either empty or false.

First, in order to give content to the notion "*x* looks red to standard observers under standard conditions," "standard observer" must mean more than "observer to whom red things look red under standard conditions." And "standard conditions" must mean more than "conditions under which red things look red to standard observers." The notion "standard observer of red" and "standard conditions for observing red" would have to be spelled out *concretely*, if the formula is not to be empty. But no one, certainly no one prior to very recent years, has ever had the slightest idea how to spell these out. Until very recently, for example, the only way to tell whether a person was a nonstandard observer of colors, because color-blind, was to note that under apparently standard conditions he apparently did not see what was red as red. Second, and far more important, even if one had every reason to believe that one was a standard observer and that conditions were standard for observing colors, if one looked and still was unable to see at all even within what *range* of color a thing was, clearly the conclusion to be drawn would not be that the thing was *not* red. Rather, one would have to admit that, despite one's well-founded beliefs about oneself and one's situation, still something *had* gone wrong.

But if the very itselfness of a property is expressed in its opposing its contraries upon certain grounds, then a test of one's ability to identify any property will be that one can also identify opposing properties and that these never do *in fact* show up upon the same ground. What evidence do I have that my ability to identify red is a genuine ability— an ability to map an outer-world property variant with an inner term? What makes me think that my word "red" has a sense? The answer that I will propose (Chapters 18 and 19) is, in part, that my evidence is my experience that red and green and blue, etc., in fact fall contrary to one another, given my current means of attempting to identify these. Their consistent contrariety is evidence for their objective reality— evidence that "red" and "green," etc., are mapping real variants in the great out-there. How could my *experience* attest to this contrariety? It has been thought by many that there is no way that anything could possibly even *appear* to be, say, both red and green at the same time.

But in fact there are many ways. There is a way of focusing one's eyes in front of identically shaped red and green marks placed a distance apart on paper such that images of these two converge, and one seems to see one mark that is both red and green. Suppose that objects often looked this way to us when we focused as usual. Suppose that the apparent colors of things changed, as it turned out, not with the situations of the things themselves but with changes in the perceiver's situation. Suppose that no one's right eye ever agreed with his left in the perception of colors, and no correlations could be found in the reports of the two eyes. Or suppose that no agreement could ever be reached between people on the colors of things, so that all attempts to reidentify the colors of things via the medium of communication with others failed. Our confidence that red and green are contraries (though probably not derived in fact from experience, but built in) is supported over and over by *empirical* evidence. And this is evidence for the objective *validity* of these concepts—for the fact that red and green *are* properties and not mere hallucinations. Or so I will later argue.

Properties are not loners like substances but enter into the world along with contrary properties. A property is itself qua in naturally necessary opposition to the rest of a property range or contrary range within which it falls, such that whatever substance has that property cannot, in accordance with natural necessity, have any properties from the rest of that range. Indeed, in the interest of clarity in ontology and the clean separation of grammar from ontology, I suggest that we take this mark to be definitional of properties and relations (two-place and three-place, etc., properties), thus distinguishing them clearly from substances, from formal determinables (having shape, having color, etc.) and from ontological categories (being a substance, being a property), etc. For example, in "tallness is exemplified by John," "is exemplified by John" does not represent a property, even a mixed or impure one, of any kind. For it has no contraries. "Tallness is *not* exemplified by John," if true, will be true not because tallness has some property that is contrary to *being exemplified by John* but because some contrary of *tallness* is exemplified by John. "Tallness" then represents a property; "is exemplified by John" says of a substance, John, that it has this property.

We need then to amend the inverse of Leibniz's law that we proposed earlier such that it requires, for properties or relations to be the same, not only that all instances of these should coincide and coincide by natural necessity but also that the instances of all contraries of these properties or relations should coincide in accordance with natural necessity. (I will not try to formalize the resulting law.)

We also need to clarify the description proposed earlier of the itselfness of individuals. If the identity of an individual is fixed by its natural insistence upon having the same properties as itself, and if the identity of a property that applies to individuals is fixed by its natural opposition to contraries upon the ground of individuals, then the identity of an individual is fixed by its refusal to admit properties that are *contrary* to one another. In accordance with natural necessity, a selfsame individual takes just *one* from each of those ranges of contrary properties correlative to which it is a selfsame individual.

Consider the following paragraph from Strawson's *Subject and Predicate in Logic and Grammar*.[8] I have substituted "property" for Strawson's "general concept" throughout.

> And here we come to a quite fundamental respect of asymmetry between spatio-temporal particulars and the [properties] they exemplify. Consider on the one hand a set of [properties] belonging to a given range and, on the other, the entire field of particulars which come within that range. Then, for any [property] of the range, we know there are other [properties] which are in logical competition with it throughout the field, i.e., no particular which exemplifies it can at the same time exemplify its competitors. But we can form no symmetrically competitive range of particulars. Indeed, we cannot find a single particular such that there is any other single particular which competes with it for [properties] throughout the [property] ranges they both come within. There are no two simultaneously existing particulars so related that from the fact that one exemplifies a [property] it follows, for every [property], that the other does not exemplify it (or does not exemplify it simultaneously).

As amended, this observation of Strawson's is, I believe, sound and important. But, as amended, there occurs within it a seemingly anomalous phrase: what is "logical competition among properties"?

Strawson's idiom was "logical competition among concepts," which has a better ring. For a very respectable tradition has it that knowlege of relations among concepts is a priori knowledge and that "logic," in the broadest sense, is an a priori science that deals with these relations. But given our description of what a "concept" is (Chapter 9), we cannot assimilate relations among properties to mere relations among concepts of properties. Properties and concepts of properties are quite different things. The relation between a concept and the world which relation makes the concept a concept *of* something—the relation that makes the inner term that the concept governs a *meaningful* term—is a relation that cannot in principle be internalized. It is a relation that lies *between* the head and the world, not in the head or mind. So general concepts do not even pair up one-to-one with properties: two concepts may correspond to one property; one concept, because ambiguous in Fregean sense, may correspond to two properties. Further, even the knowledge that a certain concept actually *is* of a property, and does not merely seem to be of a property, is never a priori and *certain* knowledge. Surely there cannot be such a thing as a priori knowledge that is *certain* knowledge of identities, differences, and incompatibilities among properties. Incompatibility among properties in a contrary range is incompatibility in accordance with natural necessity only; "competition" among properties is merely another sort of natural necessity alongside substance identity and causality. If logic is an a priori and certain science, then there can be no such thing as "logical competition among *properties.*"

It is also true that if logic is an a priori science that deals with the relations among concepts, then logical possibility and logical necessity are merely subjective appearances—chimeras—unless our concepts happen to reflect genuine natural necessities, in particular, natural identities and natural contrarieties. Logic as a study of the relations among our various concrete concepts (I am not speaking here of logic as a purely formal study) is a merely dependent science, useful only insofar as the concepts it investigates are nonvacuous and univocal. Logical incompatibility among concepts casts no light upon the world unless such a priori–conceived incompatibility reflects naturally necessary incompatibility in the world. In general, what is discovered a priori to be logically possible, impossible, and necessary cuts no ice, is of no interest at all, unless the concepts upon which these appearances of possibility and necessity rest are adequate concepts.

On the other hand, perhaps we needn't take logic to be an a priori science at all. Insofar as logic deals with relations among concepts that have themselves been tested through experience, perhaps logic is an empirical science of sorts. Especially, if one's concept of a property cannot be torn away from one's concepts of certain of its contraries, if contrariety is a natural phenomenon, and if it is also true that negation *is* just assertion of indefinite contrariety, then any concrete claim of the form "S cannot both be P and not be P" is either senseless (because the concepts "S" or "P" lack sense) or else *akin* anyway to a *true* claim about the nature of the world. (The sense in which such a claim is "akin" to a *true* claim about the world is not, of course, straightforward.) But certainly "John cannot be at the office and also not be at the office" is a claim of the sort that has traditionally been considered to be a claim within logic. Given this perspective, perhaps "logical competition among properties" is not such a bad locution after all. If logic cuts any ice at all, it *is* ice about nature.

In sum, either we must give up the idea that logic as a study of relations among concepts is a science of interest to anyone but psychologists, sociologists, and historians, or else deny the distinction of levels between "logical" and "natural" necessities, recognizing logic as continuous with the natural sciences.

If the thrust of these reflections is correct, then epistemology must include a study of empirical tests of validity in concepts—genuineness of abilities to identify—as well as the traditional study of truth in judgment. Thus we shall have to add a new dimension to traditional empiricist epistemology (in Chapters 18 and 19).

But first I would like to make a certain change in Strawson's exposition, so as to generalize it, substituting the more general notion "substance" for Strawson's "spatiotemporal particular" throughout.

Generalizing the Notion of Individual Identity to Cover All Substances

The distinction to which Strawson points between (1) entities that must select or choose from ranges of other entities just one entity from each range with which to pair in world affairs and (2) entities that need not be monogamous in this way is not an absolute but a relative distinction. Consider: if my ring is gold, it cannot be made of any contrary of gold, such as silver, brass, salt, or an amalgam of metals. Correlatively, relative to particular things like my ring, gold is polygamous. So my ring is a substance and gold is a property, relative to one another. But doesn't gold and each of its contraries also have its *own* properties, selected monogamously? Gold, for example, is malleable, has a shiny yellow color, is corrosion-resistant, is soluble in mercury, has a melting point of 1064°C, and has numerous other properties, many of them perhaps unknown. Relative to each of the large group of contrary ranges from each of which gold picks a property, the identity of gold seems to be like the identity of an individual. Granted, that is, that gold takes just one property from each of these contrary ranges in accordance with natural necessity.

Many have assumed that every entity in the world must fall in just one of two ontological categories. Everything must either be a logical *in re* subject (Frege's "objects," Russell's "particulars," etc.) or else a logical *in re* predicate (Frege's "concepts," Russell's "universals," etc.) and nothing can be both. But the theory of how language maps onto the world with which we are working invites the notion that the category *in re subject* or, as I am saying, "substance" and the category *in re predicate* or, as I am saying, "property," might turn out to be relative categories, so that a variant that occurs in some world affairs as a property of substances might occur in other configurations as a substance having properties. First, we have accorded all variants in world affairs exactly the same sorts of rights and duties vis-à-vis participation in the *actual* world. Second, there seems to be no reason to assume in advance that any one set of transformations to which a world affair may be considered to be subject articulates that world affair into any more basic or elemental variants than does any other set of such transformations; no reason to assume in advance that any one mode of representation of a world affair or of a variant in a world affair is any more perspicuous a mode of representation than any other. If what corresponds *in re* to a logical predicate is, just, a variant *considered as sensitive to the negation transformation*—a variant considered as having contraries with which it is incompatible on the ground of the *in re* subject or subjects of the sentence—other ways of considering these variants may be possible as well. The fact that gold is a property, then, need not exclude the possibility that it is also a substance. Individuals would not then be the only substances but, as Aristotle had it, merely the primary substances, being substances that are not in turn properties of anything else.

The category "substance," defined as we are defining it, is at root an epistemological category. Substances are the sorts of things that can play a certain kind of role relative to our learning and knowing about them. A substance is, just, anything that it is possible to accumulate relatively stable, relatively precise information about—typically, considerable information. Besides individuals, such things as gold, pewter, fire, *Felis domesticus*, the '69 Plymouth Valiant 100, and tuberculosis are substances. For example, any chemist's handbook tells a great many things about gold, absurdly many books have been written about *Felis domesticus* (the house cat), a handbook of considerable size describes the '69 Plymouth Valiant 100, and any physician's handbook contains considerable information about tuberculosis. In order to play this kind of epistemological role, a substance must have a certain kind of sameness or identity. It must be *one* (or close enough) relative to each of a variety of contrary ranges and be so in accordance with some sort of natural necessity (possibly necessity in situ). Substances fall into *categories*, these being defined by the contrary ranges with respect to which they are determinate. What puts *gold* and *silver* in the same substance category is *not*, or not in the first instance, some essence or property that these have in common but the fact that they are determinate with respect to the same contrary ranges: each has *one* atomic number, melting point, spectrum, luster and color, electrical conductivity, tensile strength, specific heat, specific gravity, valence, etc. What makes each a *substance* (in the case of gold and silver, a "natural kind") is not some defining essence or the fact that each participates in natural laws but the fact that each is always the same as itself relative to certain property ranges in accordance with natural necessity—regardless of the perspective from which (for example, the instance through which) it is observed.

Because a substance is something that one can accumulate relatively stable information about, typically it must be something that it is possible in principle to identify and reidentify, with fair reliability, a number of times, hence something that can manifest itself from a variety of perspectives—via various media, at various times, at various places, to various people, or in the case of substances that are also properties, as instantiated in various particulars. Some substances are perfect substances, displaying a perfect identity with respect to their coordinate contrary ranges, while other substances are imperfect or "rough" in one way or another. A perfect substance chooses just one property from each of numerous contrary ranges, exhibiting this property to the exclusion of its contraries from every perspective that can reveal members of this range. Thus it is possible to find out once and for all what property from a given range a perfect substance has so that upon (correctly) reidentifying the substance one will never discover that it manifests also contrary properties. (In a moment I will discuss change.) Knowing at one time or from one perspective what property a perfect substance has is thus knowing, period, what property it has. What use to have "knowledge" that did not *remain* knowledge—that could not be *used* as one moves to new perspectives and into the future? Imperfect substances, on the other hand, either (1) exhibit their chosen properties only for the most part or (2) exhibit, rather than exact properties, properties within a limited range or, typically, both (1) and (2). For example, the adult house cat *usually* weighs between *about* seven and fourteen pounds, whereas the adult house mouse *usually* weighs between one-half and one ounce; pewter, which covers various proportions of tin, lead, and copper in alloy, has a melting point within a certain small *range* and is "*quite*" malleable.

That one can find out once and for all what property a perfect substance has does not entail that no perfect substance has time-bound properties. If Johnny is sitting at time t_1, he may well be standing at time t_2, the bare properties "sitting" and "standing" not being members of a property range that applies to people. (It applies, however, to statues of people and of animals.) Compare: water has a melting point of 32° Fahrenheit *at* one atmosphere pressure. It does not have this melting point absolutely. But if Johnny is sitting at time t_1, then, once and for all, Johnny was sitting at time t_1. For example, he cannot be sitting at time t_1 from here or via Jane's (veridical) observations but standing at time t_1 from there or via Peter's (veridical) observations, nor can he be sitting at time t_1 by sight but not by touch or sitting at time t_1 under certain conditions but not under others. Because many contrary ranges applying to enduring individuals are ranges qualified by temporal "respects," individuals are neither the simplest examples of substances, nor are they the easiest and earliest kinds of substances that we learn to identify—to have concepts of. To have a *full* concept, at any rate, of an enduring individual, one must possess time concepts. Besides, that an individual has a certain property at a certain time is an affair of a kind upon which quite limited perspectives are available. For both of these reasons, full concepts of enduring individuals are not as accessible as are concepts of substances such as gold and *Felis domesticus*. I will discuss substances that endure through time in Chapter 17. During the rest of this chapter, I will offer comments about simpler substances—those that are also properties.

Substances that are also properties manifest themselves through their various instantiations. Such a substance, if perfect, has just one property from each of numerous contrary ranges, exhibiting one and the same property to the exclusion of all contraries in accordance with natural necessity through every instantiation of it. Consider gold. There is a group of contrary ranges—atomic weight, specific heat, spectrum, etc.— from each of which gold picks one property and sticks with this property through all perspectives upon gold including via every instantiation of gold. On the other hand, gold, in contrast to its instances, does not have a shape, a weight, a location, a temperature at each time, etc. Gold is not the selfsame as its instances, either individually or collectively. The properties of gold are not the same as the properties of its instances, yet they are of course properties that are manifested only *through* gold's instances. In order to study gold—to find out about it— one need have no ability to reidentify or think of any of its instances. To study gold one needs only to be able to recognize "gold again" when gold turns up again. Hence what one finds out about gold need not be discovered via inductive inference from things known about gold's instances, just as to discover Johnny's properties does not involve inductive inference. Yet when gold turns up again, whether one knows it or not, whether one has concepts of particulars or not, it is of course always some particular piece of gold that turns up.

Exactly what sort of identity then does the substance gold have? What kind of natural necessity holds gold together as a selfsame that must choose one property to the exclusion of others from each of a variety of contrary ranges? The answer that modern science gives is that being made of gold is having a microscopic structure of a certain kind from which each of the more superficial properties of gold flows in accordance with natural necessity. For this reason, gold has the same properties wherever it is found, hence constitutes a substance.

Contrast gold with *the round red object*. *The round red object* (take this as designating a kind) doesn't seem to be a thing about which there is anything much to say. Indeed "the round red object" is really an empty phrase or a misnomer, this particular use of "the" being reserved for turning expressions for properties into names of corresponding substances—as *Felis domesticus* may also be called "the house cat." I suppose that it is possible that there might be something that was true of all round red objects (and that was not true either of all round objects or of all red objects). Suppose, for example, that no round red object ever happens to last more than 1000 years. But unless the fact that *all* round red objects had *the same* upper limit to their life span could be explained in accordance with some kind of natural necessity—explained prior to explaining for each round red object how it happened to fall under the limit—*the round red object* still would not even begin to be a substance. Quite often simple nouns—e.g., "bachelor," "widow," "Californian," "student," etc.—like "the round red object," do not correspond to substances but merely to classes. Unlike names for substances, such words can be given analytical definitions that correspond in every sense to their "meanings." Their meanings *are* their public intensions, nothing more and nothing less; their senses are the senses of their intensions. On the other hand, red sulfur is not just sulfur that is red, and baking soda is not just soda that one bakes with. Red sulfur is an allotrope of sulfur and is a substance in its own right, as is baking soda. It is not true of red sulfur that it is red analytically or "by definition." Rather, it is true by natural necessity.

Contrast gold also with jade. Jade is either of two distinct minerals, jadite or nephrite. There are some properties that all instances of both jadite and nephrite have in common—namely, the properties of jade. But jadite and nephrite do not have these properties in common because these *must* have the same properties as one another in accordance with some kind of direct necessity. No general explanation can be given why jadite and nephrite must have the *same* properties that is prior to an explanation of why each has these *specific* properties, which specific properties, it so happens, are the same. That is, one can explain why *each* has these properties but not, more generally, why *both* must have the *same* properties. Coordinately, if one infers from the fact that a piece of jadite has a certain property to the conclusion that a piece of nephrite has that property, one might turn out to be right, but one would be right only by accident. Hence jade is not one selfsame substance any more than "the round red object" is a selfsame substance.

Now consider the 1969 Plymouth Valiant 100—"the '69 Valiant" for short. Given the inventiveness of teenagers with old cars, perhaps there is no property that every surviving '69 Valiant shares with every other unless it is shared by all other automobiles as well. But in 1969 every '69 Valiant shared with every other each of the properties described in the '69 Valiant mechanics' handbook and many other properties as well. And there is a good though complicated explanation for the fact that they *shared* these properties. They all originated with the selfsame plan—not just with identical plans but with the same plan *token*. They were made of the same materials gathered from the same places, and they were turned out by the same machines and the same workers. Or when this was not so, the materials were similar, the machines similar, and the workers similarly trained not by accident but in accordance with the intentions of certain managers and supervisors that they be similar. So it is true of each '69 Valiant that *in 1969 it had* such and such parts in such and such configurations and *was* made of such and such materials, hence that it *had* such and such strengths, dispositions, and weaknesses. That '69 Valiants share these historic properties was determined in accordance with natural laws operating this time in situ. The '69 Valiant is a kind of substance. Indeed, it is a relatively perfect substance relative to such contrary ranges as placement of distributor in 1969, size of piston rings in 1969, shape of door handles in 1969, etc.

But why is it true a mechanic knows *now*, in 1983, pretty much what to expect when he looks under the hood of the '69 Valiant or inside its door panel, etc.? Why is the '69 Valiant a rough substance with regard to its *present* properties? *Most* important, there is the fact that, other conditions remaining stable, '69 Valiants, like most other physical objects, are things that tend to persist, maintaining the same properties over time in accordance with natural conservation laws. (I will say more about such laws in Chapter 17.) Also, there are roughly stable prevailing economic and social conditions that account for rough laws true in situ in accordance with which working parts of automobiles tend to be restored or replaced with similar parts as they become broken or worn. It is no accident that working parts of '69 Valiants that have needed repair have had a tendency to get repaired or replaced with similar parts. Even though no direct natural necessity determines that one '69 Valiant must, at present, have the same properties as the next, still, with regard to many properties, it is no accident when this happens.

Another way of looking at the rough identity of the substance '69 *Valiant* is to note that it has an identity relative to certain kinds of conditional properties even when it does not relative to corresponding unconditional properties. Just as gold is neither solid nor liquid absolutely, but solid at temperatures under 1064°C and molten at temperatures over 1064°C, so the '69 Valiant tends to have certain properties if it has been subjected to certain conditions, other properties if it has been subjected to other conditions. For example, the fenders of the '69 Valiant that has not been garaged tend to rust out whereas the body stands up much better; the ball joints are liable to need replacing after relatively few thousands of miles whereas the engine, if properly cared for, is not likely to burn oil until 100,000 miles or so, etc.

Felis domesticus, like the '69 Plymouth Valiant 100, is only a rough or imperfect substance. But it is rough or imperfect in somewhat different ways and for different reasons. The '69 Valiant is very close to a perfect substance relative to numerous properties-in-1969. Newborn kittens are not nearly so much alike as '69 Valiants once were. If one considers deformed or grossly abnormal kittens among the others, this is especially apparent. But suppose we eliminate grossly abnormal kittens. After all, when the comparative anatomist or physiologist studies *Felis domesticus*, he or she studies normal members of the species only. (True, the veterinary scientist might study kittens having a certain hereditary deformity or illness, but then these kittens are treated as a special kind of their own and the data obtained do not enter into a general description of *Felis domesticus*.) But even if we eliminate grossly abnormal newborn kittens, the ones that remain still vary far more than did new '69 Valiants, both inside and outside. The characteristics of newborn kittens, rather than being perfectly determinate characteristics, fall within certain limits. Newborn kittens are similar rather than the same with respect to the various contrary ranges relative to which they form a rough identity. Compare *pewter*, which covers various proportions of tin, lead, and copper in alloy.

The *reasons* that newborn kittens are similar to one another are also different from the reasons that new '69 Valiants were like one another. Nor are kittens similar for the same reason that gold is one substance throughout all its instances. Kittens, like gold, each have their characteristics due in part to an inner microscopic structure—their genetic structure. But neither are the genes of any two kittens identical nor are the genes totally responsible for the kittens' properties. Environment has played an important role too. But there are good reasons why the genes of kittens, however different from one kitten to the next, tend to turn out similar products under conditions Normal for kitten development. Crudely, if mixing the genes in the *Felis domesticus* gene pool caused radically different kinds of animals (and other things) to be born from these mixtures, the *Felis domesticus* gene pool would have a very short life indeed! For the same reason (applied a generation earlier) it is clear why kitten genes tend to develop in similar environments. Hence the newborn kitten is a rough or imperfect selfsame substance. Further, because the genes control the development of the kitten into the cat and of the young cat into the old cat, and because the genes control the behavior of the cat so that kittens seek the same kinds of environments, food, etc., not only the newborn kitten but also the six-week-old kitten, the year-old cat, and the twelve-year-old cat are rough substances. So the whole cat-over-time instantiates, roughly, the selfsame substance as the next whole cat-over-time.

Like the '69 Valiant, *Felis domesticus* tends to get repaired—to repair itself—when it becomes worn or damaged. And like the '69 Valiant, *Felis domesticus* also has an identity relative to certain kinds of conditional properties even when it does not relative to corresponding unconditional ones. The cat that has been treated in thus and such ways will tend to behave in thus and such ways, and the cat that has contracted thus and such germs will tend to have thus and such symptoms, and is likely to be curable in thus and such ways, etc.

In sum, perfect secondary substances such as gold have an identity that is, formally, strictly the same as the identity of an individual in relation to its properties. Imperfect secondary substances such as the '69 Plymouth Valiant 100 and *Felis domesticus* have a kind of identity that is formally *analogous* to the identity of perfect substances. For example, the identity of an imperfect substance may be identity in accordance with rough laws operating in situ, rather than under all naturally possible conditions.

The identity of an ordinary individual object *qua enduring through time* is also an identity only in situ, as I will argue in Chapter 17.

Chapter 17
Notes on the Identity of Enduring Objects

The problem of the identity through time of enduring objects is in part to know to what extent it is a problem about identity in the sense that Leibniz's laws were about identity, and to what extent it is instead a problem about why we consider certain temporally extended things to be natural wholes and other temporally extended things to be mere temporal parts or to be collections rather than wholes. One way to explore this problem is to compare the way in which a thing's spatial parts are unified into a whole with the way its temporal parts are unified into one enduring thing to see how far there is an analogy. It is perfectly clear that there is no identity among the spatial parts of a thing but merely relations that gather together or unify parts of a whole. Insofar as relations among the temporal parts or stages of an enduring thing are strictly analogous to relations among the spatial parts of a thing, the problem of enduring objects is not a problem that concerns anything's identity. Let us then press the analogy between spatial and temporal parts to see how far it will carry us.

We will find that it carries us surprisingly far. Indeed, most of this chapter will be spent playing devil's advocate, showing how one problem after another that at first appears to be a problem about identity appears on closer inspection to be merely a problem about principles that unify temporal parts or stages into temporal wholes. I will do my best to convince the reader that there is no such thing as an individual's identity over or through time. But in the end I will admit that there really is such a thing as identity over time. This identity has the same sort of structure that the identity of the perfect substances described in Chapter 16 has, except that it is an identity only in situ. The ultimate purpose of this chapter will be to reinforce the claim that identity, in all its forms, is a kind of natural necessity akin to causality. Thus the law of noncontradiction is at root a law of ontology, which is why it can play the unique role that, I will argue, it does play in epistemology.

The temporal parts of an object that endures are, we suppose, momentary or nearly momentary three-dimensional objects which, properly ordered in time, compose the whole object as enduring through time. Analogously, one might slice an object into very thin spatial parts parallel, say, to the earth's parallels—or cut it into small parts in any other convenient way.

The temporal parts of an object, like the spatial parts, are no two of them the *same* part of the object. Otherwise they could not be distinguished. No matter how tight the relations are that unify various parts into a whole, these parts cannot thereby be made to be the same part but remain parts merely of the *same whole*. For example, no matter how it is that the various temporal parts of Salvadore-the-cat are related to one another to make one whole cat-over-time, still each temporal part of Salvadore is other than each other temporal part of Salvadore. On the other hand, no matter how we consider an object to be divided into parts, the whole object always remains the same as itself. Indeed, a thing need exemplify no principle of unity or wholeness whatever in order to be the same as itself. A flock of sheep is the same as itself even though the principle that unites sheep into flocks requires only a very slender relation among the members of the flock. Indeed, any arbitrary set of objects that one cares to list is the same as itself, including an arbitrary set composed of temporal slices taken at random from the histories of different objects. The unity or lack of unity among the parts of a thing or set, whether these be spatial or temporal parts, seems to have nothing to do either with the identity of any of the parts taken separately or with the identity of the whole. Indeed, why should anyone ever have thought that the problem of how momentary objects are collected into whole enduring objects in accordance with a principle or principles of unity was a problem that concerned anything's identity?

Let us try to answer that question. Suppose that an enduring object is encountered by someone at two different stages in its career—say, at t_1 and at t_2—and that someone wishes to know whether what he encounters at t_2 is the same enduring object as what he earlier encountered at t_1. Surely such a person's question is a question about identity. But a question about the identity of what? It is not a question about the identity of the momentary object-stages encountered at t_1 and t_2. No one supposes that object stages that occur at different times are ever one and the same object stage. So the question must be about the identity of the whole enduring object. To be precise, calling the two object stages S_1 and S_2, the problem seems to be this: are S_1 and S_2 stages of the *same* whole temporally enduring object? But in order to answer this question it seems clear that some principle of unity that collects momentary objects into whole enduring objects must be called upon in order to determine what sorts of relations S_1 and S_2 would have to have to one another in order to be parts of a single whole enduring object. Hence, it appears, the question that began as a question about the identity of an enduring object is in the end a question about the principle of unity that collects temporal parts into whole enduring objects; the question of the identity of the whole cannot be separated from the question concerning the principles of unity that make sets of temporal parts into enduring wholes. Further, it seems clear that there are often *alternative* ways of collecting parts into wholes, so that to answer the question whether S_1 and S_2 are stages of the same enduring whole one must first ask what *category* of whole enduring object is intended. Are S_1 and S_2 stages of the same whole enduring *what*? For example, S_1 and S_2 may be temporal stages of the same dog without being temporal stages of the same collection of atoms. So, it appears, the *selfsameness* of a whole enduring object must be relative to the category or kind under which one considers the object.

But that is a terrible muddle! Consider a spatial analogy. Suppose that while hiking we twice pass stretches of water. Since we have not changed direction during the hike, we take it that these stretches of water are not one and the same. But the question arises, are these stretches, S_1 and S_2, portions of one and the same *whole* body of water? Of course, one needs to know what kind of whole body is intended— a whole lake or a whole bay or a whole chain of lakes or a whole watershed. One needs to know what kind of principle of unity is to be used to collect stretches of water into wholes before one can answer such a question. But the *reason* for this is that the question about the stretches of water has the implicit form: is *the* body of water of which S_1 is a part the same as *the* body of water of which S_2 is a part? But the ostensibly definite descriptions "*the* body of water of which S_1 is a part" and "*the* body of water of which S_2 is a part" are *not* in fact definite but remain ambiguous at least until a specific *kind* of body of water is specified. In order to ask unambiguously whether one thing is the same as another, of course you have to specify in some unambiguous manner *which* things you are asking about. There is nothing mysterious in that. And, of course, the question whether the two things you are asking about are in fact the selfsame—the question about *identity*—remains after this clarification has been made.[1]

Now specifying the *kind* of whole K that you wish to ask about is implicitly specifying a form of unity or a principle for collecting parts into a whole. Under this principle it must fall out that the S you mention in the description "*the* whole K of which S is a part" is in fact part of one and only one whole K. Otherwise the description will be ambiguous. But the principle of unity that unites S with other parts of one and only one whole K, whether this principle requires loose or tight relations, spatial relations, temporal relations, or causal relations, etc., among these parts, seems to have nothing whatever to do with the *identity* of the whole *K*. The whole *K* might, after all, be specified by just listing all of its parts one by one and remarking that the list was exhaustive. Such a list would identify the whole without mentioning any relations among its parts—without mentioning what kind of whole it is. True, a list listing all of the momentary three-dimensional objects, past, present, and future, that compose, say, *you* would be infinitely long. And how could these parts be thought of as acquiring names, or as acquiring descriptions not mentioning the kind of whole of which they are parts, so as to be listed? But we are discussing *ontology* here, not practical problems of reference. From the standpoint of ontology a thing—a set, a whole, a collection; it makes no difference—is the same as itself quite independently of how or whether one manages to make reference to it.

Thus far the analogy between temporal parts and spatial parts seems to be clarifying. And it leads us to wonder what it is that we could want in the way of identity for an enduring object more than that the whole enduring object should be the same as itself and that each temporal stage of it should be the same as itself. We certainly do not want that one temporal stage should be the same as the next temporal stage or that any temporal stage should be identical with the whole enduring object. And what is left over after these trivial matters of selfsameness have been laid aside, it appears, is not a matter of identity at all but the matter of a form of unity that characterizes relations among temporal parts of this or that kind of *whole* enduring object. Similarly there are forms of unity that characterize relations among the spatial parts of whatever we call a whole apple, or a whole house, or a whole lake.

Consider the ancient puzzle, later adorned by Hobbes, about Theseus's ship. Theseus's ship, the ancient story goes, was repaired so many times over so many years that at the end of its life not one single tiny part of the original ship remained. In the meanwhile, Hobbes tells us, someone was collecting each original part of Theseus's ship as it was removed and replaced, and when the last of the old parts was removed, he rebuilt the ship from its original parts. Which of the two ships, Hobbes asks, was the same ship as Theseus's original ship?

Call the original ship of Theseus insofar as it stretches in time from the moment it was completed up to the time that its first part was replaced "$TS\text{-}S_o$" (Theseus's ship-stage original). Call Theseus's new repaired ship from the time of its last repair to the time of its demise "$TS\text{-}S_n$" (Theseus's ship-stage new). Call Hobbes's renovated ship "$TS\text{-}S_r$" (Theseus's ship-stage renovated). First it is obvious that $TS\text{-}S_o$ was not the same thing as $TS\text{-}S_n$ or the same as $TS\text{-}S_r$ nor was $TS\text{-}S_n$ the same as $TS\text{-}P_r$. These three were different ship-*stages*. Now reformulate the question perspicuously: Was the whole enduring ship of which $TS\text{-}S_n$ was a part the same as the whole enduring ship of which $TS\text{-}S_o$ was a part? Or was the whole enduring ship of which $TS\text{-}S_r$ was a part the same as the whole enduring ship of which $TS\text{-}S_o$ was a part? The answer cannot be given until the question is clarified. For depending upon what sort of principle you employ for gathering temporal ship-stages into whole enduring ships—and there are alternative principles that are equally natural or appealing here—the definite descriptions "the whole enduring ship of which $TS\text{-}S_o$ was a part," "the whole enduring ship of which $TS\text{-}S_n$ was a part," and "the whole enduring ship of which $TS\text{-}S_r$ was a part" shift their references, producing different *questions* to be answered. Similarly, one can easily imagine cases in which the rough principles of unity we use in collecting stretches of water into whole lakes would prove ambiguous in application—say, a narrow and long neck but with no one-way flow of water through it connects two large bodies of fresh water. Then the question, is $stretch_1$ of water part of the same lake as $stretch_2$ of water? might well prove an ambiguous question.

Yet what gives Hobbes's version of the problem of Theseus's ship its punch is not just that it is unclear whether $TS\text{-}S_n$ and $TS\text{-}S_o$ are connected by the "right" sort of principles of unity to count as parts of "one whole enduring ship" and also unclear whether $TS\text{-}S_r$ and $TS\text{-}S_o$ are so connected. What gives the problem its punch is that it seems so clear that a *choice* between $TS\text{-}S_n$ and $TS\text{-}S_r$ has to be made for appropriate connection with $TS\text{-}S_o$. For, it seems, it could not be that both $TS\text{-}S_n$ and $TS\text{-}S_r$ were parts of the *same* enduring ship, since these existed concurrently in different places. By contrast, we cannot imagine three stretches of water S_1, S_2, and S_3 so spatially connected that it was unclear whether S_1 and S_2 were parts of the same lake, unclear whether S_1 and S_3 were parts of the same lake, yet perfectly clear that S_2 and S_3 could not be considered to be parts of the same lake *on any plausible precising definition of whole-lake unity*. Have we finally hit upon an asymmetry between spatial parts and temporal parts?

$TS\text{-}S_n$ and $TS\text{-}S_r$, it seems obvious, cannot be stages of the same ship because these exist at the same time yet have different properties, occupy different parts of space, are composed of different bits of matter, etc. Indeed, Leibniz's undisputed principle that identicals are indiscernible apparently rules out that $TS\text{-}S_n$ and $TS\text{-}S_r$ are the same ship. So, it seems, whatever principle of unity one decides upon for purposes of defining "whole temporally enduring ship" has got to be a principle that prohibits two different temporal parts of the same ship from existing at the same time. It has got, for example, to prevent a whole enduring ship from "splitting" like an amoeba and still continuing to exist. Thus any principle of unity for temporal parts of whole enduring objects *must* connect with the notion of identity after all. A principle that unifies temporal parts into a whole enduring object must be such that Leibniz's law is upheld.[2]

But alas, once again we have got ourselves into a muddle! Leibniz's laws says only that the same thing must have all of the same properties as itself. It does not say, for any two parts of a whole, that *these* must have all of the same properties as one another. Why then couldn't *TS-S_n* and *TS-S_r* be two *parts* of the same enduring thing which parts happen to be simultaneous but at a remove from one another? Surely it is not *Leibniz's* law that tells us they cannot. Rather, it is the principle of *unity* for enduring *individual* objects that requires these objects each to have only one position at one time or, more clearly, to have its parts all joined together in one place at each time. It is true that we sometimes break with this general principle and allow ourselves to speak of individual objects as continuing to exist even though broken or taken apart. Still, this principle of unity tends strongly to help *define* the notion of an individual. It places a restriction on the specific principles of unity that can count as gathering spatial and temporal parts into a whole *individual* as opposed, for example, to a whole reproductively established *family*. But the requirement that an individual have all of its spatial parts joined together in one place at each time—that it not "split" in the manner of an amoeba or "split" in the more gradual manner in which Theseus's ship "split," or continue to exist after it is smashed—apparently has nothing whatever to do with the individual's identity or selfsameness. The point is difficult. Let me try to make it more graphic.

Suppose that I were to give a proper name to an amoeba-*and*-all-of-its-progeny, as this entity continues through time, splitting and then splitting again. I call this branching entity "Annabelle." First Annabelle has one spatial part, later two parts, and still later four, etc. Annabelle is an entity a bit like the John Adams *family*, about which many things are true. But the separate amoebas that compose Annabelle, as she splits apart, do not, we suppose, have their own proper names. Suppose that Annabelle has now divided herself into eight individual amoebas, and suppose that I wish to say about one of these nameless amoebas that it is living in my soup. I cannot distinguish this amoeba as a part of Annabelle *merely* by noting the time at which it lives. For example, I cannot just say "Annabelle is now living in my soup." Either "Annabelle is now living in my soup" is ambiguous, or it has got to mean that all eight current parts of Annabelle are in my soup. Now *individuals* differ from entities like Annabelle in that each has, at each time, only one undivided spatial part, so that a reference to the *time* at which any

spatially whole part of an individual exists determines that part unambiguously. But this fact about the characteristic sort of unity that an
individual exhibits through time does not seem to have anything to
do with its identity. It has to do only with what kinds of definite
descriptions will and will not do for distinguishing its parts unambiguously. Annabelle is the selfsame as herself, and each of her parts is
the selfsame as itself, despite the fact that Annabelle does not exhibit
this kind of unity.

Consider a spatial analogy. Suppose that it were convenient for some
purpose to have a term for bodies of water—say, "O-lake"—that collected stretches of water into the largest wholes possible that were
undivided across the earth's parallels. Then one could always ask of
an O-lake, how wide is it at parallel such and such? and be sure that
one's question was not ambiguous. Bodies of water that sprawled or
branched in such a way that one would go across two separated sections
of them if one followed certain parallels would not then be O-lakes.
Rather, they would divide into parts at the point of separation across
a parallel, each of these parts being a whole O-lake. O-lakes, unlike
ordinary lakes, would be such that they never had two widths at any
given parallel. But the fact that ordinary lakes sometimes do have two
widths across a single parallel does not affect their identity in any way.
Similarly, the fact that Annabelle has numerous spatial positions at
some given times does not affect her identity in any way.

Once again we seem to have demonstrated that problems concerning
the forms of unity that unite the temporal parts of various kinds of
enduring objects are quite separate from problems that concern anything's identity. It seems that principles of unity, including those that
unify an enduring individual object over time, can neither create identity
nor interfere with identity. They merely gather parts into wholes.

Consonant with this, in the case of Theseus's ship, surely the choice
among saying that the new rebuilt ship is the same as Theseus's original
ship, saying that Hobbes's reconstructed ship is the same as Theseus's
original ship, and saying that neither is the same as Theseus's original
ship is a merely verbal choice—a choice about how to define "one
whole ship over time"—whereas real confusions about identity are not
settled by making verbal choices. Indeed, the puzzles about "identity
over time" that abound in the current literature—examples of things
that "split" in one way or another, examples of things that slowly but
completely metamorphose, etc.—all seem to be puzzles *not* about anything's identity but about what principles of unity we do or should use
to divide up the world into whole enduring individuals—about how
we do use words or about how it would be best to use words. That
these examples do not pose genuine problems about anything's identity

is apparent from the fact that we understand the situations described in these examples completely; we all agree on what happened according to each example; no one is left confused about anything except what to *say*. But genuine problems of identity leave one confused about what to *think*, not merely about what to say.

And so, if I have played devil's advocate successfully, it appears that the case against genuine identity *over* or *through* time rests. There is no such thing as identity over or through time any more than there is such a thing as identity over or through space. All there is is the identity of each temporal stage of a thing with that temporal stage, the identity of the whole collection of temporal stages with that collection, and a principle of unity that collects these stages into a unified whole. For surely we do not want that one temporal stage of an object should be the selfsame as any other temporal stage. Nor do we want that any temporal stage should be the selfsame as the whole enduring object.

And yet the feeling remains that there *must* be *some* way that the very same thing—the very same book or chair—*does* exist at more than one time, and this in a sense that does not reduce merely to the fact that the thing is a unified whole having different parts at different times. *Something*, we still want to say, persists *through* time when an object persists, remaining the same even though its time changes and perhaps many of its properties change as well. A bare substratum the identity of which has nothing to do with the sameness of its properties? The thought makes us anxious, but it too persists.

Not a bare substratum, no, but a kind of sub-essence is what persists. Using the same analogy—that of spatial parts to temporal parts—let me try to show what is wrong—and what is right—about the devil's argument against enduring substances.

I have said that there is no identity over or through the spatial *parts* of a thing. But consider again the substance gold (Chapter 16, "Generalizing the Notion of Individual Identity"). Gold has an identity that persists over both space and time. This is possible because gold is not the kind of thing that *has* a spatial or temporal location and yet gold has instances that are spatially and temporally located. Gold is neither the same as any of its spatially and temporally located instances nor is it the set or collected whole of its instances. Its instances are not "parts" of it. Being gold is a property of each of gold's instances, but at the same time gold's identity as a *substance* is relative to its *own* properties, and these do not include space- or time-bound properties. In this way gold manages to be the selfsame "over" or "through" both time and space without its identity having to pass through its instances, making them the same as one another.

Now suppose that one mistakenly identified gold with the collection of all its instances. This would be a mistake. For example, the whole that consists of all the samples of gold in the world has a certain weight—more accurately, a certain mass. But gold does not have a weight or mass. And yet it is not implausible to confuse gold the secondary substance with the collection of all samples of gold. For we do say things such as "gold is more rare than iron" and "gold is seldom used for filling teeth anymore," thus using "gold" *also* to refer to the sum total of all gold or to samples of gold. Confusing the secondary substance gold with the whole that is all instances of gold, hence confusing its samples with *parts*, one might argue as follows. No part of gold is the selfsame as any other part of gold. And no part of gold is the selfsame as the whole. Therefore, there is no such thing as the identity of gold over or through space. There is only the identity of each part with itself, the identity of the whole with itself, and a principle of unity that collects the parts of gold into a unified whole. This principle of unity bundles the various parts of gold together by virtue of their all having the same *properties*, namely, the properties definitional of "gold," these properties being, of course, properties of all and only the parts of gold. Arguing this way, we would pass right by the identity of gold as a secondary *substance*—as something that, whenever and wherever it is encountered, has all of the same properties as itself in accordance with natural necessity rather than in accordance merely with a nominal definition. Gold as a secondary substance is not merely bundled together by a nominal principle of unity. It is a selfsame in accordance with natural necessity.

Is it possible that individuals have an identity over time that is analogous to the identity over space that gold has? Is there a *substance* associated with each individual enduring object that is not merely equivalent to the collection of temporal stages of that individual? This substance would have to have the same properties as itself over time in accordance with natural necessity just as gold has the same properties as itself over space in accordance with natural necessity. And besides being a substance *with* properties it would also have to *be* a property— a property of each of the temporal stages of the individual that it unifies, as being gold is a property of each of gold's instances. Call this hypothesized substance, for each individual, the individual's "subessence," for it would be a *substance* that was also the principle of unity or *essence* of that individual qua a unified set of temporal stages. And it would be a substance identity that *underlies* the unity among these temporal stages.

Paradigm enduring objects are material objects, for example, chairs and dogs and rocks rather than patches of sunlight, gravitational fields, or a tenor's high A's. Material objects are entities that retain many of their properties over time in accordance with natural conservation laws, given that nothing external to them interferes.[3] These properties perpetuate themselves through time *unless* there is a change in the situation of the object—a change in the forces acting upon it. That is, these properties are perpetuated *ceteris paribus*, and when they are perpetuated, this is in accordance with natural necessity in situ—unless, of course, they are the basic properties of an individual elementary particle, in which case they are perpetuated in accordance with natural necessity under all naturally possible conditions. Some material objects are so internally organized that they *actively* maintain many of their properties over time, reacting to certain kinds of changes in situation so as to maintain these properties. Living organisms provide the primary examples of this kind of active stability over time. Besides simple properties of a given material object that tend to perpetuate themselves over time there are also dispositional and conditional properties. Examples of dispositional or conditional properties that may perpetuate themselves over time are being brittle, being elastic, having a squeaky hinge, stopping when its brake pedal is depressed or when it runs out of gas, being able to swim (i.e., it swims when it purposes to and when conditions for this purposing are Normal), being able to write its name, remembering its name, and having a quick temper.

Consider all the properties of a certain material object O that remain the same from a time t_1 through a time t_2 in accordance with natural conservation laws operating in situ. These may be considered to be properties of a subessence S associated with O from t_1 through t_2. This subessence S is not a set of properties. S is an unique principle of natural necessity that actively *instantiates* a collection of properties over time *at a particular place or series of connected places*. It is a substance *having* properties. It chooses one property from each of a variety of contrary ranges and exhibits that property to the exclusion of its contraries in accordance with natural necessity. S is the sort of thing that one can find things out about from one perspective upon it and then use this information or reaffirm it from another perspective, for example, by catching it again later on. As in the case of gold, although S never exhibits itself except through its "instances"—its temporal stages—one need have no concept of any of its instances in order to have a concept of it—in order to reidentify it and learn about it via various perspectives upon it.

Now almost any stage of any enduring object (except elementary particles) has more than one subessence associated with it. For, since not all of the conservation laws operating in situ that perpetuate properties of a thing depend upon the same external conditions holding constant, most things encounter vicissitudes that change some of their naturally stable properties, at least in minor ways, before others, i.e., before the thing disintegrates entirely. For example, where t_1 to t_{10} are times three months apart occurring in sequence, Salvadore the cat will undoubtedly retain different sets of properties in accordance with conservation laws from t_1 to t_2, from t_1 to t_3, from t_1 to t_{10}, and from t_5 to t_{10}. So a temporal stage does not by itself determine any particular subessence as *the* subessence that must unify it with other temporal stages into one whole enduring thing over time. The decision how to divide up the world into discrete individual temporally extended wholes that begin at one time and end at another cannot then be determined but can only be *limited* by the existence of individual subessences that are selfsames over time.

The principle of strict indentity over time is not strong enough by itself to divide up the world into a determinate set of enduring objects. Or, more accurately, it divides the ongoing world into chunks that are far too numerous, overlapping, and crisscrossing to try to keep track of. So a great deal of room is left for decision on our part as to how to divide the world into sensible-sized and sensibly unified temporally extended wholes to be recognized and honored by coordination with common and/or proper names. A study of the various kinds of principles of unity that we do refer to in recognizing various kinds of temporally extended wholes is not necessary to the argument of this book. But let me make a few somewhat random or unstructured observations about them before we pass on to the subject of epistemology.

First, just as it is convenient to recognize with natural kind terms secondary substances such as the '69 Plymouth Valiant 100 and *Felis domesticus* that are rough or imperfect, so it is convenient to recognize temporally extended wholes that are unified by imperfect subessences. Some properties are not perpetuated *exactly* over time in accordance with conservation laws but instead are very slowly transformed into merely similar properties over time. Thus many of Salvadore's exact properties slowly change as he grows from kitten to cat until very few of his exact original properties remain. As a tadpole slowly turns into a frog, most of its initial properties are slowly replaced by quite different properties, and yet, for certain purposes, it is reasonable to recognize the temporally extended whole that includes all these stages, indeed, even all the stages from egg to tadpole, under the common name "example of *Rana catesbeiana*."

Second, although some properties of a temporal stage of a thing may perpetuate themselves independently of other properties, sometimes there are large sets of properties that are related to one another as the properties of gold are related to one another, all depending upon some one underlying structure or property. In that case, a vicissitude that destroys this core property will destroy many others as well. Such a complex of properties is a natural to use for determining the subessence that defines a recognized temporally extended whole. For example, living organisms come to an end, very naturally, when they die because then, very suddenly, nearly all their properties stop perpetuating themselves. Such complexes are, in general, examples of natural kinds.

Third, and correlative to points one and two, it is productive to recognize temporally extended wholes that exemplify either exact or rough natural kinds. For then we will be recognizing wholes about which much may be known, either with certainty or with high probability, without the bother of an individual examination. Thus it is reasonable to treat Salvadore, from birth to death, as one temporally extended whole, since all the time he remains, in accordance with natural necessity in situ, a *cat*, and because cats form a rough natural kind or substance. And it is reasonable to treat Kermit that way, even as he grows from egg through tadpole to frog. But it would not be so reasonable to treat a kitten that metamorphosed, through some rare accidental circumstance, into what was in all respects like a typical frog as all one temporally extended whole. For this whole would not be one of a natural kind about which one might presume to know anything at all in advance of examining it individually. But it is also reasonable to cut up Kermit the example of *Rana catesbeiana* into several smaller temporally extended wholes, namely, Kermit the egg, Kermit the tadpole, and Kermit the frog. For frog eggs, tadpoles, and frogs each form a more perfect natural kind than, simply, *Rana catesbeiana*. I suggest that this third observation accounts for the tenacity with which some hold the view that individuals *as such* fall under defining natural kinds.

Fourth, we do have a very strong tendency to ignore subessences that "split apart" in space. For example, if one lists all the properties of a certain temporal stage of Salvadore which properties tend to endure through time *ceteris paribus*, this list will include many properties that characterize the concurrent stage of the collection of matter that Salvadore is then composed of. But Salvadore and Salvadore's matter will slowly separate over time. Hence we distinguish Salvadore's naturally enduring properties from the naturally enduring properties of his matter, considering these to compose separate subessences. Thus it is that Salvadore at any given time *is* his matter at any given time, yet Salvadore the temporally extended whole is not the temporally extended whole that is Salvadore's matter. Similarly, it might be true (I am not sure about this) that when an amoeba splits, certain of its properties are perpetuated as properties of *each* resulting sister amoeba in accordance merely with conservation laws in situ. Thus, all the temporal stages of all the parts of our friend Annabelle might be recognized as constituting a single temporally and spatially extended whole determined by a single subessence. But it is not our tendency to cut the world up that way, and for good reason. Very few things are like Annabelle, and we need to employ principles that are applicable with a high degree of generality so that they can easily be *learned* if we are to communicate with one another. Further, we need to divide the ongoing world into wholes the parts of which can easily be identified as parts of the same whole, whereas the parts of Annabelle would be hopeless to keep track of.

Last, there is plenty of room for enduring-object categories that are carved out only by *analogy* to categories that follow contours of genuine identity over time—rough spatial and temporal continuity being an obvious guide for such analogy. A pile of sand, partially used and partially replenished, may not contain any of the same grains of sand that it did a year ago. And a pile of sand does not replenish itself, the new sand retaining, say, the location of the old in accordance with any conservation laws. Yet the pile may be considered all along to be the same pile of sand, say, pile 27 at the sand quarry. Similarly, Theseus' new repaired ship, though it does not have the same structure as the old in accordance with any inner principle that perpetuated this structure, may be considered to be the same as the original because it has continuously retained its original structure for other reasons. Convert the ship to steam, then to nuclear power, slowly altering its shape and size and construction and material accordingly, and it will not be so clear that it might be called the same ship. But even here, the chain of overlapping true identities over time, based on each stage having most of the same properties as the last in accordance with conservation laws, and the rough spatial and temporal continuity of the whole might still lead us, in certain moods, to call it the same ship.

These observations on the principles in accordance with which we carve out temporally extended wholes to recognize and talk about are very rough and ready. My purpose in making them at all is only to try to make clearer a basic point that we need to have very firmly established before venturing into epistemology: there is a difference of great importance between identity, in all its forms, and the mere unity of wholes. There are many kinds of salfsames in the world, including all the selfsames that are arbitrary sets of temporal thing-stages, arbitrary sets of properties, or arbitrary sets of anything else you wish to name. Unity is something quite other than and over and above identity. Yet unity is far less fundamental than identity. For all *principles* of unity must make reference to prior selfsames of some kind—selfsame properties, selfsame relations, selfsame substances, selfsame subessences, etc. Principles of unity whereby one "cuts up the world" into unified wholes are principles that can be chosen at one's convenience. But the identity of a thing is *not* something that rests on convenience or convention. Principles of selfsameness are discovered in nature, not created by language or thought.

The first problem of epistemology must then be to understand how it is that we are able to learn to recognize objective identity. For only if we can recognize the various objective identities there are in the world can we carve up that world into bite-sized wholes in accordance with sensible principles of unity, or carve up ranges of properties into bite-sized property areas. In order to carve up the world, one must first *find* the world—one must first *have* an objective world to carve up. And finding the objective world is, just, finding some of the objective identities that it contains.

Chapter 18

Epistemology of Identity: The Law of Noncontradiction

Departing from traditional realist theories, I have distinguished three questions about the nature of thought. First, there is the question what it is for a thought to be about something. The theory of intentional icons, developed in Part II, offered an answer to this first question. Second, there is the question what it is to *know* what one is thinking of—what it is to identify the referents of one's thoughts. The theory of the act of identifying, presented in Chapter 15, offered an answer to this second question. The third question remains. What criteria do we use to separate empty ideas from valid ones and to sort correct from incorrect dispositions to identify? In Chapter 8 I suggested that the criterion used during the invention and development of concepts to sort out those that are governing term tokens that map from those that are not is the law of noncontradiction. But in order to understand why such a criterion might be effective, certain assumptions must be made about ontology. Chapters 16 and 17 sketched these assumptions. At last we can turn to epistemology.

Unlike hubots, the inner vocabulary that we use is not genetically wired in—certainly not most of it. We must be capable of "coining" inner terms. Perhaps we coin for ourselves all the inner terms we use, each person thinking entirely in his or her own idiosyncratic inner language. And the mechanisms that coin inner terms must invent adequate programs to govern the iteration of the terms they invent such that the sentences containing them map onto the world. What must be explained is how humans Normally do this. What test do humans use to decide whether their concepts are adequate? And why does this test Normally work?

Notice that this statement of the epistemological problem that needs to be solved differs in a very important way from usual formulations of the epistemological problem faced by realists. The epistemological task, viewed from our standpoint, is not to show that there are inner tests that determine absolutely whether one's inner sentences map onto the world. We need only show that there might be tests that, *when* applied under conditions Normal for the devices that administer them, determine whether *concepts, when* applied under conditions Normal for them, are producing sentences that map. If man qua knower is a natural creature, we have no reason to suppose that the way man knows is any more infallible than the way man manages to do anything else. Indeed, we *are* assuming (1) that whatever tests man uses in order to monitor his term-producing programs are *not* infallible tests and (2) that a specific program for iterating a term in inner sentences can be a good program without being one that works under *all* conditions, either possible or actual. It need only work under conditions Normal for it.

Tradition has it that if correspondence is not the test of truth, coherence must be. But tradition now also has it that all our concepts and beliefs are bound up together in a comprehensive system such that none can be tested without at the same time testing all the others. An *efficient* generate and test routine would have to test what had been generated piece by piece. Otherwise the concept-learning process would mimic natural selection too closely, taking eons to make tests on all the possible combinations that might be generated. Compare how the heart is tested by natural selection—along *with* the kidneys and *with* the brain, the pineal gland, the clavicle, and the index finger, etc.—and how long this takes! Moreover we are assuming that the tests by which concepts are tested are not infallible and that term-iterating programs are not themselves infallible even when good ones. Hence inconsistency in inner sentences need not always indicate that concepts are inadequate. If it were also true that no inner term-iterating program could be tested without testing all of one's other term-iterating programs simultaneously, the problem of weeding out empty or faulty concepts from the system by the test of coherence would certainly be a completely hopeless one.

True, our stance is not that of the Cartesian epistemologist who wants a demonstration that the only "logically possible" way of accounting for coherence in a system of thought (or system of apparent thought—stuff that feels like thought) "after all the evidence is in" would be by postulating that this system maps onto an outer world in a systematic way. We are not trying to understand how a test such as coherence would necessarily be an infallible test of the mapping of inner terms in every possible world. We are only trying to understand how there might be a test that *in this world* has historically been applied to humans' concepts, the results of this test correlating, for reasons that we can give, with adequacy—with a tendency to generate term tokens that map. And yet we seem to be handicapped in a way that the traditional epistemologist is not handicapped. We will have to understand coherence to be a test that has exceedingly often proved to be an adequate test in the past even though "all the evidence" has never been anywhere near in for any human. And it is not merely an understanding of the possibility of *truth* in human belief that hinges on this. The very possibility of meaningfulness or intentionality in human thought is apparently at stake.

Why the test of noncontradiction can be an efficient test will be the topic of Chapter 19, in which I will argue that epistemological holism is false. Why the test of noncontradiction, if it *could* be applied to but a small group of concepts at once, would be a relatively effective test for the adequacy of concepts is the topic of this chapter.

An adequate concept governs production of inner-term tokens that perform their proper functions in accordance with a Normal explanation when they correspond to some particular real-world variant. Production of a series of inner-term tokens of the same type is a preliminary act of identification of the representational values of those tokens (see Chapter 15, "The Act of Identifying"). An adequate concept, cooperating with Normally functioning cooperative interpreting devices, produces correct acts of identification of the referents of the term tokens it produces. To develop an adequate concept is, in part, to learn how to identify as-the-same-again something in the world. If conformity to the law of noncontradiction is the test whereby we evaluate the performance of our concepts, then this test is both a test for the mapping of the terms governed by these concepts and a test of our abilities correctly to identify the values of these tokens. That is why I have collapsed the two questions, how do we know that our ideas are not empty and how do we know that we are identifying their values correctly. How might the law of noncontradiction serve as a test for the correctness of acts of identifying?

The problem faced by an organism that needs to learn how to identify *as* the same what objectively *is* the same is not the problem, to which it is often assimilated, of learning how to "cut up the world" into bite-sized chunks in a nonarbitrary way or in the same way that others in a language community do. It is not the problem that Quine calls "setting conditions for identity" or "dividing of reference. . . . : how far you have the same apple and when you are getting into another."[1] Setting conditions for how far you have the same apple and when you are getting into another is the problem of determining principles of *unity* that will govern one's kind terms for individual wholes. The identity of the parts of a unified whole and of the whole itself is presupposed in order for there to be anything definite to be unified by a principle of unity. Similarly, the problem of learning to identify properties correctly is not the problem of deciding how to divide up a contrary range, such as the range of colors, into bite-sized areas. It is not the problem of setting conditions for when you have red again and when you are getting into orange. It is the problem of learning to identify red again, say, from diverse angles and under diverse lighting conditions, through the media of various language representations ("red," "rouge," "rot," etc.), as the referent of a variety of definite descriptions ("The color of blood," "a nose like a cherry," "emitting wavelength such and such") and perhaps by the use of instruments (e.g., wavelength measurers), etc. The problem of learning to identify a person again is that of learning to identify her at various distances, from various angles, in various postures, by her walk, by her voice, by her name, by her handwriting, by characteristic signs that she leaves behind (my youngest's characteristic mess in the bathroom), and by a variety of definite descriptions, etc. The problem of learning to reidentify a given whole or a given property or of learning general principles by which wholes or properties of a certain kind may reliably be identified is a problem that is not solved either for an individual or for a community by making linguistic decisions either of an arbitrary or of a thoroughly reasonable sort. It is a problem that, with each individual act of identifying, one has either solved or not solved, for each such act is objectively either correct, incorrect, or senseless (i.e., the apparent representations of which one attempts to identify the values have no mapping values).

The basic sorts of things that one must learn to identify in order to have nonempty theoretical beliefs are substances and properties. (Among properties I am including relations and acts such as sitting and hitting.) The identities—the very itselfnesses—of substances and of properties, I have argued, are two among other kinds of natural necessity to be found in the natural world. That is why we must *find* identity rather than deciding or making it. The identities of substances and of properties have structure; these identities are structured in relation to one another. This structure is exhibited in the refusal of a property to admit any of its contrary properties onto the ground of any substance that it qualifies. Alternatively, this structure is the insistence of a substance upon having its properties to the exclusion of properties that are contrary. If we read the negative as I have argued (Chapter 14) that it must be read—as operating upon logical predicates of sentences only—this structure is exactly expressed by the law of noncontradiction. In the outer world, substances and properties display an abstract structure showing systematic exclusion of property and contrary property upon common ground. This parallels inner consistency in belief. Coherence can be a test of correspondence because coherence in thought corresponds to an abstract feature of the world. The law of noncontradiction reflects the (or a) structure of being. It is a template of the general structure of world affairs as it should reflect in thought—a template at least of that kind of world affair that language having subject-predicate structure is designed to map.

Consider an analogy. The lens of an eye, when properly focused, takes light that has been scattered from a single part of an object to hit different parts of the eye and bends this light so that it returns again to a single point on the retina. Thus effects or manifestations of the same point on the object which have been separated and scattered are returned to have a unitary impact upon the seeing organism. But the organism that has lens eyes must focus its eyes in order to achieve this effect. So it must have some way of "knowing" when its eyes are focused on an object—some way of "knowing" when this unitary impact is in fact occurring. It must have a knowledge, as it were, of what the world *ought* to look like so as to know when focus has been achieved. Whether animals learn to focus their eyes or whether this comes with maturation, the problem is the same. The infant must have some way of knowing when he has an object in focus vs. when he still needs to adjust his focus so as to see an object more clearly. Somehow he must know what an in-focus object—any in-focus object—is supposed to look like. (This "knowing" is, of course, a knowing how.) There must then be features that characterize typical *clear* images of objects so that these can be distinguished from unclear images. And contemplating images that have these clarity features must be rewarding to the infant so that he will maintain focus on an object once he finds that focus. (This is how he manifests his knowing how.) The patient work of modern ethologists and experimental psychologists has revealed that this sort of wired-in knowledge and wired-in interest is one of the cornerstones upon which the possibility of learning other things about the world is built.

Through the act of identifying, effects or manifestations of a single thing that have been dispersed via different media to impinge upon our senses in different ways are, as it were, gathered together so that the effect of these upon our thoughts and actions is unitary. But to the extent that we learn to identify rather than being preprogrammed to identify, we must have some way of knowing when we have achieved a focus upon some substance or property in the world. We must have some way of knowing what the world should look like—think like— when it is in focus for thought. (Again, this "knowing" is of course a knowing *how*.) Conformity of our beliefs to the law of noncontradiction is our preconceived notion of focus in thought. Normally it is because one's concepts are producing inner-term tokens that consistently map the same in accordance with consistent explanations that one's belief set is coherent. So we develop new concepts by tuning our methods of term iteration until they are producing consistent inner maps for us.

This sketch of concept development makes sense only granted two conditions. First, it must be possible to test evolving concepts in small enough groups that there is some chance of locating the cause of the trouble when contradictions begin to arise. That this is possible will be argued in Chapter 19. Second, there must be plentiful opportunity for contradictions to arise as we develop concepts.

Contradictions can arise only if the same judgment is attempted more than once so that consistency in result vs. lack of consistency in result can be established. Basic concepts, insofar as these are learned, must be concepts of things that we can have more than one opportunity to make the same judgment about. These things must thus be elements in world affairs that can manifest themselves to us in more than one way, from more than one perspective, through more than one medium, or at least at more than one time. It must be possible to have concepts of these things that consist of more than one intension, say, that consist of abilities to recognize the same element through the medium of more than one sense or from different angles or perspectives via the same sense or by different marks via the same sense. Or, if one's concept of a thing consists of just one intension, then the thing must be such that it can be observed at more than one time via that intension, as can individuals that preserve their identity through time.

This second requirement forces us to depart radically from those models of concept formation that presume our first and surest concepts or thoughts to be concepts or thoughts of sensory data. Rather than being ideal objects for thought to take its first hold upon, the momentary events that take place where the various senses meet the world would be the most difficult of all things to focus upon—as well as the least useful to have knowledge of. Suppose, for example, that there were such things as the sense data hypothesized by the logical atomists and early verificationists. Each such sense datum presents itself to one sense at a time and then vanishes forever without a trace. Any affair involving a sense datum could be viewed from exactly one perspective via exactly one sense at exactly one time. To develop concepts that would allow us to make judgments about sense data would be quite impossible, there being no way to test programs designed to iterate terms for these data and for the properties of these data. It would be impossible, at any rate, unless one were *simultaneously* to develop a full-scale theory about lawful connections among sense data so as to predict as well as to observe their occurrences. But such an attempt would snag immediately upon the first requirement we mentioned for the possibility of concept development. Concepts must be tested in small groups so that one has some idea which iteration programs need to be adjusted when contradictions begin to arise.

The problem involved in trying to develop a language about sensation is not then quite what Wittgenstein thought it was. It is not that *private* languages cannot be developed. Rather, languages that speak of what can be viewed only once and from only one perspective cannot be developed. Adding comprehension of a public language to one's repertoire of ways to gain multiple perspectives on the world is just one more way, though one with profound implications, as we will soon see, to manage to make the same judgment over again.

The substances and correlative properties of which it should be easiest to develop concepts are enduring individual objects that retain many of their properties over a considerable period of time, that are middle-sized so that one can navigate around or manipulate them, and that can be sensed via several or all of the senses. Also, natural kinds and natural materials that display a variety of properties easily accessible to our senses should be relatively easy to form concepts of. *Mother*, *milk*, and *cat*, for example, should all be easily accessible to the infant. Small children's concepts of individual substances such as *Mother* and *our house* undoubtedly have the same kind of simple internal structure— the same sorts of implicit intensions—as do their concepts of kinds and materials. For the difference between the failure of kinds and materials to have properties from certain ranges that their *instances* have properties from (gold is not square although some pieces of gold are) and the failure of an individual object to retain over time certain properties that it has at *given* times—that its temporal stages have— is not a discernible difference until time, hence endurance through time, is comprehended. Small children's concepts of individual objects cannot be of these objects as persisting uninterruptedly through time and as having time-bound properties, since small children do not conceptualize time. (Children do not usually acquire time concepts until about age four.)

Extrapolating from the findings of ethologists, the chances are good that a considerable repertoire of abilities to identify or abilities that would make learning to identify easy are either built into humans at birth or mature sometime relatively soon after birth. These would not necessarily be abilities to produce thought tokens having subject-predicate structure. But there is already evidence from the work of experimental psychologists that the coordination of visual, tactual, and kinesthetic images required for eye-hand coordination is innate; that the ability to track an object with the eyes is innate; that the knowledge where to look to find the source of a sound is innate; that the ability to recognize geometric objects to be the same whether they have been inverted, rotated, or moved nearer or farther away is innate; and most interesting of all, that the ability to discriminate boundaries among some, perhaps all, of the forty or so phonemes that represent all phonemes in all human languages is innate. Also, newborns seem to possess both "feature detectors" by which to detect human faces and a natural disposition to study these faces. Moreover, face recognition is processed separately in the brain from recognition of ordinary objects; lesions affecting face recognition or face-name associations do not necessarily affect recognition of other objects. This suggests that although we do not of course come into the world programmed to recognize any particular person, we may well be carefully programmed to *learn* to identify particular people *by* their faces. Similarly, although the ability to track a moving object with the eyes is not yet an ability to identify anything, this ability is ideally suited to help us to accomplish the task of learning what various kinds of objects and properties look like at various distances and angles, under different lighting conditions, etc.

In beginning to construct theoretical concepts we do not then begin from scratch. But it is equally important to note that we are not left with no recourse but to trust in our maker with regard to adequacy of the concepts we develop out of these materials. Over and over our concepts are tested, as the simple observations we make about simple things in the everyday world are made over, hold up, and remain stable, testifying over and over that we possess genuine abilities to identify certain kinds of substances and to identify properties from certain ranges as in opposition to their contraries. We do not in fact keep finding that this or that simple observation is not so after all when we observe from another perspective or via another sense—or when we hear from another person.

Besides the enormous boost that inborn capacities undoubtedly give us toward the development of adequate concepts, there is language, the power of which it is impossible to overestimate. In Chapter 19 I will argue that believing what one hears is exactly like any other way of gaining knowledge by perception without inference. Between the seen world and the ordinary seeing of it or between the heard world and the ordinary hearing of it, etc., lie very complicated mechanisms— eyes, ears, and specialized parts of the nervous system, etc.—that have been designed by nature. Between my seeing of it and what I see in a mirror lies, besides these natural mechanisms, a very simple man- made instrument. The fact that the mirror was made by man does not change the fact that I can *see* myself in the mirror and hence know by perception without inference whether or not my face still has paint on it. If it is a pair of glasses, a magnifying glass, a microscope, or a telescope that lies between my seeing of something and what I see, still I simply *see* the thing, gaining knowledge of it by perception without inference. And so for the use of recording devices, TV sets, voltmeters, gas gauges, oscilloscopes, and a thousand other man-made instruments that allow us to perceive what, by the use of our unaided senses, we could not perceive. A difference between ordinary perceiving and many of the latter ways of perceiving is that in the former case not merely some affair in the world but one's relation *to* that affair is perceived, whereas in many of the latter cases (e.g., TV, recordings) one must know, if one knows, what one's relation to the perceived is by independent means. Perception as used to guide action requires that the relation between perceiver and perceived should show in the perception. But this difference between the former and the latter cases is not relevant to the difference between gaining knowledge by perception alone and gaining knowledge by inference. Coming to know something by believing what someone else says is making use of another instrument that extends perception—an instrument that is hardly an artifact. This instrument is the carefully adjusted perceptual and cognitive systems of another person, through which some portion of the world has been carefully focused and then projected again via a medium one knows how to interpret. My eyes can play tricks on me, my instruments can get out of adjustment, and others may misinform me. But when things go Normally, none of these misfortunes occurs.

Children are born with the disposition to attend closely to speech sounds as distinguished from other sounds and with the ability to distinguish boundaries between the phonemes employed by human language. That is, they are born, or soon mature, to recognize as same and as different just those samenesses and differences that define the same-difference schemes their elders are using in producing speech representations. Crudely, same-word-again knowledge, in its outlines, is built into human infants. Noam Chomsky speculates that even a knowledge of rules to which the syntaxes of all human languages conform is built into human infants, although little straightforward experimental evidence for this has yet been brought forth. In any event, it is clear that the ability to identify the same again by internalizing outer language terms must be well developed in very small children. Thus the child is provided with a vast array of *inner* terms the values of which he knows how to identify, although at first these inner terms may have only language-bound intensions (see Chapter 9).

In Chapter 9 I argued that many of the terms we adults employ have, for most of us, only or mainly language-bound intensions and that this does not preclude our "knowing their meanings." Often one would have to ask the experts or undergo specialized training, for example, in the laboratory of some science, in order to move beyond having mere language-bound intensions for terms that one is nonetheless happy to employ in everyday thought and speech. But a child slowly acquires full-bodied intensions for thousands of words *without* asking the adults about their full-bodied intensions and without directed training. Yet it is unlikely that the child would ever have developed many or most of these concepts without using the handle of language. How does language effect the teaching of concepts? Why does it afford so much leverage to the developing mind? How does it possess the power to hand down to new generations not just the accumulated *knowledge* of previous generations but the whole battery of accumulated concepts upon which this knowledge is based? If language is just *one* medium by which a child perceives and hence identifies things in the world alongside a variety of *other* potential ways of identifying these same things, why is this particular extra perspective upon the world so powerful?

The reason is that the child can *rely* upon this particular means of discovering the existence of and of reidentifying a thing, using it as a standard by which to adjust other programs for identifying that thing in those cases in which knowing how to identify via other routes is not built in or easily acquired. If developing concepts requires experimenting with a variety of ways to iterate what one hopes may turn out to be a mapping term until one either finds ways that agree with themselves and each other or abandons the attempt, it must be inestimably valuable to the child to have *one* way that he knows is reliable of inventing and iterating inner terms that are not empty, hence that he can use as a standard against which to develop other means of iterating the same term. How likely is it that a child would discover for himself the identity even of that common but diverse species *dog* or of the material *iron*, these discoveries entailing discoveries of various nonobvious contrary ranges with respect to which Normal dogs and pieces of iron are identities, without the steadying hand of language to hold onto?

Both Quine and Wittgenstein (in *Philosophical Investigations*) are aware of the importance of language as a guide during conceptual development. But they conceive of the role of language quite differently from the way I have described it. Wittgenstein, concerned that there must be some criterion for correctness or justification for acts of identifying that is independent of one's unfettered natural urges to say or not to say the same again, hands this function to language. To identify correctly *is* just to identify as others in one's language community do, saying what others do or would when others do or would. Clearly Wittgenstein thinks of learning to identify as learning to divide up the world into the same bits and chunks as one's fellows do for purposes of communication—for the sake of playing important social "games" made possible thereby. Learning how to identify is like learning what units of length or scale of temperature one's fellows are using when measuring, and learning to report the results of one's measurements in these standard units. Now of course it is true that one must learn to divide up the world with words as others in one's language community do. For example, one must use the same principles of unity for determining whole lakes and whole persons-over-time, the same units of measurement, and draw roughly the same line between red and orange, etc. But before reaching the point at which such lines can be drawn, one must first have a hold upon the objective world that is to be so sectioned. And that world is not of course the world of sensation but the world "out there." Agreement in judgments is not an index of agreement in ways of responding to stimulations. Seldom if ever do two people say the same as a result of undergoing identical stimulations. Nor is agreement in judgments *just* an index of agreement about how to carve up the world out there. Normally it is a sign that each speaker has indeed made contact, in his or her own way, *with* the world out there—the world *between* them. It is a sign that each is mapping something *real*, as well as the *same* something real as the other, with his mutterings.

Quine devotes section Two of *Word and Object* to "The Objective Pull; or, E Pluribus Unum." The possibility of sharing an observation language, he claims, requires that a compromise be drawn in word usage between word responses that are easy to learn because stimulated by subjectively similar stimulation patterns and word responses that are trainable because teacher and learner are liable simultaneously to have stimulation patterns that occasion the same word or sentence.

> In general, if a term is to be learned by induction from observed instances where it is applied, the instances have to resemble one another in two ways: they have to be enough alike from the learner's point of view, from occasion to occasion, to afford him a basis of similarity to generalize upon, and they have to be enough alike from simultaneous distinct points of view to allow the teacher and learner to share the appropriate occasions. A term restricted to squares normal to the line of sight would meet the first requirement only; a term applying to physical squares in all their scalene projections meets both. And it meets both in the same way, in that the points of view available to the learner from occasion to occasion are likewise points of view available to teacher and learner on simultaneous occasions. Such is the way with terms for observable objects generally; and thus it is that such objects are focal to reference and thought.

Now it is clear that at least these requirements would have to be met in order that two speakers of a language should speak in unison. But choral speaking is not communication. Indeed, in the paradigm case of communication, the hearer *learns* from the speaker rather than agreeing with him. Nor is it clear just what relevance the ability to engage in choral speaking in response to stimulations is supposed to have to "reference and thought." Quine seems to take it that the purpose of thought, the criterion of good thought, is that it allows one to predict the shape of patter upon one's afferent nerve endings in advance. How is the learning of response patterns that facilitate choral speaking supposed to help accomplish this?

What is lacking in Wittgenstein and in Quine is close enough attention to what agreeing in judgments really amounts to. It is not, for example, speaking in unison; failure to say the same or to be disposed to say the same at the same time is not disagreeing in judgments. If you look at the sky and say "Fine weather tomorrow" whereas I, unable to read weather signs in the sky, remark only "Gorgeous sunset," we do not disagree in judgments. Agreement in judgments is saying the same *about* the same; it is the same *subject* about which the same is said, not the same *occasion* on which it is said. And agreement in judgments is of interest because it precludes *disagreement* in judgments—saying something *contrary* about the same subject. Disagreement in judgments can arise only because judgments have subject-predicate structure and admit of *negation*.

The importance of the structure *subject-predicate-negation* is completely overlooked by Wittgenstein and Quine. Indeed, Quine goes so far as to introduce "Ouch!" under the heading "one-word sentences" and to claim that the distinction between a word and a sentence comes down in the end to "printers' practice, however accidental."[2] Nor does it occur to him that what he terms the "positive stimulus meaning" of an observation sentence might *conflict* with what he calls the "negative stimulus meaning."[3] But if our thesis is correct (1) that the negate of a sentence is evidenced not by the absence of evidence for its affirmation but by positive findings, (2) that the primary evidence for our hold upon the objective world is that we do not find ourselves wanting to affirm and negate the same sentence, and (3) that having discovered how to make judgments in such a way that we do not find ourselves wanting to affirm and negate the same sentence is having discovered where a natural necessity lies in *nature*, then it is necessarily true that the set of all *possible* stimulation patterns would contain numerous members that would be members of both the positive and the negative stimulus meaning of any meaningful observation sentence. For if our thesis is correct, lack of contradiction in judgment at every level including the level of observation judgment rests *essentially* upon the ontological structure of the *actual* world.

Because Wittgenstein and Quine pay no attention to subject-predicate structure with negation, the structure upon which the possibility of agreement vs. disagreement in judgments rests, neither sees the true significance of agreement in judgments. Normally, agreement in judgments is not just getting together with one another; it is getting together with the world. Agreement in but one positive judgment would be a striking thing. For it should not be thought that agreement and disagreement in positive judgment are two equally probable possibilities. There are, in most cases, many more ways for a sentence not containing the negative to be false than for it to be true. And when a whole fabric of agreeing positive judgments appears, covering a domain such as that of the colors and shapes of mundane physical objects, the evidence that we are mapping the same domain of affairs out there with our independent judgments, hence that each of us is mapping *a* domain of affairs out there with his or her judgments, is overwhelming.

The world viewed through that instrument that is the speech of another—the world perceived via natural teleperception—is sometimes the only second perspective one has upon a domain of world affairs. I can look at the same table numerous times from numerous angles, and I can touch it here and there, thus establishing for myself that the methods that I use in reidentifying it and its shape apparently agree with themselves and one another, hence that they may indeed be general methods of reidentifying objective things. But consider time concepts. It is hard to see how one could gain more than one perspective upon an affair concerning *when* this or that happened, or develop the notion of a linear time sequence for events at all, without turning to the aid of others who confirm one's judgments. Only because my judgments of time sequence nearly always match those of others do I have reason to believe that I have an objective *ability*, not merely a seeming ability, to fit things remembered into a time sequence and that objective time sequences exist at all. The medium that is another person who speaks to me provides at least the most accessible way of having more than one perspective upon time. True, concepts of time might be developed along with theories about causal processes, the two together providing me with a kind of second perspective upon individual times. But when concepts of entities can be tested only along with *theories* about these entities, the process of concept formation is bound to be far less efficient, as is attested by the strenuous exercise that has been required to develop concepts of various of the marginally observable entities with which the most abstract of the sciences deal.

Taking a more familiar example, Wittgenstein was undoubtedly right that the possibility of making introspective judgments about myself—the possibility of developing concepts of my thoughts and sensations and feelings—depends upon the fact that *others* can sometimes perceive, with fair reliability, what I think and how I feel using independent methods.

Chapter 19

Epistemology of Identity: Concepts, Laws, and Intrusive Information

Every concept or range of concepts that a child develops only with the aid of language some earlier child or man or woman or cooperating group must have managed to develop without the guidance of established language. This possibility depends upon the possibility that concepts can usually be developed in relatively small groups. How small might these groups be?

First, the concept of a property cannot be developed unless at the same time the ability is developed to recognize at least some portion of what is contrary to it *as* contrary, even if not as divided into definite properties to be identified in their own right. Although it is not necessary to suppose that concepts of various definite contraries of a property are always developed along with the concept of that property, it is reasonable to suppose that this usually happens. Second, the concept of a property cannot be developed unless concepts are developed of some substances that exemplify properties from its range—substances that exemplify it or its negation. Third, some general method of recognizing for at least some members of the category of substances to which a property's range applies that they *are* members of this category must be developed along with the concept of that property. Discovery that both a property and its negation apparently applied to a substance would not indicate a conceptual failure unless the relevant property range *ought* to apply to that substance in accordance with one's tentative concepts. Thus rough substance categories must enter our conceptual schemes right at the start. Fourth, to grasp a substance category is, in general, to have at one's disposal some reliable means of learning to reidentify particular members of that category. For example, grasp of the category "person" is likely to include knowing how to learn to recognize particular people by studying their *faces* rather than their postures or locations; grasp of the category "tree" is likely to include knowing how to learn to recognize particular trees by studying their locations and "postures" rather than their "faces," these "faces" changing from season to season. And fifth, substance categories are of interest primarily because their instances are determinate with respect to a number of contrary ranges, not just one. A paradigm substance is a subject of many kinds of knowledge; one can find out many things about it. In sum, the group of concepts that we must suppose to be developed together will include concepts at least of several kinds of properties along with at least some of their contraries, concepts of at least one open-ended range of substances to which these properties and their contraries apply, the ability to recognize in advance at least some portion of these substances as substances to which these contrary ranges should apply, and an ability to learn, by some relatively efficient and reliable means, how to reidentify these particular substances as themselves.

That sounds like a lot of concepts and abilities to be developed all at once. But Nature has apparently handed us quite proficient inborn abilities tailored to the development of concepts at the very least of ordinary physical objects, people, and certain properties of these. And once one has learned how to identify a substance category reliably, development of concepts from additional contrary ranges applying to members of that category is enormously simplified. Likewise, having learned to identify a certain range of properties reliably, both the development of concepts of additional substances, for example, secondary substances, to which that range applies and the development of concepts of derivative conditional and perspective-bound properties is much simplified. For example, given a grasp of certain classes of ordinary physical objects as identities with respect to shape, size, color pattern, and weight, the more difficult concepts of mass, of having a size or a weight at-a-time, then of having other time-bound properties such as charge and temperature, could emerge. Mass and charge in turn are properties of the secondary substances "the electron" and "the proton," etc., concepts of which were developed of course only along with theories about the laws that govern these substances. But it is unlikely we would have developed these concepts at all had the notions of mass and of charge not been already on hand.

Now the prevailing view in this century has been that *the* mark of a concept's adequacy is just the fruitfulness of that concept in helping to predict and explain. According to the phenomenalists, applying a concept by making a judgment was equivalent to asserting that certain laws would hold within one's ongoing experience—laws correlating sense data. According to what was for many years the received view of science, concepts of "theoretical entities," i.e., entities that are not "directly observable," are defined in part by the natural laws that are taken to govern these entities, so that testing these laws is part of testing these concepts. But a concept's involvement in laws necessarily involves it with other concepts, all the concepts that make up one theory being tested together. Indeed, many have concluded, in the end all our concepts are embedded in one overall system of laws—system of inference dispositions or, as Quine has it, of dispositions to associate sentences—the validity of each concept in the system being just its ability to contribute to the effectiveness of the system as a whole in helping to make prediction and explanation possible. Hence every concept is tested and validated only along with every other concept that we have. The origin of the notion that a concept is defined by inference rules is, of course, the notion that meaning is intension. And although that is not the position of this book, still, concepts are composed of intensions so that testing for the validity of a concept *is* testing its intensions. If it were true that even the most basic intensions of terms characteristically are explicit and hence involve applications of prior concepts and that, in the end, the intensions of all terms are intertwined, then our position would indeed snag on the second condition that we laid down (see Chapter 18) for the plausibility of our interpretation of the role of the law of noncontradiction in testing concepts—that concepts should be testable in small enough groups that the source of the trouble can be located when contradictions begin to arise.

A preliminary point is perhaps worth making before the view is examined that concepts can be tested only along with other concepts to which they are connected by inference rules in a system. However it is that concepts are tested in the end, it is not by predicting the occurrence of sensory data.

Perhaps it is no longer necessary to argue that we do not predict the occurrences of sensory data in order to corroborate judgments. The dominant view seems to be that we do not in fact have a language, either inner or outer, that describes sensory data except as that language depends upon prior concepts of the external things that Normally cause these data.[1] I myself have already argued that concepts of mental states are not very easy to come by. But it will not hurt to add one more argument to the case against an inner protocol language in which predictions that test concepts are ultimately expressed.

If man, natural creature that he is, could perfectly well get along without such a language, including that he could develop and test concepts of outer things without it, then the frugality of Nature argues that man does get along without such a language. What practical purpose, after all, would such a language serve? Making thought-maps of occurrences at our sensory surfaces or, alternatively, of the maps that are our percepts, would surely be a waste of neural energy. Impacts upon our nerve endings are not things we can manipulate directly or things that it would be of any use to manipulate or to know about in order to pursue our practical concerns in the world. We have no more need to think of sensory data as we go about our daily affairs than we have to think about or to predict the patterns on our retinas. As for *predicting* sense data or stimulations, it is our bodies and our projects in the world that we use our knowledge of the world to sustain, and this does not require being in a state in which the actual input from our afferent nerves provides only redundant information. We map the world with inner pictures in order to affect it, not predict it. Of course, it is often useful to us to be able to predict happenings in the world in order that we may prepare to affect the world. But that is not at all the same as predicting happenings at the ends of our afferent nerves. It is enough if we are able to interpret our experience as that experience comes along, if we find our interpretations to be consistent, and if we can learn how to *act* appropriately as guided by this interpreted experience. Only if it were necessary to predict sensory data in order to corroborate judgments, hence to test our concepts of things in the world, would it be plausible to assume that we have concepts of sensory data prior to concepts of things in the world.

But it is not necessary to predict or to infer the occurrences of sensory data in order to corroborate ordinary perceptual judgments, hence, presumably, in order to corroborate any judgments. All that is necessary is to make the judgment again by the use of different implicit intensions, or at a later point in time hence, of course, based upon a different set of stimulations. All that one must predict in order to corroborate, for example, that there is a book in one's lap is that there is a book in one's lap. A perceptual judgment implies, first of all, itself. Corroboration of a judgment may be stumbled upon as one goes about other tasks or it may be purposefully induced, but in neither case is inference from the judgment to data required. Two moves from data to judgment are all that is involved. Consider an analogy. I wish to verify that this rectangular container before me holds just one liter. So I measure its three dimensions and determine the product to see if its volume is indeed 1000 cm³. The evidence that I start with in order to verify its capacity is knowledge of each of its three dimensions. But there is no need to predict what each of these three dimensions will measure or to think of the disjunct of all the possible trios of numbers that would multiply to 1000 in order to verify that it holds one liter. Similarly, it is not necessary to predict what sensory data will be forthcoming in order to verify a perceptual judgment. It is enough to move from whatever data turn up to a judgment.

Indeed, even if we did predict sensory data in the process of corroborating perceptual judgments, nonoccurrence of the predicted data would neither falsify the judgment nor necessarily impugn the concepts responsible for the judgment, and this for two reasons. First, discovering that a judgment is false is not the same as not discovering that it is true. One would have to encounter sensory data from which a *contrary* of the original judgment could be manufactured in order to disconfirm the judgment. Second, concepts of things in the world do not need to consist of infallible intensions in order to be valid concepts. Concepts are abilities, and abilities have Normal conditions for exercise which Normal conditions need not always obtain. It takes a great deal more than the appearance of one contradiction to impugn the validity or general adequacy of a concept.

Granted that it is not necessary to make inferences from judgments to sensory data in order to test concepts, is it necessary to make any inferences at all? First let us ask whether it is necessry to make inferences *from* sentences that contain term tokens governed by a concept in order to test that concept. Is it necessary to have a theory about the natural laws that govern an entity in order to test a concept of that entity?

Obviously properties must participate in laws or they could not be identifiable at all. For to be identified, they must have consistent effects at least upon our sensory apparatuses. And substances are identifiable only because they have properties by which they can be identified. Moreover, why would it be of any use to know there was a thing that had a certain property unless something followed from that fact? Surely knowing facts about the world outside us is of use only as a preface to knowing how to use these facts, knowing what to do with or because of them, knowing what to expect as a result of them, etc., for purposes of action. And this kind of knowledge would be impossible if the facts did not participate in laws. But it does not follow that one must *know* the laws of nature either in order to develop and test concepts of the things that obey these laws or in order to use these concepts productively. For example, there is no question that my ability to identify a substance—any substance—depends upon the fact that the substance has certain characteristic properties that affect me in lawful ways. It does not follow that I must employ *concepts* of these properties in order to identify that substance. In fact, I do not have the slightest idea what properties it is of paint enamel vs. porcelain enamel that allow me to tell the one substance from the other by tapping these with my teeth, but that's how I tell nonetheless. I can tell a birch from a poplar at a very considerable distance, but how or on the basis of what properties I do not know at all. Certainly I cannot *identify* these properties in these contexts, which is the same as to say that I employ no concepts of these properties in these contexts.

Similarly, although there are surely natural laws that help account for my ability to distinguish red from green—laws about light and about my macro and micro physiology—surely I had been distinguishing red from green for years before I learned anything about these laws. And even now my ability to distinguish red from green in no way depends upon the partial knowledge that I have of these laws. Just as a child rides a bicycle knowing nothing of the laws of dynamics that make this possible, we identify substances and properties without using knowledge of the laws that make these identifications possible.

Likewise, knowing how to use facts one knows in the context of practical activities typically does not involve knowing the laws that make this know-how possible. The child learns that fire is hot. And he learns ways to tell when other things are hot. When he knows that a thing is hot, he avoids close contact with it. But knowing to avoid what is hot is not knowing any laws about heat or about hot things. It is merely knowing what to *do* in the presence of hot things. It is knowing how to be guided by the fact of a thing's hotness, not necessarily what to infer from this fact.

Consider color concepts. What laws are there that a person not trained in physics knows about colors? Does redness participate in any superficial natural laws? True, there are certain fruits that are unlikely to be ripe unless red. But for the most part it is handy to be able to recognize colors not because these participate in superficial causal laws but because there are many things that can be identified in part by color. "It's the *red* book over there that has the pictures of Yorkshire you wanted to see." Such sentences can convey very useful information even though one may know no laws about redness.

There seems then to be no reason to believe that one must develop beliefs about the laws that a substance or property participates in in order to develop and to use a concept of that entity. However, that a property one thinks one is identifying seems to participate in simple causal laws is surely additional grounds for believing in its reality. And if one takes a thing to have a property but then that thing refuses to obey a well-established law that one believes having that property entails, this is surely good grounds for wondering whether the intension, explicit or implicit, that one used in apparently identifying that property in that case is an entirely reliable intension, or for wondering whether the conditions under which one made the property judgment were Normal. Also, from the fact that there is no reason to believe that one must always develop beliefs about the laws that a substance or property participates in in order to develop and use a concept of that entity it does not follow that no concepts of entities are ever developed or ever have to be developed along with theories about those entities. Science may not be entirely continuous with common sense in the way it develops concepts, or certain branches of science may not be. After all, the purpose of a good portion of science *is* to predict and explain. And our ordinary ways of validating concepts by developing alternative routes to the same domain of judgments—diverse perspectives upon the same domain of world affairs—just may not be directly applicable, for example, to the domain of world affairs that have elementary particles as variants or that have as variants values of the real state variables— if there be any such—that characterize the economic systems of modern industrial nations.

But we have still to determine whether it is true that concepts that depend upon other concepts figuring in their explicit intensions depend upon these in such a way that all are tested only together. That is, we must determine whether the prior concepts expressed in judgments *from* which application of a concept is inferred are tested along with that concept. And it will help to determine as well how common it is for the only intensions that compose a concept to require the application of prior concepts.

Tradition has it that not just a few but a very large proportion of our concepts are not of things we observe directly but of things the effects of which we observe on *other* things. Indeed, the very use of language to gain what I have called "another perspective on the world," which perspective I take to be so important, is not usually taken to be a method of direct perception. And it is surely true that a great many of our ways of identifying things involve manipulating, testing, and probing these things to see what effects they have upon other things. We test for acidity by checking effects upon litmus paper or by seeing what happens when we add phenolphthalein. We check for hardness of minerals by seeing what other minerals they will scratch, etc. But where a thing A is identified by observing its effects upon B and C, isn't both the validity of the concepts of B and of C and the validity of the theory that attributes the observed effects to the influence of A tested along *with* the concept of A? The answer is no, and for two reasons.

First, from the fact that the only intensions I have for a term A are explicit intensions—intensions that require applying prior terms B and C from which the applicability of the term A is inferred—it does not follow that the validity of the concepts governing B and C is tested when the concept governing A is tested or vice versa. It does not follow when the explicit intensions of A are ordinary definite descriptions ("the first president of the United States") nor does it follow when the explicit intensions of A represent what is taken to be only causally related to A's referent ("mercury in the thermometer placed here has risen to the number seventy" as an intension for "the temperature here is seventy degrees"). True, a term that has only explicit intensions is governed by a concept that apparently rests upon various other concepts.

Valid concepts are abilities—abilities to reidentify a selfsame. Such a term then is coordinate with an ability that apparently rests upon prior abilities. Compare: my ability to make a cake apparently rests in part upon my abilities to recognize and to break eggs and upon my abilities to recognize and to sift flour, etc. But consider: if I find that I cannot make good cakes with reliability, is this evidence that I do not know how to recognize or how to break eggs or that I do not know how to recognize or to sift flour? These prior abilities have prior and completely independent tests, and if they pass these tests, my inability to make a cake does not bring them into question. And it is equally true that if it should turn out that I am able to make good cakes reliably and yet, oddly, that I have in fact no real ability to recognize eggs at all, this would only lead us to suspect that my ability to make cakes did not after all rest upon an ability to recognize eggs. Perhaps making good cakes is possible by mistaking the right kinds of things *for* eggs in accord with some intension that I merely thought was a good way of recognizing eggs. In fact the intension captures other things than eggs but still good for making cakes. However unlikely this story, still the test of good cake making and the test of good egg recognizing are entirely separate tests.

And so it is with testing concepts that seem to rest entirely upon other concepts. That the various independent ways we have of measuring temperature (mercury thermometers, alcohol thermometers, gas thermometers, coil thermometers, etc.) agree with one another and themselves and that various substances have always the same melting points and boiling points as themselves according to these measures is sterling evidence that temperature is an objective property range. If these uniformities did not hold, however, this would not cast doubt upon our abilities to recognize whether mercury lines are or are not opposite certain numbers and whether these or those are or are not "thermometers" in the sense of being constructed in accordance with such and such specifications. Moreover, the uniform results we get when measuring temperature by various methods is direct evidence that temperature is a real thing and could not be undermined even by a bizarre discovery that our ways of determining temperatures do not, to our surprise, proceed by way of any prior *genuine* conceptual abilities but are *sui generis*.

Second, the notion that a large proportion of our concepts are not of things we observe directly but of things of which we observe only effects on other things is itself mistaken. The notion that in each instance of observation either we observe a thing directly or we observe it only via its effects on other things is confused. We never observe anything except via its effects upon other things, in the first instance, upon our sense organs and nervous systems. We observe the shapes and colors of things using our eyes only via the effects these shapes have upon light that strikes objects, and we observe the words people articulate only via the effects these have upon sound waves, etc. The distinction that needs to be drawn is not between observation that proceeds via effects of the observed on other things and observation that proceeds "directly." It is between gaining information about a thing only via *knowledge* of its effects upon other things and gaining knowledge of a thing without such intermediary *knowledge* of other things. But here we must be extremely careful. For the fact that one has knowledge of, or is in command of concepts that would allow one to gain knowledge of, the effects of something on intermediary things does not imply that one *uses* this knowledge during the process of judging about this something on the basis of observation.

Take the example of seeing the shapes of things. Nowadays many people have a general knowledge of the way shapes affect light patterns and of how light patterns are then affected by the lens of the eye, hence how the retina comes to be affected as it is when one sees shapes. But no one ever *uses* this knowledge in the process of telling the shapes of things by eye. Similarly, we have concepts of photographs, we understand the processes whereby photographs are turned out, and we are able to describe the two-dimensional patterns of light and dark that photographs exhibit should we need to. But when we see a person in a photograph, none of this knowledge and none of these concepts is called into play. We do not first make judgments about two-dimensional patterns and then infer to their causes. Rather, we see the person directly, focusing with the mind *through* the photograph upon the person-affairs behind. We see directly that the person wears a hat or that she smiles. What we do not see directly is the temporal and spatial relation to *us* of those world affairs that show through the photograph. So looking at people through photographs does not yield all the same kinds of information about them that looking at them more directly yields. But looking at people in photographs is no less direct perception for that. And so it is with the use of many instruments. One who is familiar with microscopes, telephones, voltmeters, gas gauges, and thermometers sees the affairs these instruments are designed to reveal directly. Yes, sounds can be *seen* on a sound spectrograph if the viewer has a practiced eye.[2]

Similar reflections apply to those cases in which we manipulate and probe and test for the effects of a thing on other things in order to identify it. First, manipulating, probing, and testing are part of every perceptual process. One of the most important mistakes that it is traditional for epistemologists to make is the mistake of viewing perception as passive—as a receiving of information rather than as a gathering of information. In fact we begin to perceive only as we begin to proceed with such small doings as focusing the eyes, making (unconscious) rapid eye movements to determine the orientation of lines, and moving the eyes. We move on to grosser doings such as turning the head, turning the body, approaching the object to be observed, reaching out to feel it, squeezing it, poking it (Is it alive? Does it move?), lifting it, turning it, tapping it, smelling it, tasting it, biting it (Is it genuine gold?), rubbing it (Does it shine now?), attempting to bend or deform it, attempting to crumble it, breaking it open to look inside, looking at it under a magnifying glass, trying to see it better with binoculars, applying a match to see if it burns, putting litmus paper in it, measuring it, weighing it, etc. Use of these ways of testing and probing does not necessarily involve entertaining hypotheses about the laws of nature. Often we simply know *how* to manipulate ourselves and other things into relations or into situations that make identifications possible. Such abilities *are* what implicit intensions *are*. Thinking of implicit intensions as being merely "stimulus meanings" would be an error of magnitude. Also, highly consistent results among tests that test for the same substance or property indicate directly that there is indeed some objective substance or property that these tests are testing for whether or not we have used theories about the underlying causal mechanisms that account for the effectiveness of these tests in interpreting results. *That the tests work can be known independently from knowing how they work.*

We adults all have concepts of beliefs and intentions, concepts of words and of sentences, concepts of sound waves, and concepts of eardrums. And we are aware that when we learn by listening to what others say this Normally comes about because what we learn about in this way has affected the beliefs of the speaker, which beliefs, coupled with an intention to impart information, have caused words and sentences to be uttered, which words and sentences are, physically speaking, sound waves, which sound waves affect our eardrums, etc. But small children understand speech without knowing any of this. And adults understand speech in exactly the same way that small children do. They understand it without using any of this knowledge. Usually, believing what one hears is also gaining knowledge by direct perception.

But surely, it will be said, we adults *do* use at least some of this knowledge. If I have reason to believe that a person has had no opportunity to gain true beliefs about a certain subject, I will not believe what he says about it. And if I have reason to believe that a person may not desire to impart information but has reason to impart misinformation instead, I will not believe what he says. Similarly, if I have reason to believe that a photograph was made by a trick photographer, I will not believe what the photograph seems to show. And if I have reason to believe that I am in the presence of a talented magician or that someone has just slipped LSD into my coffee, I may doubt almost everything I would otherwise have been sure I'd seen. In order to be confident of anything I seem to perceive, must I not first believe that conditions are Normal for the mode or method of perception I am using? Doesn't what I take myself to be observing at any given time always depend upon what Quine called "collateral information"? When I believe myself to be in my own house, I perceive a certain sound as the sound of Salvadore the cat demanding to come in by hurling himself headlong against the outside door. But if I were to hear the same sound knowing I was in someone else's house, I would not interpret it even as the sound of a cat, for most people's cats do not have such strong heads. What I would normally perceive as a cake, when it is in a bakeshop window, I may perceive instead as a decorated piece of plaster. Doesn't all this show that even concepts that can be applied by direct perception are entwined in the end with our general theories about the ways of the world and with all our beliefs about the disposition of particular things in the world as well? Then how can it be said that any concepts are validated independently of all the rest?

In "Two Dogmas of Empiricism" Quine sums up the outcome of the empiricist tradition after Carnap with the words "our statements about the external world face the tribunal of sense experience not individually but only as a corporate body."[3] In that new dogma of empiricism there is this much truth. No belief, no matter how well grounded in experience, is totally immune to possible challenge in the face of new beliefs based on new experience. Further, there is no way of ruling out in advance challenge from *any quarter*. Any belief that I now have might conceivably be brought to bear, given new theory, new beliefs, and/or new concepts, in such a way as to help challenge any other belief that I now have. No matter how certain I am when I utter even "Lo, a rabbit," it is always possible that I may later find evidence that the supposed rabbit came out of a magician's hat, the magician having fooled me in accordance with such and such principles then quite unfamiliar to me. And there is no belief that I have that could not conceivably end up *helping* to do the work of convincing me that I was wrong about that rabbit. On the other hand, not all of my beliefs *do* end up interacting with one another in such a way that they either help support one another or help discredit one another. Indeed, an enormous number of one's beliefs never face a trial at all; they are never either challenged or confirmed in any way. That I nearly ran over a squirrel on a tight curve on my way to school this morning I firmly believe; but it is unlikely that this belief will ever be either challenged or supported by any other beliefs. It is supported only by my confidence in my squirrel-recognizing abilities, a confidence that derives from *other* occasions of this ability's use. But still, the more fully one develops one's theory of the world, of what is in it and where and of how it all works, the more one's beliefs do tend to interact with one another, supporting or challenging one another. Our beliefs are entwined, and each always faces the possibility at least of a trial by peers, if not by an independent tribunal.

But from the fact that our beliefs are entwined in this way it does not follow that our *concepts* are similarly entwined. *The epistemology of identity or of concepts is prior to and in important ways independent of the full epistemology of judgment.* That one can be solid in knowing *that* one means and in knowing *what* one means in making a judgment without that judgment being itself true is clear. Indeed, it is so clear that the tradition has insistently mistaken this distinction of degree for a distinction of kind, holding either that grasp of meaning, unlike grasp of fact, is not the sort of thing that *can* fail, or that it is tested by armchair reflection rather than by experience. But the fact that collateral information may lead us to withhold or withdraw an observation term or, alternatively, may encourage us to apply it *on a particular occasion*—the fact that our beliefs based on observation are sometimes supported by or challenged by other beliefs—does not imply that our observation terms are originally *validated* only relative to collateral information or that their having sense is ever brought into question when collateral information intrudes to inhibit or encourage their applications on particular occasions. For example, whether or not I will come to believe that a magician manipulated me into exclaiming or thinking "Lo, a rabbit," hence whether or not I end by rejecting my belief in that rabbit, is quite irrelevant to the question whether the term "rabbit" has a sense.

Using collateral information as an aid in knowing when and when not to apply an observation term is using knowledge about Normal conditions for exercise of that term's associated concept, or for employment of certain of its implicit intensions. To gain knowledge of Normal conditions for the exercise of any ability and to be able to recognize the presence vs. the absence of these conditions is a step toward perfecting that ability. But perfection is not required in order to have an ability, nor is it required in order to have all the evidence one needs to be justifiably certain that one's ability *is* an ability. Basic ability programs, including basic concepts, are applied for the most part either without knowledge of their Normal conditions for proper performance or without using this knowledge if one has it. (Compare

Chapter 3 on the implausibility of interpreting Gricean intensions as mechanisms.) And those abilities that do appear to rest upon abilities explicitly to recognize conditions that are Normal for their exercise are still known to be genuine abilities by their fruits and cannot be impugned just by impugning the concepts or judgments upon which they apparently rest.

But concepts are unlike most other abilities in this important respect. When one tries to swim or to turn on the lights or to start the car, one usually knows immediately whether one has succeeded or failed. When we apply concepts, however, we often do not have any way of knowing immediately or even in the long run whether we have identified correctly in this instance or not. When I nearly ran over that (presumed) squirrel this morning, I had one brief chance to exercise my ability to identify squirrels, and surely I will never be able to check on whether that exercise was successful. All I have to go on in being so sure I did almost run over a squirrel is the fact that in the *past*, when I *have* had chances to check on my squirrel-identifying abilities—by tracking the squirrel and looking again, noting its behavior, talking with others who confirmed what I saw, etc.—I have found these abilities to be highly reliable. Because specific concept applications often are not checked or not easy to check, collateral information, even when gained long after the time at which a concept was applied, when this information implies that conditions for that concept's application were not Normal at the time of application, may justifiably cause one to change one's mind on an observation. Indeed, any information that has been acquired using conceptual abilities that one trusts as much as one trusts the abilities in accordance with which one originally applied a concept, but which information conflicts with the result of that concept's earlier application, may justifiably raise doubts or change one's mind. But it is not relevant to determining whether a concept is a *valid* concept to determine whether or not one understands and can correctly judge the conditions for its Normal application. Hence it is not true that observation concepts are tested only along with concepts used in judging that their Normal conditions hold. All that is required in order to evidence the validity of an observation concept is that there be some core methods—some core intensions for it—that allow it sometimes to be applied more than once in the making of the very same judgment, and that when it is so applied, the results are highly, though not necessarily infallibly, consistent. That is enough for us to be as certain as we can be (which is not of course to be utterly certain) that the concept really is a concept *of* something, hence to have good evidence when we apply it on other occasions, using perhaps less reliable or less well tested intensions or using explicit inductive inference, that whether the resulting judgments turn out true or false, at least they are not senseless.

I opened this book with the claim that it is not necessary to accept the dichotomy *either* foundationalism *or* holism. In this chapter I have tried to show that the root evidence we have for the sense having of our observation terms does not rest upon or await the development of any theories that use these terms. At core, coherence is just noncontradiction. If contradiction can arise without theories—without inference—lack of contradiction or coherence can be a test of conceptual adequacy prior to the development of theories. But, given our description of what a concept is, to say that a concept is adequate is to say that a reasonable proportion of *judgments* made by applying it are true. Moreover, since it is often possible to make an observation judgment over again, single judgments are often tested by the coherence test without any inferences at all having been made. Hence coherence can be said to be a test also of truth and without invoking holism.

With the development of small and then larger theories, additional evidence can accumulate that challenges or supports particular judgments, and observation concepts may be amplified, altered, disambiguated, etc., so as to become more adequate. Nor do I wish to claim that there is no way that an observation concept can ever be shown to be empty or senseless as the result of developing theory. But it is not my purpose here to reconstruct large portions of epistemology. These last chapters on epistemology, like the entire book that precedes them, are intended to be suggestive. I will be satisfied, for the moment, if I have succeeded in pointing in a direction to explore.

Epilogue

... there can exist nevertheless a certain material falsity in ideas, as when they present that which is nothing as though it were something. [But] ... this idea of God ... is very clear and distinct and contains more objective reality than does any other, so that there is no other which is more true from its very nature, nor which is less open to the suspicion of error and falsity.

(Descartes, Third *Meditation*)

Translate: knowledge that an idea has a sense is armchair knowledge.

It is an established maxim in metaphysics, *that whatever the mind clearly conceives includes the idea of possible existence,* or in other words *that nothing we can imagine is absolutely impossible.*

(Hume, *A Treatise of Human Nature,* Part II, Section II)

Translate: knowledge of logical possibility and knowledge that our ideas have sense is armchair knowledge.

In the very essence of an experience lies determined not only *that,* but also whereof it is a consciousness, and in what determinate or indeterminate sense it is this.

(Husserl, *Ideas,* para. 36.)

Translate: consciousness provides its own affidavit both *that* it means and about *what* it means.

If the world had no substance, then whether a proposition had sense would depend on whether another proposition was true.

(Wittgenstein, *Tractatus Logico-Philosophicus,* 2.0211)

Wittgenstein of course denies the consequent of this hypothetical: that a proposition has sense *cannot* depend upon whether another proposition is true. In other words, that a proposition has sense must be a priori knowledge, or at least cannot be empirical knowledge.

> The terms '9' and 'the number of the planets' name one and the same abstract entity but presumably must be regarded as unlike in meaning; for astronomical observation was needed, and not mere reflection on meanings, to determine the sameness of the entity in question.
>
> (Quine, "Two Dogmas of Empiricism," *From a Logical Point of View*)

Translate: knowledge of synonymy of terms must be a priori knowledge.

> Cut the pie any way you like, "meanings" just ain't in the *head*!
>
> (Hilary Putnam, "Meaning and Reference," *Journal of Philosophy*, 1973)

A new line? Or only a sheep in new lion's clothing?

During the course of this book I have made many controversial claims. For the most part I have avoided engaging in polemics for fear of diverting the constructive argument or obscuring its central lines, difficult and complexly interwoven as they were. But if I had to fling down the gauntlet before just one opponent, that opponent would be the meaning rationalist. For the meaning rationalist stands behind nearly every other opponent.

This epilogue is headed with quotations from six meaning rationalists: Descartes, Hume, Husserl, Wittgenstein, Quine, and Putnam. Why Putnam is on the list I will soon explain. Why nearly every other philosopher who has ever written on language or on thought is not on the list is only that I didn't happen on a succinct quotation at the right time. Meaning rationalism has gone unquestioned to such a degree that, to my knowledge, no arguments have ever been advanced to support it.

Meaning rationalism is not a single doctrine but a syndrome. The paradigm meaning rationalist believes that intensions can't be wrong or mistaken and that mere (seeming) thoughts-of, as opposed to judgments about, cannot be senseless. Or at least he believes that any lapses from sense into nonsense are entirely avoidable given enough patient and intelligent armchair work. He also thinks that if one is careful enough, there need be no such thing as being confused about *what* one is thinking of. He thinks this, that is, if he thinks that thoughts have correspondents at all—if he thinks that thoughts are *of*. Otherwise, *of course* he thinks there is no problem about knowing what one is thinking of. He thinks that ambiguity in thought is determined by armchair reflection, and that synonymy or lack of synonymy between terms in one's idiolect is determined in the same way. He takes it that there is something called "logical possibility" that is real, that is grasped by a priori reflection, and that is in no way rooted in how the world actually is. He believes some or all of these things, and as a result he may believe any of various other more obviously queer things as well.

To think of a thing, in the meaning rationalist view, implies knowing what one is thinking of, where "knowing" is rationalist "knowing." That is, one's subjective certainty concerning what it is that one is thinking of must match an objective truth in this matter not just in fact but of necessity. How could this be possible? It would be possible of course if thinking of a thing were having it or its nature before diaphanous consciousness and nothing more, and if consciousness were fundamentally epistemic. If this is what thinking of a thing consists in, then there could not, in principle, be such a thing as making a mistake about what one was thinking of. Thus meaning rationalism motivates the classical realist view of the nature of the act of thinking-of, the consequences of which view we examined in Chapter 15. It motivated Platonic realism; it motivated phenomenalism; it motivated verificationism. Indeed, it helped to motivate philosophical analysis in nearly all of its classical and modern forms. But there are two contemporary doctrines or ways of thinking that it motivated in an especially direct and obvious way, without passing through classical realism, that I would like to mention.

If one cannot misunderstand *what* a term in one's idiolect represents, or be wrong in thinking *that* it represents, then whatever criteria one uses in applying it cannot of course be mistaken criteria. Rather they must *define* its meaning in the sense of stipulating it. The meaning rationalist thus is forced to take the meaning of a term to be determined by its intension. But ambiguity in meaning is discerned by a priori reflection. Hence, unless these are "logically equivalent," no term can have two or more intensions. Each term must have a criter*ion*, not criter*ia*. Also, if the term is to have a determinate meaning, since whether it has a determinate meaning has to be knowable a priori, the intension that the term has must always amount to a "necessary and sufficient definition." "Necessary and sufficient definitions" of terms are definitions that purport to cut cleanly not just between those *actual* things in the world that do and that do not fall under a term but between all "logically possible" things. Compulsive searching for "necessary and sufficient definitions" by which to define certain puzzling terms and engaging in the pastime of inventing fictitious "counterexamples" to these definitions is one of the clearest symptoms of meaning rationalism.

A second doctrine or way of thinking that meaning rationalism motivates, though not quite so directly, is nominalism. According to the meaning rationalist, any lapses from sense into nonsense in thought, any confusions about what one is merely thinking *of*, must be detectable a priori. Hence if there is something that I *could* be mistaken about, even after careful reflection, it must be that, perhaps despite all appearances, this something corresponds not to a thinking-of but to a judgment. So long as I am careful, concepts cannot err. All errors are errors of judgment. So, it appears, many things that we otherwise would have thought were mere concepts or thoughts-of must really be implicit judgments. For example, since I cannot tell just by a priori inspection that my apparent idea-of-Shakespeare is an idea of anything real, it must be that thinking of Shakespeare is really thinking *that* something having such-and-such characteristics exists. But judgments cannot be made without employing prior concepts. So not all concepts can be analyzed as implicit judgments. Some concepts at least must stand on their own feet. Some concepts, it seems, must be of things known to be real by a priori inspection. Traditionally these basic concepts were taken to be or at least to include all concepts of properties, simple and complex; exactly why need not concern us here. The important thing is that meaning rationalism led to the conclusion that all our genuine concepts are of things that have a most peculiar ontological status. They are things that *are* and that can be *known* to be, yet that have no necessary relation to the actual world. They are things that do not need the world about which we make ordinary judgments in order to be. They must be Platonic forms, or reified "concepts" or reified "meanings" or things having "intentional inexistence" or reified "possibilities"—or else they must be *nothing at all!*

Nominalists drew the only reasonable conclusion. These basic concepts correspond to nothing at all. Thinking-of, certainly thinking-of-properties, is not thinking *of* anything. Realism is just wrong.

I have argued that it is not realism that is wrong but meaning rationalism. Now, Hilary Putnam says boldly that " 'meanings' just ain't in the head." Offhand one would think that if meaning were not in the head, then inspection of the contents of one's head would not be sufficient to determine whether or not one was meaning anything. One would think that *Putnam* at least was not a meaning rationalist. Yet Putnam too has finally forsaken realism. Has he found arguments against realism then that do not depend upon meaning rationalism?

In "The Meaning of 'Meaning' "[1] Putnam argues that, in the case at least of natural kind terms such as "water" and "gold," intensions do not determine extensions. Intensions of course are what is "in the head." He argues that it is possible that natural kind terms having identical intensions might still have different extensions. Assuming that terms that have different extensions must have different meanings, i.e., that whatever meaning is it *must* determine extension, he concludes that meaning is not in the head.

Putnam's argument here is that of a realist. The assumption that whatever meaning is, it must determine reference or extension is the very essence of realism. The realist's position is that what it *is* for a term to mean is for it somehow to correspond to something—if not to something actual, at least to something *real* such as a Platonic form or a "real possibility" or an extension. If the meaning of a term did not determine a referent or a real correspondent or at the very least an extension for it, realism would just be wrong. So if meanings are not intensions, then they must be shown to be something *else* that *can* determine reference or extension. Otherwise realism collapses.

Now Putnam asserts that the reason the intensions of natural kind terms do not determine their extensions is that, despite appearances, natural kind terms are indexical. And indeed, the tradition that meanings are intensions has always had problems with indexicals. But there is no need to wrestle with tradition on this issue. (Indeed, tradition has left us shockingly little to wrestle with.) The thing that is utterly clear about indexicals is that their referents are determined in part by a relation between the term token (or the speaker) and the referent. And Putnam believes that the extension of "water" or of "gold" is likewise determined by a relation between the term token and its extension. That is why he (mistakenly) says that these terms are "indexical."

But saying that natural kind terms are "indexical" is merely to label a problem, not to solve it. So a relation between the term "gold" and its extension determines this extension. But *which* relation? (Putnam falls back upon the use of prior indexicals in discussing this.) And what determines which relation it must be between a term and the world that constitutes the reference relation? If this problem cannot be solved, realism collapses.

In "Realism and Reason"[2] Putnam argues that this sort of problem cannot be solved, hence that "metaphysical realism" does collapse. True, he defines "metaphysical realism" in what is, to my mind, an odd way. The realist position of this book, for example, does not fit his description. But, I will soon argue, it fits his description of the alternative, "internal realism," equally badly. In any event, Putnam argues that the notion that truth is correspondence to "THE WORLD," and that our terms refer by corresponding one by one to elements in THE WORLD, is incoherent.

Putnam begins by pressing a problem that we first addressed in Chapter 5, namely, that a *pure* correspondence theory of truth is vacuous. A pure correspondence theory will not work because mathematical mapping relations are ubiquitous whereas representation-represented relations are not. The theory that truth consists merely in there being *a* mapping relation between a full set of true representations and the world is empty. If any correspondence theory of truth is to avoid vacuousness, it must be a theory that tells what is different or special about the mapping relations that map representations onto representeds. —And so, Putnam asks, "what further constraints on reference are there that could single out some [one] interpretation as [the] (uniquely) 'intended' [one] . . . ?"

Putnam's characterization of the elusive correct interpretation or correct mapping function as the one that is "intended" tips his hand. He is thinking that this relation must be one that is determined by being thought of or mirrored *in* the mind:

> Notice that a 'causal' theory of reference is not (or would not be) of any help here: for how 'causes' can uniquely refer is as much of a puzzle as how 'cat' can, on the metaphysical realist picture.
>
> The problem, in a way, is traceable back to Occam. Occam introduced the idea that concepts are (mental) *particulars*. If concepts are particulars ('signs'), then any concept we may have of the *relation* between a sign and its object is *another sign*. But it is unintelligible, from my point of view, how the sort of relation the metaphysical realist envisages as holding between a sign and its object can be singled out either by holding up the sign itself, thus
>
> $$\boxed{\text{COW}}$$
>
> *or* by holding up yet another sign, thus
>
> $$\boxed{\text{REFERS}}$$
>
> or perhaps
>
> $$\boxed{\text{CAUSES}}$$

Putnam has explicitly spelled out the meaning rationalist assumption: in order to mean something determinate in the world we must at the same time *know* that and what we mean and "know" this with a rationalist gloss on "know." The entire relation *between* the head and the world that connects the world with the head must be mirrored in the head. And this entails that the relation between the mirror of that relation and that relation also be mirrored in the head, and so forth *ad infinitum*. The only way out of this regress would be, as Putnam immediately comments, "to be led back to a direct (and mysterious) grasp of Forms." That is, the only way out would be to put the relation between the head and the world that constitutes reference where the classical realist put it, namely, inside the head, by placing the referent (or its nature) directly before the mind. Then the relation need not be mirrored at all.

The position of this book has been that the relations between the head and the world that constitute reference and meaning are genuinely between the head and the world. Coming to understand just what these relations consist in does nothing toward *founding* meaning and reference; these relations do not need to be intended or thought of in order for us to mean and to refer.

But it may be asked what *makes* these particular relations "reference" and "meaning" relations whereas other mapping relations are not. And then it may be asked why *this* is what makes them reference and meaning relations rather than something else.

Consider the original paradox: mapping relations are ubiquitous whereas representation-represented relations are not. Now surely one of the reasons that representation-represented relations are not ubiquitous is that *representations* are not ubiquitous. The category "representation" is a very special category among things. And shouldn't it be obvious that there is no way of making out what determines the mapping rules that count as the reference rules and meaning rules for representations unless one first understands what representations are, what distinguishes them from other things, say, sneezes? My argument has been that to discover what a representation *is* is to discover that it is, by virtue of being a representation, supposed to map, and it is to discover what determines the mapping function in accordance with which it is supposed to map. It is because a representation is a *representation* that it is supposed to map and in accordance with certain rules and not others—rules that have been determined by the same history that makes it to be a representation at all.

Now I seem to see Putnam knowingly nodding his head. Your theory, he seems to say, of what a representation is, of what truth and reference are, is just *another theory*. What you have offered is merely an "internal realism"—a theory of reference *within* our theory of the world. And that, I (Putnam) have been hoping we could do all along.

Certainly I have offered a theory of meaning, of reference, of truth and hence *of what theories are* that places all these within the natural world. In that sense the theory I have offered is a theory "within" our theory of the world. It is a theory that stands beside and hopefully in agreement with many of our other theories concerning what all is in the world. I have made *all* theories "internal"; all our theories (as well as everything they are about) are in the world rather than in some prior place. Is there then some alternative to an "internal" theory? Putnam holds a different theory of what a theory is—a theory that conflicts with mine. Is his theory also a theory about the place of theories *in the world*? If so, his theory of theories is "internal" in exactly the same sense that mine is; his anti-metaphysical-realist position is an "internal" theory too. If not, where *does* he think theories are? In what sort of prior place? Where does he think he is standing? On some ground that is *not* in the world?

Descartes and then Locke, it is said, opened an era in which philosophers sought vainly to reach the world through a "veil of ideas" (or, alternatively, to pull the world in behind the veil). They placed themselves behind this veil by beginning with a vision or theory of mind as a realm in which ideas lived but which was outside the world these philosophers wished to reach with their ideas—the world, at least, of nature. Today, influenced especially by Wittgenstein and Quine, there is a new school of philosophers who live behind a veil of "theories," entangled in "language games" or in the "logical order." They too have placed themselves behind a veil by beginning with a certain vision or theory, this time a theory about language; a theory about theories—a theory entailing that theories can be meaningful theories while (like old-fashioned "ideas" and "minds") floating loose from the rest of the world. This veil, I have suggested, is composed of (1) a rationalist theory of meaning, hence the absence of any solid theory of what representations are, hence of what theories are, *as attached parts of the world*, (2) an unnecessary and mistaken epistemological holism, and (3) the failure to see how logic might fit into the world of nature. I have thrown out an alternative view—a sketch of how we, our language and thought and theories too, are in the world, and of just *how* a theory must be attached to the rest of the world in order to be a theory at all. What would make such a sketch "internal" or "merely"? The fact that it cannot be given Cartesian foundations? The fact that we just never will KNOW? For surely someone *will* come along with *another* sort of theory?

Of course we could never KNOW in a rationalist or foundationalist sense that any such theory was true. Such a theory implies a theory of knowledge that emphatically excludes such a KNOWING. But having denied the very *sense* of the Cartesian quest is not at all the same as being left behind a veil, hence in the position of having to pull our realism inside after us. Rather, we can climb out on the shoulders of our realism. It supports us not by *grounding* our knowledge and certainly not by grounding it in some prior order—some order other than the natural order. It supports it by explaining what our knowledge is and what it is not and, schematically, how we came to have it. That such an explanation can be given does not *ground* anything. But certainly it should make us feel more comfortable. Put it negatively. If we could give no explanation at all of what our knowledge is or of how we come to have it, surely we would have reason to contemplate being skeptics.

To explain how knowledge is possible is to answer Kant's legitimate question. But to answer a legitimate question is not always to answer it in the exact spirit in which it was asked—within the same view of the possibilities for an answer that the questioner envisioned. Kant expected the answer to his question to supply a foundation for knowledge. And in a certain sense our answer does, but not in the sense of propelling our knowledge to be any more real or closer to some ideal of knowledge than it was before. The answer supplies a foundation for our knowledge by enabling us to understand what foundation—what solid natural-world rock—it had been resting on all along.

Notes

Introduction

1. I use "Cartesian certainty" throughout this essay to denote that final sort of certainty that Descartes yearned for but, it seems, did not actually claim was possible. See his *Replies to Objections II*, "Fourthly . . . " (Richard Lee pointed this passage out to me.)
2. Richard Rorty, *Philosophy and the Mirror of Nature*, Princeton University Press, Princeton, N.J., 1979, p. 176.
3. For a clear statement of this problem, see Hilary Putnam, "Why Reason Can't Be Naturalized," *Synthese* 52 (1982), pp. 3–23.
4. Would the history of recent philosophy have been different if Quine had discovered "the paradox of the indeterminacy of meaning and translation" while Goodman had offered "the theory of the irrationality of induction"?
5. The relation of the question asked in this paragraph to Putnam's distinction between "metaphysical realism" and "internal realism" is addressed in the Epilogue. There I maintain that the distinction cannot be maintained without retreating to a position that puts theories themselves someplace other than in the world, thus reintroducing the veil of ideas in the form of a veil of theories.
6. More accurately, most forms of nominalism will be denied. If all it takes to be a nominalist is that one refuses to allow properties *in re* to be independent *objects*, then I have no quarrel with nominalism.
7. For readers who may be inclined to leap ahead here I must warn that the Normal explanation referred to is not one that reaches back to the causes of production of the sentence. I am not going to develop a "causal theory" of meaning or of reference in any familiar sense, although important aspects of the theory will be "causal-historical" in their own way.

Chapter 1

1. My thanks go to Bernard Williams for coining the awkward but indispensable term "reproductively established families" for me. (If Williams can't think how to say something gracefully either, the problem must be real.) I am very grateful to Professor Williams for urging me to introduce technical terms into this essay. His advice was the more compelling as he himself writes so admirably clearly with ordinary English.
2. The reader familiar with David Lewis's *Conventions* (Harvard University Press, Cambridge, Mass., 1969) may be troubled that I do not relate the ideas in these two paragraphs to Lewis' work. In Chapter 3 I will argue that language is not conventional in the way Lewis describes, for Gricean intentions do not drive language use in the ordinary case. These arguments will be broad enough to constitute a critique of Lewis's analysis of conventions generally.

Chapter 2

1. This term is not ideal. Especially, it calls to mind evolutionary adaptation which is a long process rather than an affair of the moment. The primary meaning of "adapt" is simply *to make fit or suitable, to adjust*. Unfortunately none of these synonyms have graceful forms parallel to all of those that will be needed of "adapt." Besides, there is a special similarity between the meaning of "adapted" as I will use it in the context "adapted device" and the evolutionary sense of "adapted." In each case we have something that is both determined by and fitted to its environment such as to serve, in that environment, some invariant function—ultimately, in each case, survival or reproduction.
2. Think of "adaptor" vs. "adapted" as analogous to "the prosecutor" vs. "the prosecuted" or of "counselor" vs. "counselee." The difficulty here is that no matter what terms are used, we tend to think of the organism (or of what it does) rather than the environment as the agent when the organism adjusts or comes to fit the environment. But of course the environment is a causal agent here too, indeed, an agent that is prior to anything the organism does in response to its agency. In my usage "adaptor" makes reference to this agency of the environment. But I must *force* it to do that. There simply is no term that would do that job without forcing, I believe.
3. Jonathan Bennett, *Linguistic Behavior*, Cambridge University Press, Cambridge, 1976, p. 45.

Chapter 3

1. The primary sources here are: H. P. Grice, "Meaning," *Philosophical Review* 66 (1967), pp. 377–388. H. P. Grice, "Utterer's Meaning and Intentions," *Philosophical Review* 78 (1969), pp. 147–177. H. P. Grice, "Utterer's Meaning, Sentence Meaning, and Word-Meaning," *Foundations of Language* 4 (1968), pp. 225–242. P. F. Strawson, "Intention and Convention in Speech Acts," *Philosophical Review* 73 (1964), pp. 439–460. David K. Lewis, *Convention: A Philosophical Study*, Harvard University Press, Cambridge, Mass., 1969. Stephen R. Schiffer, *Meaning*, Oxford, Clarendon Press, 1972. Jonathan Bennett, *Linguistic Behavior*, Cambridge University Press, Cambridge, 1976. Kent Bach and Robert M. Harnish, *Linguistic Communication and Speech Acts*, The MIT Press, Cambridge, Mass., 1979.
2. See, for example, *Linguistic Behavior*, p. 8.
3. The argument originates in Strawson's "Intention and Convention in Speech Acts" and is incorporated in Lewis's *Conventions* and in Schiffer's *Meaning* and, covertly, in Bennett's *Linguistic Behavior*. Strawson's argument was designed to show that "meaning$_{nn}$" as Grice originally explained it could not serve as a complete analysis of what lies behind *sentence* meaning but would need, at least, to be amended. Here I recast the basic argument to serve my own purposes. The fallacy to which I direct attention does not infect Strawson's original argument against Grice's original thesis. But those who have concluded that since the Strawsonian counterexamples to Grice's original thesis are indeed counterexamples, it must be that the normal use of natural language requires of the speaker that he have an infinitely nested, or even just a nested, set of *positive* intentions, *have* fallen into this fallacy.
4. Daniel Dennett, "Brain Writing and Mind Reading," *Brainstorms*, Bradford Books, 1978.
5. *Linguistic Behavior*, p. 194.
6. Konrad Lorenz takes this position in *Behind the Mirror*, Harcourt Brace Jovanovich, New York, 1977.

Chapter 4

1. Donald Davidson, "On Saying That," *Synthese* 19 (1968–1969), pp. 130–146.

2. Compare here Putnam's compatible discussion of the "division of linguistic labor" in "The Meaning of 'Meaning'," *Minnesota Studies in the Philosophy of Science*, vol. VII, Keith Gunderson ed., University of Minnesota Press, Minneapolis, 1975. An abbreviated version appears as "Meaning and Reference," *Journal of Philosophy* 70 (November 1973). The examples that I use here are taken from Putnam.

3. Sellar's general position on the translation-rubric sense of "means" is central to large portions of his thought and is variously explained in his papers. The early sources are reprinted in his *Science, Perception and Reality*, The Humanities Press, New York, 1963, especially Chapters 4 ("The Language of Theories"), 5 ("Empiricism and the Philosophy of Mind"), 6 ("Truth and 'Correspondence' "), 8 ("Grammar and Existence: A Preface to Ontology"), and 10 ("Is There a Synthetic Apriori?"). Later there is, for example, "Notes on Intentionality," *Journal of Philosophy* 61 (21) (1964) and *Science and Metaphysics*, Routledge and Kegan Paul, Humanities Press, New York, 1968, especially Chapters III and IV.

4. Sellars ultimately uses "sense" in such a broad way that "and" at least and probably also "alas!" has a sense. If Sellars were to embrace my views he would likely be happy to call any stabilizing proper function a "sense." Frege's original examples of *Sinn* are examples of identifying descriptions having different *Sinn* but the same *Bedeutung*. Such identifying descriptions *do* have different direct proper functions or, in accordance with Sellars's ideas, different "roles." Hence the possibility of identifying *Sinn* with role or stabilizing function, and the possibility of taking "alas!" to have *Sinn*. On the other hand, I will later argue that identifying descriptions having different *Sinn* but the same *Bedeutung* differ from one another also in that although both are "supposed to" correspond to what is in fact the same thing, the mapping rules from which these "supposed to"'s are derived are different for the two descriptions. This seems to me to be a more relevant difference, and more like what Frege had in mind. But if this is the difference to which *Sinn* corresponds, then such words as "and" and "alas!" do not have *Sinn*.

5. *Science, Perception and Reality*, p. 110.

6. *Science, Perception and Reality*, pp. 314–315.

7. Sellars's later accounts of "means" are mainly in "Notes on Intentionality" and *Science and Metaphysics*.

Chapter 5

1. Professor Hector-Neri Castañeda has given me a great deal of help with this chapter by asking deep questions about it. I fear that he will still find some of my reflections, especially the ones on his accidental double, rather wild. But disagreement does not trouble Professor Castañeda. He is one of those who would rather see philosophy flourish than gather disciples.

2. Daniel Dennett has suggested that I really need not make this stark and unintuitive claim. And it is true that the appearance of such a double would be more than absurdly unlikely; it is almost certain that no such event could come to pass within the confines of the laws of nature. Correlatively, a thing's history *does* show in its present constitution. But I must stubbornly hold my ground. No matter how true it is that a thing's present constitution shows and must show its history, still it is not the present constitution but the history that makes a thing have proper functions. My claim will be that beliefs and desires and intentions are such by virtue of their proper functions, hence of their histories.

As my story unfolds, however, it will turn out that any newly created double of yours would very soon *come* to have beliefs, desires, and intentions. For it would soon come to be true that his "concepts," or ways of iterating inner elements in inner representations, had survived *due* to having served the same sorts of functions that yours do. (See Chapters 6, 8, and 9.)

A similar situation occurs whenever a mutant appears on the scene. Even though what is new in the mutant may serve a very useful function, hence help the mutant to survive and to produce progeny that survive, etc., still this new aspect has, in the case of the very *first* mutant member of the community, and sometimes for a considerable time thereafter, no proper function at all. It takes time to acquire a direct proper function—time for a thing to have become correlated with a function and to have continued to be reproduced on *that* account.

Chapter 6

1. One reader objected that I treat "intentionality" in this passage as though it were an ordinary rather than a technical term. But the question before us has nothing to do with how many people or which people use the term "intentionality," nor am I doing linguistic analysis. "Intentionality" has been defined variously by various philosophers and most often not defined at all but just used. Here I am concerned to describe the kinds of *phenomena* that I believe people have been after with the term "intentionality"— especially, to capture the phenomena that Brentano was after when he introduced the term into our modern vocabulary.

2. Acts of identification occur only when something *like* inference is going on. If performing inferences is tantamount to having reasons and having reasons marks off rational creatures from others, then I am agreeing with Bennett about *why* bees are not rational (Jonathan Bennett, *Rationality*, Routledge & Kegan Paul, London, 1964). Bennett claims also that (although bees don't have beliefs) a creature *might* have beliefs without being rational. I will claim that a creature may harbor inner intentional icons or be disposed to produce outer ones without being rational. But the reader is encouraged *not* to think of inner intentional icons as beliefs and intentions. What bears a sufficient similarity to *human* beliefs to count as also being "beliefs" is a matter to be decided in accordance with theoretical considerations of clarity and elegance *once we actually have a theory of what human beliefs are.* (I am flouting linguistic analysis as a useful program for casting light on the phenomena that need uncovering here.) According to the theory that I will offer of what human beliefs are, these have absolutely crucial characteristics that perhaps very few intentional icons have, the *first* of which is that human beliefs are representations. I would incline then to say that nothing has beliefs that does not draw inferences from these beliefs—nothing has beliefs that is not rational. But that would be a decision about *sensible usage*, not just a theory about the world and certainly not just a thesis about ordinary usage.

3. Far from being members of reproductively established families, there is no reason to assume that these mechanisms, as occurring in different speakers and hearers from the same language community, are *alike* with regard to either constitution or disposition. For example, after Quine, we have no reason to think, indeed much reason to doubt, that the same term always corresponds to the same "stimulus meaning" when used by different speakers of the same language (*Word and Object*, MIT Press, Cambridge, Mass., 1960, Chapter 2). More on this in Chapter 8.

4. L. Wittgenstein, *Tractatus Logico Philosophicus*, Routledge & Kegan Paul, London, 1922 (with corrections, 1933).

5. I purposefully introduce a vague term here—"world affair"—so that I can slowly mold its sense unhampered by opposing preconceptions. I trust that the term conveys enough of what is meant that I can use it as I proceed to articulate it more clearly and while

dealing with matters that press upon us more immediately than does ontology. I will venture into ontology in Chapters 16 and 17.

Chapter 7

1. This chapter was written before I made the acquaintance of Fred Dretske's *Knowledge and the Flow of Information* (Bradford Books/MIT Press, Cambridge, Mass. 1981). Had it been written after, I would have used something like Dretske's characterization of "information" at certain points in discussing nonlanguage signs. Dretske describes what he calls the "channel" of communication: "The channel of communication = that set of existing conditions (on which the signal depends) that either (1) generate no (relevant) information, or (2) generate only redundant information (from the point of view of the receiver)." (p. 115.) The channel apparently consists of conditions that mediate or properties of that which mediates between a source of information and a signal that carries information, which conditions and properties are not "capricious" (p. 115). I would prefer to define the "channel" through which information is carried merely as a set of conditions that were actually present from which, if these are taken as givens, a natural law in situ can be derived showing why the signal had to map onto its source. What constitutes "*the* channel" vs. "*the* source," then, is not a given in nature but a matter of what kind of explanation one is interested in at the moment. And "the channel" may well be "capricious" in that at another moment in time it may in fact be other than it was at the time for which the explanation is given. Instruments are *designed* to supply designated kinds of information through designated kinds of channels. It is for that reason that it is always possible to distinguish *the* proper channel from *the* proper source of information in their case. And of course the channel of an instrument is designed not to be capricious over time.

Chapter 8

1. See W. V. Quine, *Word and Object*, MIT Press, Cambridge, Mass., 1960, Chapter 2.
2. The expression is Brian Loar's, *Mind and Meaning*, Cambridge University Press, Cambridge, 1981, p. 44.
3. Analogy with the "functions" that computers have begs the question of course since what count as a computer's "functions" are, just, what it has been designed in accordance with *some person's explicit intentions* to do. Insofar as some functionalists have probably had design via evolution in mind as delineating what counts as a brain's "functions," they have not faced the fact that this entails that such "functions" are determined by a thing's history, hence that if intentionality is determined by "function," intentionality does not reside in a mechanism but in its history. To my knowledge, only Daniel Dennett has proposed, *in this context*, an independent account of a mechanism's "functions"—in "Beyond Belief," Andrew Woodfield ed., *Thought and Object: Essays on Intentionality*, Oxford University Press, 1982, pp. 1–95.
4. Speaking perfectly strictly, it is not the term tokens themselves that have correlated with a function, for no alternatives to these tokens have been tried. It is the program that produces the tokens in sentences that has as a proper function to produce what will pass the consistency testers; it survived because it did this better than competing programs. Hence, speaking perfectly strictly, it is not a direct but a derived proper function of the term tokens to help the sentences in which they are embedded to pass consistency tests. Again, intentionality is not strictly of a piece, even in paradigm cases.
5. Bradford Books/MIT Press, Cambridge, Mass., 1981.

Chapter 9

1. I have argued that simple adjectives and verbs refer in the same way that proper names refer (Chapter 6). But in order to include the case of common nouns, the reader should read "refer or denote" for "refer" throughout this chapter.
2. W. V. Quine, *Word and Object*, The MIT Press, Cambridge, Mass., 1960, p. 8.
3. In "Reference and Proper Names" (*Journal of Philosophy* 70 (1973)) Tyler Burge circles around the fact that the intension of a proper name such as "Aristotle" includes the intension "the one called 'Aristotle'." From our point of view, Burge makes the following mistake. He interprets "Aristotle" when functioning as a singular term to have in part the same sense as "Aristotle" in "An Aristotle joined the club today." Compare: "I just discovered another bolt. There's a bolt of cloth, a bolt that a nut goes on, a bolt of lightning, bolting the door and bolting out the door, and there's also an herb that's a bolt." "An Aristotle" in the context "An Aristotle joined the club today" means *a thing called "Aristotle,"* and that in turn means *a thing the name of which has an "a" then an "r" then*—etc. Similarly for "bolt" in "I've just discovered another bolt" as used above. Burge then takes it that "Aristotle" in "Aristotle was a philosopher" must have the sense of *"that* Aristotle"; it must contain an implicit "indexical" that points to that one of the things having a name beginning with "a" followed by "r," etc., that is meant. A parallel would be to interpret "bolt" in "Please bolt the door" as containing an implicit indexical element pointing to which thing called "bolt" was meant. But as I will later interpret quotation marks (Chapter 13), the quoted token of "Aristotle" in "the thing called 'Aristotle'," *where this last gives an intension for "Aristotle"* qua *name of The Philosopher,* refers to its own least type or reproductively established family *branch*—and *not* to a string of letters. When quotes are used in this way, there is only one thing called "Aristotle," namely, the man named by the reproductively established family branch from which I just copied *that* token of "Aristotle." For a discussion of these two uses of quotation marks, see Chapter 13.
4. Hilary Putnam, "Meaning and Reference," *Journal of Philosophy* 70 (November 1973), p. 706.
5. We should also note that there are some terms—"bachelor" is the favorite example—that do seem simply to be shorthand for their standard public intensions. Unlike most terms, they do not denote natural kinds or, as I will call them, "substances" (see Chapter 16). The fact that "bachelor" is such a favorite with which to illustrate the classical conception of the relation of a term to its intension suggests that terms of this kind are not in fact very common.
6. Knowing an infallible intension for a term would not be the same as possessing an infallible means of identifying its referent. "Chemical element with the atomic number seventy-nine" may be an infallible intension for "gold." But there may be no perfectly reliable method of determining whether something is a chemical element with atomic number seventy-nine. And even if there is such a method, one could never know, with Cartesian certainty, that one had indeed applied it.

Chapter 10

1. These Normal conditions may obtain in a particular case even though not reflecting a Normal causal relation between the color pattern and its adaptor. Remember the sick chameleon that has been placed by a sympathetic friend on someting that it matches. In this case, what the chameleon sits on is not in fact the adaptor for its color pattern even though it matches as it ought. For the color pattern was not produced by the chameleon's pigment-arranging devices in response to what it sits on.
2. It is true, however, that in the "temerity" case what I mean is ambiguous in *another*

way. The programs in me that have reproduced the public term "temerity" from other tokens of its type have as proper functions to produce tokens that map in accordance with *public* language rules. Hence my "temerity" has as a background derived sense the sense *boldness* as well as the derived sense *timidity*.

Chapter 11

1. Bertrand Russell, "On Denoting," *Mind* 14 (1905); reprinted in *Readings in Philosophical Analysis*, Herbert Feigl and Wilfrid Sellars eds., Appleton-Century-Crofts, New York, 1949, pp. 103–115.
2. P. F. Strawson, "On Referring," *Mind* 59 (1950); reprinted in *New Readings in Philosophical Analysis*, Herbert Feigl, Wilfrid Sellars, and Keith Lehrer eds., Appleton-Century-Crofts, New York, 1972, pp. 35–50.
3. Keith S. Donnellan, "Reference and Definite Descriptions," *Philosophical Review* 75 (July 1966); reprinted in *New Readings in Philosophical Analysis*, pp. 59–71. Also see "Putting Humpty Dumpty Together Again," *The Philosophical Review* 77 (1968), pp. 203–215.
4. Strawson, "On Referring."
5. "Speaker Reference, Descriptions, and Anaphora," *Contemporary Perspectives in the Philosophy of Language*, Peter A. French, Theodore Uehling, Jr., and Howard K. Wettstein eds., University of Minnesota Press, Minneapolis, 1979, pp. 28–44.
6. Saul Kripke, "Speaker's Reference and Semantic Reference," *Contemporary Perspectives in the Philosophy of Language*, pp. 6–27.
7. Daniel Dennett comments (private correspondence) that using a description that pins down one's man can be enough for libel even though the description is grammatically indefinite. But, I suggest, this is because libel has to do with the successful, nasty, and obvious intent of the speaker, not with the stabilizing functions of the idioms he uses.

Chapter 12

1. G. E. Moore, "The Nature of Judgment," *Mind*, 1899.
2. Panayot Butchvarov, *Being Qua Being; A Theory of Identity, Existence, and Predication*, Indiana University Press, Bloomington, 1979.

Chapter 13

1. For an illuminating discussion of alternative theories of mention quotes, see Donald Davidson, "On Saying That," *Synthese* 19 (1968–1969) pp. 130–146; reprinted in Donald Davidson and Gilbert Harman eds., *The Logic of Grammar*, Dickenson Publishing Company, Encino, Calif., and Belmont, Calif., 1975. Davidson's own theory of mention quotes is given in "Quotation," *Theory and Decision* 11 (mr 1979) pp. 27–40, and will be discussed shortly.
2. Op. cit.
3. "On Saying That."
4. "Reference and Modality" in *From a Logical Point of View*, Second Edition, Harper & Row, New York, 1953, 1961, p. 141.
5. "Quantifiers and Propositional Attitudes," *The Journal of Philosophy* 53 (1956), pp. 177–187. Reprinted in *The Logic of Grammar*.

Chapter 15

1. " . . . nothing of which we can form a clear and distinct idea is absurd and impossible." *Treatise on Human Nature*, Part I, Section VII, para. 6.

Chapter 16

1. Baruch A. Brody, *Identity and Essence*, Princeton University Press, Princeton, N.J., 1980.
2. Recent discussions of such cases may be found in Brody, *Identity and Essence*, pp. 14–20; D. M. Armstrong, *Nominalism and Realism* vol. I, *Universals and Scientific Realism*, Cambridge University Press, Cambridge, 1978, pp. 95–97; Robert Merrihew Adams, "Primitive Thisness and Primitive Identity," *Journal of Philosophy* 76 (1) (January 1979), pp. 5–26; Ian Hacking, "The Identity of Indiscernibles," *Journal of Philosophy* 72 (9) (May 1975), pp. 249–256; David Wiggins, *Sameness and Substance*, Harvard University Press, Cambridge, Mass., 1980.
3. "Primitive Thisness and Primitive Identity."
4. Lawrence Sklar's discussion of this issue in *Space, Time and Spacetime*, University of California Press, Berkeley, Calif., 1974, suggests that Hacking's point is quite familiar to philosophers of geometry.
5. *Nominalism and Realism*, p. 96.
6. "Primitive Thisness and Primitive Identity."
7. D. M. Armstrong, *A Theory of Universals, vol. II, Universals and Scientific Realism*, Cambridge University Press, 1978, p. 11.
8. P. F. Strawson, *Subject and Predicate in Logic and Grammar*, Methuen & Co., Ltd., London, 1974, p. 18.

Chapter 17

1. For a very detailed and patient refutation of the doctrine of relative identity—of the view that whether an *x* and a *y* are the selfsame depends upon the category of sameness specified, e.g., same man vs. same official vs. same collection of atoms—see David Wiggins, *Sameness and Substance*, Harvard University Press, Cambridge, Mass., 1980, Chapter 1.
2. Compare Wiggins's principles D(iii) and D(vi), *Sameness and Substance*, Chapter 2. What follows is intended in part as a rough comment upon these principles.
3. The idea that identity over time has something to do with causal connections between a thing at one time and the same thing at another is not at all new. For an interesting recent formulation of this position, see Sidney Shoemaker, "Identity, Properties and Causality," *Midwest Studies in Philosophy*, vol. IV (*Studies in Metaphysics*), Peter French, Theodor Uehling, Jr., and Howard Wettstein eds., University of Minnesota Press, Minneapolis, 1979, pp. 321–342. What has not been argued before is that causal connections among the temporal stages of a thing have to do with identity in the same sense that Leibniz's laws were about identity.

Chapter 18

1. W. V. Quine, *Word and Object*, MIT Press, Cambridge, Mass., 1960, p. 115.
2. *Word and Object*, p. 14.
3. *Word and Object*, p. 32.

Chapter 19

1. For classic statements of this position, see Wilfrid Sellars, "Empiricism and the Philosophy of Mind," *Minnesota Studies in the Philosophy of Science*, vol. I, Herbert Feigl and Michael Scriven eds., University of Minnesota Press, Minneapolis, 1956, pp. 253–329, and the opening pages of W. V. Quine, *Word and Object*, MIT Press, Cambridge, Mass., 1960.

2. Paul Churchland makes the point that is rehearsed in this paragraph extremely vividly in *Scientific Realism and the Plasticity of Mind*, Cambridge University Press, Cambridge, 1979, Chapter 2.

3. *From a Logical Point of View*, Harvard University Press, Cambridge, Mass., 1953.

Epilogue

1. Hilary Putnam, "The Meaning of 'Meaning'," *Minnesota Studies in the Philosophy of Science*, vol. VII, Keith Gunderson ed., University of Minnesota Press, Minneapolis, 1975. An abbreviated version, from which the quotation at the head of this chapter was taken, appears as "Meaning and Reference," *Journal of Philosophy* 70 (November 1973).

2. Hilary Putnam, *Meaning and the Moral Sciences*, Routledge & Kegan Paul, London, 1978.

Index of Technical Terms

Analytical Index

"a" or "an," 176, 182, 189
abNormal members of reproductively
   established families, 29, 42
abstraction: classical theories of, 246
Adams, R. M., 261, 262
adapted devices, 40–41, 49, 336 (Ch. 2,
   n. 1)
adaptors, 40–41, 49; immediate, 40–41;
   original or ultimate, 41, 49
"adaptor" vs. "adapted," 336 (Ch. 2, n.
   2)
adrenalin: as an intentional signal,
   116–18
Alan's bouquet, 51, 52, 60, 64, 68, 77,
   95, 120–23 passim, 167
"all." See universal descriptions
alternative articulations of world affairs,
   108
ambiguity, 10, 157–58, 273, 326, 340–41
   (Ch. 10, n. 2); in Fregean sense, 128,
   131–32, 137, 141, 170; in dictionary
   sense, 132, 170
ancestor of a member of a reproductively
   established family, 27
Aristotle, 11, 233, 245, 275; view of
   contraries, 268–69
Armstrong, D. M., 262, 266
Austin, J. L., 2

Bach, Kent, 336 (Ch. 3, n. 1)
baptismal ceremonies, 81–82
bee dances, 13, 39–45 passim, 71, 95,
   123; as intentional icons, 97–99
   passim, 107–8; as simultaneously
   indicative and imperative, 115;
   compared to hubot inner language,
   128; as not manifesting rationality, 336
   (Ch. 6, n. 2)

belief: as a proper function category,
   139–40
beliefs, 62, 127, 338 (Ch. 6, n. 2); as
   connected with rationality, 13; false,
   17–18, 94; used in doing vs. had while
   doing, 63; as capacities to produce
   explicit beliefs, 63–64; as supporting
   an activity, 65; as members of proper
   function categories, 93–94; as inner
   sentences, 138; as intentional icons,
   138–146; as representations, 140, 242
"believes that." See intentional contexts
Bennett, Jonathan, 60, 65–66, 336 (Ch. 2,
   n. 3; Ch. 3, nn. 1–3), 338 (Ch. 6, n. 2)
biological categories, 17, 29
Blanchard, Brand, 7
body organs: compared to language
   devices, 2–3, 48–49
Bradley's paradox, 108
Brentano, Franz, 86, 338 (Ch. 6, n. 1)
Brody, Baruch, 259
Burge, Tyler: on reference and proper
   names, 340 (Ch. 9, n. 3)
Butchvarov, Panayot, 193

calling someone by name, 118
Carnap, Rudolf, 153, 193, 199
Cartesian certainty, 6, 10–11, 87, 92, 289,
   335 (Intro., n. 1)
Castañeda, Hector-Neri, 337 (Ch. 5, n. 1)
categories. See ontological categories
causal theory of reference, 335 (Intro., n.
   7)
chameleons, 39–45 passim, 118, 161–63
   passim
chemical messengers in the body, 116–18
Chomsky, Noam, 22, 97
Churchland, Paul, 343 (Ch. 19, n. 2)